D0857437

Encounters with Biomedicine

Health, Society and Culture

A series edited by Hans A. Baer, *Department of Sociology and Anthropology, University of Arkansas at Little Rock*

Volume 1 **Encounters with Biomedicine: Case Studies in Medical Anthropology**

Edited by Hans A. Baer

Additional volumes in preparation

This book is part of a series. The publisher will accept continuation orders which may be cancelled at any time and which provide for automatic billing and shipping of each title in the series upon publication. Please write for details.

Encounters with Biomedicine

CASE STUDIES IN MEDICAL ANTHROPOLOGY

Edited by

HANS A. BAER

Department of Sociology and Anthropology
University of Arkansas at Little Rock

GORDON AND BREACH SCIENCE PUBLISHERS
New York   London   Paris   Montreux   Tokyo   Melbourne

© 1987 by Gordon and Breach Science Publishers S.A., Post Office Box 161, 1820 Montreux 2, Switzerland. All rights reserved

Gordon and Breach Science Publishers

Post Office Box 786
Cooper Station
New York, New York 10276
United States of America

Post Office Box 197
London WC2E 9PX
England

58, rue Lhomond
75005 Paris
France

14–9 Okubo 3-chome
Shinjuku-ku, Tokyo 160
Japan

Private Bag 8
Camberwell, Victoria 3124
Australia

Library of Congress Cataloging in Publication Data
Encounters with biomedicine.
  (Health, society and culture, ISSN 0891-7795; v. 1)
  Includes bibliographies.
  1. Medical anthropology — Case studies. 2. Social medicine — Case studies. I. Baer, Hans A., 1944–II. Series. [DNLM: 1. Anthropology. 2. Cross-Cultural Acceptance of Health Care. GN 296 C337]
GN296.C37   1987   306'.4   87–11988
ISBN 2–88124–195–6 (France)

No part of this book may be reproduced or utilized in any form or by any means, electronic or mechanical, including photocopying and recording, or by any information storage or retrieval system, without permission in writing from the publishers.
Printed in the United States of America.

Contents

About the Contributors   vii

Preface to the Series   xi

Introduction   xiii

Section 1. Health Services, Health Problems and Health Policy

Does Access to Health Services Guarantee Improved
Health Status? The Case of a New Rural Health Clinic in
Oaxaca, Mexico   3
  KENYON RAINIER STEBBINS

Institutional Factors in the Implementation of a Health
Care Program for the Elderly in Rural Utah Towns   29
  HANS A. BAER and CHARLES C. HUGHES

Type II Diabetes Mellitus, Technological Development
and the Oklahoma Cherokee   43
  DENNIS WILLIAM WIEDMAN

The Ethnography of Policy: Florida's Mental Health Act   73
  MICHAEL V. ANGROSINO and ANGELA E.
    SCOGGIN

Section 2. International Visitors: Coping with American Society and Its Health System

On Being Sick Away from Home: Medical Problems and
Health Care Needs of International Students   101
  MARY K. SANDFORD

Pregnancy and Motherhood among Micronesian Students
in the United States   119
    JULIANA FLINN

Prevailing Over Adversity: The Story of a Vietnamese   147
Physician's Internship in an American Community Hospital
    WILLIAM RITTENBERG

Section 3. Medical Encounters: The On-Going Saga of the Physician-Patient Relationship

A Close Encounter with a Court-Ordered Cesarean   185
Section: A Case of Differing Realities
    BRIGITTE JORDAN and SUSAN IRWIN

The Militarization of Cancer Treatment in American   201
Society
    DEBORAH OATES ERWIN

Owning CF: Adaptive Noncompliance with Chest   229
Physiotherapy in Cystic Fibrosis
    ANNA W. BELLISARI

Cure, Care and Control: An Ectopic Encounter with   249
Biomedical Obstetrics
    MERRILL SINGER

Section 4. Applications and Research in Clinical Settings

Consultation Psychiatry as Applied Medical Anthropology   269
    THOMAS M. JOHNSON

Fieldwork in a Clinical Setting: Negotiating Entree, the   295
Investigator's Role and Problems of Data Collection
    JOAN J. MATHEWS

Biomedicine as a Cultural System: An Anthropologist in   315
the Kingdom of the Sick
    SUSAN M. DiGIACOMO

Index   347

About the Contributors

HANS A. BAER received his Ph.D. in anthropology from the University of Utah in 1976. His early fieldwork took place among Hutterites in South Dakota and among the Levites, a Mormon schismatic group which established the Eskdale commune in the Great Basin. More recently, his fieldwork has been among Black Spiritual churches and osteopathic physicians and chiropractors in the United States and Great Britain. Dr. Baer is Associate Professor of Anthropology at the University of Arkansas at Little Rock. He is the author of *The Black Spiritual Movement: A Religious Response to Racism* (University of Tennessee Press, 1984) and coeditor of *Toward a Critical Medical Anthropology*, a Special Issue of *Social Science and Medicine* (1986). In the area of medical anthropology, his interests are Afro-American ethnomedicine, medical pluralism, and the political economy of health.

MICHAEL V. ANGROSINO is Professor of Anthropology and Public Health and Chair of the Department of Anthropology at the University of South Florida. He has conducted anthropological fieldwork in the West Indies as well as the United States. His current areas of interest are applied medical anthropology, particularly in the development of public policy affecting the delivery of mental health services, and in factors associated with community adjustment on the part of deinstitutionalized mentally retarded adults.

ANNA W. BELLISARI earned her Ph.D. in anthropology at Ohio State University in 1984. Her research interests include chronic diseases of children, childhood growth and development as well as the growth, development, and behavior of nonhuman primates. Dr. Bellisari teaches in the Department of Sociology and Anthropology at Wright State University.

SUSAN M. DiGIACOMO earned her Ph.D. in anthropology at the University of Massachusetts, Amherst. She has done research on women factory workers in the United States and Spain, gypsies in Barcelona, and Catalan nationalist politics. Dr. DiGiacomo has taught at Colby College and presently teaches in the Department of Anthropology at Cornell University.

DEBORAH OATES ERWIN is Research Associate and Cancer Information Coordinator for the Arkansas Cancer Research Center and Adjunct Instructor of Humanities at the University of Arkansas for Medical Sciences. She received her Ph.D. in anthropology from Southern Methodist University in 1984.

JULIANA FLINN is Assistant Professor of Anthropology at the University of Arkansas at Little Rock. She earned a Ph.D. in anthropology from Stanford University in 1982 and an M.P.H. from Columbia University in 1984. She has conducted fieldwork on Pulap Atoll in Micronesia and among Pulap migrants both in Micronesia and the United States.

CHARLES C. HUGHES is Professor of Behavioral Sciences and Director of Behavioral Sciences and Director of Graduate Studies, Department of Family and Community Medicine, and Professor of Anthropology in the Department of Anthropology, University of Utah. In addition to being a coauthor of *People of Cove and Woodlot: Communities from the Viewpoint of Social Psychiatry* (Basic Books, 1960), he has published extensively on Inuit culture as well as many areas in medical anthropology. Dr. Hughes is a Past President of the Society for Medical Anthropology.

SUSAN IRWIN is a doctoral student in anthropology at Michigan State University. Her research interests include face-to-face interaction in medical and educational settings.

THOMAS M. JOHNSON is Assistant Professor of Anthropology at Southern Methodist University and Clinical Assistant Professor of Psychiatry at the University of Texas Health Sciences Center — Dallas. He has conducted research on strategies to reduce pain in burn care, the process of medical education, physician-patient interaction, and high-risk obstetrics. Dr. Johnson has been a member of the Education Committee of the Association for the Behavioral Sciences and Medical Education and served as the Editor of the *Medical Anthropology Quarterly*, the official publication of the Society for Medical Anthropology, from 1983 to 1986.

BRIGITTE JORDAN is Associate Professor of Anthropology with an adjunct appointment in the Department of Pediatrics and Human Development at Michigan State University. Her research interests include the design of culturally appropriate health care delivery systems, women in international development, research methodology, and the structure of knowledge systems. She is best known for her work in cross-cultural obstetrics and is the author of *Birth in Four Cultures* (Eden Press, Montreal, 1983) for which she received the Margaret Mead Award of the Society for Applied Anthropology.

JOAN J. MATHEWS is Coordinator of Staff Development at Foster G. McGaw Hospital of the Loyola University Medical Center. She earned her Ph.D. in anthropology from Northwestern University.

WILLIAM RITTENBERG is Assistant Professor of Pediatrics and Human Development at Michigan State University. He earned his Ph.D. in anthropology at the University of California at Los Angeles in 1977. His research has focused on Thai peasants in Southeast Asia and American and overseas physicians in the United States.

MARY K. SANDFORD is Assistant Professor of Sociology and Anthropology at the University of Southwestern Louisiana. She earned her Ph.D. in anthropology from the University of Colorado. Her primary area of interest is the interaction of biological, cultural, and environmental factors in producing health and nutritional problems in past and present populations.

ANGELA E. SCOGGIN is a graduate student in the Department of Anthropology at the University of South Florida. As an occupational therapist, she has worked extensively with physically handicapped and autistic children. Ms. Scoggin is currently conducting fieldwork in Lima, Peru, on evaluating intervention strategies to encourage development among hospitalized children.

MERRILL SINGER is a Research Associate at the Hispanic Health Council in Hartford, Connecticut, and a lecturer at the University of

Connecticut Medical School. He is coeditor of *Toward a Critical Medical Anthropology*, a special issue of *Social Science and Medicine*. In the area of medical anthropology, Dr. Singer has conducted research on ethnomedicine among the Black Hebrews of Israel, Christian Science healing, an *espiritismo* centro, hypoglycemia, and alcoholism among Hispanic youth in the United States.

KENYON RAINIER STEBBINS is Assistant Professor of Anthropology at West Virginia University. He received his Ph.D. in anthropology from Michigan State University in 1984. His case study is dedicated to the Chinantec people in Oaxaca, Mexico, among whom he did field-work between 1980 and 1982.

DENNIS WILLIAM WIEDMAN is Research Associate in the Department of Sociology and Anthropology at Florida International university (Bay Vista Campus) and an Adjunct Instructor in the Department of Psychiatry at the University of Miami School of Medicine. He earned his Ph.D. in anthropology from the University of Oklahoma in 1979.

Preface to the Series

The Health, Society and Culture series, of which this is the first volume, aims to document concretely and specifically, through case studies, commentaries, theoretical overviews, and monographs, the value of social scientific perspectives in understanding health, disease, illness, and medical systems in a wide variety of sociocultural settings, and the potential of these perspectives in contributing to the improvement of health and health care.

While the first volume in the series includes case studies on a broad range of topics, several more volumes relying heavily but not exclusively on the case study approach are planned. The first of these will focus on the social production of illness. Case studies to be included will consider diseases and illnesses generated by environmental and industrial pollution, agricultural practices, poverty, unemployment, and stresses in the workplace and modern life. Another volume will examine professionalized heterodox health systems in Western societies. Due to a variety of factors, including dissatisfaction with biomedicine, the cost of high-technology medicine, and the inability of biomedicine to treat certain medical complications, health clients as well as health policy makers are giving increasing attention to a variety of heterodox health systems, such as osteopathy, chiropractic, naturopathy, homeopathy, Christian Science and a wide array of other therapeutic systems that fall under the umbrella of what is often referred to as the "holistic health" movement. Still an additional volume will present a comparative examination of national health systems. This volume will reflect the growing interest within the medical social sciences to link social units at the macroscopic and microscopic levels.

I urge colleagues who are interested in contributing to any of the planned volumes or are interested in editing volumes of their own or writing mongraphs on specific health-related issues to contact me.

Hans A. Baer

Introduction

As should be the case, medical anthropologists have borrowed the frameworks that guide their teaching, research, and applications from a larger corpus of anthropological theory as well as a number of paradigms that cross-cut disciplinary boundaries. In a long overview of medical anthropology, David Landy (1983: 185) observes "that the human group that calls itself by the name medical anthropology is a lively, heterogeneous community, busily engaged in myriad activities, studying, thinking, and writing about behaviors of human collectivities and individuals in understanding and coping with disease and injury." In the United States, medical anthropology as a subdiscipline has grown in recent decades to such an extent that the Society for Medical Anthropology now constitutes the second largest unit of the American Anthropological Association. Four journals, *Medical Anthropology, Social Science and Medicine, Culture, Medicine and Psychiatry*, and the *Medical Anthropology Quarterly* (New Series) serve as the major forums for anthropologists interested in health-related issues. In addition, many medical anthropologists publish in other anthropological as well as sociological, behavioral science, medical, nursing, public health, and health policy journals. This volume and many of the subsequent volumes in the series on Health, Society and Culture, hopefully will fill a need for case studies in medical anthropology and other medical social sciences that are to be longer than most journals will permit but that are to be shorter than is required for a monograph. The idea for a volume of case studies examining health-related issues originated with Julio F. Ruffini, the editor of Volumes 1 and 2 of *Advances in Medical Social Science* (also published by Gordon and Breach). I eventually inherited the project of editing what evolved into *Encounters with Biomedicine: Case Studies in Medical Anthropology* after Dr. Ruffini decided that other responsibilities interfered with carrying it out himself.

In commenting upon the strong emphasis that anthropologists place on case studies, Hunter and Whitten (1976: 18) observe that

"Few anthropologists are content solely with masses of data subjected to complex statistical analysis; rather, they look for the concrete social fact — the item of behavior, the description of a recognizable experience — on which to anchor an understanding of social processes." For the purposes of this volume, a case refers to a concrete example of health institutions, situations, events or interactions in which medical anthropological perspectives, insights, data, or techniques could be useful in understanding and improving health and health care. Some cases are "successes," others are "failures," and still others are a mixture of both. Nevertheless, each case study will attempt to demonstrate the value of medical anthropology in understanding what determined success or failure. Case studies will discuss health-related situations at the macroscopic, intermediate, or microscopic levels (e.g., national and community health programs, health and illness behavior and/or attitudes of specific groups, interactions between healers and patients in a variety of medical settings). All of the case studies attempt to provide a rich narrative so that readers may acquire a keen comprehension of the institution, program, setting, or event described.

In addition to the descriptive narrative, contributors will provide an analysis and commentary, either at the end of the case, or interwoven throughout the narrative. Each analysis will discuss the theoretical and/or practical implications of the case. When appropriate, analyses will include generalizations and demonstrate the applicability of the particular case for other similar situations. The essays in this volume represent only a small sample of the topics of interest to and a portion of the approaches employed by anthropologists interested in health-related issues. Readers undoubtedly will observe that most of the case studies herein focus on aspects of health and biomedical care in American society. To a large degree, the case studies in this volume are the pick of the draw solicited through the *Anthropology Newsletter*, the *Medical Anthropology Quarterly* (Old Series), and professional contacts. They also reflect the increasing tendency for anthropologists to conduct research within their own society and, in many instances, local community. This volume is intended to serve as a "teaching and research guide" for undergraduate and graduate students in medical anthropology and other medical social science disciplines, for students in the health sciences, and for teachers in these areas who wish to use the case study book as a supplement to assigned textbooks or as a resource for preparing lectures to illustrate and document concepts and models presented in class.

In my role as editor, the contributors have taught me much about the complexity of health, disease, illness and medical systems and the need to elucidate these phenomena from a variety of perspectives. Conversely, I hope that contributors have benefitted from my editorial comments, which at times were drawn from my commitment to the development of a critical medical anthropology which attempts to link phenomena at the micro- and intermediate levels to those at the macro-level, namely the political economy of health.

Despite the global diffusion of biomedicine, health statistics reveal the wide prevalence of high infant mortality rates, low life expectancy, infectious diseases, and malnutrition in most Third World countries. Drawing upon innovative programs in the People's Republic of China and World Health Organization's goal of "health for all by the year 2000" (World Health Organization 1978), many Third World nations have embarked upon an array of primary health programs, including ones serving rural areas. In the opening case study of Section 1 on Health Services, Health Problems, and Health Policy, Kenyon Stebbins explores the nature of the government-sponsored COPLAMAR health program, which is directed toward providing health services in Mexico's rural sector, particularly in the Oaxacan village of Amotepec (pseudonym). Created in 1977, the program by 1980 encompassed 2,105 new rural health clinics, each of which was theoretically staffed by a *pasante* (a fifth year medical student serving a year-long tenure of social service). In the eyes of Amotepecans, the COMPLAMAR clinic falls far short of their initial expectations for various reasons, including the *pasante's* chronic absenteesim, the inferior quality of many of the pharmaceuticals dispensed, and the clinic's inability to cure persisting ailments stemming from poverty, malnutrition, and unsanitary conditions in the village. Following a political-economic perspective, Stebbins argues that the COMPLAMAR program ultimately serves the Mexican ruling class more than the rural masses by contributing, at least in part, to an improvement of functional health, which in turn creates a more productive labor force, and to the dissipation of social unrest in the countryside.

In commenting upon the many contradictions of Mexican capitalism, Cockcroft (1983: 3) observes, "Half of the nation's deaths occur without medical attention, yet there are 80,000 medical students, 20 percent more than in the United States. Some 16,000 doctors are employed in greater Mexico City, yet almost half the urban and rural municipalities have no doctors at all." As Stebbins argues, meaningful improvement in the health status of the rural population

as well as the teeming urban masses will require a drastic transformation of Mexico's peripheral capitalist economy (Also see Horn
1985).

While rural-urban disparities in health services are most severe in
the Third World, they also occur in both advanced capitalist as well
as socialist-oriented societies. In the case of the United States, a
host of rural health programs, including extension services provided
by medical schools, the National Health Service Corps, and the
utilization of nurse practitioners as a first point of medical contact,
have been developed in recent decades to ameliorate this disparity
(Haynes 1984). The underdevelopment of rural America has contributed to a high concentration of elderly people in small towns and
the countryside as young people migrate to the cities in search of
better economic opportunities. Despite the dispersal of Hill-Burton
monies beginning in the 1940s for the construction of rural hospitals,
it is now apparent that the rural elderly are in greater need of
primary care physicians and intermediate-care facilities than acute
care units. Reforms that attempt to correct such contradictions, as
Hans Baer and Charles Hughes demonstrate in their case study of
the Utah Cost Improvement Project, can be difficult to implement
at the local level, especially when federal and state health and social
service agencies are unaware of the peculiarities of each target
community.

While the provision of health care under the auspices of the
federally-operated Indian Health Service has contributed to a decrease in the incidence of tuberculosis, trachoma, and other ende-
mic diseases, biomedicine has not been able to prevent the onset of
certain "diseases of civilization" among Native Americans. In the
next case study, Dennis Wiedman argues that the shift from subsistence agriculture to wage labor in an industrial economy led to a
sedentary lifestyle, heavier reliance upon processed and high-calorie
foods, and a concomitant rise in the incidence of Type II diabetes
mellitus. Ironically, diabetes has often been viewed as a disease
emanating from an affluent diet (Eckholm 1977). In the case of
the Oklahoma Cherokee as well as many other Native American
groups, however, pervasive poverty, which induces individuals to
consume a relatively inexpensive low protein, high calorie diet as
opposed to a high protein, medium calorie diet in order to obtain
the necessary energy level, appears to be a much more important
factor in the high incidence of diabetes.

The Key Symposium on "Contemporary Health Policy Issues and
Alternatives: An Applied Social Science Perspective," at the 1984

Annual Meeting of the Southern Anthropological Society in Atlanta perhaps signalled more than any other event the growing interest of medical anthropologists in health policy decision-making processes. In the final case study of Section 1, Michael Angrosino and Angela Scoggin examine the role that grass-roots groups played in the passage of the Florida Mental Health Act of 1971, which legally guaranteed due process and other civil rights and called for the deinstitutionalization of patients in mental hospitals. Following Anthony F.C. Wallace's model of administrative structures, the authors chronicle in detail the process of "decay and reorganization" by which an idealistic movement was transformed into a conservative bureaucracy that made access to treatment in institutional settings available to only the most severely disturbed individuals. In interpreting the actions of state mental health lobbies, Brown (1979: 647) argues that while they had a progressive side in that they "challenged the century-old snake-pit asylums ... ⟨the⟩ community mental health staff overestimated the extent to which they could change the basic social problems faced by their clients." Due to the increasing fiscal crisis of the state, community mental health programs were unable to provide the innovative services that they promised. Many of the patients discharged from state hospitals now reside in nursing homes and boarding homes of questionable quality, while others wander the streets of our cities in search for morsels of food and a place to spend the night. As Scull (1985: 551) so aptly observes, "the switch to community treatment has in all probability not changed the situation of most chronic mental patients for the better, and the balance of political forces in our society suggests that there is only a slight chance of major initiative being undertaken to mitigate or eliminate the deficiencies of existing mental health policy."

Section 2 consists of case studies dealing with specific problems encountered by international students attending American colleges and universities and a Vietnamese physician undergoing an internship in a Midwestern public hospital. In the first of these, Mary Sandford, by focusing on Latin American students and Nigerian Igbo students at a Southern university, demonstrates the variability in the responses of international students to the American health care system. Apparently buttressed by an indigenous emphasis on self-treatment, the Igbo students are less disturbed by the assembly-line operation of the university health clinic than are the Latin American students who are accustomed to the personalism and the relaxed pace of physicians back home. In keeping with the increas-

ing emphasis in medical anthropological research on practical results, even modest ones, Sandford's findings were utilized in the
writing of a brochure orienting international students to the American health system, and in establishing a special clinic for international students. She concludes that the improvement of international
student health services ultimately rests upon the creation of a
"sensitive medical community." Unfortunately, as long as medical
schools continue to socialize physicians to be "disease-centered"
rather than "person-centered," such an achievement seems unlikely
(Lynaugh and Bates 1973).

In an effort to tighten its hegemony over the Trust Territory of
Micronesia, the United States government has promoted not only
educational facilities there but also opportunities for young Micronesians to study on the American mainland. Juliana Flinn's case
study focuses on one specific coping mechanism, namely becoming
pregnant, that some young women from the atoll of Pulap use in
overcoming the stresses of migration and American college life.
Ironically, whereas pregnancy is regarded as a natural process on
Pulap, it takes on dual medical connotations in American society as
part of the medicalization of birthing and as a quasi-sick role that
releases the young women from unpleasant social demands. As
opposed to the situation in the United States, the young woman
returning to Pulap with her infant faces complete social acceptance
and does not need to admit to having been unable to bear the
pressures of a competitive social system thousands of miles across
the ocean.

Due to a drastic shortage of physicians in certain sectors of the
American health system, the 1960s and 1970s witnessed a large
influx of foreign medical graduates (FMGs), particularly from the
Third World, into the United States. As William Rittenberg's case
study indicates, one major dilemma deriving from the presence of
FMGs in American hospitals is often not technical incompetence
but rather the inability of some of the FMGs to communicate
effectively with patients. While Dr. Thieu (pseudonym) obviously is
a dedicated physician, his privileged status within South Vietnamese
society blinded him to the atrocities committed by the nationalist
forces and their American collaborators against countless numbers
of Vietnamese people, as well as his part in a process that drains
many underdeveloped countries of badly needed health providers.
Ironically, most FMGs intern in inner-city municipal hospitals
serving the poor, or in smaller community hospitals, neither of
which can otherwise fill their internships because American medical

gradautes prefer to work in more prestigious community hospitals. Yet, the growing number of American medical graduates relative to the population has been accompanied by an intensification of gatekeeping efforts that restrict the licensing of FMGs. Unfortunately, as Irigoyen and Zambrana (1979:782) observe, "there are historical and situational factors which account for the fact that FMGs are represented at the lowest levels of the hierarchy, and perhaps have been blamed unjustly for problems that are a result of the inefficient management by the US health system in general."

The healer-patient constitutes the core dyad upon which other medical interactions as well as medical institutions *per se* are structured. Despite the voluminous literature that already exists on this topic, it continues to hold considerable fascination for medical, social and behavioral scientists. Although there has been a tendency for anthropologists to focus on the healer-patient relationship in tribal societies, peasant communities, or ethnic enclaves, as is evidenced by the four case studies in Section 3, they have joined their colleagues in sociology in studying medical encounters within the corridors of biomedicine.

As is apparent in Brigitte Jordan and Susan Irwins' case study, anthropologists, however, have been more likely to examine medical encounters exhibiting a cross-cultural dimension. Even if we account for the large influx of foreign medical graduates and the increase of female medical students during the past decade or so, the vast majority of physicians in this country remain Euro-American males. In contrast, not only are the majority of patients female, but a large percentage of patients in American medical settings fit into one or more of several other minority categories. The West African woman who refused to undergo a Cesarean section exhibits a "trible minority" status in the context of American society, namely as a foreigner, as a black, and as a woman. In insisting upon her desire to undergo a normal birth while defying medical advice, she came face to face not only with the power of the medical establishment, but of the state as well. As Jordan and Irwins' case study illustrates, the ability of biomedicine to impose its hegemony over ordinary people's lives is not absolute but is ultimately delegated by elites in the larger society. The "tendency to warp the birth experience, distorting it into a pathological event rather than a physiological one for the normal childrearing woman" (Haire 1978:187) manifests our society's belief that our problems can be solved by technological tinkering.

What Deborah Oates Erwin aptly terms the "medical militarization of cancer treatment" in the next case study constitutes yet another manifestation of the American commitment to the technological fix. In the war against cancer, the soldier-patient faithfully obeys the orders of his or her commanding officer-physician, no matter how tough the battle becomes or bad the odds for victory are. Yet, as the author indicates, medical militarization contributes to a form of "false consciousness" by urging Americans to fight the disease head-on rather than by altering the economic, political, and social conditions necessary to prevent it. According to Samuel Epstein (1979), 70 to 90 percent of human cancers are environmentally-induced, and thus ultimately preventable. As is required for the eradication of most diseases in the Third World, however, an effective prevention program against cancer will require major social structural changes in American society.

Medical militarization as a *modus operandi* extends to various other complications, including perhaps cystic fibrosis. In that chest physiotherapy (CPT), which loosens and removes the thick mucus obstructing the patient's lungs, is of limited effectiveness over the long run, physicians, respiratory therapists, patients, and patients' parents, as Anna Bellisari shows in the next case study, face a monumental battle in combatting still another incurable disease. In contrast to most of the social scientific literature on the issue of patient compliance (See Gold 1977), the author argues that non-compliance may be an adaptive strategy that cystic fibrosis patients and their parents adopt in balancing their estimates of the appropriateness and efficacy of CPT and a desire for a normal childhood which CPT grossly interferes with.

In the final case study in Section 3, Merrill Singer analyzes a non-compliant patient's frustrating experiences with the obstetrics/gynecology department of a health maintenance organization (HMO). In addition to having to deal with the belief among the HMO staff that women are incapable of diagnosing their own pregnancy, both she and her obstetrician find themselves victimized by a corporate structure, which with its emphasis on cost effectiveness, limits the length of their interaction to a few minutes. As Salmon (1984: 143) observes, during the 1980s, "nationwide and multinational corporations will become prominent providers of health services, with their primary goal being profit." As this transformation unfolds, patients will continue to be, even more so than in the past, consumers whose health care will be dictated by their financial means, and physicians will undergo a process of "proletarianization" (McKinlay and Arches 1985).

Section 4 consists of three essays that discuss various approaches anthropologists can employ in working in clinical settings, either as applied anthropologists or ethnographers. In keeping with Weaver's (1968) assertion that medical anthropology is "a branch of applied anthropology," many medical anthropologists in recent years have been attracted to a growing subfield called "clinical anthropology." Some time ago, based upon a case study of a traditional Navajo man who was institutionalized as a psychotic in a California state mental hospital, Jewell (1952:36) noted that "The need to consider emotional adjustment with respect to cultural factors has long been recognized. It has, however, been somewhat of an academic acknowledgement which demands greater practical application on the clinical level." In drawing insights from a comparable case study of a traditional Native American woman hospitalized for alcoholism-related complications, Thomas Johnson discusses the complexities and dilemmas associated with working in psychiatric settings. Although he recognizes that because of their systemic perspective anthropologists often have a better understanding of the sociocultural origins of mental disturbances than do psychiatrists, Johnson argues that, given the organizational structure of hospitals, it is unrealistic to think that anthropologists can "take over" consultation psychiatry. Instead, he suggests that anthropologists serve on consultation-liaison psychiatry teams, and provide psychiatrists with anthropological perspectives and ethnographic skills.

In addition to doing "anthropology in medicine," medical anthropologists will hopefully continue to develop the "anthropology of medicine." Yet, as opposed to the relatively easy access that anthropologists have had to the "little peoples of the world" (e.g., tribal villagers, peasants, ethnic minorities, subproletariats), they find that entree into the medical arena for research purposes tends to be much more problematic "due to the predominance of elites in the setting" (Danziger 1979:514). In her case study, Joan Mathews relates how she repressed the anti-doctor bias that she had acquired during her twenty-year stint as a nursing educator and administrator in order to adopt a posture of 'affective neutrality' that she feels was essential in her study of information exchange processes among physicians, nurses, and patients in a university hospital. The author delineates a series of specific guidelines that medical anthropologists may find useful in obtaining entree to and conducting research in medical settings. In reality, the "value-free" approach that Mathews aspires to is an elusive one (See Pflanz 1975). As Riska and Vinten-Johansen (1981:595) argue, "By using a clinical model, the medical leadership has managed to force behavioral scientists into limited roles as social engineers providing technical expertise within the parameters largely defined by the medical profession alone."

In the search for ways of studying biomedicine without legitimizing its power relations, Susan DiGiacomo argues in the last case study in this volume that anthropologists can in some instances utilize their own sense of outrage as a valid research strategy. Whereas her earlier research focused upon Spanish labor politics, the author turned to an analysis of biomedicine as a cultural system so that she could cope with the frightening ordeal of undergoing treatment for Hodgkin's disease. Although initially she had to fight her oncologist for much of the information on her condition, in time he came to enjoy the collaborative relationship that she demanded. Hopefully DiGiacomo's innovative approach to conducting fieldwork in the clinical setting will inspire other anthropologists to shift their endeavors from social engineering on behalf of the experts to one of patient advocacy.

Hans A. Baer

REFERENCES

Brown, Phil, 1979. The Transfer of Care: U.S. Mental Health Policy in World War II, *International Journal of Health Services* 9: 645–662.

Cockcroft, James D, 1983. *Mexico: Class Formation, Capital Accumulation, and the State*. New York: Monthly Review Press.

Danziger, Sandra, 1979. On Doctor-Watching: Fieldwork in Medical Settings, *Urban Life* 7: 513–532.

Eckholm, Erik P., 1977. *The Picture of Health: Environmental Sources of Disease*. New York: W.W. Norton.

Epstein, Samuel S., 1979. *The Politics of Cancer*. Garden City, N.Y.: Anchor/ Doubleday.

Gold, Margaret, 1977. A Crisis of Identity: The Case of Medical Sociology, *Journal of Health and Social Behavior* 18: 160–168.

Haire, Doris, 1978. The Cultural Warping of Childbirth, in *The Cultural Crisis of Modern Medicine*, John Ehrenreich, (ed.), pp. 185–200. New York: Monthly Review Press.

Haynes, Terry, L., 1984. Rural Health in the United States and Canada, in *Advances in Medical Social Science, Volume 2*, Julio L. Ruffini, (ed.), pp. 187–267. New York: Gordon and Breach.

Horn, James J., 1985. The Mexican Revolution and Health Care or the Health of the Mexican Revolution, *International Journal of Health Services* 15: 485–499.

Hunter, David E., and Phillip Whitten, 1976. *The Study of Anthropology*. New York: Harper and Row.

Irigoyen, Matilde, and Ruth E. Zambrana, 1979. Foreign Medical Graduates (FMGs): Determining their Role in the U.S. Health Care System, *Social Science and Medicine* 13A: 775–783.

Jewell, Donald P., 1952. A Case of a "Psychotic" Navaho Indian Male, *Human Organization* 11: 31–36.

Landy, David, 1983. Medical Anthropology: A Critical Appraisal, in *Advances in*

Medical Social Science, Volume 1, Julio L. Ruffini, (ed.), pp. 185–314. New York: Gordon and Breach.

Lynaugh, Joan E., and Barbara Bates, 1973. The Two Languages of Nursing and Medicine, *American Journal of Nursing* 73: 66–69.

McKinlay, John B., and Joan Arches, 1985. Towards the Proletarianization of Physicians, *International Journal of Health Services* 15: 161–195.

Pflantz, Manfred, 1975. Relations Between Social Scientists, Physicians and Medical Organizations in Health Research, *Social Science and Medicine* 9: 7–13.

Riska, Elianne Riska, and Peter Vinten-Johansen, 1981. The Involvement of the Behavioral Sciences in American Medicine: A Historical Perspective, *International Journal of Health Services* 11: 583–596.

Salmon, J. Warren, 1984. Organizing Medical Care for Profit, in *Issues in the Political Economy of Health Care*, John B. McKinlay, (ed.), pp. 143–186. London: Tavistock.

Scull, Andrew, 1985. Deinstitutionalization and Public Policy, *Social Science and Medicine* 20: 545–552.

Weaver, Thomas, 1968. Medical Anthropology: Trends in Research and Medical Education, in *Essays on Medical Anthropology*, Thomas Weaver, (ed.), pp. 1–12. Athens: University of Georgia Press (Southern Anthropological Society Proceedings, No. 1).

World Health Organization, 1978. *Primary Health Care*, Geneva: World Health Organization.

Health Services, Health Problems and Health Policy

Does Access to Health Services Guarantee Improved Health Status? The Case of a New Rural Health Clinic in Oaxaca, Mexico

KENYON RAINIER STEBBINS

West Virginia University Department of Sociology and Anthropology

INTRODUCTION

The improvement of health status is a goal shared by individuals, national governments, and international health agencies. The World Health Organization, for example, opened the 1980s by calling for "health for all by the year 2000." Underdeveloped countries around the world are responding to this call in a variety of ways. This essay examines what one country in Latin America has recently attempted to do about the poor health status prevalent among many of its citizens.

The case of Mexico is especially interesting for at least two reasons. First, since 1917 the post-Revolutionary Mexican constitution has guaranteed all of its citizens the right to health, a guarantee that has not yet been realized by millions of Mexicans. Second, since the latter part of the 1970s, the Mexican government has implemented significant health programs with the explicit purpose of improving the health status of millions of its most marginalized citizens.

This article critically evaluates these health services from both "above" and "below," i.e. from the viewpoint of the health services planners and implementers, and from the perspective of the health services recipients. This critical evaluation of the impact of new health services on the poor demonstrates the important contributions which anthropological insights can make.

Centralized program planners and implementers generally rely on

3

macro-analyses of health needs. The perspectives of the scattered recipients of health services are much less readily available, and are accordingly basically *assumed* by health services officials. In this article I suggest that anthropologists can make essential contributions toward understanding health, illness and disease, and medical systems, and I also suggest that anthropological information can add significantly to the possibilities for improving both health status and health services delivery.

Anthropologists are well suited to investigate how *recipients* preceive the delivery of health services. By incorporating the viewpoints of not only outsiders (e.g. the health planners and the anthropologist) but also the insiders (e.g. the recipients of health services), anthropological investigations provide a much more complete understanding of circumstances at the receiving end of government programs.

While medical anthropological studies employ a wide variety of theoretical perspectives, this case study utilizes a political economic perspective (Baer 1982). In considering health issues, a political economic perspective looks less to the individual for an explanation of his or her sickness, and looks more to the causal roles played by the larger political, economic, and social systems which affect the individual. In Third World countries such as Mexico, improving the health of the poor majority may have much less to do with medical systems than with political and economic constraints (Gish 1979: 210).This article shows how the health services and health status of the population under consideration are critically affected by political and economic factors at both the macro- and micro-level.

HEALTH STATUS AND HEALTH SERVICES IN MEXICO

Prior to the Mexican Revolution of 1910–1917, the Mexican government provided very little in terms of health services for its people. The revolutionary constitution of 1917 not only addressed the peasants' demands for "land and liberty," but also made health an "abstract right" of the people (Musselwhite 1981: 120–121, 146), and guaranteed health care for all Mexicans (Kreisler 1981: 9, 91). Unfortunately, these constitutional guarantees have yet to be realized by millions of Mexicans, especially poor and rural Mexicans who suffer from malnutrition, ill health, and scarcity of health sustaining resources.

Health statistics for Mexico reflect an urban bias in terms of health and sanitation services and environmental conditions (Cañedo 1974, England 1978, Lopez Acuña 1982). For example, rural Mexican children under the age of five are approximately twice as likely to be malnourished as urban Mexicans. Roughly 50 percent of Mexico's urban population benefit from sewage facilities, as compared with only 0.25 percent for Mexico's rural inhabitants (Lopez Acuña 1980b: 21). Access to potable water is also much more scarce in rural Mexico. While 87.5 percent of all residents living in cities of greater than 50,000 population have potable water available to them, only 34.4 percent of all Mexicans living in localities with fewer than 2,500 inhabitants enjoy potable water (Rameriz 1981: 85).

However, the advantages found in urban areas as compared to rural areas are disproportionately enjoyed by the elite minority, (England 1978: 154) leaving vast numbers of urban residents no better off than Mexico's rural poor (Chávez 1982, Lopez Acuña 1980b). Accordingly, a much more realistic dichotomy exists between *poor* Mexicans (whether in urban or rural areas) and *rich* Mexicans (living mainly in urban areas).[1]

In terms of the availability of health sevices, Mexico's Secretary of Health and Welfare stated that roughly 15 million of Mexico's 71 million people have "no access to [biomedical] health services of any kind," and Mexico's National Union of Doctors stated that perhaps the figure was closer to 20 million neglected Mexicans (*New York Times*, June 17, 1983). A political scientist who interviewed numerous government health officials during a year of research in Mexico City goes even further, stating that "[Mexican] government officials have admitted that *half the population* has never received [biomedical] health care services of any kind as late as the late 1970s" (Musselwhite 1981: 91, emphasis added).

In the early 1970s, the government began placing greater attention on health services for Mexico's rural sector. Even so, as recently as 1976 only eight percent of the Ministry of Health budget was for rural areas (Marta Fernandez, personal communication, March 7, 1980). New approaches to rural health services were tried and they served as pilot projects for what followed in the late 1970s in rural Mexico.

In early 1977, the COPLAMAR[2] program (the focus of this

article) was created by Presidential Decree. The principal stated objective of the COPLAMAR development agency was to allow the "marginal people in the deprived zones" of Mexico to "participate more equitably in the national wealth" (COPLAMAR 1978: xvi–xvii).

While the primary orientation of COPLAMAR is the development and extraction of marketable resources, it does include a widely publicized health component. By 1980 the COPLAMAR program included 2,105 new rural health clinics. Each clinic was designed and located with the expectation that it would "cover" a population of roughly 5,000 "marginal people" living in Mexico's most "deprived zones." Thus, over ten million rural Mexicans were said to have recently become "covered" by these new health clinics. I will focus on the impact of these new clinics on the health status of the target population.

METHODOLOGY AND RESEARCH SITE

Over 40 percent of Mexico's population lives in 97,615 rural localities, each with a population smaller than 2,500. The findings reported here are based on fieldwork which I conducted between 1980 and 1982 in a small highland Chinantec municipio (political subunit) in the northern part of the state of Oaxaca.[3] With the exceptions of the village school teachers, the clinic's doctor, and myself, all of Amotepec's (pseudonym) 2,179 residents habitually spoke Chinantec, and spoke Spanish (if at all) only when necessary.

The overwhelming majority of the field data were collected in the village, where I lived for fifteen months. This was done by participant-observation, open-ended informal interviews, and copying of official documents (especially at the health clinic). In addition to time spent in the research site, I spent two more months in Oaxaca City and Mexico City making valuable contacts and obtaining important archival information.

The Amotepec villagers live on steep hillsides at approximately 7,000 feet above sea level (about 17 degrees north of the equator). Sub-subsistence farmers, their primary crops (corn, beans, and squash) are entirely dependent upon rainfall for water. Due to the lack of adequate quantity and productivity of agricultural lands, nearly all Amotepec families supplement their incomes by seeking income outside of the village. Accordingly, Amotepecans typically spend great portions of their lives (ranging from several months to several years) working in cities in a variety of occupations. As will be seen below, the villagers' land scarcity and familiarity with urban Mexico greatly influence how they experience their new village health clinic.

THE COPLAMAR DEVELOPMENT PROGRAM

The COPLAMAR development program emphasizes resource extraction and development. For example, in the state of Oaxaca, four-fifths of the COPLAMAR budget for 1978–1982 was proposed for agriculture, timber, industry, communications, and transport, with only 7.4 percent of the funds targeted for the health sector. Nevertheless, the construction, staffing, and supervising of over 2,000 new rural health clinics represents an enormous allocation of funds by the Mexican government. In addition to the clinics, 41 rural hospitals have been constructed throughout the republic to serve those patients whose health needs cannot be met in their rural clinics.

The rural clinics are intended to provide (free of charge) the following services: general outpatient consultations, pharmaceuticals, mother-infant care and family planning, health education, nutritional information, sanitation promotion, immunizations and control of communicable diseases. The rural hospitals are designed to provide (also free of charge) the following services for referral patients: special outpatient consultations, hospitalization, pharmaceuticals, obstetrical and gynecological care, pediatrics, surgery, internal medicine, preventive medicine, and dental services (COPLAMAR 1978, 1981). While patients receive these services at no *out-of-pocket* expense, each head of household must provide up to ten days of unpaid labor per year for any clinic-related tasks that are asked of them.[4]

Prior to the construction of COPLAMAR'S 2,105 new rural health clinics, Mexico had only 1,700 health centers providing services to its 30 million rural residents. These pre-COPLAMAR health centers were easily accessible to only 15 percent of the rural population, leaving 25.5 million rural Mexicans without reasonably available health care in 1977 (Correu Azcona *et al.* 1980:247–248).

By October of 1980, the 2,105 new COPLAMAR rural clinics were operating in 31 federal states[5] covering 20,000 communities. These new clinics were serving 11.3 million Mexicans

(COPLAMAR 1981:43), or nearly half of the population cited above who were without such services in 1977.

Of these 11.3 million Mexicans supposedly covered by the CO-PLAMAR clinics, 4.3 million (or 38 percent) were "captured" during the program's first year (September 1, 1979 to August 31, 1980). The "captured" population refers not only to all of the patients who attended any clinic during the first year, but also all of the family members of any patient. During the program's first year there were 3,266,273 patient-visits recorded in all of the COPLA-MAR clinics combined.[6] These patients received 3,334,873 prescriptions, which were filled immediately at the clinic. Nearly half (47 percent) of all patient-visits included an injection.

Despite the fact that the COPLAMAR family planning program is a "national-level priority," only 12,017 births were attended by clinic pasantes during the first year (an average of 5.7 births per clinic), and only 36,744 women participated in the family planning program (an average of 17 per clinic) (COPLAMAR 1981:100). Those states with greater indigenous populations (especially Oaxaca, Chiapas, Veracruz, and Guerrero) reported even less frequent participation in the family planning program.

A COPLAMAR (1981) report which surveyed all of the 746,130 family dwellings covered by COPLAMAR's 2,105 clinics provides some insight into the living conditions of the target population: 80 percent are one or two room dwellings, 76 percent have dirt floors and walls of mud or adobe, 30 percent have access to piped water, and only 13 percent have sewage disposal. The village of Amotepec mirrors these statistics in most respects, but differs in that there are no sewage disposal facilities in the village. (There is piped water available to all residents in Amotepec, but it is doubtful that it is potable).

With this brief background, we turn now to consideration of the kinds of health problems encountered in Amotepec, and the kinds of treatment strategies pursued by the villagers. This will be followed by discussion and analysis of the impact of COPLAMAR's services on the health status of its target population.

HEALTH STATUS AND TREATMENT STRATEGIES IN AMOTEPEC

Amotepec was selected as a recipient for a COPLAMAR clinic because of the village's size and perceived need for such services.

Amotepec was the largest locality in the region without any govern-ment health services, and had been soliciting various state and federal agencies for a health clinic for several years.[7] The federal government provided all the necessary equipment and construction supervision, and the localities provided the unpaid laborers for the construction of each new COPLAMAR clinic. Each clinic is staffed by a pasante (a fifth-year medical student serving his or her required year of social service) and a local bilingual female auxiliary who functions primarily as a linguistic translator, but also performs minor record-keeping and medical functions, such as injecting patients.

The overwhelming majority of Mexico's 97,580 localities remain without the services of a locally available physician or pasante. Prior to 1979, Amotepec had never had a resident pasante, and rarely had been visited by one. Amotepecans. like people elsewhere in Mexico, relied in the past on a variety of indigenous healing techni-ques. How people in Mexico have chosen from a variety of curing options has been the focus of many investigations (McClain 1977; Young 1978, 1980, 1981a, 1981b; Young & Garro 1982). The re-search conducted for this study revealed that people in Amotepec share a characteristic reported by the above-noted scholars, namely that of pragmatism. In other words, Amotepecans did not view their treatment alternatives as mutually exclusive. Instead, they combined aspects of various healing resources whenever they perceived it to be to their advantage to do so.

In Amotepec there is a strong historical tradition of, and con-tinued appreciation for, herbal medicines. This preference may be accounted for by two factors. First, a great variety of flora is readily available in this "luxuriant" northern end of the Central American tropical rain forest (Schultes 1941). Second, the great distance from Amotepec to the nearest physician (two or three days' walk until recent decades), not to mention the costs involved, made it impera-tive that some other manner for responding to illness and disease be locally available.

There are presently five part-time healers (*curanderos*) in Amotepec, three males and two females. One curandero is particu-larly renowned for his exceptional skills, including not only know-ledge of herbal remedies, orations, and pulsing, but also familiarity with injections and patent medicines. He is often absent from Amotepec for weeks at a time, working in his fields some three hours' walk downslope from Amotepec. While he is occasionally sought out when he is not in the village, more often people will seek other local healers or healers residing in nearby villages.

Despite the fact that no physician had ever been available in Amotepec prior to the arrival of the COPLAMAR pasante in 1979, villagers have long been very familiar with biomedicine. Their familiarity derives not only from their experiences with physicians located throughout urban Mexico, but also because of the medical services and pharmaceuticals provided by two linguist-missionaries who lived in Amotepec periodically for over 20 years before 1979. These providers (who were trained in basic medicine, but were not physicians) were widely appreciated not only for their medical "expertise" but also for their ability to communicate with the villagers in their own language, and their (albeit incomplete) understanding of the Chinantec's world-view.

The nature of the illness complaint influences the choice of healer sought. For example, virtually all villagers know that physicians (whether in Amotepec or elsewhere) are untrained in certain illnesses experienced in Amotepec (and throughout Mesoamerica) (such as *susto*, *mal ojo*, *mal aire*, *envidia*, and *brujeria*).[8] Amotepecans also know that physicians are ignorant of herbal medicines, as well as pulsing and cleansing. Therefore, illness complaints requiring knowledge of the above are almost never taken to physicians. Instead, family members, friends, or one of the village healers are sought out. If the patient is not cured by one of these village residents then he or she is often transported to a nearby Chinantec-speaking village for treatment by a healer. Or, if the patient has the strength and the financial resources, an urban healer might be visited.

Although people in Amotepec bring a wide variety of illnesses and diseases to the COPLAMAR clinic, before they go to the clinic most Amotepecans are first likely to try a home remedy for their ailment, and/or consult a local healer, depending on the nature of the ailment. In many instances the afflicted person (or responsible parent) is sufficiently satisfied with this treatment, and the clinic is not utilized. For example, when one of Amotepec's past presidents (a man age 40 who was active in the efforts to bring a clinic to the village) seriously cut his hand with a machete, he preferred to bandage it himself with his own unsterile cloth rather than visit the clinic which is a mere ten minute walk from his house.

Home remedies often involve medicinal herbs, and/or things purchased in the village. The small general stores in Amotepec stock a limited supply of items (such as alka-seltzer, and *Mejoral* [a sort of aspirin]) which are frequently utilized. Since the nearest pharmacy is located about a five hour bus ride from Amotepec, many villagers stock a few patent medicines.

Amotepecans utilize various treatment options in an eclectic and pragmatic way, taking advantage of the available resources as they see fit. Their eclecticism may be seen in the things they use (prayers, patent medicines, herbal medicines, eggs mixed in beer, to name a few) and in the personnel they seek out (local and extra-local healers, the local clinic pasante, and distant physicians) in their attempts to relieve pain and suffering. Despite the 2,889 visits made by patients to the clinic during its first 32 months (an average of three patients per day), there is widespread dissatisfaction with the personnel and the pharmaceuticals dispensed there (explained below).

THE COPLAMAR CLINIC IN AMOTEPEC

Having presented a general overview of the COPLAMAR program to deliver health and health services to millions of "marginal" Mexicans by means of 2,105 rural clinics, we turn now to an examination of one specific clinic located in the highland Chinantec locality of Amotepec. I will first describe the particular clinic, and then I will compare its "reality" with the "ideal" clinic designed by the COPLAMAR program's planners. We will see that while much of what exists and occurs in the Amotepec clinic closely parallels official regulations, several differences exist as well, despite voluminous regulations and monthly visits to the clinic by supervisors.

The COPLAMAR clinic in Amotepec opened in September of 1979, and has had an average of 100 patients each month since. Patient visits are carefully recorded in the clinic, and (with certain restrictions for confidentially) I was able to see these records with little difficulty. Males and females are seen as patients in approximately equal numbers. While villagers of all ages come to the clinic, the majority (54%) of the patients are under the age of sixteen. This concentration of patients in the younger age brackets reflects the youthfulness of the general population in Amotepec.

The most common physical ailments reported in Amotepec bear sad resemblance to those reported in the rural areas of underdeveloped countries elsewhere. Undernutrition, gastrointestinal, and upper respiratory ailments (the classic "diseases of poverty") are most frequently encountered by the clinic personnel. Roughly two-thirds of the children under the age of five in Amotepec were found to be undernourished, and 38 percent of them are second- and third-degree undernourished (meaning that they are at least 25 percent below their theoretically desirable body weight).[9]

Analysis of the COPLAMAR clinic's first 2,889 patient-visits during the clinic's first 32 months of operation reveals that 58.3 percent of all clinical diagnoses were for gastro-intestinal and upper respiratory problems The remainder of patients were treated for numerous different ailments, including (listed in descending order of frequency): rheumatoid arthritis, diabetes, scabies, back pain, dental caries, skin ailments (various), epilepsy, and a broad variety of miscellaneous injuries and afflictions.

As noted above, the Amotepec clinic was often in variance with COPLAMAR regulations. For example, each COPLAMAR clinic is designed to serve 5,000 people, none of whom is expected to live farther than one hour's walk from the clinic. The clinic in Amotepec, like many other COPLAMAR clinics, fails to meet these ideals. The Amotepec clinic officially serves a population of 3,159, fully half of whom live in outlying hamlets averaging two hours' walk from the clinic. Because of their distance from the clinic, these "covered" beneficiaries almost never receive any benefits from the COPLAMAR clinic in Amotepec.

Similarly, each COPLAMAR clinic is supposed to be located no more than 3 hours' walk or ride from the referral hospital. However, for the people in Amotepec, the referral hospital involves a seven-hour bus ride on a bus service that runs only twice a week. Given the time, distance, and expense involved, it is perhaps not surprising that during the clinic's first 2½ years of operation, only one Amotepecan ever utilized the referral hospital, and that was only because the patient was transported to it directly by the clinic supervisor (in his Jeep) at the urging of the supervisor. Other Amotepecans who have needed emergency care have stopped in Oaxaca City and sought the services of other physicians, rather than travel farther to Tlacolula, despite the costs involved in Oaxaca.

Any villager hoping to be treated at the referral hospital must be prepared for yet another encumbrance. COPLAMAR regulations require that all patients must have a signed note of authorization from their rural clinic pasante in order to be admitted to the hospital. Thus, if you become ill while in Oaxaca City, you may not simply ride the bus one hour to the free health services of the referral clinic, but instead you must endure the lengthy bus ride back to Amotepec to obtain the proper papers from the pasante (who may not even be in the village!).[10] COPLAMAR officials told me that there are numerous clinics whose circumstances are much less favorable than those faced by Amotepecans.

Official COPLAMAR regulations require their clinics to be open daily from 8 a.m. to 1 p.m., and from 3 p.m. to 6 p.m., Monday through Saturday. Pasantes are required to work in the clinic during these times unless visiting an outlying "covered" hamlet on work-related business. Working in the clinic on Sundays is optional, but the pasante must be in the community on Sundays in case of emergencies. Each pasante is allowed four days vacation per month, plus three days per month to attend a required meeting in the state capital. An additional 14 days of vacation is granted annually. Thus, a pasante should be in the village about 265 days (or 73 percent) of the year.

Absenteeism is common among urban-trained pasantes who often find little to interest them in the rural settings where they are compelled to reside for a year. During my research time in Amotepec, the clinic was often closed to the public, or was open even though the pasante was absent. Amotepec's pasante took great liberties with the COPLAMAR regulations. During his year in the village he was out of the village 58 percent of the time, an absentee rate more than double that allowed by regulations. This pasante not only ignored the required work days and working hours, but often would be publicly drunk during working hours. Thus, villagers became unable to rely on the clinic being open, or the pasante being present and sober.[11]

While such clinics as the one in Amotepec may have the potential to provide rural Mexicans with their constitutionally guaranteed right to health, the reality of the Amotepec clinic shows that such potential is far from being realized. As will be suggested below, COPLAMAR clinics like the one in Amotepec, while not adequately meeting their stated objectives, are serving other functions. We turn now to analysis of various perspectives on such rural health clinics.

THE VILLAGERS' VIEW OF THE COPLAMAR CLINIC

As early as 1603, the highland Chinantec Indians were forced to destroy their homes and sacred idols, and were made to relocate their residences and to worship a new god at the insistence of the Spanish Crown (Cline 1949, 1955). In more recent times the Mexican state has actively penetrated the region for both economic and

political reasons. In the mid 1950s an all-weather road was constructed into the highland Chinantec area because of the nation's
interests in the region's timber resources. During the 1970s new
roads, schools, potable water, electricity, and health clinics reached
into remote villages for the first time, thus providing the nation with
several new forms of linkages with the rural population.

Over the centuries, the Chinantec people have, not surprisingly,
developed considerable distrust for outsiders whose policies and
activities affect their lives. Villagers in Amotepec continue to be
almost universally distrustful of, and cynical about, government
intervention in their lives. In spite of this, they are quick to express
appreciation for the various state-subsidized amenities which have
reached Amotepec in recent years (including a new road, electricity,
potable water, a CONASUPO food-staples store, a new school, and
the new health clinic). Yet they are also quick to share their complaints about each of these state-supported "improvements."

Amotepecans' great familiarity with urban Mexico (because of the
land scarcity which forces them to work outside the village), makes
them keenly aware of their second-class status when compared to
many urban Mexicans. One might expect that these feelings of
inequality vis-à-vis Mexico's urban-based power sector might be
soothed by the arrival of a modern government health facility.
These expectations could logically be reinforced by the fact that
Amotepecans were now receiving services which they had been
requesting for many years. The villagers wanted the health clinic not
only because they hoped that it might improve their health status,
but also because local-level political rivalries made it advantageous
for Amotepec to have as many impressive amenities as possible (See
Stebbins 1986a for elaboration of this point).

Due to past experiences with government participation in their
daily lives, however, the villagers of Amotepec accepted the CO-
PLAMAR clinic with suspicion and ambivalence. Several informants told me that prior to the opening of the clinic most villagers
did not believe that its services and pharmaceuticals would be free,
even though they had been told this all along.

At the time of my fieldwork, the COPLAMAR clinic had been
functioning for more than two years. What were the villagers
perceptions about their clinic at this time? They repeatedly con-
veyed to me their disappointment with what they had received, and
they also repeatedly reflected their deep-felt cynicism about the
government bureaucrats which provided them with it. The villagers
did not view their new health clinic as an indication of government

benevolence. Instead, they once again felt betrayed by the promises made to them (in official proclamations) which led them to believe that they were equally as deserving of first-class services as anyone in Mexico.

The villagers expressed their anti-government, anti-clinic sentiments in a variety of ways, including the following:

> The government doesn't do anything unless there is money in it for them. The government helps [rural people, with a clinic, for example] if there is money put in their hands — big bundles of money. The government is maintained by the money which pueblos like ours give it. Pueblos like Amotepec are not helped very much by the government. The government bureaucrats "eat" twenty percent of whatever funds are supposed to go toward helping the marginal pueblos.

> The government collects taxes on our houses every year. They keep most of the money we give them, and return just a little of it for such things as roads and electricity [and clinics].

> The tax collectors come to town twice a year collecting taxes from all the home owners. Can you imagine having to pay a tax on something you already own?

> In order to get anything from the government it is necessary to continually pester them about your desires. Otherwise they'll forget you (spoken by the village president, recalling Amotepec's decades of soliciting the government for a clinic).

> The Mexican government doesn't help the [rural] people one bit. Even though the CONASUPO, the clinic, the school, and the electricity are beneficial, it is wrong to say that the government helps the people. Instead, the government *exploits* the people. Government people get their positions through family connections or money, regardless of whether they are qualified, and they respond only to bribes (spoken by Amotepec's immediate past-president).

> The government exploits peasants, but it knows that it better not exploit them *too* much, because if the government makes our lives too difficult, who will grow the corn [and other important foodstuffs] for them?

> The soldiers are really just slaves [*mozos*] for the rich. Just look at the banks where the rich people keep their money. You see soldiers guarding it with rifles.

> There is no justice in Mexico, and especially in Oaxaca. The millionaires can kill peasants, and then easily buy their freedom from the government officials.

> The government runs everything in Mexico, and keeps the profits for itself. The government controls the petroleum, the lumber, the sugar cane, and tobacco, and doesn't pay a fair wage for the work done, or a fair price for the timber [for example] bought. These rich people run everything.

Accordingly, the people of Amotepec feel strongly that they have a right to a health clinic, and they feel that they are constantly paying for it with their labor and taxes. Now that they have a locally-available government health clinic (which they feel they have *earned* through their financial contributions to the government), Amotepecans have found it to fall short of their expectations and desires in a number of ways. Their complaints include dissatisfaction with the clinic's pasante, the clinic's pharmaceuticals, and most importantly, the clinic's frequent inability to cure persisting ailments.[12] It is to this most important complaint that we now turn.

DO IMPROVED HEALTH SERVICES GUARANTEE IMPROVED HEALTH STATUS?

The health needs of the rural Mexican population have long been neglected, despite constitutional guarantees of health. The leading causes of death in Mexico are similar to those experienced in the United States during the early 1900s. More than 30 percent of all deaths in Mexico are from pneumonia, influenza, enteritis, and diarrheal diseases (Daschbach and Connolly 1977: 564–565). All of these diseases are closely associated with lack of potable water, unhygienic environments, inadequate housing, and undernutrition, conditions which prevail in rural Mexico.

In recent years[13] the Mexican government has attempted to improve these conditions, but their efforts have unfortunately not significantly improved living conditions for the vast majority of the rural population (Grindle 1981). The recent government development of 2,105 COPLAMAR health clinics represents an enormous commitment to the provision of health services in Mexico's rural areas. Nevertheless, the health services provided by the clinic in Amotepec fall far short of what is deemed necessary and desirable by the recipients of the services. The COPLAMAR clinic in Amotepec does a reasonable job of providing patient care and pharmaceuticals to the half of the "covered" population that lives near the clinic. The preventive health services listed as part of the COPLAMAR program are scarcely evident in Amotepec, and there is little reason to believe that conditions are significantly different in the other COPLAMAR clinics. COPLAMAR documents recognize the importance of environmental factors, nutrition, and "social" medicine (COPLAMAR 1981: 125, 132, 166), but in Amotepec these components of health services are not delivered. Instead, the clinic there operates basically as a part-time emergency first-aid station, while at the same time adding to the frustrations of the villagers.

While the highly trained curative medical treatment which is sporadically available in Amotepec is not without merit, it comprises only part of what is required to improve the villagers' health status. At least as important, and probably more so, is the need for public health programs which would significantly improve the undernutrition and unsanitary environmental conditions which prevail.

By choosing to emphasize curative (rather than preventive) medical services, the conditions which contribute to the onset, persistence, and recurrence of Amotepec's most common diseases are left largely unaffected. It is perhaps ironic that, if the Amotepec villagers were allowed to voice their sentiments as to what form of emphasis they would like their government-provided health services to take, they would in all likelihood express a preference for a highly-trained and experienced physician (This is because many of them believe that "modern" medicine should be able to make them healthy). This expressed preference for biomedicine should not be mistaken as disinterest in public health or paramedical programs. What Amotepecans want most of all regarding matters conerning health and illness is to be *healthy*. How they achieve this status is largely unimportant to them. From the villagers' perspective, physicians have the potential to cure ailments, and that is why they express a desire for a physician. But when Amotepecans say that the doctor in their village should know how to *cure* people, they are not expressing a preference for *curative* medical services so much as they are expressing a desire to be free of their persistent ailments (See Stebbins 1986b for further discussion).

The fact that their ailments persist should not be blamed on the COPLAMAR pasantes. Greater responsibility for the poor health indices among rural Mexicans (including Amotepecans) lies with the health planners and the medical institutions which train pasantes to work primarily in highly technical urban settings, with almost no preparation in public health measures or low-technology health care delivery in cross-cultural settings. At an even higher level of analysis, the particular material and social conditions of life observed for dependent capitalist economies such as Mexico's are greatly affected by the world economy and peripheral capital accumulation (Chossudovsky 1983).

The nature of the political and economic linkages between developed and underdeveloped countries in Latin America results in much of the resources of the poor countries being siphoned into the wealthy countries. Referring to developed capitalist countries as metropoles and to underdeveloped capitalist countries as satellites, Frank (1969: 14–15) writes that "the metropolis expropriates economic surpluses from its satellites and appropriates it for its own economic development. The satellites remain underdeveloped for lack of access to their own surplus ..." and because of similar conditions within the satellite's domestic economy. In other words, the dependency relations between developed and underdeveloped countries serve not only to enrich the former, but also to impoverish the latter. Furthermore, within capitalist underdeveloped countries such as Mexico the process of capital accumulation serves to benefit the capitalist class at the expense of the lower classes (Cockcroft 1983a).

While the villagers of Amotepec derive some benefits from their COPLAMAR clinic, Mexico's ruling class is also benefitting from this investment in rural Mexico. Their benefits include: 1) potentially facilitating the extraction of valued resources from rural areas (especially if the clinics could attend to the dominant problems of infectious disease and undernutrition [Laurell 1981]), 2) providing for the possibility of a healthier reserve supply of labor in both urban and rural workplaces, and 3) publicly demonstrating the ruling class' commitment to the rural sector, thereby reducing the possibility of unrest or revolt in the countryside.

From World War II until very recent times, Mexico's annual economic growth has averaged 6.3 percent, an exceptional rate of economic expansion (Kate and Wallace 1980: 1). However, despite this incredible sustained economic growth, it has been estimated that 67 to 80 percent of the population of Mexico City cannot afford basic food, shelter, and health care (Musselwhite 1981: 51).

The contrasts in living standards between the wealthy and the poor in Mexico are striking. Amidst Mexico's islands of prosperity there are oceans of poverty. Despite being the fourth largest producer of petroleum in the world (Street 1981: 374), Mexico continues to have millions of undernourished and underemployed citizens. Much of the wealth generated during Mexico's post-World War II economic growth has been extracted by transnational corporations centered in developed countries, especially in the United States (Cockcroft 1983b). The wealth which is not exported out of Mexico is far from equally distributed among all Mexicans. In fact, few countries in the world have a more unequal income distribution than Mexico (Felix 1977: 111).

In an insightful essay on the maldistribution of human health resources in Latin America, Navarro (1974) demonstrates that the underdevelopment of health is inseparably associated with the region's dependency relationships with the dominant capitalist world system, and with the economic and political control of resources by the ruling class. The linkages connecting transnational corporations with Mexico's ruling class are explained by both parties' shared interests in accumulating capital and maximizing wealth.

The capitalist class in the less-developed countries, as elsewhere, is governed by the logic of capital accumulation that dictates profit maximization in the case of individual capitalists as well as state policies in the interest of collective profit maximizing for the class as a whole (Szymanski 1981: 416).

This interpretation helps to explain what has happened in Mexico in recent years. Despite significant oil revenues, during the 1970s things continued to worsen for the poorest Mexicans (Gonzales Casanova 1980: 202). In spite of widespread government programs to aid rural areas, the plight of the peasantry continued. For example, a 1979 study by Mexico's National Nutrition Institute found that nearly 90 percent of Mexico's rural population suffered various degrees of calorie and protein deficiency and that (with the exception of the north of Mexico) the level of calorie consumption had declined or remained unchanged for rural Mexicans over the previous 20 years (cited in Grindle 1981: 33). Similarly, environmental and economic conditions (such as employment, education, housing, and health) were also not noticeably improving during the 1970s in rural Mexico (Grindle 1981: 33).

Poverty conditions (especially unsanitary living conditions and inadequate nutrition) can have serious health consequences. The COPLAMAR program recognizes the disadvantaged situation of millions of rural Mexicans, and represents an unprecedented investment in Mexico's "deprived zones and marginal areas." The rural clinics and referral hospitals represent a part of this commitment. However, as has been pointed out by the experienced residents of Amotepec, the *promise* of an improved standard of living in the countryside is *no guarantee* that improvements will be realized.

The provision of health services such as those incorporated in Mexico's COPLAMAR development program is an example of an activist, politically centralized state penetrating into its rural hinterlands. The nature of state penetration in Mexico is heavily influenced by the priorities of the nation's political elite. While the primary orientation of the COPLAMAR program involves wealth-producing resource development and extraction, COPLAMAR's health services program provides the ruling elite with certain benefits, as noted above. For example, significant propaganda value is derived from COPLAMAR's efforts. To this end, government officials proudly proclaim that the 2,105 new COPLAMAR clinics are proof that the constitutional guarantee of health for all Mexicans is finally being realized by millions of long-neglected rural residents. However, for Amotepecans we have seen that such is not the case.

Nevertheless, the *appearance* of doing something about rural health conditions may be quite beneficial to the ruling class, regardless of the effectiveness of the services provided. By virtue of *appearing* to address past injustices in the countryside, the COPLAMAR program is, in effect, telling the peasantry that things are getting better for them, and that meaningful change is underway and must not be jeopardized by complaints. At the same time, the COPLAMAR program tells the larger Mexican population that the government it actively working to improve the lot of the disadvantaged rural sector.[14] In this way, the potential for rural unrest is reduced, and the legitimacy for suppressing rural instability is increased. Such political stability is especially important given the nature of Mexico's economic growth strategy, which is dependent on "nervous" capital (Musselwhite 1981: 265–266).[15] Despite the peasants' complaints about the COPLAMAR clinic and their hostility toward the Mexican government, the widely disseminated propaganda extolling the virtues of the COPLAMAR clinics serves to reduce public support for the peasants' complaints, while legitimizing the use of government force to supress any serious attempts to publicly protest their situation.

The COPLAMAR health clinics potentially benefit Mexico's ruling class in several other ways in addition to those noted above. For example, the family planning programs which are intended to be a major component of COPLAMAR's health services (COPLAMAR 1981), if effective, would be of enormous benefit to the government, because of its concern about feeding, housing, and employing its future population. Also, such new clinics may potentially serve to encourage rural residents to postpone or abandon plans to migrate to already overcrowded urban centers.

The medical establishment also benefits from COPLAMAR's perpetuation and expansion of the biomedical model, emphasizing curative treatment. This is so because curative medicine provided by highly trained physicians perpetuates their dominant view of how to treat ailments, in contrast to public health personnel or paramedical healers who represent an alternative approach to the same issues.

Since the end of the nineteenth century, "scientific medicine" has become an ideological tool utilized by the medical profession to control not only the training of new physicians, but also the orientation of health care delivery (Brown 1979).[16] Medical professionals, closely allied with Mexico's ruling class, tend to promote ideological paradigms that benefit primarily their own privileged class. The biomedical paradigm which dominates technological medicine today benefits the limited economic and social interests of various medical groups who are unlikely to voluntarily surrender the powerful status they presently enjoy.

Pharmaceutical interests, for example, benefit from supplying the 2,105 clinics and 41 regional hospitals with their products. Mexico's health care orientation in 1973 was found to be "highly dominated by the influence of the drug and medical supplies industries" (Lopez Acuña 1980a: 88). This 1973 survey on health research in Mexico showed that only 4.3 percent of the research projects were in the field of public health, while most research was clinically based and mostly sponsored by drug companies (Lopez Acuña 1982: 205).

Finally, the introduction of biomedicine (through the COPLA-MAR clinics) into indigenous communities represents yet one more intrusion on the part of the capitalist-oriented national economy into the lives of traditionally subsistence-oriented people (who are now also part-time workers in urban areas). The Chinantec people of southern Mexico, like indigenous people throughout the world, are regular recipients of externally imposed ideological paradigms which are often foreign to their world-view.[17] The COPLAMAR clinics represent yet another form of state penetration (Corbett and Whiteford 1983) which aids (both subtly and overtly) the government's long-standing goal of "Mexicanizing" the Indian population (Warman 1970).[18]

SUMMARY AND CONCLUSIONS

This analysis of health status and health services in rural Mexico demonstrates the value of anthropological data-gathering techniques (including micro-level data) and the importance of political and economic considerations (especially at the macro-level) when evaluating local-level realities. The case of a new rural health clinic in Oaxaca, Mexico illustrates how people at the local community level are affected by macro-level policies which penetrate into their daily lives in a number of ways through a wide variety of linkages, including government-directed health clinics.

This paper has shown that macro-level information (in the form of government documents, media accounts, and interviews with bureaucratic officials) does not necessarily conform with data obtained at the micro-level (as for example in the village of Amotepec). This essay has also noted that the Mexican government's recent impressive improvements in rural health care services (in the form of 2,105 rural clinics and 41 rural hospitals) do not necessarily mean that the "beneficiaries" of these new *services* will enjoy improved health *status*. However, this paper suggests that even if impressive new rural health facilities fail to add to the well-being of Mexico's rural population, they do provide certain political and economic benefits to the nation's ruling elite, including enhanced possibilities for political stability.

This essay has also shown that rural villagers in Mexico (like those elsewhere) are very familiar with biomedicine, and they definitely want it available to them in their village. However, they want *effective* medicine and *effective* personnel, neither of which they feel has yet been provided to them. Most importantly, they want to be free of their persistent and recurring ailments once and for all, and they feel that their government has an obligation to do so. As we have seen, until the *causal* factors (especially unsanitary environmental factors and inadequate nutritional intake) of their persistent ailments are addressed, preventable health problems will persist.

Improving the health status of rural Mexicans requires significant redistribution of health-sustaining resources (especially food-related) and improved environmental conditions (especially pure water, adequate housing, and proper sewage disposal). These kinds of structural changes involve concerns outside of the medical establishment, including land redistribution programs, water agencies, education, roads, agricultural extension services, and financial assistance. In dependent capitalist economies such as Mexico's, the conflicts between class interests prevent the lower classes from enjoying a representative share of the country's health-related resources.

The COPLAMAR services described in this paper are presently being provided in the absence of any accompanying social, political, or economic transformations, and thus the status quo is left basically intact. One health planner who has compared health development strategies of socialist economies with those in dependent capitalist economies has stated that it is a myth to think that

> governments are universally committed to improving the health of their populations .... In many countries, few things could be farther from the truth. Technical knowledge is one thing — and an essential one — but without political will it is of little use. Where there is presently no such political will because governments represent the more powerful and the more healthy rather than the less powerful and the less healthy, then development will occur only through demands by the latter on the former (England 1978: 158).

Despite Mexico's ongoing revolutionary rhetoric about providing health for its rural masses, the implementation of such glowing political promises remains unaccomplished. Until such time as Mexico's impoverished rural population gains more favorable access to important health-sustaining resources such as those outlined above, there is little reason to believe that their health status will improve beyond what they currently experience, in spite of the recent provision of great numbers of health clinics and hospitals specifically targeted for their benefit. With Mexico's economic development aspirations so closely linked to its uncertain oil revenues (Horn 1983: 36), and with "austerity" measures increasingly being mandated from the highest levels, the outlook for improved health status for the poor is even more problematic.

Anthropologists concerned with health-related matters are in a unique position to provide policy-makers and the general public with important information that might otherwise not be obtained, especially information about how the rural and marginalized sector of an underdeveloped country is being affected by government programs. Those social scientists who employ a political-economic perspective in their analyses provide a more thorough explanation of the forces which impact upon the lives of impoverished people.

Anthropologists who utilize a political-economic perspective, by virtue of the careful attention they pay to the marginalized population, are able to convey an even more complete understanding of the plight of the poor. Those anthropologists who provide health-related policy-makers with such information are possibly enhancing the chances that the serious health needs of the underclass will be quickly and reasonably addressed. However, because the interests of these policy-makers are so closely aligned with those of Mexico's corporate elites and government bureaucrats, any significant change in the health status of the masses is more likely to come from below than from above. Anthropologists, therefore, may affect more meaningful change by working at the grass-roots level rather than at the level of the government bureaucracy.

NOTES

1. It is also misleading to suggest that a clear-cut dichotomy exists between rural and urban populations because, as Uzzell (1976) has noted, Mexico's "rural" population frequently visits and/or lives in urban areas for extended periods of time, and therefore does not contrast completely with the "urban" population.
2. COPLAMAR stands for Coordinacion General del Plan Nacional de Zonas

Deprimidas y Grupos Marginados, or the General Coordinating Board for the National Plan [to aid] Depressed and Marginal Groups.

3. This paper reports on some aspects of research conducted for a doctoral dissertation in medical anthropology. For elaboration of points made here, as well as additional information, see Stebbins (1984).

4. Ten days of unpaid labor would not be met with enthusiasm by rural Mexicans. However, during the period when this research was gathered, Amotepec household heads were being obliged to donate only about 2 days of labor per year.

5. The more "Indian" states of Chiapas, Oaxaca, Puebla, Tlaxcala, Hidalgo, San Luis Potosi, and Guerrero account for 49 percent of the COPLAMAR clinics. Ethnically, 38.4 percent of the covered population are Indians ("indigenas") and 61.6 percent are non-Indians ("mestizos") (COPLAMAR 1981: 95).

6. It is impossible to estimate how many different *patients* this figure includes, because some patients made more than one visit to a clinic during the year.

7. How Amotepec was chosen from among so many other potential villages is not entirely clear. Certainly, Amotepec was among the largest communities in the region without any kind of government clinic. COPLAMAR officials told me that their decisions relied heavily on the recommendations of the National Indigenous Institute (INI). It should not be forgotten that the primary criteria for locating new government services are often based on the political motives of government officials more than on the needs of the population (Grindle 1980, see especially Chapter 8).

8. These illness categories can be loosely translated as "magical fright" (susto), "evil eye" (mal ojo), "evil winds" (mal aire), "envy" (envidia), and "witchcraft" (brujeria).

9. This finding is based on data obtained between September 1981 and April 1982, when the clinic personnel weighed a total of 149 children who came to the clinic for whatever reason (even if only to accompany their mother or a sibling). Their weight was plotted against their age, and their degree of malnutrition was recorded. There is no reason to believe that nutritional status for Amotepec's children has improved since this finding.

10. It is possible (but certainly not guaranteed) that these requirements would be waived in an emergency situation.

11. While such reports are not uncommon, the reader should understand that not all pasantes neglect their responsibilities toward their patients. In fact, some pasantes are extremely dedicated, and in certain cases have accidentally lost their lives while trying to reach their remote health posts.

12. The villagers' widespread dissatisfaction with their pasante is explained by his chronic absenteeism and his frequent drunkenness. The villagers' complaints about the clinic's pharmaceuticals are explained by the fact that they do not cure their persistent ailments, a point now addressed in the text. It is encouraging to report that Amotepec's most recent pasante is very diligent about her responsibilities in the village (personal observation, June 1986). However, as this paper attempts to convey, in order to cure the persistent health problems of rural Mexicans, much more than a diligent pasante will be required.

13. The presidency of Luis Echevarría (1970–76) marks the beginning of the recent emphasis on rural services. These services were extended during the presidency of José Lopez Portillo (1976–82), largely because of unparalleled petroleum revenues. The economic crises and accompanying austerity measures of the presidency of Miguel de la Madrid have resulted in cutbacks in many rural services.

14. In addition to the state health programs, Mexico's ruling class has numerous other linkages with the rural sector through a variety of state-directed programs, including the schools, the CONASUPO food-staples program, public transportation systems, public utilities, and the major media channels.

15. Investment capital is extremely concerned about the potential for unrest, especially given Mexico's proximity to its "volitile" Central American neighbors to the south.
16. Brown's (1979) discussion of the historical development of medicine in the United States provides interesting parallels with the situation described in this essay concerning health care delivery in underdeveloped countries. Central to Brown's thesis is the long-standing close association between American medicine and industrial capitalism. For an enlightening discussion of relationships between public health programs and capitalist extraction of resources in underdeveloped countries, see Brown (1976).
17. The impact of dominant peoples on indigenous cultures can be severe. The Papaloapan River Commission constructed two large dams in the 1950s which displaced tens of thousands of lowland Chinantec and Mazatec Indians in what has been called a "program of ethnocide" (Barabas & Bartolomé 1973: 13).
18. In the case of the health clinic, the goal of assimilating the ethnic populations throughout the republic is quite subtle and almost coincidental to the stated goals of the COPLAMAR program. Nevertheless, the clinic reflects the national culture, the national world-view and Western scientific understandings of health and disease, and shows virtually no knowledge of, interest in, or sensitivity to, the Chinantec culture and world-view.

REFERENCES

Baer, Hans, 1982. On the Political Economy of Health, *Medical Anthropology Newsletter* 14(1): 1, 2, 13–17.

Barabas, Alicia, and Miguel Bartolomé, 1973. Hydraulic Development and Ethnocide: The Mazatec and Chinantec People of Oaxaca, Mexico, *IWGIA Document*. Copenhagen.

Bossert, Thomas, 1979. Health Policies in Africa and Latin America: Adopting the Primary Care Approach, *Social Science and Medicine* 13C: 65–68.

Brown, E. Richard, 1976. Public Health and Imperialism: Early Rockefeller Programs at Home and Abroad, *American Journal of Public Health* 66(9): 897–903.

Brown, E. Richard, 1979. *Rockefeller Medicine Men: Medicine and Capitalism in America*. Berkeley: University of California Press.

Cañedo, Luis, 1974. Rural Health Care in Mexico? *Science* 185: 1131–1137.

Cháves, Adolfo, 1982. 'Nutrición: Problemas y Alternativas. In *México, Hoy*. eds. Pablo Gonzales Casanova and Enrique Florescano. Mexico City: Siglo XXI Editores.

Chossudovsky, Michel, 1983. Underdevelopment and the Political Economy of Malnutrition and Ill Health, *International Journal of Health Services* 13(1): 69–83.

Cline, Howard F., 1949. Civil Congregations of the Indians in New Spain, 1598–1606, *Hispanic American Historical Review* 29(3): 349–369.

Cline, Howard F., 1955. Civil Congregations of the Western Chinantla, New Spain. 1599–1603, *The Americas* 12: 115–137.

Cockcroft, James D., 1983a. Immiseration, not Marginalization: The Case of Mexico, *Latin American Perspectives* 10(2, 3): 86–107.

Cockcroft, James D., 1983b. *Mexico: Class Formation, Capital Accumulation and the State*. New York: Monthly Review Press.

Coplamar, 1978. *Region Mixteca de Oaxaca*. Programas integrados, Vol. 22. Mexico City: Presidencia de la Republica.

Coplamar, 1981. *Primera Reunión Anual de Análisis del Desarrollo del Programa IMSS-COPLAMAR: Unidades Médicas Rurales*. Mexico City: Instituto Mexicano del Seguro Soccial.

Corbett, Jack, and Scott Whiteford, 1983. *State penetration and development in Mesoamerica, 1950–1980. In Heritage of conquest: Thirty years later*, p. 9–33. Eds Carl Kendall, John Hawkins and Laurel Bossen Albuquerque: University of New Mexico Press.

Correu Azcona, Sergio, 1980. Agent Characteristics and Productivity in the Mexican Rural Health Program, *Studies in Family Planning* 11(7–8): 247–254.

Daschbach, Charles, and Robin J. Connolly, 1977. Medicine in Mexico: Health Indices, *Arizona Medicine* 34(8): 564–565.

England, Roger, 1978. More Myths in International Health Planning, *American Journal of Public Health* 68(2): 153–159.

Felix, David, 1977. Income Inequality in Mexico, *Current History* 72(425): 111–114, 136.

Frank, Andre Gunder, 1969. *Capitalism and Underdevelopment in Latin America*. New York: Modern Reader.

Gish, Oscar, 1979. The Political Economy of Primary Health Care and "Health by the People": An Historical Explanation, *Social Science and Medicine* 13C: 203–211.

Gonzales Casanova, Pablo, 1980. The Economic Development of Mexico, *Scientific American* September, 192–204.

Grindle, Merilee S., 1980. *Politics and Policy Implementation in the Third World*. Princeton: Princeton University Press.

Grindle, Merilee S., 1981. Official Interpretations of Rural Underdevelopment: Mexico in the 1970s. University of California at San Diego Working Paper No. 20.

Horn, James J., 1983. The Mexican Revolution and Health Care, or the Health of the Mexican Revolution, *Latin American Perspectives* 10(4): 24–39.

Kreisler, Robert, 1981. Politics and Health Care in the Republic of Mexico: A study of the Dynamics of Public Policy. Ph.D. Dissertation, Columbia University.

Laurell, Asa Cristina, 1981. Mortality and Working Conditions in Agriculture in Underdeveloped Countries, *International Journal of Health Services* 11(1): 3–19.

Lopez Acuña, Daniel, 1980a. Health Services in Mexico, *Journal of Public Health Policy* 1(1): 83–95.

Lopez Acuña, Daniel, 1980b. *La Salud Desigual en México*. Mexico City: Siglo XXI Editores.

Lopez Acuña, Daniel, 1982 'Salud y Seguridad Social: Problemas Recientes y Alternativas.' In *México, Hoy*. eds. Pablo Gonzales Casanova and Enrigue Florescano. Mexico City: Siglo XXI Editores.

McClain, Carol, 1977. Adaptation in Health Behavior: Modern and Traditional Medicine in a West Mexican Community, *Social Science and Medicine* 11: 341–347.

Musselwhite, James C., 1981. Public Policy, Development, and the Poor: Health Policy in Mexico. Ph.D. Dissertation, Johns Hopkins University.

Navarro, Vicente, 1974. The Underdevelopment of Health or the Health of Underdevelopment: An Analysis of the Distribution of Human Health Resources in Latin America, *International Journal of Health Services* 5: 5–27.

Navarro, Vicente, 1976. *Medicine under Capitalism*. New York: Prodist.

Ramirez, Carlos, 1981 'El Plan Nacional de Empleo Preve su Propio Fracaso'. In *Planes sin Planificación: Reportajes y Análisis de los Reporteros de Proceso*. 73–87. José Luis Ceceña Cervantes, *et al.* Mexico City.

Schultes, R.E., 1941. The Meaning and Usage of the Mexican Place-Name '*Chinantla*', *Botanical Museum leaflets*, Harvard University 9(6): 101–116.

Stebbins, Kenyon R., 1984. Second-Class Mexicans: State Penetration and its Impact on Health Status and Health Services in a Highland Chinantec Municipio in Oaxaca. Ph.D. Dissertation, Michigan State University.

Stebbins, Kenyon R., 1986a. Politics, Economics and Health Services in Rural

Oaxaca, Mexico, *Human Organization* 45(2): 112–119.

Stebbins, Kenyon R., 1986b. Curative Medicine, Preventive Medicine, and Health Status: The Influence of Politics on Health Status in a Rural Mexican Village, *Social Science and Medicine* 23(2): 139–148.

Szymanski, Albert, 1981. *The Logic of Imperialism*. New York: Praeger.

Ten Kate, Adriaan, and Robert Bruce Wallace, 1980. *Protectionism and Economic Development in Mexico*. Hampshire, England: Gower Publishing Company.

Uzzell, Douglass, 1976. Ethnography of Migration: Breaking Out of the Bi-Polar Myth, *Rice University Studies* 62(3): 45–54.

Young, James C., 1978. Illness Categories and Action Strategies in a Tarascan Town, *American Ethnologist* 5: (1): 81–97.

Young, James C., 1980. A Model of Illness Treatment Decisions in a Tarascan Town, *American Ethnologist* 7: 106–131.

Young, James C., 1981a. Non-Use of Physicians: Methodological Approaches, Policy Implications and the Utility of Decision Models, *Social Science and Medicine* 15B: 499–507.

Young, James C., 1981b. *Medical Choice in a Mexican Village*. New Brunswick: Rutgers University Press.

Young, James C., and Linda Young Garro, 1982. Variations in the Choice of Treatment in Two Mexican Communities, *Social Science and Medicine* 16: 1453–1465.

Institutional Factors in the Implementation of a Health Care Program in Rural Utah Towns

HANS A. BAER
University at Ankansas at Little Rock

CHARLES C. HUGHES
University of Utan

INTRODUCTION

Since the 1950's, there has been a growing recognition of the need to consider the social and cultural characteristics of target populations in the introduction of health programs. Although these studies often are not considered in the implementation of health programs, social scientists have gained a relatively good understanding of the sociocultural factors that may determine their acceptance or rejection by potential recipients. Conversely, as Foster and Anderson (1978: 233) observe, "as time has gone on we have slowly come to accept a disquieting thought; at least as many of the resistances encountered in the promotion of scientific medicine are rooted in the medical profession and in health bureaucracies as in the target peoples." This realization has promted various scholars and social activists, such as Ehrenreich and Ehrenreich (1970), Illich (1976), Navarro (1976) and Waitzkin (1983) to scrutinize the class, bureaucratic, and ideological aspects of the medical establishment in the United States and in other industrial nations, and determine how they affect the nature and distribution of health care.

Although our analysis will not be as ambitious as these studies, we hope it will contribute to an understanding of the factors which influence health care delivery in a complex society. We will delineate institutional factors that need to be considered in the imple-

29

mentation of health programs in rural American communities. For purposes of our analysis, the term "institutional" will refer to those social arrangements and normative patterns which take on a fixed and distinctive character in a community and serve as a locus of vested interests or group identity.

The factors identified are derived from part of an evaluation of the Utah Cost Improvement Project. Utah Cost Improvement Project (UCIP) was supported by a contract between the Social Security Administration and the Utah State Division of Health establised to develop and implement an experimental program permitting rural hospitals to accept extended care patients in their acute care facilities.

Because of the few medically-licensed, long-term care facilities in rural Utah, elderly people needing extended care are often required to seek such care in skilled nursing facilities in the Salt Lake City area or in other urban areas perhaps as far as two or three hundred miles away from their homes and families. In addition to the obvious inconveniences and hardships imposed by such an arrangement, extended care patients, who require perhaps no more than a few months of skilled nursing care, may face a psychological trauma in being placed in a nursing facility, even one close to a home.

Rural Utah, particularly the southern part of the state, is characterized by a low population density with a widely variable demand for medical services. As a result of this situation and liberal capital expenditures in the erection of hospital facilities since the Hill-Burton Act, rural Utah hospitals generally have chronically low occupancy rates. UCIP was established as a pilot program by the Utah Division of Health to alleviate some of these problems. The stated primary goal of the program was to aid rural hospitals by increasing their occupancy rates and lowering both hospital operating cost and medicine costs. Other objectives of the UCIP included the provision of means of payment for extended care patients who are unable to obtain skilled nursing care locally because of the absence or shortage of such services; the provision of a continuity of care by retaining the patient under the same physician; and the broadening of the functions and an increase in the effectiveness of rural hospitals.

The effectiveness of UCIP was evaluated by the Department of Preventive Medicine at the University of Colorado. Part of this evaluation was directed by Charles C. Hughes, who supervised the work of three other anthropologists. This anthropological team was to assess the awareness of the project in nine of the twenty-five participating communities, particularly among physicians, other health personnel, social service workers, and hospital trustees. The research team was also assigned to define the health care needs, health problems, and social structural and cultural characteristics of the communities. One of the authors (Hans Baer) gathered data for an evaluation of the UCIP in three southern Utah towns during the summer of 1975. The institutional factors considered in this paper will be based largely on data gathered in these three communities.

A DESCRIPTION OF THE THREE COMMUNITIES

The three communities of immediate concern will be referred to as Collegeville, Scenic, and Railroad Center. Collegeville (population 11,000) is a state regional commercial center with several small manufacturing and mining operations. It is the site of small state college and the regional headquarters for several federal land agencies. During the summer months many tourists pass through and stay in Collegeville because of its proximity to a number of national parks and national forests and its annual drama festival.

Scenic (population 1,400) is the seat of one of the largest counties in the country and is near the Navajo reservation. It is a jumping-off spot for recreational activities in several national parks and forests. During the 1950s Scenic experienced a short-lived uranium boom which resulted in a doubling of its population and subsequent decline to its present population. Presently, Scenic has a number of small manufacturing and processing concerns and is a commercial center for the surrouding area.

Railroad Center (population 1,300) is a division point on the railroad line between two relatively large Western cities. Railroad employment in the Railroad Center area has decreased appreciably during the past several decades due to several factors, including the advent of more efficient railroad operation, the decrease in iron shipments from a neighboring county, and the closing of the railroad locomotive round house. The shutdown of a nearby copper mining and processing operation further adversely affected the community's economy. Despite a declining economy and the loss of about four hundred residents during the 1960s and 1970s, many Railroad Center residents felt that their area would experience a giant economic boom due to local alunite and geothermal exploratory projects.

Like most rural Utah communities, the bulk of Collegeville's and Scenic's residents are Mormons and conservative Republicans.

Except for a small Paiute community consisting of about two hundred people, almost all of Collegeville's residents are Whites. Although about one-half of the surrounding county's population is Indian, there are only a few Indian families who reside in Scenic. Ten percent, or possibly slightly more, of Scenic's population consists of Spanish-Americans who first moved into the area from New Mexico and southern Colorado. Despite the fact that most of Railroad Center's residents are Mormons, it is an atypical rural Utah community in that it has a relatively high percentage of non-Mormons (referred to as "Gentiles") and tends to be Democratic in its political orientation. A frequent complaint of Gentiles and some inactive Mormons in Collegeville and Scenic was that the active Mormons tightly control the social, economic, and political activities of their communities. Since the Mormons do not greatly outnumber the Gentiles in Railroad Center, the tension between the two groups was much reduced in comparison to many other Utah communities.

DEFINITION OF HEALTH SERVICES

The hospitals in all the communities considered in this essay were relatively new; at the time of the study the oldest one having been erected in 1960. The occupancy rate of the Collegeville hospital hovered around 40 percent, having dropped in the early 1970s. Among the factors for this were the erection of a hospital in a nearby county, the erection of still another hospital in an adjoining state near Collegeville, the loss of medical specialists to a neighboring community, and the increasing costs of hospitalization. An intermediate nursing facility is located a block away from the hospital and another intermediate nursing facility is located in the county seat north of Collegeville. Collegeville was characterized by a lack of medical specialists, although efforts had been made to acquire them. The county seat (population 1,400), about twenty miles from Collegeville, had no physicians, partly because they preferred to reside close to the hospital.

The Scenic Hospital serves most of the communities in the county, with the exception of the Navajo reservation, which is served by an Indian Health Service hospital in Arizona and a sectarian hospital in the southern portion of the county. Except during the winter months, when there are more illnesses, the Scenic Hospital operated at about a fifty percent occupancy rate in 1975. Although the Scenic Hospital permitted Navajo medicinemen to visit

patients, little else was done to accommodate Indians, who comprised about one-third of the hospital's patient load. The hospital operated a skilled nursing facility in a town about twenty miles south of
Scenic, which will be referred to as Mesa. Although health personnel admited that it would be more efficient to have the nursing
home adjacent to the hospital, its location resulted from an intense
rivalry between Mesa and Scenic. Because the county seat and
hospital were located in Scenic, the placement of the nursing home
in Mesa were intended to appease its citizens. The Mesa nursing
home generally operated at near or completely full capacity, but
generally only had a few Indians at any given time. Although the
Mesa physician visited the nursing home at least once a week, the
two Scenic physicians generally did not visit it more than once every
three months or even more.

Despite the relatively small population (approximately 3,800) of
the county within which Railroad Center is located, there is also a
hospital located in the county seat, about thirty-five miles away.
Railroad Center Hospital serves farm communities in the surrounding valley and also two tiny communities west of it, one of them
being in another state. Adjoining the hospital's acute care unit is a
skilled nursing facility; the former operated at a fifty percent occupancy rate and the latter at a 75–80 percent occupancy rate in 1975.
The Railroad Center Hospital was served by one physician who was
assisted by a Medex. The hospital in the county seat did not operate
a skilled nursing facility but did administer a housing unit for elderly
people not requiring constant nursing care.

INSTITUTIONAL FACTORS

In the evaluation of UCIP, it became very apparent that the nature
and degree of the program's acceptance was affected strongly by
local institutional factors.

1. Channels of Communication

Open channels of communication on a number of levels are essential in the successful implementation of any health program. The
need for full understanding of the purposes and implication of a
program applies both to those persons who would be the ultimate
recipients of care, their families, and those persons located at intermediate stations along the communication channel, such as the
hsopital administrators, members of the hospital board, physicians,

staff nurses, and aides. A break at any point could imperil the entire operation.

The State Division of Health apparently considered each participating administrator the "gatekeeper" to the hospital and, as such, assumed that he would communicate the details of UCIP, not only to members of his hospital staff, but also to physicians and the community at large. Some administrators neither fully understood the way the program was intended to function, nor communicated important details to others. The Scenic Hospital administrator resented what he considered interference by the State Division of Health, but did not object to the program as long as he had considerable flexibility in deciding how to use it. The Collegeville Hospital administrator had serious reservations about the program, largely because he felt that the payments made for services rendered to extended care patients were insufficient. In addition, he maintained that he had been both pressured and misled by the State Division of Health into accepting the program. The Railroad Center Hospital administrator stated that although he approved of UCIP, he did not think that his hospital had a great need for it.

It appears that the attitudes of the administrators toward the program, which ranged from mild hostility to indifference, affected the manner in which its details were communicated to hospital personnel. For example, in the three communities under consideration both physicians and nurses were generally not acquainted with the term "Utah Cost Improvement Project" but referred to the program as "SNF" (meaning "skilled nursing facility") program. Furthermore, little information about the details of the program were known to the physicians or nurses. In the case of the Railroad Center Hospital, the only nurse familiar with the program in any form whatsoever was the nursing supervisor. It is particularly interesting to note that the assistant administrator of the Collegeville Hospital indicated no recognition of UCIP by name and was only vaguely familiar with the program, as were personnel of the various state regional health districts, social service agencies and nursing homes serving the three communities. Local mass media, such as radio stations and weekly newspapers, were not effectively used to inform the public about the health program.

Closely related to the problem of communication was the manner in which the program was administered at the local level. Because nurses often were not clear about the type of care that extended care patients should receive, there was often a tendency on their part to provide the former with the same type of care that is given to acute care patients. Almost all administrators, physicians, and nurses who were asked about the matter maintained that extended care patients often require as much or more attention as acute care patients. Considering the elderly age of most extended care patients, it is quite possible that these claims were accurate. Some nurses noted that when an attempt was made to inform extended care patients that their care should be less intensive than that for acute care patients, the former felt that they were being neglected or receiving inferior services. Although most hospital personnel felt that payments for extended care patients were insufficient, including two administrators who felt that their hospitals were losing money on the program, no effort was made to conduct an in-depth cost analysis to determine the effect of the program on hospital operating costs.

2. Nature of Interaction Within the Local Health Care Delivery System

A significant factor affecting channels of communication and ultimately the acceptance of a health program is the nature of interaction within the local health care delivery system. One dimension of the organization of the community general hospital which is relevant to this issue is the presence of "two lines of authority" (Smith 1955; Coe 1970: 269–272). Although, at least in theory, the ultimate authority and overall responsibility for the hospital rests in the hands of the board of trustees, it in turn delegates the day-to-day management of the organization to the hospital administrator. However, the medical staff controls matters concerning patient care and exercises substantial influence throughout the hospital structure at nearly all organizational levels. This arrangement of dual authority lends itself easily not only to conflict between the hospital administration and its physicians, but also to a confusion of role expectations among other health personnel, particularly nurses.

While the relationship between the administrator and the medical staff appeared to be relatively congenial at both the Scenic and Railroad Center Hospitals, it was extremely strained at the Collegeville Hospital. Younger physicians particularly disliked the administrator, whom they felt was incompetent. Some physicians vehemently complained that the administrator resisted the purchase of much needed hospital equipment. This tension extended into one between the physicians and the three county commissioners who served as the only voting members of the hospital's board of trustees. The physicians desired voting privileges on the hospital board, of which they are ex-offico members, but the commissioners refused to grant them this request.

The potential conflicts inherent in dual system of authority are dramatically illustrated by the controversy which resulted from the firing of the Collegeville Hospital pharmacist. The pharmacist claimed that he discovered a nurse stealing narcotics and demanded her immediate dismissal, but the administrator postponed this dismissal for ten days pending an investigation of the alleged incident. The pharmacist became upset about this delay, resulting in an angry exchange of words between him and the administrator. Although the accused nurse was dismissed, the pharmacist was also fired on the grounds that he was insubordinate and created a turbulent atmosphere in the hospital. A large number of nurses signed a statement supporting the administrator's firing of the pharmacist. Several nurses noted that the pharmacist was a difficult person to work with, and one nurse stated that the pharmacist often accused nurses of stealing drugs and other items. The former hospital pharmacist had in his possession an unsigned statement which he claimed was given to him by the hospital medical staff. The statement expressed the appreciation of the medical staff for the services of the former pharmacist and requested that they and the fired pharmacist be informed of the reasons for his dismissal. Although the hospital physicians did not take a public stand on the dismissal of the pharmacist, a series of articles on the controversy in a local weekly newspaper reminded people of the tensions which existed at the hospital, including those between the administrator and the medical staff.

The nature of collegial relations among physicians in the three communities seemed to be related to the number of physicians in the vicinity. Because Railroad Center had only one physician at the time of our study, this particular issue was not relevant. Scenic had two physicians, the senior physician being a Chinese-American and a pillar in a local Protestant church, and the junior physician being a staunch Mormon with ultra-conservative political views. Although they differed greatly both temperamentally and in social background, the two men shared a private clinic and appeared to have a smooth working relationship. In contrast, Collegeville, which had twelve physicians, was characterized by a considerable degree of collegial conflict. Some younger physicians felt that the methods of the older physicians were outdated; one young physician, for example, stated that he could not possibly cooperate with some Collegeville physicians because of their inferior medical procedures and standards. An intense rivalry existed among the four physicians' clinics, resulting in bruised and angry feelings if a patient switched clinics. Some physicians resented the refusal by two general practitioners to share their contracts to perform physical examinations of employees of several companies and the national parks in the areas.

Although Collegeville had a hospital radiologist, an opthamologist, a psychiatrist, and an internist, the general practitioners affiliated with the four private clinics generally did not welcome the arrival of medical specialists to the community. Freidson (1972: 347) notes that "the danger of losing patients by referring them to a young internist seems to have led at least some general practitioners to avoid referring patients at all." One hospital worker maintained that the general practitioners would not welcome an obstetrician or a pediatrician to the community because of the great amount of work local physicians do with young children and women of childbearing age. Because of its large Mormon population, which tends to value large families, and its rapid influx of young families, Collegeville would offer these specialists most lucrative practices. The resistance of the general practitioners resulted in the discontinuation by several specialists, including an anaesthesiologist, an orthopedist, and a surgeon, of their practices in the community and/or at the hospital. It is interesting to note that in his study of the hospital in "Dockston," a semi-rural, economically depressed river town in Appalachia, Ingman (1975: 123) also found that the general practitioners opposed the addition of specialists to the medical staff.

The relationship between the public health sector and other medical services in American society is in many ways characterized by separation, competition, and antagonism (Fry 1969: 167–168; Glogow 1977: 204; Starr 1982: 181–185). Furthermore, as Reynolds (1973: 201) notes, public health departments "are greatly dependent upon the cooperation of solo practitioners and are not related to them or to patients in any direct and systematic way." All three communities considered here experienced some degree of conflict between the private health sector and local public health departments or quasi-public health departments.

Of the three communities, probably the most severe tension between private physicians and a regional public health district existed in the county where Railroad Center is located. Railroad Center's physician and his counterpart in the county seat objected to the attempts of the public health district to establish immunization clinics, well baby clinics, and to perform the physical examinations of the county's school children. The Railroad Center physician maintained that these services were only a duplication of the services that the county's physicians had been performing for years under the old county public health system and were willing to continue under the new one for a nominal fee. On the one hand, he complained about the failure of the health district to direct attention to health problems which the local physicians were unable to deal with effectively. On the other hand, the physician-director of the public health district complained that the physician in the county seat called him a "socialist tyrant," and that the physician in Railroad Center viewed the health district as an infringement on his own scope of activity." The county community nurse noted that the county physicians were not "public health-minded," and claimed that she did not receive many referrals from them.

Interaction between private physicians and the state regional health districts was marked by a moderate to a pronounced degree of conflict in all three communities. Although it is the responsibility of physicians to provide public health nurses with referrals for home nursing patients, the public health nurse stationed in Scenic stated that few such referrals had been made and also complained that physicians in the area were not "public health minded." Physicians in Scenic and Collegeville viewed the public health district as a form of economic competition. In the case of the Scenic-Mesa area, two physicians objected strongly to the clinics sponsored by a quasi-public agency which is governed by an Anglo-American executive director and a nine-member Navajo advisory board. Nevertheless, a spirit of cooperation existed between the public health department and this agency.

Personnel affiliated with the health district serving the Collegeville area were extremely upset that they were "evicted" during the previous winter from the hospital, the location of their offices, allegedly to make room for a new radiology laboratory. Despite the opposition of Collegeville physicians to public health department-sponsored immunization and well baby clinics, some physicians consistently referred patients to the home health agency of the public health department.

While there existed a certain degree of cooperation among various personnel in the health care delivery systems of Scenic, Collegeville, and Railroad Center, we have focused upon areas of conflict because of their implications concerning the implementation of new health programs. These conflicts often exhibit the self-interests of the parties concerned rather than a concern about the delivery of adequate health care. It is difficult to determine the actual effect of conflict within the various local health care systems on the implementation of UCIP, but it certainly was not helpful.

3. Political Philosophy of Influential Community Leaders

It has been argued that the political ideologies, which often are broader than specified vested interests, may play a crucial role in determining the nature of health policy (Swanson 1972). Because of the lack of awareness that political leaders in the three communities had of the UCIP, however, there was no significant opposition to the program from this sphere of influence. However, it appears that the political attitudes of local community leaders can potentially affect the implementation of public health programs. Two county commissioners, who were members of the Collegeville Hospital's board of trustees, were politically ultraconservatives. Because of the vote of these two commissioners, the county in which Collegeville is located was withdrawn in 1975 from a state regional association which coordinated social services, including mental health care, for several counties. The commission chairman, who was also the chairman of the hospital's board of trustees, stated that the social services association is a form of "regionalism" which takes away power from the county commission and places it in the hands of "socialistic" social service employees. During the summer of 1975, the commissioners from the Scenic-Mesa area announced their unanimous decision to withdraw their county from the regional public health district. Earlier in 1975 the three commissioners of the county where Railroad Center is located voted unanimously to withdraw the county from another regional public health district, upon the recommedation of the county medical society.

Due to the prominent position of many physicians in rural communities, as we can see from the case of the county where Railroad Center is located, their political leanings may have a significant effect on the acceptance or rejection of various health programs. Physicians in the three communities were generally opposed to national health insurance and some physicians vehemently objected to UCIP on these grounds. It appears that Collegeville physicians tended to feel that an increase in federally-funded health programs is an inevitable phenomenon which, although from their perspective undesirable, cannot be halted. For the most part, Collegeville physicians expressed little opposition to UCIP, but one physician from a neighboring community (who occasionally sees patients in the Collegeville Hospital) referred to it as "another form of unwarranted government intervention" in the health field.

The junior physician in Scenic and a physician who practiced in Mesa but used the facilities of the Scenic hospital also expressed opposition to federally funded health programs. The former, who was the leader of a small, but extremely vocal group of ultraconservatives in the community and also left copies of *American Opinion* magazine in his waiting room for his patients to read, referred to UCIP an another government "give away program" and "boon doggle." The Mesa physician, who worked primarily with Navajos and Utes, qualified his remarks by noting that government-sponsored health programs are necessary for Indians because the larger society has placed them in a state of economic dependency.

Of all the physicians in the three communities, the physician in Railroad Center departed the most from the conventional image of the small town doctor. His liberal views on many social and ethical issues as well as his casual dress style, which included blue jeans and somewhat long hair by rural Utahn standards for a middle-aged man, antagonized or disturbed some conservative members of the community. Conversely, although the Railroad Center physician was favorable toward UCIP and saw no apparent problems with it, he was generally opposed to the concept of national health insurance. Like many other health personnel, including some in the public sector, he complained at length about many of the regulations and the amount of paperwork which the federal government formulates for rural hospitals. Although the Railroad Center physician had not been sympathetic to many of the objectives of the regional public health district, he emphasized preventive medicine rather than a type of medicine which is oriented to the treatment of specific symptoms. For example he purchased the unused movie theatre in the community and intended to convert it into a cardiopulmonary testing and exercising area. Plans also were made to provide opportunities for residents to develop interests in art, music, yoga, and meditation.

CONCLUSIONS

Thus far, we have not alluded to the problems faced by the UCIP in the other rural towns investigated. Suffice it to say, however, that field data indicate that many of the issues outlined above applied equally well to the other places, modified, of course, by local political and sociocultural circumstances. The one area that was clearly different was the hospital which served the predominantly Navajo population; here the entire cultural situation — both of health care providers and recipients — was so different as to mark it off for special treatment (as well as having special problems). But the general problems areas — those of incomplete communication, political infighting in the socio-medical sphere, and the importance of understanding the dynamics of community politics — were shared by all.

The significance of the finding that these three obstacles to implementation were operative in all three communities studied is, of course, interesting, but its import pertains not so much to content as to method and basic conceptual framework. Rather than an approach that searches for significant discrete variables, this essay has emphasized another type of methodology — an inductive, holistic investigication that attempts to delineate an approximation of the overall system properties and institutional pattering of each community. The importance of such a system is not, of course, unfamiliar in the literature on health systems research and public health; speaking of diseases as the entities to be studied but in terms that have implications for the present paper and its approach, Henrik Blum (1979: 251) has noted:

> Those of us in public health are accustomed to focusing on problems revealed by measurement of incidence or prevalence of disease in a given geopolitics area. At the same time, the nature and quantity of services intended to control the problem have been built to standards essentially unrelated to the nature or frequency of the problems as they occurred locally. Often the standards were devised at the national level by experts-away-from-home and conventionally built around the notion of the single agent as the etiologic cause of each condition (the Arden House syndrome). The programs usually have been unrelated to the activities needed for effective intervention in each condition in any given community. (1973: 603).

Bruhn carries this exemplification of the need specific knowledge at the local level even further in his discussion of health planning the context of the data base necessary for social change:

> Pathways to health goals are not narrowly defined. They are closely related to the non-health goals of the community. Health care cannot be planned with out considering how economic, political, social, religious, geographic and other factors influence its need, modes of delivery and utilization. The visibility of health problems varies from community to community and their visibility is deeply entangled with other features of community life. "Real" problems to outside observers. Yet the effectiveness of the planner's approach in helping the community identify more covert health needs is largely dependent upon their ability to assess the interplay of the numerous community sub-systems an they related to the total functioning of the community. Planning is too often viewed as planning for institutions, organizations, agencies and the convenience of the people who work for them, rather than for the needs of the consumer.

This paper has been an attempt to illustrate the importance of understanding the interplay of such community factors with reference to the implementation of a specific proposed change in the health care system.

ACKNOWLEDGEMENTS

The research reported in this paper was supported by Social Security Administration Contract No. 600–74–0386, with The Center for Health Services Research, University of Colorado Health Services Center.

REFERENCES

Blum, Henrik L., 1974. *Planning for Health: Development and Application of Social Change Theory*. New York: Human Sciences Press.

Bruhn, John G., 1973. Planning for Social Change: Dilemmas for Health Planning, *American Journal of Public Health* 63 (7): 602–606.

Coe, Rodney M., 1970. *Sociology of Medicine*. New York: McGraw-Hill.

Ehrenreich, Barbara and John Ehrenreich, 1970. *The American Health Empire: Power, Profits, and Politics*. New York: Random House.

Foster, George M. and Barbara Gallatin Anderson, 1978. *Medical Anthropology*. New York: John Wiley & Sons.

Friedson, Eliot, 1972. The Organization of Medical Practice. In *Handbook of Medical Sociology (Second Edition)*, eds. Howard B. Freeman, Sol Levine, and Leo G. Reeder.

Fry, John, 1969. *Medicine in Three Societies: A Comparison of Medical Care in the USSR, USA and UK*. London: Billings & Sons.

Glogow, Eli, 1977. Community Participation and Sharing in Control of Public Health Services. In *The Consumer and the Health Care System: Social and Managerial Perspectives*, eds. Harry Rosen, Jonathan M. Metsch and Samuel Levey, 203–216. New York: Spectrum.

Illich, Ivan, 1976. *Medical Nemesis: The Expropriation of Health*. New York: Random House.

Ingman, Stanley R., 1975. Static Dynamics in Medical Organization. In *Topias and Utopias in Health: Policy Studies*, eds. Stanley R. Ingman and Anthony E. Thomas. The Hague: Mouton.

Navarro, Vincente, 1976. *Medicine under Capitalism*. New York: Prodist.

Reynolds, Janice M., 1973. The Medical Institution: The Death and Disease-Producing Apprendage. In *American Society: A Critical Analysis*, eds. Larry T. Reynolds and James M. Henslin, 198–224. New York: David Mckay.

Smith, Harvey, 1955. Two Lines of Authority Are One Too Many, *Modern Hospital* 85: 48–52.

Starr, Paul, 1982. *The Social Transformation of American Medicine*. New York: Basic Books.

Swanson, Bert, 1972. The Politics of Health. In *Handbook of Medicine Sociology, Second Edition*, eds. Howard B. Freeman, Sol Levine and Leo G. Reeder, 435–455. Englewood Cliffs, NJ: Prentice Hall.

Waitzkin, Howard, 1983. *The Second Sickness: Contradictions of Capitalist Health Care*. New York: Free Press.

Type II Diabetes Mellitus, Technological Development and the Oklahoma Cherokee

DENNIS W. WIEDMAN

Florida International University
University of Miami School of Medicine

INTRODUCTION

Medical reports over the past thirty-five years indicate that Type II diabetes is a new disease for Oklahoma Native Americans. Previous to 1940, there were no reported diabetic cases among Oklahoma Native Americans, but by the 1960s this disease reached epidemic proportions. By 1965, in Oklahoma, there were over two deaths per capita due to diabetes among Native Americans for every one death per capita among persons classified as "White" (Oklahoma State Department of Health 1943 to 1970).

Investigating the evidence that diabetes dramatically increased among Native Americans after 1940, I began a study to detail the cultural changes which occurred among the Oklahoma Cherokee. The resulting diachronic assessment of the culture history and ecological context of the Cherokee tested the hypothesis that the increase in type II diabetes was associated with rapid industrialization.

Two bodies of medical literature provided the basis for the formation of this hypothesis. The first was the continuous reports that Native Americans in Oklahoma, and elsewhere in North America, were experiencing a dramatic increase in this disease which was unknown to them prior to 1940. The second body of medical literature dealt with populations throughout the world who were experiencing a similar epidemic and pointed to the general conclusion that populations which migrate to urban settings, and others which acculturate to European foodstuffs, experience an increase in diabetic prevalence.

A basic question focused the research. If the Cherokee had been acculturating to European technology for over 200 years, and acculturation to European foodstuff was a factor, then why didn't the Cherokee gradually exhibit the onset of diabetic symptoms? From the two bodies of literature, it was hypothesized, before entering the field, that the Oklahoma Cherokee had experienced rapid technological cultural change around 1940 and this resulted in the sudden increase of this disease. Both of these bodies of literature will be reviewed before the presentation of the research findings and discussions, but first, a brief overview of Type II diabetes and its etiology.

ETIOLOGY OF DIABETES

Diabetes mellitus is a chronic, hereditary disease characterized by an abnormally high level of glucose in the blood and urine. It results from either an inadequate production of insulin by the pancreas, or underutilization of insulin at the cell membrane. Insulin facilitates the transport of glucose, a basic energy source, into cells.

There are two major forms of diabetes: Type I, or insulin dependent, previously known as "juvenile diabetes," usually appears in childhood; Type II, or non-insulin dependent, previously known as "maturity-onset diabetes," usually does not produce symptoms until after the age of thirty. In both types the complications are mainly vascular, and lead to a marked disability in the arteries of the brain, heart, kidneys, feet, and eyes. The initial outward characteristics of both types are excessive urination and thirst (National Diabetes Group 1979, West 1979a). Native Americans rarely, if ever, develop Type I diabetes, so this paper deals with type II, the maturity-onset form.

Three treatments are at present used by physicians to control this chronic disease. In mild cases, the treatment consists of dietary restrictions and weight control. Dietary restrictions may be supplemented with oral hypoglycemic agents, or in severe cases with subcutaneously injected insulin.

THE INCREASE OF DIABETES MELLITUS AMONG NATIVE AMERICANS

Oklahoma Native Americans
In 1974, the late Kelly West, physician and epidemiologist, reviewed evidence dealing specifically with diabetes and Oklahoma Native

Americans. He concluded that the disease was a rarity prior to 1940. He based his conclusion partially upon his review of medical reports by civilian and military physicians who served Native Americans in Oklahoma from 1832 to 1939. These medical case notes indicated no evidence for the presence of diabetes. In addition, West interviewed well-informed, educated elders from more than twenty Oklahoma tribes; only two cases of diabetic symptoms prior to 1940 could be recalled, none prior to 1936 (West 1978a: 32). His review of 700 diabetic cases at Lawton Indian Hospital in 1973 revealed that none had exhibited symptoms of diabetes prior to 1940 (West 1974b).

Before 1940 physicians should have identified this disease since excessive urination and thirst have been known to European medicine as symptoms of diabetes since the second century A.D. Excessive sugar in the urine, another symptom, was known even earlier. Also, by 1910 the urine test for diabetes was standardized, and the blood glucose tolerance test was in use by 1923 (Papaspyros 1964). This lack of evidence is also noteworthy because prior to 1940, Native Americans were often treated by the same physicians who diagnosed diabetes in Euroamericans (West 1974b).

One might attribute the absence of diabetic symptoms among Native Americans before 1940 to their low utilization of biomedical facilities. But Oklahoma Native Americans, because of their treaty rights, have received health care from the United States Government for 100 years. In 1870, five military posts with attending physicians served Indian and Oklahoma Territories; by 1880 each Indian agency had a diplomaed physician (Crockett 1953). Eight Federal Indian hospitals served Oklahoma Native Americans by 1940.

According to the Oklahoma State Health Department, adult-onset diabetes has been a leading cause of death among Oklahoma Native Americans since 1953. Since 1943, the average number of deaths due to diabetes in Oklahoma per year, per 100,000 population, was 15 for Euroamericans, 22 for Blacks and 27 for Native Americans. For each of the past 34 years there has been an average of one death among Euroamericans from diabetes as compared to two among Native Americans in Oklahoma in proportion to their populations. In 1980, 2,651,144 Euroamericans and 169,464 Native Americans lived in Oklahoma (Oklahoma State Department of Health 1943 to 1980).

The earliest study calling attention to the high rate of diabetes among Oklahoma Native Americans was a comparison of hospital admission complaints during the period 1951–1955 for the Lawton Indian Hospital and two non-Indian hospitals. The Indian hospital had four times as many admissions for diabetes as the two non-Indian hospitals. This study identified the characteristics considered typical of Native American diabetics: 68% were female, 32% male, and 76% were between the ages of 50 and 80. As with other Native Americans, there was no case of Type I, juvenile-onset diabetes (Sochet 1958). Additional reports indicate that most Oklahoma Native American populations, including the Oklahoma Seminole (Mayberry and Lindeman 1963, Elston et al. 1974); the Pawnee (White 1966); and the Choctaw (Drevits 1965) have high rates of diabetes.

Kelly West assessed the prevalence of diabetes among Oklahoma Native Americans by surveying client records at each of the Indian Hospitals in Tahlequah, Talihina, Tishomingo, Claremore, Pawnee, Shawnee, Clinton and Lawton. Even after considering under-reporting, he concluded that by the early 1970s, five to six percent of the total Oklahoma Native American population were diabetics, even though forty-six percent of the population were under the age of twenty, and therefore not prone to diabetes. He estimated fifteen Oklahoma tribes to have a high rate of diabetes and no tribe to have a low rate (West 1974b).

Next, West conducted standardized blood glucose tests in three Native American communities in Oklahoma: the Cherokee in Tahlequah, Seminole and Creek in Shawnee, and Kiowa and Comanche in Lawton. All of the communities showed a high rate of diabetes. On the basis of Indian Health Service Hospital records and the blood glucose level in these communities West concluded: "In the aggregate our observations on the rates of occult and known diabetes suggest that roughly one-third of Oklahoma full blood Indians over thirty years of age have diabetes" (West 1974b: 847).

Native Americans Outside Oklahoma

A health status report on diabetes issued in 1955 by the United States Public Health Service, indicated that the rate of death of Native Americans due to diabetes had equaled that of Euroamericans (West 1974b). The increasingly high rate of diabetes among Native Americans outside of Oklahoma has subsequently been documented by numerous researchers [e.g., the North Carolina Cherokee (Stein et al. 1965); the Florida Seminole (Westfall and Rosenbloom 1971); the Alabama Coushatta (Johnson and McNutt 1964); the Mississippi Choctaw (West 1974b); the Seneca of New York (Frohman 1969, Judkins 1976); and the Passamaquoddy of Maine (Ede 1966)].

Southwestern Native Americans have attracted a great deal of attention from medical scientists concerning the dramatic increase in the diabetic rate. Between 1934 and 1939, Joslin (1940) conducted a survey of diabetes in Arizona and found the diabetic rate for Indians and whites relatively the same at 10%. He indicated that of Indian diabetics, the Pima had a higher rate. Subsequently, the Pima have been found to have the highest rates yet for a population; 27% of the women, and 19% of the men were diabetic. Furthermore, there was an extraordinarily high rate of 68% for women between the ages of 55 and 64 (Miller et al. 1968). Since Joslin's study in 1940, the increasing rate of the disease has been well documented among Southwestern Native Americans (Seivers 1966, Cohen 1954, Henry et al. 1969, Bennett et al 1971).

Relatively low rates of diabetes have been reported for the Eskimo (Schaefer 1969), and among the Athabaskan natives of Alaska (Mouratoff et al. 1969). Their results indicated the disease amongst these relatively unacculturated Native Americans is well below the average for the United States.

Overall, this trend toward an acceleration of diabetes amongst Native Americans was documented by Hill and Spector (1971), who compared vital statistics of United States populations of whites and non-whites with American Indians. They found a 40% increase in the rate of diabetic deaths among Native Americans between 1955 and 1967.

At a 1968 World Health Organization meeting, Niswander (1969) discussed the problems of diabetes and Native Americans. From records of the United States Public Health Service he analyzed 250,000 discharge diagnoses for the period 1963 to 1967. For the forty-six Indian Hospitals in the United States, a mean frequency of 2.2% of the discharges dealt with diabetes, as compared to the general non-Indian hospital discharge rate of 1 to 1.5%

CULTURE CHANGE AND DIABETES MELLITUS

Since the early 1970s adult-onset, Type II, diabetes mellitus has been recognized as a recent disease, and characterized as "The Price of Civilization" (Prior 1971). It has been suggested that migration to urban or industrial settings is the basis of the increase of diabetes among Australian Aborigines (Wise et al. 1970, Odea et al. 1980 and 1982), Yeminite Jews (Cohen et al. 1972), Japanese migrants to Hawaii (Kawate 1979), Indians who moved to Africa, and Zulu who moved to an urban environment (Cleave and Campbell 1969). All of these studies deal with populations which underwent a rapid nutritional and lifestyle change following their migration to a new setting.

The level of acculturation to European culture and foodstuffs has been specifically implicated in the high diabetic rate among South Pacific populations (Zimmet 1979 and 1981), Maori in New Zealand and Polynesia (Prior 1974), for Pima (Bennett et al. 1971), and Native Americans in general (West 1974b). Eaton, in a 1977 issue of *Medical Anthropology*, concluded that diabetes is a disordered physiological and psychological adaptation to rapid culture change, which increases as cultures undergo lifestyle evolution from hunter-gatherer to agrarian to urban to industrial societies.

Physiological changes must have resulted from the cultural change and multiple physical factors have to be considered in the development of Type II diabetes mellitus. It is still unknown what physiologically causes the beta cells of the pancreas to secrete an inadequate amount of insulin or the underutilization of insulin at the cell level. This deficiency could be due to genetic factors, to the infective virus coxsacki B and rubella, or to environmental factors such as chemical agents (Fajans 1981, Toniolo et al. 1982). Geneticists now consider Type II diabetes to be not one but several differeent diseases, each exbiting a different inheritance pattern involving either a principal gene. with modifiers, or genes at several loci with approximate additive effects (Rotter and Rimoin 1979, Kobberling and Tattersall 1982). This genotype may even be the basis of several metabolic disorders which occur more often among Native Americans (Weis et al. 1984).

Each food group has at one time or another been suggested as the cause of diabetes. The correlation of fat intake was originally hypothesized in the 1930s by Himsworth (1936). Yudkin (1963) contended that the cause was carbohydrates, especially sugar, as did Cleave and Campbell (1969) and A. Cohen et al. (1972). Currently the most common explanation for the increase of Type II diabetes is obesity resulting from caloric excess and indolence. Degree of obesity can be assigned by measuring subscapular skinfold thickness, or relative weight for height by age and sex using a population based mode as a standard (West 1979a). Using this measure of obesity a World Health Organization sponsored study of over eleven countries used standardized tests and procedures to control for various factors, including nutritional intake (West and Kalbfleisch 1971),

West 1974c, Keen and Grabouskos 1979). Their findings show that increased consumption of fats and sugars may not be independent of each other as a cause for Type II diabetes, as this study expicates an impressive and consistent association between the prevalence of diabetes and adiposity or body fat — irrespective of the source of calories.

METHODS

Although the relationship between body fat and diabetes seemed clear, it remained to be determined why diabetes appeared in Native Americans after 1940. In order to delineate factors related to onset of Type II diabetes during a traditional society's acculturation to an industrial society, a comprehensive analysis of a single group's cultural development was necessary. This analysis was carried out as part of the work of an interdisciplinary team consisting of ethnologists, archaeologists, geologists, geographers, and botanists who conducted cultural, historical and ecological analyses of prehistoric and historic people, in an eighty square-mile river drainage area in the Oklahoma Ozarks. The findings on Cherokee historic adaptations presented here are a synopsis of data collected during 1977–1979 (Wiedman 1979). This cultural analysis, which affords an account of 150 years, from 1828 to 1978, focuses upon land use, technological development, and population changes.

The three methodologies of historic archeology, ethnography and historiography were used. With historical archeology methods we located, and in many cases dated, former living and work sites. Ethnographic methods were used by living in the study area, by participating in social activities, and by conducting oral history interviews. Interviews focused upon the individual's geographic location at particular points in time which placed historic sites into a series of population movements and settlement pattern changes. This method also generated genealogical information which placed people in a social and historical continuum. Information about occupation, education, and health care was assembled along with cultural data about the family and community. Historiography provided us with written documents which linked archeologically located sites to specific individuals. Each of these methodologies generated questions which could not be answered by any single methodology. These three research methodologies, when added to those of the other interdisciplinary team members, enabled us to correlate and validate various pieces of information.

Overall, we located a total of 276 habitation sites; identified 1912 people, both living and dead; and compiled forty-four family genealogies. Seventy percent of the genealogies were four to five generations deep, beginning with the Cherokee removal in the 1830's. With limited time in the field, we incorporated 47 percent of the identified individuals into the genealogies.

The conclusions derived from the data collected with these methods were then compared to other reports on the Ozark Cherokee. General population statistics and agricultural data confirmed that similar patterns of adaptations and demographic changes occurred in the four other Cherokee Ozark counties. Thus, this research provides an overall description of technological change in the Cherokee Ozarks from 1838 to 1980.

CHEROKEE TECHNOLOGICAL DEVELOPMENT

At the time of historical contact in the 16th century, the Cherokee were situated in the Southern Appalachian mountains. They hunted mammals, especially deer, which provided the major portion of their required dietary fat and animal protein. The cultivation of corn, beans, and squash, plus the collecting of wild species of plants, provided the carbohydrates needed for proper nutrition. The Cherokee began to utilize domesticated plants around 500 A.D., when horticultural technology, based upon the cultigen corn, diffused from Mesoamerica. Their traditional tools were made from the natural stone, clay, and fibers found in their environment, or traded from other Native American groups. European technological items gradually were introduced into the Cherokee culture after the settlement of the Carolinas by the English. Guns and iron tools were the first items to be introduced, as was the horse in 1740 and the cow thirty years later. Cotton, coffee, and potatoes were also added during this time (Mooney 1975).

Warfare with surrounding Native Americans and European colonists increased Cherokee political unity. From a group with villages dispersed along the river and creek bottoms of Southern Appalachia they gradually formed aggregates of politically united villages which, by 1760, dealt with the Europeans as a single political unit (Gearing 1962).

As the Cherokee were confronted by the increasing population of European settlers, many Cherokee moved further west, where they established a settlement in the Ozark Mountains of north central Arkansas. In this location, they continued their lifestyle based on the hunting of animals and the cultivation of corn, beans, and squash. They supplemented their diet by the gathering of wild vegetable products. By 1838, nearly the entire Cherokee population of Georgia, Tennessee, Alabama and South Carolina was forced to move its traditional homelands to Indian Territory, in the western Ozark Mountains (Foreman 1975).

When the Cherokee arrived the region was completely forested, except for small prairies on the tops of hills and mountains. Since it had not been intensively used since prehistoric agriculturalists departed three hundred years earlier, it was rich in resources. In adapting to the Ozark Mountains the Cherokee changed their settlement patterns from villages of log cabins along the river bottoms to dispersed settlements of extended family units. Our historical archeology survey revealed that house sites were consistently built in three ecotone locations: at the edge of open prairies on the tops of the mountains (uplands); at the base of the mountains in the talus zone adjacent to the flood plain; or on the edge of a river terrace between two flood plains. In these three ecotone locations, where there was an abrupt change between two larger ecological zones, they efficiently exploited the adjacent zones by hunting animals and cultivating corn, beans, and squash. All citizens of the Cherokee Nation held the land in common. Each could fish, hunt, and cut timber in all places not occupied by farms or towns. An "open range" policy allowed livestock, marked with the owner's brand, to roam at will. The open range mandated that each farm, in order to have a successful crop, had to be fenced from the wandering livestock.

The Cherokee population increased over a twenty-year period. With the advent of the United States Civil War the improvements made to the land were destroyed, and the population greatly decreased and scattered. Since a portion of the Cherokee sided with the losing cause of the Confederacy, the self-governing power of the Cherokee Nation was greatly restricted by treaty agreement with the Federal government (Woodward 1963).

The decrease in population after the Civil War left parcels of land underutilized. Gradually, the Euroamerican frontier reached the Ozarks and the population increased as new settlers began to move in, even though it was illegal for people of European background to enter and settle in Indian Territory. Throughout this time the Cherokee and the Euroamericans remained in dispersed households that were based on hunting and corn cultivation. The farms averaged 10 acres, two thirds of the crop land were usually planted in corn and in some cases a few acres of wheat or oats. In addition, the farms at the higher elevations also had a half acre or so with fruit trees. Each winter the farmer cleared trees and rock from the adjacent land, expanding the acres under cultivation. The expansion of farms in the uplands was limited by level ground and soil composition. Expansion of bottom lands was limited by the amount of time one family could expend in cultivation and maintenance of the rail or rock fences needed to prevent destruction by ranging livestock.

About 1880, newly invented technological items, such as the sod breaking plow and barbed wire, enabled the Euroamerican frontier to move further west, past the Ozarks, onto the Great Plains. The sod breaking plow made cultivation easier and faster; barbed wire efficiently fenced the agricultural plots from the ranging cattle and hogs (Webb 1931). After 1892, when wire fencing became legal in the Cherokee Nation, the small Cherokee farms in the bottom lands expanded as additional acres were cleared, fenced with wire and plowed. Because of limited level land the farmsteads in the uplands were unable to expand their acres under cultivation.

Like frontiers in general, this was a time when people are highly transient, and technological innovations are very frequent as the people adapt to the new frontier environment (Wiedman 1976). Euroamericans who moved into Indian Territory could not legally own land, so they leased or share cropped land from the Cherokee. These people cleared lands which had never, in historic times, been open to cultivation. Euroamericans planted similar crops as the Cherokee, but they utilized more rangeland for cattle and hogs.

By the 1890s the railroads crossed Indian Territory. This event made cotton into a major export crop for the farms on the flood plain of the Arkansas River and its tributaries extending into the Southern Ozarks as far north as Tahlequah. With the completion of the railroads in the 1890s cotton, forest products and timber for railroad ties could now be exported. These exports enabled Cherokee families to obtain credit or cash for the purchase of manufactured products, such as farm equipment, tools, and kitchen utensils. Steam-driven cotton gins were established at this time. Not only did they process cotton and grind corn for local consumption, they became the focal point for the dispersed farmsteads. Around the cotton gin settled a few mixed blood or Euroamerican families, whose home became general stores, inns for travelers and post offices. Similarly, small villages developed along well traveled wagon routes, usually at ten-mile intervals, the distance a wagon could travel in one day (Ragland 1957).

By 1900, we find that the mixed blood and Euroamerican farms situated on the bottoms were organized around the cultivation of corn and cotton. The land cleared for cultivation usually was around 15 to 20 acres. Although many incorporated up to fifty acres, these required hired labor or a large family. The typical farm consisted of a log cabin on the edge of the cleared field. Around this living structure was a cook house, an outhouse and a smoke house used to preserve and store foods. The fields were usually divided into three sections: corn, cotton and pasture. Corn was not only the staple food crop, but in addition to hay cut from the pastures, it was also the energy source provided the livestock during the winter months. The cows and pigs were let loose to forage in the uplands where the acorns and other nuts provided subsistence for the pigs, and the grasses under the trees provided for the cows. During the winter, the livestock were allowed to graze the remains of the cultivated fields and their manure provided the only fertilizer to the farmed land. Cherokee usually had fewer cattle and hogs than the Euroamericans, thus they devoted fewer acres to pasture. Cherokee generally have a distaste for dairy products so they primarily used cattle as a meat source after the game began to become scarce. As compared to the Euroamericans, they relied to a greater extent upon the gathering of wild fruits: blackberries, dewberries, strawberries and huckleberries.

The continued immigration of Euroamericans into Indian Territory made law enforcement impossible; by 1900 Euroamericans outnumbered the Cherokee 2 to 1. The Cherokee Nation could not impose its laws on United States citizens, and the United States courts in surrounding territories could not maintain control over Euroamericans in Indian Territory. With this as one rationale, the United States convinced Native Americans in Indian and Oklahoma Territories to allot their lands individually. Once allotted, the land was owned by individuals, and could be sold with the approval of the Indian agent. As long as the land remained in the ownership of the original allotee or the heirs, it could not be taxed by the county. When the state of Oklahoma came into existence in 1906 the power of the Cherokee Nation in governing its people was further reduced.

Beginning in the teens much of the land was leased to oil and gas companies who began to explore for mineral resources to no avail. From the time of allotment to about 1925 woodcutting and the production of railroad ties and stave bolts took the place of hunting as a primary occupation of male Cherokee. In the late teens, much of the upland acreage was leased to lumber companies based in Arkansas and Missouri which began to harvest the rich timber resources.

The densest population of Euroamericans and mixed bloods in the five Cherokee Ozark counties was along the Arkansas River bottoms of present day Sequoyah and Cherokee counties. This population, supported by the intensive cultivation of cotton and corn, increased from the 1880s to the 1920s. From 1920 to 1929, the population in the bottom lands north of the Arkansas river and south of the Ozark Mountains quickly decreased. Primarily this dramatic decrease was due to the arrival of the boll weevil and to the depletion of soil nutrients from continual planting of cotton without fertilizers. The two Cherokee Ozark counties, (Sequoyah and Cherokee), with a large proportion of their land area composed of Arkansas river bottoms, rapidly declined in population and number of farms between 1920 and 1930.

In 1929 the United States economic system collapsed in the stock market crash. Families who lived in nearby towns were greatly affected by the Depression and many chose to move to the rural countryside. Thus all five of the Cherokee Ozark counties witnessed a 15% increase in population from 1930 to 1940 derived from both the cities and from the Arkansas River bottoms. Most of these people, both mixed blood Cherokee and Euroamericans, attempted the small farm strategy of relying upon several acres in corn, cotton, a small vegetable garden, and a few hogs and cattle ranging in the wooded zones. Many of the newcomers either rented or share cropped the agricultural lands from Cherokee owners. With this influx of people the cultivated lands were broken up into smaller farms, and vast areas of marginal lands were cleared of forest, resulting in an increase in the number of farms and an overall intensification of land use.

Around 1929, almost ten years after the boll weevil's introduction to the Arkansas river bottoms, the Southern Ozark Mountains suffered cotton crop failure. After the cotton failure the acreage was planted by mixed blood and Euroamericans primarily in corn or pasture grasses and the newly introduced varieties of sorghum, oats and wheat (Hewes 1940). As more land was cleared and farmed, more topsoil was washed away by the spring rains and flooding streams. Even with increased mechanization, crop diversification and rotation, the overpopulation of the land quickly reduced the natural resources.

With many people living in poverty conditions, farming small unproductive lands, the drought conditions of 1936 forced a great number of families to find another means of livelihood or move out.

Livestock production was an alternative adaptation. A few Euroamerican families began pig lots. The pigs were fed excess corn and after the yearly growing season, were released into the fields to root in what was left of the cultivated crop. In this way the agricultural produce was more thoroughly used, the soil was fertilized with manure and the soil was broken up for the next planting. Pig production developed after the cotton failure in 1929 as alternate method of livelihood, and reached a peak in the late 1930's and early 1940s. Several Euroamericans who had housesites in agriculturally marginal rocky and hilly locations, specialized in goats instead of pigs, but this strategy was much less frequent. During the years from 1936 to 1946 Cherokee and Euroamerican farmers increased their production of sorghum and small sorghum mills began operation.

Of the many new subsistence strategies bootlegging was the most legendary. With the increased reliance upon sorghum and corn, a number of Cherokee and Euroamericans began to distill these agricultural products into alcohol. This was the time of prohibition, and this home industry became a profitable business for many of the people who lived a distance from the main roads. In a move by the Federal government to restrict the overuse of agricultural lands the Agricultural Adjustment Act was implemented. This act attempted to restrict the number of livestock and acres planted in particular crops. Not only did the government agricultural agent force the farmer to restrict the planted acres, but they herded together the ranging cattle, slaughtering and burying them.

During the late 1930s, the Cherokee Nation together with the Federal Government implemented work projects, which provided jobs for people to support their families. These public work projects involved the building of schools, bridges, and roads. Most of the roads before this time were little more than trails which followed surface features and most Cherokee either walked, traveled on horseback or in wagons. A major result of the straightened roads and new bridges was that families who lived in the now-inaccessible valleys and hilltops began to move their households to the improved roads for easy access to outside resources by car or truck. Both

Cherokee and Euroamericans now worked for stave mills and cut timber for railroad ties, or they began to commute to larger towns to obtain work. Nonproductive and inaccessible lands fell into disuse. Lands which had been purchased by Euroamericans or Cherokee from the original allotees became county property when the taxes were not paid. Land owners did not begin to forfeit their property until 1939; then the county gained possession and the properties were auctioned off to the highest bidder. From this time until 1943 numerous properties were auctioned by the county because of failure to pay taxes.

Many of the upland farm sites originally settled by the full bloods in the 1830s were in operation all the way into the 1940's. As noted earlier, these ecological locations, primarily because of limited level land, were not as productive as the bottom lands. Many of the full blood families were able to adapt because at allotment time they received both upland and bottom land. They chose to live in the uplands, while they leased the bottom lands to mixed bloods or Euroamericans. With rent and lease money as a source of income they could remain in the upland locations farming corn along with a small vegetable garden and few fruit trees. When the agricultural bottom lands began to decrease in production, the Cherokee landowners were affected by the loss of income from these properties. Most of the upland housesites in the study area, long occupied by full blood Cherokee, were abandoned shortly after 1940.

Beginning in 1936 many Cherokee and Euroamericans moved to California and the Gulf coast where war related industries were in need of manpower. Therefore, after 1936 the number of farms in all five Cherokee Ozark counties declined a dramatic 15% from 1935 to 1940, and starting in 1936, and especially after 1940 the outmigration was greater than the in-migration, and the region began to decrease in population. For all five counties of the Cherokee Ozarks, the population decreased nearly 20% from 1940 to 1960 (Peach et al. 1964).

Heavy rains and severe flooding in 1946 caused the last of the subsistence agriculturalists to give up. In 1946 the last of the bottom lands in the study area were cultivated, and most of the Cherokee and Euroamerican population had either moved out or relocated along the graveled and maintained roads built by the Federal or tribal work projects.

As the county auctioned off forfeited land for taxes, several Euroamericans from outside the area placed bids on the land. The purchases were extensive; by 1950 some tracts included over 9,000 acres. The big landowners used the land for cattle ranching which was an extension of the ranging cattle strategy of the previous settlers. Ranches were operated by a manager who hired local men to seasonally work the cattle. Large ranches formed where previously many small farmsteads existed.

Large ranches lasted until the late 1960s, when the State of Oklahoma began to enforce the law making ranch owners responsible for ranging cattle. With cattle ranching less profitable, these owners began to open bottom lands for farming soybeans. Large mechanized tractors and trucks, plus the use of fertilizers, enabled them to produce good crops, where forty years previously the soil was depleted of nutrients.

Beginning about 1960, people began moving into the Ozarks, desiring to live in the rural environment. Many were the same individuals who had left for California during the period from 1936 to 1956. They moved into houses along the improved roads and commuted to jobs in the larger towns. Some families purchased 50 to 500 acres and began to raise cattle. In many cases, the lands they purchased were those of the large ranchers. In a few cases, these were the same lands their families had lost in the 1940's.

DISCUSSION

For 1,400 years after the introduction of corn, Cherokee culture was based on hunting and the cultivation of corn, beans and squash. This adaptive strategy lasted until the 1930s, when overpopulation, the continuous cultivation without fertilizers or crop rotation, and soil erosion destroyed subsistence agriculture. From 1936 to 1946, a major technoeconomic change occurred. The number of farms fell and population decreased as people migrated out of the Ozarks. The remaining Cherokee abandoned their hilltop and valley housesites and built homes next to the newly established roads. Cherokees no longer walked great distances but relied upon cars and trucks for transportation. The small farmstead which had corn as its major crop became practically nonexistent. Instead the Cherokee still in the Ozarks cut timber, worked at several ranches, or commuted to the larger towns for jobs. This major change in a ten-year period transformed the Cherokee agricultural infrastructure into one based on an industrial technology and a cash economy.

Cash income freed the Cherokee from the restraints of the immediate environmental resources and made it possible for them to purchase foods from a wide array of environments. Nutritionally, the primary change was in the decreased consumption of corn and the increased consumption of refined corn meal, wheat flour and other refined products which have a higher caloric value. For example, whole ground cornmeal, which served as the basic food item for these 1,400 years, contains 435 calories per cup, whereas refined cornmeal, degermed and enriched contains 500 calories — a 13% increase (United States Department of Agriculture 1975: 20). They also increased their intake of fats when they changed from boiling and broiling on woodburning stoves and in open fireplaces to deep frying on gas and electric stoves. Also, as canned foods became more prevalent, the home canning and bottling of vegetables and fruits decreased as did the time and energy expended in gardening. Additionally, the Cherokee no longer walked great distances but traveled in cars and trucks, and new appliances reduced many of the arduous household chores. Overall, in a relatively short period of time the Cherokee experienced a major technoeconomic change which included not only a nutritional shift from natural, self-produced foods, to industrially refined, high calorie food products, but also a less strenuous lifestyle. Soon after this shift in nutrition and lifestyle, in the Cherokee Ozarks, the first Native American death due to diabetes mellitus was recorded in 1942. From this year until 1977, the average death rate per year, per 100,000 population, was 16.27 for Euroamericans, 19.62 for Blacks and 26.23 for Native Americans (Oklahoma State Department of Health 1943 to 1977). By 1974, among 4000 Cherokee over thirty-four years of age in the Tahlequah district of the Indian Health Service, 13% were known diabetics. In a clinical study of the general population of Tahlequah, Kelly West (1974b:847) administered the blood glucose tolerance test to 124 Cherokees over the age of 30; these were age matched to Euroamericans from the same community. Over 20% of the Cherokee had two-hour blood glucose values exceeding 149 mg. per 100 ml, as compared to 8% of the Euroamericans. These data support the hypothesis that with the transition to an industrial technology a relatively significant proportion of a human population will begin to exhibit detrimental diabetic symptoms.

Prolonged obesity, resulting from caloric excess, is now considered a precipitator of detrimental Type II diabetic symptoms. Recently, Fajans (1981) concluded that 60% to 90% of Type II diabetics are obese and that obesity may precede the recognition of abnormal carbohydrate tolerance. The degree of obesity appears to have some predictive effect (O'Sullivan and Mahon 1965 and 1968);

Keen et al. (1982a) noted a "delayed diabetogenic effect" of obesity, becoming evident only in the second five years of observation. Not only is adiposity now considered a prime cause of diabetes, but, more specifically, persons who have fat primarily in the upper body are more likely to develop diabetes (Kissebah et al. 1982, Szathmary and Holt 1983).

Historical photographs of Cherokee individuals and families from the study area reveal that in the early part of this century most Cherokee were lean. Now, however, the Cherokee are quite obese, especially in the upper torso, a consequence of the caloric excess relative to energy expenditure that came with the shift to the industrial lifestyle. Thus body fat was stored, obesity ensued and diabetic symptoms began to appear.

Two recent studies provide further understanding of this relationship between industrial technology and diabetes. A low diabetic prevalence rate of 2.7% was recorded in the Polynesian population of Wallis Island where the food was produced by subsistence agriculture or fishing, without mechanization, and prepared by traditional methods. Diabetes prevalence was found to be less than half for those classified as participators in "heavy laboring" in the gardens, regardless of sex (Taylor et al. 1983). In the second study, Odea et al. (1980) studied urban Australian Aborigines who had returned to a hunting diet and increased physical activity. They documented a marked reduction in plasma insulin concentration, associated with a small improvement in glucose tolerance. This study followed the earlier studies by Wise et al. (1970, 1976) which had indicated an increase in diabetes after Aborigines moved to the urban setting.

Generally, relatively few individuals in preindustrial societies are able to maintain a caloric expenditure lower than caloric intake, the basis for obesity and the onset of detrimental diabetic symptoms. But with industrial development a relatively significant proportion of people will begin to show diabetic symptoms if they are genetically predisposed and become obese owing to an excessive caloric intake.

Several social and cultural factors have been identified which could compound or even maintain diabetic prevalence once a population becomes industrialized. Although much more research is needed to refine our understanding of socio-cultural factors in the complex etiology of type II diabetes, preliminary research reveals several factors of special importance.

Diabetic prevalence seems to be compounded if in an affluent industrialized country a population is living in poor socio-economic conditions. A study in England and Wales has shown a markedly higher incidence of type II diabetes in towns with the worse socio-economic conditions (Barker, Gardener and Power 1982). Also, diabetic patients in Denmark's lowest social class have a signficantly greater risk for diabetic complications (Ellman et al. 1984). In the United States, data from the 1973 Health Interview Survey indicate that rates are substantially higher where family income is low (Editorial, *Lancet* 1982). These findings are contrary to reports of diabetes as a disease of the rich in ancient India, China, Java, in pre-1940s England, Wales and the United States, and also among contemporary people living in poor countries (West 1978: 274–277). Recent studies focusing on factors related to diabetes and poor socio-economic conditions are lacking, but the high rate of obesity, especially among women with income below the poverty level, is suggested by the work of West (1973). It could be surmised that in affluent industrialized countries poor socioeconomic conditions restrict dietary intake to inexpensive processed foods rich in calories.

Among the Pima where diabetes is extremely prevalent, Reid et al. (1971) documented that their diet met or exceeded the National Research Council's recommended allowances for calories, protein, calcium, iron and magnesium. As compared to the general population of the United States, the Pima derived a greater percentage of calories from starch and a greater percent of protein from vegetable sources, mainly beans. Both of these are inexpensive foods. Judkin's nutritional study of the Seneca characterizes their diets as very high in overall caloric consumption, however, as compared to the national average a low percentage of these calories were derived from protein sources, a high percentage from carbohydrates and fats (Judkins 1974). Poor socio-economic conditions may result in a diet rich in carbohydrate calories in order to get the same energy that would be derived from a more expensive high-protein, medium-calorie diet. In another study, however, Florida Seminoles were found to have diets without vitamin deficiencies, and in most cases more than adequate in animal protein. High income families ate expensive meats more often, but the diet of low income families were ample in calories and protein. The obese Seminoles consumed 250 to 1,600 calories more than required for persons of the same age, sex, height and activity (Joos 1984: 228). These studies point to the fact that relative to energy expenditure, the excessive consumption of calories derived from fats and carbohydrates is a major cause of Native American obesity. Technological changes, as noted earlier, have promoted the deep frying of foods in fat and socio-economic conditions promote their consumption of inexpensive carbohydrates such as fried potatoes and breads. Added to these foods is their over consumption of carbohydrates in the form of refined sugars, especially soft drinks and "junk food." Decreased consumption of these high calorie foods could significantly reduce Native American obesity and the diabetic epidemic.

Certain social and cultural behaviors of North American Indians may promote overeating and obesity. At most Oklahoma Indian social gatherings eating and food exchange are the focal points of the communal occasions. More frequently though, are the daily visits to the homes of friends and relatives where the consumption of a meal, regardless of the time of day, is a sign of hospitality and friendship. Similar eating patterns have been noted for the Florida Seminole (Joos 1984), and the Sioux (Lang 1985). These social and cultural behaviors contribute to the overconsumption of food and make weight loss and control of blood sugar almost impossible.

Additionally, once adiposity becomes the norm, diabetic prevalence could be maintained in the industrialized population if they have an obese body image as a cultural theme (Wiedman 1979). Every social group has an ideal body image expressed in everyday behavior and verbal statements. If a population considers an obese body as healthy and sexually appealing, then this obese body image can be considered a "cultural theme" (Opler 1945): their perceptions maintain the body weight by verbal approval or disapproval stated in everyday interactions. With this theme recurrently stated, a person who maintains a lean body weight would be consistently reminded of his unhealthy appearance. In a preliminary survey of contemporary non-industrialized populations I found that in most cases extra pounds are preferred not only for a healthy appearance, but because extra body weight is an indication that the man is a good provider and the women a good cook. Many preindustrial societies may have highly valued and sought obesity, but given the technology and environmental resources few were able to do so. Only when the industrial lifestyle and foods are introduced can a majority of people obtain the cultural theme of having extra pounds to spare.

This idea was tested by West (1979b) among the Kiowa and Comanche. The mean weight of 557 diabetics was 140% of ideal body weight as determined from height. These same diabetics had been 105% above ideal at age 18, and 159% at diagnosis of diabetes. Non-diabetics from the same population were asked how much they would like to weigh: the mean preferred weight was 127% of ideal weight. Similar findings were reported for the Florida Seminole (Joos 1984). Although preliminary, these studies indicate that if a population has an obese body image as a cultural theme these cognitive preceptions could be a factor in the diabetic epidemic. Socioeconomic conditions, cultural patterns of food consumption, and obese body images are important sociocultural factors which should be considered in the treatment and control of this disease.

THEORETICAL CONSIDERATIONS

Up to this point, we have shown that Cherokee cultural and demographic data supports the conclusion that as a human population changes to an industrial economy the diabetic prevalence increases dramatically. Considering that an industrial infrastructure is relatively recent for every human population, the diabetic genotype must have produced a phenotype with a selective advantage throughout earlier human evolution. This may also be the case with mammals since many develop detrimental diabetic symptoms when held in captivity (Howard 1982, Coleman 1982).

The "thrifty gene," proposed by James Neel in 1962, and updated in 1982, is the most accepted evolutionary explanation for the occurrence of the diabetic genotype. Additionally, two selective factors have been identified which could increase or maintain this "thrifty gene" in a population: repeated periods of starvation and multiparity.

Repeated periods of stavation was proposed by Neel in his original formulation of the thrifty gene explanation. He hypothesized that the "thrifty gene" equipped hunters and gatherers to survive a feast-and-famine pattern of food intake, but which become detrimental as they adapted to civilization. For 99% of human evolution, while man:

> ... existed as a hunter and gatherer, it was often feast and famine. Periods of gorging alternated with periods of greatly reduced food intake. The individual whose pancreatic responses minimized post-prandial glycosuria might have, during a period of starvation, an extra pound of adipose reserve (Neel 1962: 355).

Starvation as a selective factor is supported by research with a genetic strain of predisposed diabetic mice. When compared with a control group of normal mice, Coleman found that the diabetic strain was able to survive starvation significantly longer. Phenotypically, the mice had a different blood-insulin concentration, and their fat pads oxidized glucose more slowly than in normal mice. In other words, once the food energy is stored as fat in diabetic mice, it is released much more slowly. This trait, Coleman (1979: 665) contends, could provide "... a selective advantage when food was scarce and yet not be deleterious when food was abundant."

Current diabetic research, which uses evolutionary theory, is often based on the assumption that virtually all of man's existence as a hunter-gatherer has been lived in a precarious and arduous feast-and-famine cycle (most notably Zimmett 1977 and 1979, Coleman 1979 and 1982, Knowler et al. 1983). Hence, a "thrifty gene" would allow a person to survive recurrent famines and starvation. Weis and coworkers (1984) have postulated that the combination of food scarcity and migration may have increased the "thrifty" genotype among Native Americans who migrated from Asia to the New World and the Polynesians who voyaged to the Pacific islands. Cross-cultural data, however, indicate most hunter-gatherers use a wide variety of reliable food sources and do not have feast and famine cycles characterized by gorging alternated with periods of starvation. Generally speaking, hunters and gatherers have "hungry seasons" when fewer resources are available. This seasonality is true even in environments where plant resources are abundant, providing greater security through diversity, because many species ripen at the same time of the year (Lee and Devore 1968, Damas 1969a and 1969b, Bicchieri 1972). Dunn (1968) concludes that malnutrition and starvation are rare among hunters and gatherers. Thus, human starvation may not be as important a selective factor for the Type II diabetic genotype as medical researchers have assumed. More often, however, seasonal variation in the food supply would be a factor in selection.

The second selective factor, multiparity, formulated by Wiedman (1983), proposes that the "thrifty gene" was an adaptive advantage in hunting and gathering populations because females with the gene would have a phenotype which efficiently stores body fat and subsequently metabolizes that fat more slowly during seasonal variations in resources, thereby increasing the likelihood that a female with this gene would produce more viable offspring per lifetime. The "thrifty gene" is hypothesized to affect fecundity and fertility of a population in several ways. First, the increased ability to gain body fat would facilitate maternal weight gain during pregnancy, and after pregnancy, the mother would maintain body weight to provide for a sufficient lactation duration. And secondly, it would produce a child with a slightly greater birth weight, one who could better survive childhood.

Diabetic females have often been shown to have a greater birth rate than nondiabetics but this association has been interpreted as evidence that the recurrent stresses of pregnancy increases the risk of diabetes (Keen and Jarrett 1982b). Numerous studies in diverse countries indicate that increased births are associated with diabetes (Baird 1982).

A greater frequency of births by diabetics was explained by Mosenthal and Bolduan in 1933 as due to the recurrent stresses of pregnancy. They proposed the hypothesis that the chance of developing diabetes would become greater with increasing parity. Many studies suppported this hypothesis with data indicating greater diabetic parity (Joslin et al. 1936, Munro et al. 1949, Pyke 1956). Their conclusions, however, have been questioned by Steinberg (1958), and Vinke et al. (1959) whose statistical investigations of Dutch women indicated no relationship between the number of pregnancies and pathogenesis of diabetes.

Several recent studies, however, have produced statistically significant differences in parity between diabetics and non-diabetic females. O'Sullivan and Gordon reported the parity distribution for 3267 women examined by the Health Examination Survey of the United States Public Health Survey. Overall, they reported that "... the mean parity for diabetic women ages 18–79 years was higher than the mean parity for non-diabetic women. This difference is statistically significant at a level of 5 percent ...." (O'Sullivan and Gordon 1966: 3). Mean parity was also elevated in diabetic women, even when the parity count was restricted to live births.

Greater parity in diabetic Polynesian females than their non-diabetic counterparts (P⟨0.001) was found by Zimmet and others (1977). Even though the younger age group had a significantly greater parity, they attributed the parity differences to the older age of the diabetics. Stanhope and Prior in their study of Polynesians from the Island of Tokelau found diabetic females produced more offspring. The excess parity of diabetic Tokelauans over nondiabetics was significant for both those who remained on the Island and those who migrated to New Zealand. They calculated:

> ... the number of total pregnancies and live births of definite and known diabetic females expected if their reproductive behavior did not differ from nondiabetic females, taking age into account. There were 14 percent more live births ($X_1^2 = 4.474$; $P = 0.034$), and 15 percent more total births than expected ($X_1^2 = 6.192$, $P = 0.013$) (Stanhope and Prior 1980: 420).

Although West (1978b) concluded that parity did not increase the risk of diabetes, additional research will have to be conducted before we can say that the stress of multiple childbirths results in a greater risk for diabetes, or the opposite interpreation, that the diabetic genotype increases the possibility of more children per lifetime.

The birth of larger offspring to females with the diabetic genotype is hypothesized to be the basis for the improved reproductive fitness. We know that diabetic females in industrial populations give birth to larger neonates who often have congenital complications. But in preindustrial populations, the diabetic genotype female would not have maintained a prolonged period of obesity, so they will not manifest detrimental diabetic symptoms. Theoretically, the offspring will be born without complications and will be of slightly greater birthweight. If this is true, then one would expect prediabetics in an industrial society, those who develop diabetic symptoms later in life, to produce slightly larger neonates. Studies of the Pima Indians strongly suggest that the prenatal environment of the offspring of prediabetic women results in children born with a slightly greater birthweight than offspring of non-diabetics.

> ... although prediabetic women respond normally to glucose-tolerance tests, they may have some subtle abnormalities in glucose disposal at times during their pregnancies — abnormalities causing their offspring to have a slightly higher mean percentage of desirable weight than the offspring of non-diabetics (Pettitt *et al*. 1983: 244).

Excessive fetal and neonatal morbidity and mortality are commonly associated with diabetic mothers, and this would seem to disprove the likelihood of the diabetic genotype's having a multiparity advantage. However, West (1978b) reviewed the literature regarding the birth of larger babies to diabetic mothers and concluded that excessive birth weight and neonatal mortality are not manifestations of prediabetics; rather, they are associated with excessive adiposity and the age of diabetic mothers. Moreover, he stated that the risk of fetal and infant mortality is very low in prediabetics, when blood glucose levels are normal or very near normal. Detailed medical studies among the Pima found congenital anomalies to be less frequently encountered in non-diabetic and prediabetic than in diabetic pregnancies. Furthermore, "... among prediabetic pregnancies — pregnancies occurring in women before the onset of diabetes — the rates were no different than in the non-diabetic pregnancies" (Bennett et al. 1977). Multiple congenital malformations are attributed to the severity of metabolic derangement in the early stage of pregnancy, and are not related to genetic factors (Freinkel and Metzger 1979).

Theoretically, because starvation and malnutrition happens infrequently among hunters and gatherers, these negative factors would be of secondary importance to multiparity which would be a positive selective factor operating on every generation.

SUMMARY

This case study in medical anthropology detailed the technological developments which happened concurrently with the first detrimental symptoms of type II diabetes mellitus among the Cherokee. Ethnographic, historic and archeologic evidence documented the Cherokee's rapid cultural change from an agricultural to an industrial economy in a matter of ten years, from 1936 to 1946. This infrastructural change resulted in nutritional and lifestyle changes which contributed to obesity and the onset of detrimental diabetic symptoms. Third World countries which are just now undergoing a transition to an industrial society can expect a dramatic increase of this disease.

Although diabetic manifestations are now detrimental, the genotype in our evolution may have provided a selective advantage for the human species. In evolutionary terms the diabetic "thrifty" genotype would be beneficial in hunting and gathering populations since improved reproductive fitness would result in multiparity and a population increase; or secondarily, individuals with the gene would be more likely to survive periods of starvation or the more frequent seasonal variations in nutritional resources. However, with industrial development, or migration and acculturation into an industrial society, a relatively significant proportion of a hunting and gathering or agricultural population will begin the onset of detrimental diabetic symptoms if they become obese owing to excessive caloric intake. Furthermore, an increased prevalence of Type II diabetes mellitus may occur if they live in poor socioeconomic conditions, and a high rate could be maintained if the population has an obese body image as a cultural theme.

REFERENCES

Baird, J.D., 1982. Is Obesity a Factor in the Aetiology of Non-Insulin Dependent Diabetes. In *The Genetics of Diabetes Mellitus*, Sirono Symposium Vol. 47, (eds.) J. Kobberling and R. Tattersal, 239. New York: Academic Press.

Barker, D.J., M.J. Gardner and C. Power, 1982. Incidence of Diabetes amongst People Aged 18–50 years in Nine British Towns: A Collaborative Study, *Diabetologia* 22: 412–425.

Bennett, Peter H., T.A. Birch and Max Miller, 1971. The High Prevalence of Diabetes in the Pima Indians of Arizona, U.S.A. In *Diabetes Mellitus in Asia 1970*, (eds.) Tsugi, S., and M. Wade, 33. Amsterdam: Excerpta Medica.

Bennett, P. *et al.*, 1977. Congenital Anomalies and the Diabetic and Prediabetic Pregnancy. In *Pregnancy Metabolism, Diabetes and the Fetus*, 209. Ciba Foundation Symposium 63 (New Series).

Bicchieri, M.G., 1972. *Hunters and Gatherers Today*. New York: Holt, Rinehart and Winston.

Cleave, T.L. and G.D. Campbell, 1969. *Diabetes, Coronary Thrombosis and the Saccharine Disease*. 2nd Ed. Bristol: John Wright and Sons Ltd.

Cohen, A.M., A. Teitelbaum and R. Saliternik, 1972. Genetics and Diet as Factors in Development of Diabetes Mellitus, *Metabolism* 21: 235–240.

Cohen, Burton, 1954. Diabetes Mellitus among Indians of the American Southwest: Its Prevalence and Clinical Characteristics in a Hospitalized Population, *Annals of Internal Medicine* 40: 588.

Coleman, Douglas, 1979. Obesity Genes: Beneficial effects in Heterozygous Mice, *Science* 203: 663–665.

Coleman, D., 1982. The Genetics of Diabetes in Rodents. In *The Genetics of Diabetes Mellitus*, (eds.) J. Kobberling and R. Tattersall, 183–195. New York: Academic Press.

Crockett. B.N., 1953. *The Original Development of Public Health in Oklahoma 1830–1930*. Durant, Oklahoma.

Damas, David, 1969a. *Contributions to Anthropology: Band Societies*. Bulletin 228 Ottawa: National Museums of Canada.

Damas, David, 1969b. *Contributions to Anthropology: Ecological Essays*. Bulletin 230. Ottawa: National Museums of Canada.

Drevets, Curtis, 1965. Diabetes Mellitus in Choctaw Indians, *Journal of the Oklahoma State Medical Association* 58: 322–29.

Dunn, L., 1968. Epidemiological Factors: Health and disease in hunter-gatherers. In *Man the Hunter*, ed. R. Lee, Chicago: Aldine Publishing Co.

Eaton, Cynthia, 1977. Diabetes, Culture Change and Acculturation: A Biocultural Analysis, *Medial Anthropology* 1(2): 41–63.

Ede, M.C., 1966. Diabetes and the Way of Life on an Indian Reservation, *Guy Hospital Report* 115: 455–461.

Editorial, 1982. Diabetes Mellitus and Socioeconomic Factors, *Lancet* ii: 530–531.

Ellemann, K., J. Soerensen, L. Pedersen, B. Edsberg, and O. Anderson, 1984. Epidemiology and Treatment of Diabetic Ketoacidosis in a Community Population, *Diabetes Care* 7: 528–532.

Elston, R., K. Namboodiri, H. Nino and W. Pollitzer, 1974. Studies on Blood and Urine Glucose in Seminole Indians: Indication for Segregation of a Major Gene, *American Journal of Human Genetics* 26: 13–34.

Fajans, S., 1981. Etiologic Aspects of Types of Diabetes, *Diabetes Care* 4: 69–75.

Foreman, Grant, 1975. *Indians and Pioneers*. Norman: University of Oklahoma Press.

Freinkel, N. and B. Metzger, 1979. Pregnancy as a Tissue Culture Experience: Critical Implications of Maternal Metabolism for Fetal Development. In *Pregnancy Metabolism, Diabetes and the Fetus*, 3–23. Ciba Foundation Symposium 63.

Frohman, Lawrence, Thomas Doeblin and Frank Emerling, 1969. Diabetes in the Seneca Indians, *Diabetes* 18: 38–43.

Gearing, Frederick, 1962. *Priests and Warriors: Social Structures for Cherokee Politics in the 18th Century*. American Anthropological Association, Memoir 93.

Henry, R., T. Burch, P. Bennett and M. Miller, 1969. Diabetes in Cocopah Indians, *Diabetes* 18: 33–37.

Hewes, Leslie, 1940. The Geography of Cherokee Country. Ph.D. Dissertation, University of California, Berkeley.

Hill, Charles Jr., and Mozart Spector, 1971. Natality and Mortality of American Indians Compared with U.S. Whites and Non-Whites. Health Services and Mental Health Administration, *Health Reports* 86: 229–46.

Himsworth, H.P., 1936. Diet and the Incidence of Diabetes Mellitus, *Clinical Science* 2: 117–148.

Howard, C., 1982. Non-Human Primates as Models for the Study of Human Diabetes Mellitus, *Diabetes* 31: Sup. 1: 37–42.

Johnson, John and C. Wallace McNutt, 1964. Diabetes Mellitus in an American Indian Population Isolate, *Texas Reports of Biological Medicine* 22: 110–125.

Joslin, Elliot, 1940. The Universality of Diabetes, *Journal of the American Medical Association* 115: 2033.

Joslin, E., *et al.*, 1936. Studies in Diabetes Mellitus. IV, Etiology, Part 1, *American Journal of Medical Science* 191: 759.

Joos, Sandra, 1984. Economic, Social, and Cultural Factors in the Analysis of Disease: Dietary Change and Diabetes Mellitus among the Florida Seminole Indians. In *Ethnic and Regional Foodways in the United States*, (eds.) L. Brown and K. Mussell. Knoxville: U. of Tennessee Press.

Judkins, Russell, 1976. Diet and Diabetes among the Iroquois: An Integrative Approach. *Actas Del XLI Congreso Internacional De Americas*, Vol. III, Mexico.

Kawate, R. *et al.*, 1979. Diabetes Mellitus and its Vascular Complications in Japanese Migrants on the Island of Hawaii, *Diabetes Care* 2: 161–170.

Keen, H. and V. Grabauskas, 1979. The WHO Multinational Study of Vascular Disease in Diabetes, *Diabetes Care* 2: 175–186.

Keen, H. and R. Jarrett, 1982. Environmental Factors and Genetic Interactions. In *The Genetics of Diabetes Mellitus*, (eds.) W. Creutzfeldt, J. Kobberling, and J. Neel. New York: Springer-Verlag.

Keen, H., R. Jarrett and P. McCarthney, 1982. The Ten-Year Follow-Up of the Bedford Survey (1962–1972): Glucose Tolerance and Diabetes, *Diabetologia* 22: 73–78.

Kissebah, A., N. Vydelingum, R. Murray, *et al.*, 1982. Relation of Body Fat Distribution to Metabolic Complications of Obesity, *Journal of Clinical Endrocrinology and Metabolism* 54: 254–260.

Knowler, W., D. Pettitt, P. Bennett and R. Williams, 1983. Diabetes Mellitus in the Pima Indians: Genetic and Evolutionary Considerations, *American Journal of Physical Anthropology* 62: 107–114.

Kobberling, J. and R. Tattersall, 1982. *The Genetics of Diabetes Mellitus*. Academic Press, New York.

Lee, Richard and Irving Devore, 1968. *Man the Hunter*. Chicago: Aldine Publishing Co.

Mayberry, Ruben and Robert Lindeman, 1963. A Survey of Chronic Disease and Diet in Seminole Indians in Oklahoma, *American Journal of Clinical Nutrition* 13: 127–134.

Miller, Max, Peter Bennett and Thomas Burch, 1968. Hyperglycemia in Pima Indians: A Preliminary Appraisal of Its Significance. In *Biomedical Challenges Presented by the American Indian*, Pan American Health Organization 165.

Monro, H., J.C. Eaton and A. Glen, 1949. A Survey of a Scotish Diabetic Clinic, *Journal of Clinical Endrocrinology* 9: 48.

Mooney, James, 1975. *Historical Sketch of the Cherokee*. Chicago: Aldine Publishing Company.

Mosenthal, H. and C. Boulduan, 1933. Diabetes Mellitus-Problems of Present Day Treatment, *American Journal of Medical Science* 186: 605.

Mouratoff, George, Nicholas Carroll and Edward Scott, 1969. Diabetes Mellitus in Athabaskan Indians in Alaska, *Diabetes* 18: 29–32.

National Diabetes Group, 1979. Classification and Diagnosis of Diabetes Mellitus and other Categories of Glucose Intolerance, *Diabetes* 28: 1039–1057.

Neel, James, 1962. Diabetes Mellitus: A "Thrifty" Genotype Rendered Detrimental by "Progress"?, *American Journal of Human Genetics* 14: 353–362.

Neel, James, 1982. The Thrifty Genotype Revisited. In *The Genetics of Diabetes Mellitus*, Serono Symposium No. 47, eds. Kobberling and R. Tattersall. New York: Academic Press.

Niswander, J.D., 1969. Some Special Medical Problems of Indian Populations — Discussion on Diabetes. In *Biomedical Challenges Presented by the American Indian*, World Health Organization, Pan American Health Organization Publication 165.

O'Dea, K., *et al.*, 1980. Some Studies on the Relationship between Urban Living and Diabetes in a Group of Australian Aborigines, *Medical Anthropology* 4: 1–20.

O'Dea, K., R. Spargo, and P. Nestel, 1982. Impact of Westernization on Carbohydrate and Lipid Metabolism in Australian Aborigines, *Diabetologia* 22: 148–153.

O'Sullivan, J. and T. Gordon, 1966. National Center for Health Statistics: Childbearing and Diabetes Mellitus. *Vital Health Statistics*. No. 1000, Series 11, Number 21, 3. Public Health Services, U.S. Government Printing Office, Washington.

O'Sullivan, John and Clare Mahan, 1965. Blood Sugar Levels, Glycosuria, and Body Weight Related to Development of Diabetes Mellitus: The Oxford Epidemiology Study 17 Years Later, *Journal of the American Medical Association* 194: 6: 117–122.

O'Sullivan, John and Clare Mahan, 1968. Prospective Study of 352 Young Patients with Clinical Diabetes, *New England Journal of Medicine* 278: (19): 1038–1041.

Oklahoma State Department of Health, 1943 through 1970. *Public Health Statistics*. Oklahoma City.

Oklahoma State Department of Health, 1971 through 1985. *Oklahoma Health Statistics*, Oklahoma City.

Opler. Morries E., 1945. Themes as Dynamic Forces in Culture, *American Journal of Sociology* 51: 198–206.

Papaspyros, N.S., 1964. *The History of Diabetes Mellitus*. Second Edition. Stuttgart: Georg Thieme Verlag.

Peach, W., R. Pool and J. Tarver, 1964. *County Building Block Data, For Regional Analysis: Oklahoma*. Research Foundation, Oklahoma State University, Stillwater, Oklahoma.

Pettitt, D., B. Baird, K. Aleck, P. Bennett and W. Knowler, 1983. Excessive Obesity in Offspring of Pima Indian Women with Diabetes, *New England Journal of Medicine* 308: 244.

Prior, I., 1971. The Price of Civilization, *Nutrition Today* 6: 2–11.

Prior, I., 1974. Diabetes in the South Pacific. In *Is the Risk of Becoming Diabetic Affected by Sugar Consumption?*, Eighth International Sugar Research Symposium, 4–13.

Pyke, D., 1956. Parity and Incidence of Diabetes, *Lancet* 1: 6927: 818.

Ragland, H., 1957. Historical Series, February through July. Sequoyah County Times, Salisaw: Oklahoma.

Reid, J., S. Fullmer, K. Pettigrew *et al.*, 1971. Nutrient intake of Pima Indian Women: Relationships to Diabetes Mellitus and Gallbladder Disease, *American Journal of Clinical Nutrition* 24: 1281–1289.

Rotter J. and D. Rimoin, 1979. Diabetes Mellitus: The Search for Genetic Markers, *Diabetes Care* 2: 215–226.

Schaefer, Otto, 1969. Glycosuria and Diabetes Mellitus in Canadian Eskimos, *Canadian Medical Association Journal* 99: 201–206.

Seivers, M.L., 1966. Disease Patterns among Southwestern Indians, *Public Health Reports* 81 (12): 1075–83.

Sochet, Bernard, 1958. Five Year Experience with Diabetes Mellitus at the U.S. Public Health Service Indian Hospital, Lawton Oklahoma, *Journal of the Oklahoma State Medical Association* 51: 459–462.

Stanhope, J., and I. Prior, 1983. The Tokelau Island Migration Study: Prevalence and Incidence of Diabetes Mellitus, *New Zealand Medical Journal* 92:673: 417–431.

Stein, Jay, K. West, J. Robey *et al.*, 1965. The High Prevalence of Abnormal Glucose Tolerance in the Cherokee Indians of North Carolina, *Archives of Internal Medicine* 116: 842.

Steinberg, A., 1958. Heredity and Diabetes, *Diabetes* 7: 244.

Szathmary, Emoke and Nasha Holt, 1983. Hyperglycemia in Dogrib Indians of the Northwest Territories, Canada: Association with Age and a Centripetal Distribution of Body Fat, *Human Biology* 55: 493–515.

Taylor, Richard, Peter Bennett, George LeGronidec *et al.*, 1983. The Prevalence of Diabetes Mellitus in a Traditional-Living Polynesian Peoples: The Wallis Island Study, *Diabetes Care* 6: 334–340.

Toniolo, A. *et al.*, 1982. Virus-Induced Diabetes Mellitus: Glucose Abnormalities Produced in Mice by the Six Members of the Coxsakie B Virus Group, *Diabetes* 31: 496.

United States Department of Agriculture, 1981. *Nutritive Values of Foods*. U.S. Government Printing Office, Washington D.C.

Vinke, B., W. Nagelsmit, F. Van Buchem and L. Smid, 1959. Some Statistical Investigations in Diabetes Mellitus, *Diabetes* 8: 100.

Webb, W., 1931. *The Great Plains*. Ginn Publishers.

Weis K., R. Ferrell, and C. Harris, 1984. A New World Syndrome of Metabolic Disease with a Genetic and Evolutionary Basis, *Yearbook of Physical Anthropology* 27: 153–178.

West, Kelly, 1973. Diet Therapy of Diabetes: An Analysis of Failure, *Annals of Internal Medicine* 79: 425–434.

West, Kelly, 1974a. Culture, History and Adiposity, Or Should Santa Claus Reduce?, *Obesity and Bareatric Medicine* 3: 48–52.

West, Kelly, 1974b. Diabetes in American Indians and other Native Populations of the New World, *Diabetes* 23: 841–855.

West, Kelly, 1974c. Epidemiologic Observations on Thirteen Populations of Asia and the Western Hemisphere. *Eighth International Sugar Research Symposium.*

West, Kelly, 1978a. Diabetes in American Indians, *Advances in Metabolic Disorders* 9: 29–48.

West, Kelly, 1978b. *Epidemiology of Diabetes and Its Vascular Lesions*. Holland: Elsevier.

West, Kelly, 1979a. Standardization of Definition, Classification, and Reporting in Diabetes Related Epidemiologic Studies, *Diabetes Care* 2: 65–76.

West, Kelly, 1979b. Detailed Study of an Epidemic of Obesity and Diabetes. Paper presented at the annual meetings of the Ameican Diabetic Association.

West, Kelly and John Kalbfleisch, 1971. Influences of Nutritional Factors on Prevalence of Diabetes, *Diabetes* 20: 99–104.

Westfall, David and Arlan Rosenbloom, 1971. Diabetes Mellitus among the Florida Seminole, *Health Services and Mental Health Adminisration Health Reports* 86: 1037–41.

White, W.D., 1966. Diabetes in the Oklahoma Indian. Abstracted Proceedings, First Joint Meeting of the Clinical Society and Commissioned Officers Association. 21,. U.S. Public Health Service, Baltimore.

Wiedman, Dennis, 1976. The Individual and Innovation in the Process of Sociocultural Adaptation to Frontier Situations, *Papers in Anthropology* 17: 106–116.

Wiedman, Dennis, 1979. Diabetes Mellitus and Oklahoma Native Americans: A Case Study of Culture Change in Oklahoma Cherokee. Ph.D. Dissertation, Department of Anthropology, University of Oklahoma.

Wiedman, Dennis, 1983. The Diabetic Genotype as an Adaptive Advantage in Human Evolution: A "Multiparity" Hypothesis. Paper presented at the Annual Meetings of the American Anthropological Association, Chicago.

Wise, P., F. Edwards, D. Thomas *et al.*, 1970. Hyperglycaemia in the Urbanized Aboriginal: The Davenport Study, *The Medical Journal of Australia* 2: 1001–1006.

Woodward, Grace, 1963. *The Cherokees*. Norman: University of Oklahoma Press.

Yudkin, John, 1963. Nutrition and Palatability with Special Reference to Obesity, Myocardial Infarction and other Diseases of Civilization, *Lancet* 1: 1335–1338.

Zimmet, P., 1979. Epidemiology of Diabetes and its Macrovascular Manifestations in Pacific Populations: The Medical Effects of Social Progress, *Diabetes Care* 2: 144–153.

Zimmet, P., A. Seluka, J. Collins, P. Currie, J. Wicking and W. DeBoer, 1977. Diabetes Mellitus in an Urbanized, Isolated Polynesian Population: The Funafuti Survey, *Diabetes* 26: 1106.

Zimmet, P. et al., 1981. The Prevalence of Diabetes in the Rural and Urban Polynesian Population of Western Samoa, *Diabetes* 30: 45–51.

The Ethnography of Policy: Florida's Mental Health Act

MICHAEL V. ANGROSINO
ANGELA E. SCOGGIN
University of South Florida

INTRODUCTION: ANTHROPOLOGY AND PUBLIC POLICY

In two recent critical essays, Thomas Weaver has summarized the tentative steps which anthropology has taken in the direction of becoming a "policy science," that is, a discipline whose findings are regularly incorporated into the decision-making processes of the public and private sector. He notes that "the failures of anthropology as a policy science have been more apparent than its successes" (Weaver 1985a: 103) and cites "unfamiliarity with the politics, administration and the nature of policy formation" as among the reasons for these failures. In his discussion of training needs in the field (Weaver 1985b: 199), he goes on to insist that "the anthropologist must understand the structure of policy makers' organization and how decisions are made."

Policy-oriented anthropologists have characteristically been interested in studying the impact of policy on selected target communities, but they have had relatively little to say about where policy directions come from, how policy is formulated, and how it gets implemented. The purpose of this paper is to demonstrate the application of some standard ethnographic data-collection methods (participant-observation in relevant agencies and target communities; key informant interviewing) and some anthropological concepts to the study of policy. We will focus on the Florida Mental Health Act and will explore:

1) the political, social, and economic context in which the policy took shape;

2) the legislative history of the Act;

3) the ongoing dynamic interrelationship between lawmakers and communities affected by lawmakers' decisions.

Two key factors in our analysis may be highlighted at the outset:

1) Although public policy has sometimes been described as "whatever governments choose to do" (Dye 1972: 1), we reject the notion found in some traditional political science literature that governments act in a vacuum. We will look at policy as a *social* process in which legislators respond to community initiatives as much as they impose their will on those communities. In sum, policy is not made *for* clients *by* government — it is the result of a balance of interests negotiated between these two interest groups.

2) This interaction results in a developmental *cycle* of policy, rather than in discrete, end-point decisions. This position is embodied in the work of Jones (1984) and may be summarized by saying that in the policy cycle, any short-term decision taken to satisfy one set of perceived needs inevitably generates new and unforeseen problems which must result in decisions about new actions to be taken.

MENTAL HEALTH POLICY: THE NATIONAL CONTEXT

A considerable body of literature exists which addresses the role of culture in either sustaining mental health, or, in some cases, promoting mental illness.[1] The life conditions of mentally ill people in the U.S. have been treated descriptively by ethnographic means (Estroff 1981), as have the lives of mentally retarded citizens (Edgerton 1967). Anthropologists have also engaged in stimulating debate over the desirable shape of public policy affecting those populations (Landy 1983; Scheper-Hughes 1983). However, these studies tend to accept policy as a top-down process. There has been relatively little anthropological attention paid to the question of how policy is established in the first place, and how the needs of those served can be translated to decision-makers. In the absence of such analysis, it will be difficult, as Weaver suggests, for the applied anthropologist to act as an effective advocate for policy change.

Before examining the specific case of Florida's Mental Health Act, we must describe the national context in which state policy developed. Specific policy directed toward the mentally ill in the U.S. may be said to have begun in the mid-nineteenth century under the influence of the social reformer Dorothea Dix. Guided by the reforms in penology inaugurated in France by Pinel, Dix instigated the establishment of state mental hospitals in thirty states. Although her goal was "moral treatment," the hospitals soon developed into warehouses in which the mentally ill were shut away with little treatment and scant hope of discharge. Through the weighty bureaucracy of the state hospitals, state governments played the major role in determining the fates of the mentally ill until 1946 when the National Institute of Mental Health was created. For the first time, the federal government assumed an important directive role in mental health policy.

The National Institute of Mental Health may be said to have represented a new interest in *prevention* of mental illness, an emphasis that reflected new trends in psychotherapy, principally the development of medications that made it possible to maintain even formerly "intractable" patients in a functioning state. NIMH also became a focus of research and training, both of which were opened to academic disciplines and professions beyond the biomedical fields. By the mid-1950s, a citizens' advocacy movement, expressing concern over the anti-therapeutic nature of the state hospitals, had come to prominence. The Joint Commission on Mental Illness and Health[2] published its report in 1961, and it advocated, among other innovations, the deinstitutionalization of chronic patients who, with proper medication, could live in "natural communities" where aftercare and other rehabilitative services would be available.

Because of the strong personal interest of President Kennedy in mental health issues, the Community Mental Health Centers Act of 1963 became a centerpiece of New Frontier/Great Society legislation. By mandating a federally supported network of community-based services, this Act threw the weight of the federal government behind a policy of deinstitutionalization. This term, which has had various applications, may best be summarized as a move to: prevent unnecessary institutionalization; deinstitutionalize those who could properly be maintained in the community; and improve inpatient care for those still requiring hospitalization.[3]

The second of these two goals has attracted the greatest amount of scholarship and media attention, and has also been the focus of policy directions in states such as Florida. The general consensus in the literature is that deinstitutionalization become a kind of moral crusade, one which flourished in the era of civil rights movement and other efforts to secure political, economic, and social equality for various disadvantaged groups (Williams, Bellis, and Wellington 1980). It is also the case that deinstitutionalization was often promoted as a cost-cutting measure, thus giving it economic as well as political appeal, but these purported economic benefits have never been clearly established (Miller 1982: 48). Local politicians and business people often pushed for deinstitutionalization because they believed it would bring both local control and federal monies to services in their communities. But these motives tended to be undercut in most states by the continuing political clout of the state hospital administration and staff who feared loss of jobs and so lobbied against developing community service programs. In at least one state, Tennessee, a compromise was reached whereby the directors of the state mental hospitals were made the direct supervisors of the community service coordinators. Miller concludes that there were, in effect, so many different, and potentially conflicting motives among political and business leaders that the advocacy community, representing a single-minded moral position, tended to define the terms of the debate and, more often than not, win the day with extensive lobbying tactics.

Nevertheless, deinstitutionalization was rarely accomplished without the stresses of lawsuits, conflicts with receptor communities, and considerable debate within the various helping professions about the extent and characteristics of non-institutional services (Halpern, et al., 1980: 11–17). Sociologist Leona Bachrach (1976) identifies the key problems that inhibit effective implementation of deinstitutionalization programs.

1) Discharged patients have not been prepared to function independently in the community.

2) Many programs are insensitive to the special needs of minority and other special interest groups within the general deinstitutionalized population.

3) Communities have not been able to provide an adequate range of services to support deinstitutionalized clients.

4) Clients have not been able to attain easy access to services scattered over a service delivery region, even when such services are in existence.

5) There continues to be a prejudice against the mentally ill on the part of the mainstream community.

6) Fiscal responsibility for care of patients is so parcelled out among federal, state, and local authorities that the patient is often caught in a web of conflicting rules and guidelines.

7) Deinstitutionalization was sometimes mandated in the face of hesitation or even opposition by key groups (e.g., service professionals) who did not subscribe to its goals.

One result of these problems has been the increasing visibility of chronicity. The sheer number of chronically mentally ill people is increasing in part because schizophrenia, which characteristically appears in young adulthood, has been on the increase with the maturation of the baby boom generation (Bachrach 1980). But a further problem exists: since these people came of age in the era of deinstitutionalization, the likelihood is that they have never been institutionalized, and hence were never socialized into a routine of compliance. They therefore form an increasingly large, mobile, ill population with few ties to the organized mental health system (Bachrach 1982). The national media attention focused on "bag ladies" (merely one of many varieties of chronically mentally ill people unattached to the mental health system) illustrates the policy process which is at the heart of this paper: a remedy, deinstitutionalization, was proposed and effectuated in order to deal with a perceived problem (the anti-therapeutic nature of hospital care); but unforeseen flaws in the implementation of deinstitutionalization created the social conditions that led to a newly recognized social problem, that of homeless or otherwise unattached chronically mentally ill people. The trend in current policy is therefore aimed at reaching the chronically mentally ill. In Florida, as elsewhere, there is talk of a need to give serious consideration to a policy of "reinstitutionalization." The national mood, too, has changed. "Community-based care" was heavily subsidized by federal monies, and hence has come to be seen as an artifact of the "big govenment" syndrome currently in political disfavor. It is ironic that the state hosptial, at one time the very symbol of repression, has come to stand, for political theorists of a certain stripe, as a refuge from the "excesses" of the supposedly failed liberal experiment of deinstitutionalization.

FLORIDA'S MENTAL HEALTH POLICY

Before the passage of the Florida Mental Health Act in 1971, the procedure for involuntary placement of a mentally ill individual into a state mental hospital was considered part of the same judicial procedure with the declaration of incompetency. According to Flaschner (1972: 345), "there was a tendency to confuse incompetency with commitment, whereas hospitalization itself should not involve suspension of civil rights." In addition, "an adjudication of incompetency [was] a condition precedent to a judicial order of hospitalization" (Flaschner 1972: 346). Before the enactment of the Mental Health Act, Florida's mental health policy seemed to be a confusing mixture of what should have been separate procedures concerning the mentally ill. That policy was "a serious mental health law anachronism" (Flaschner 1972: 346).

The new Florida Mental Health Act, drafted by House Representative Maxine Baker,

> ...was designed to reduce the occurrence, severity, duration, and disabling aspects of mental, emotional, and behavioral disorders. It provides for emergency services, temporary detention for diagnosis and evaluation, and short-term community inpatient treatment as a means of limiting the need for admissions to state hospitals (Hays 1982: 2).

The Act addressed four major concerns: 1) responsibilities of the state's Department of Health and Rehabilitaive Services relating to the mentally ill; 2) designation of approved treatment facilities; 3) patient rights; and 4) participation and liability of mental health professions. The section addressing patient rights was the most extensive. Indeed, the Baker Act had the strictest requirement for involuntary placement of any state in the nation at the time of its enactment. Florida's publicly funded mental health system was, at the time, composed primarily of four large state hospitals. The Act called a whole new service system into being. That system was ultimately to be coordinated by an umbrella state agency, the Department of H.R.S., but was administered through a series of local district boards, which tended to be dominated by a fragile coalition of client advocates and mental health professionals.

The Baker Act substantially strengthened the due process and other civil rights of clients, and took up the national call for community-based, as opposed to hospital-based treatment. Involuntary confinement was limited to those clients who were judged to be "dangerous to themselves or others." Prior to the Act, a person could be placed in a state hospital if three people signed affidavits and secured the approval of a judge. The jailing of the mentally ill while commitment was being considered, once a common practice, was prohibited by the Baker Act.

THE FLORIDA CONTEXT

The single most important characteristic of Florida as a political and economic entity is its rapid growth and its emergence as an overwhelmingly urban state. Since World War II, its population has more than tripled, and this trend, largely the product of in-migration rather than increased birth rate, is expected to continue into the twenty-first century. Florida's demography is marked by the increasing number of retirees. By 1980, the percent of the population over age 65 was nearly 20%, twice the national average.

Tourism continues to be a major source of state revenues, but agriculture — which has become an increasingly large-scale corporate enterprise — is also important. The mining of phosphates, a major growth industry in the 1960s and early 1970s, is currently in a long period of decline.

There is a general push emanating from the state leadership to attract more high-tech industries to the state. "Glamor" industries, such as film and TV production, are also being courted. But the relative lack of a manufacturing sector means that the role of labor unions has been relatively weak in Florida. Unions have traditionally been strong only among employees in the building trades and among public employees.

These factors may be taken to mean that Florida lacks a true "liberal" constituency. However, as even the "conservative" constituencies are committed to modernization and growth, there is considerable pressure in the direction of upgrading government structures and providing educational and social services that will be attractive to the high-tech industries that are seen to be the wave of the future. Because of the state's rapid growth, traditional elites (centered in the rural, agrarian north of the state) have been displaced; but as the quest for "manageable growth" has not yet settled into a clearcut pattern of economic or political dominance, no new elites have emerged to definitely lead Florida's decision-making processes. It is thus possible that a "humanitarian" movement such as deinstitutionalization was in the late 1960s and early 1970s could find an advocacy constituency and get itself established as policy without real "elite" support. The "powers-that-be" never were perceived as "owning" mental health services, and so its bureaucracy grew largely on its own terms, which meant that it increasingly grew away from its natal constituency in the advocacy groups.[4]

MENTAL HEALTH SERVICES IN FLORIDA: PREHISTORY OF THE BAKER ACT

In Florida the treatment of the mentally ill came to be seen as a social problem as early as 1954 when a special committee reported to Acting Governor Charley E. Johns that the mental health crisis in the state was more acute than had been generally realized. However, serious attention to the problem was not forthcoming until the mid-1960s when a series of articles was published in the *Sun Sentinel*, a newspaper serving the Broward-Palm Beach area; these articles exposed "discrepancies" in the Florida mental health system (Curella 1966). These so-called "Snake Pit 1966" articles described the plight of the mentally ill in hospitals and jails, and demonstrated the inadequacy of existing laws to protect the rights of such people.

Delivery of mental health services in Florida was confined to large institutional facilities, as was the case in most states. Florida's first state mental hospital was established at Chattahoochee in 1877 in an old government arsenal. Chattahoochee was Florida's only state mental hospital until one was built in the remote rural town of Arcadia in 1947. These "insane asylums" were deliberatedly located in desolate areas. A hospital was not built in an urban area (Dade-Broward counties) until 1957.

When Maxine Baker, a fledgling member of the Legislature in the late 1960s, visited the state mental hospitals, she regarded them, at best, as severely overcrowded and, at worst, as places that seemed more punitive than therapeutic. Patients had no privacy, and no provision was made for them to have personal belongings. Men and women patients were not allowed to fraternize with each other. Patients could not wear street clothes, even if they were ambulatory. Mail was read, and patients were allowed to write to only one person. Since the hospitals were usually far from the patients' home communities, visits were few, and contacts with relatives and friends were quickly lost. In these facilities, treatment was minimal, apart from tranquilizing the patients; the staff did little therapy or rehabilitation. There was a high percentage of foreign-born and foreign-trained doctors on staff; their professional competency was seriously compromised by their inability to communicate effectively with non-medical staff and patients.

These problems were, to be sure, all too common in the mental hospitals of all the states in that era. However, when the conditions were revealed to idealistic politicians who sincerely felt them to be unacceptable in "our fair state," a process of change could be initiated.

At the same time that Baker and a few allies were viewing the state hospital system with alarm, Florida was beginning to feel the first tentative results of national mental health legislation and treatment trends. The advent of psychotropic medications, and the passage of the Community Mental Health Centers Act allowed for the discharge of many patients from state institutions. But in Florida, most counties were unprepared to meet the needs of deinstitutionalized patients. Since most commitments in Florida at the time were involuntary, most institutional patients had been declared incompetent and had consequently lost their civil rights. As a result, not only were they cast adrift in communities without adequate provision for services, but they were people of uncertain civil status.

A milestone in Florida's expanding consciousness of mental health issues was the Donaldson case which began in 1957 and reached the Supreme Court in 1972. The Supreme Court ruling in this case established the concept of "right to treatment" for disabled clients. (See Miller 1976: 20–3 for a full discussion of this case.)

Prologue to the Baker Act

Florida's mental health policy was fraught with real problems in the early 1970s. Despite the appointment of a legislative subcommittee in 1966 to look into mental health issues, nothing much came of the effort until Maxine Baker was elected to the legislature, carrying her concerns for the protection of the rights of disadvantaged groups like the mentally ill with her. But her ability to affect change required a major shift in Florida's political climate.

The problem in the 1960s was the overrepresentation of rural districts in a state that had dramatically increased its urban population. The "Snake Pit 1966" articles suggested that many of the problems with the system were due to inadequate appropriations and the unwillingness of the rural legislators to support a broadening of the system beyond the remote hospitals which were located in districts they represented. A shift in legislative power to representatives of urban districts occurred as a result of the Supreme Court's 1966 ruling on reapportionment.

THE POLICY CYCLE

"Policy" may be thought of as a statement of the philosophy or ideology guiding social action. The process by which such an abstraction becomes implemented can best be described as a *cycle* rather than as a linear sequence of events. Such a processual framework, consisting of eleven steps, has been developed by Jones (1984). The eleven steps of the policy cycle will be used to describe the history of the Baker Act. Jones (1984: 28) notes that:

The policy activities listed can be grouped in sequence of government action. The first five are associated with getting the problem to government and the next three with direct action by the government to develop and fund a program. Implementation is really the government returning to the problem, and the last two activities ... can be thought of as returning the program to government (for review and possible change).

Perception

In order for the policy cycle to begin, there must be an issue or situation that is perceived as a problem by one or more individuals. The treatment of the mentally ill in Florida had been an area of controversy for several years. In the years immediately preceeding passage of the Baker Act, many groups, including county and state Mental Health Associations with allies in the media, raised the issue over and over.

Maxine Baker (D-Miami) is usually credited with being the "driving force" that made this popular question into a defined political issue. She told us that it was her visit to the Dade County courthouse where mentally ill people were held while awaiting transfer to a hosptial that fixed her resolve. The lofty abstractions of humanitarians had become a vivid, and painful reality to her, and a general social concern had become a personal crusade.

Baker's perception of the problem intensified as she began visiting institutions and mental health facilities around the state. She discovered that "there was practically no interaction between local mental health facilities and the hospitals," and that the institutions were "severely overcrowded, with little privacy." Perhaps the most startling thing Baker discovered was the very large number of patients who were involuntarily committed to state institutions. Within the first two years of her legislative career, Baker had begun to perceive Florida's mental health policies as in need of change, and had taken on that reform as a personal crusade. The high number of involuntary commitments, and the holding of the mentally ill in jails while awaiting transfer to hospitals were two specific issues which she felt were in need of immediate change.

Aggregation

The second step in the policy cycle, aggregation, involves getting other people to join in a crusade, to agree that one person's perceived issue really is a problem in need of a collective soluation. After she had established herself in the Legislature, Baker was appointed to chair an interim mental health committee charged with amending the existing mental health laws. Several amendments were, in fact, proposed and enacted, but few really touched the essential issues of structural reorganization of the system as a whole, and the reorientation of that system away from institutional and toward community-based care. Baker says that "we did do some reorganization of the Department of Mental Health, but very little. And when I became Chairman of the Mental Health Committee, I began to realize that it was a waste of time to keep amending this old, old antique Mental Health Act."

Attempting a complete revision of the Act was no easy task. Baker even had some difficulty gaining adherents among her own committee members, so she took drastic action. She notes wryly that the Mental Health Committee was not considered a plum assignment as all the legislators wanted to sit on the FINANCE, TAXATION, INSURANCE, and other "big" committees. To pump some commitment into her colleagues, she took them to the county jail in Tallahassee and arranged with the sheriff to have them locked up in the cells where mentally ill people were kept while awaiting transport. "And that impresed them," she chortled. Baker's forthright advocacy and "shock" tactics ultimately convinced others that here was an issue crying out for resolution.

Organization and Representation

Baker and her committee were, of course, in a position to affect policy change, but at the grassroots level, the Mental Health Associations combined to form an influential organization in support of the changes the legislators were examining. It was imperative that opinion be mobilized and organized in the communities of Florida, or else Baker's reforms would come to nothing. The Mental Health Associations were particularly disturbed with the 1963 repeal of a law which allowed emergency admissions to state hospitals without having to wait for court-ordered commitments. The Florida Mental Health Association was a major force behind the passage of the Baker Act, as it demonstrated a popular base of support for reform, the radical nature of which probably would not have set well with conservative legislators if backed solely by Baker and her little group. So the Association needed the legislators to pass the reform measures, but the legislators needed the Association to demonstrate that there was, in fact, a social and political base of support for the reforms.

As chair of the Mental Health Committee, Baker was the pivotal person in this intersection of interests, but two other positions on the Appropriations and Rules Committees also contributed to her effectiveness.

Agenda-Setting

Agenda-setting is a process that moves an issue from the status of an interesting curiosity (a "human interest" filler on the evening news) to that of an item demanding some resolution by policy-makers. Jones (1984: 73) notes that "labelling, widespread interest, limited (or neutralized) resistance, a persistent advocate in high places, media attention, and professional or technical analyses are a few of the conditions for agenda setting."

The issue of mental health reform in Florida would seem to fit these conditions. First, the issue did have an impact on large numbers of people. The increasing population of Florida, particularly in urban areas, made the problem of the mentally ill more visible. The reapportionment of the legislature required that the state allocate representation based on population. This shift established a base of support within the policy-making body that appreciated the impact that Florida's mental health policy could have on the new urban population centers.

Recognition of the problem with Florida's mental health policy had been increasing during the several years preceeding the proposed reforms and has already been discussed. But it is important that there be a perceived solution to the problem. Issues that seem to be either too vague, or too complex to suggest a workable solution tend to fall out of the public's attention and hence off the decision-makers' agenda. The policy changes envisioned by Baker and her colleagues were radical for Florida, but consonant with the system being implemented nationally as a result of the Community Mental Health Centers Act, so that there was ample evidence that community-based treatment could be developed that was based on concern for the rights of clients.

Formulation

As we have seen, it took several years and a combination of individuals and organizations, operating in a changing social and political climate, to get the specific issues reflected in the Baker Act to the point where they could be acted on by the government. The next three steps in the policy cycle involve reactions by the legislative body per se. Formulation is the first policy development phase; it means that specific means are proposed to solve the perceived problem.

In formulating a new Florida Mental Health Act, Baker and her committee utilized several strategies, including enlisting expert legal advice, comparing the mental health laws of other states, encouraging input from citizens' groups, and educating possible supporters and opponents. Attorney Doris Householder worked extensively with the Mental Health Committee in the development of the Act, and, in fact, drafted the bill that went before the Legislature. As they began working on the bill, Baker and Householder realized that they would have to deal with some potentially strong opposition. Baker's strategy was to enlist the aid of groups affected by the legislation, such as the Mental Health Associations, the psychiatric and psychological communities, American Association of University Women, League of Women Voters, and various civic clubs around the state.

Legitimization

The process of legitimization is one in which the group advocating for changes establishes *its* solution as the most feasible or desirable. In this case, policy legitimization resulted in approval and passage of the newly drafted mental health bill. Baker notes that the main opposition was from the county judges and their allies on the Judiciary Committee who feared that the bill would too greatly centralize mental health authority. With the help of attorneys representing the interests of the groups mentioned above, the bill was revised so as to de-emphasize the centrality of Tallahassee in limiting the judges' discretionary powers. With those objections thereby deferred, the solution of community-based care came to be seen as the most humane and workable alternative to the discredited state hospital system, even by people not theretofore entirely convinced that change should be in that direction. After the bill was passed, the chairman of the Senate Judiciary Committee said that the presentation of the bill before his committee was the best his committee had ever heard. He thereby voted to name it the "Baker Act," the title by which it is still most widely known.

With the passage of the Baker Act, years of preparation and a combination of social and political factors had culminated in the acceptance of a new mental health policy and the establishment of a new service system.

Budget

It is a truism of policy analysis that nothing is really policy unless someone is paying for it. Former Senator Louis de la Parte, who chaired the Ways and Means Committee, told us that simple passage of the Baker Act did not guarantee that his committee would vote to fund it. In fact, throughout his legislative career he had to fight to get fair appropriations for the health and rehabilitative services in general.

However, Baker was Vice-chairman of the Mental Health Appropriations Subcommittee when the Act was passed, so she was in a position to exert some influence on the allocation of funds. Even though she notes that mental health allocations have never been adequate, she was able to make sure that her bill was allocated sufficient funds to enable the new mental health system to get started. Without the budgetary commitment, the Act would simply have been a pious sentiment demonstrating Legislature's concern, but devoid of public impact.

Implementation, Evaluation, and Adjustment

The policy steps of implementation, evaluation, and adjustment follow the actual passage of the Act and encompass the effects of the legislation on the communities, individuals, and those groups entrusted with implementation of the policy. These factors, along with the ongoing evaluation and adjustment process as reflected by amendments to the Act, will be discussed in a separate section below.

Immediately following passage of the Act, educational programs, publication of public awareness materials, meetings with Mental Health Boards, and regional seminars for law enforcement officials were begun. The implementation that began with the passage of the Baker Act has been marked by the development of public receiving facilities, community mental health centers, and creative treatment programming with the goal of facilitating the adjustment of deinstitutionalized mental patients to the community. Evaluation of these programs is built into the process by the Florida Sunset Law which require periodic review and justification for continuation of funding. Not only has this requirement influenced all state services, but it has also ensured frequent and early response to perceived lacunae in the provisions of the Baker Act. The perception of such lacunae through the ongoing evaluation process begins the policy cycle anew.

MENTAL HEALTH POLICY: AN ANTHROPOLOGICAL PERSPECTIVE ON THE EVOLUTION OF A SERVICE BUREAUCRACY

In a previous section we characterized the deinstitutionalization movement as an offshoot of national civil rights concerns. While different interest groups had their own diverse political, economic, or social reasons for backing deinstitutionalization, formal policy emerged in the 1960s largely because of moral pressure brought to bear on sensitive political decisionmakers by consumer advocates, supported by advances in psychomedical technology.[5] However, this movement, founded in idealism, has become something of a bureaucratic tangle, one which often works against the best interests of patients caught in the complexities of the system; it is a system which has by and large failed to anticipate demographic and attitudinal changes in the service population. In sum, an idealistic movement based on sensitivity to client needs has become a complex, sometimes unresponsive, conservative bureaucracy against which public opinion is growing, to the extent that the main ideological tenents of the movement are being called into question. How did this evolution — which, as we shall see, occurred in Florida in a parallel fashion — come about?

One of the few anthropological theorists to have addressed the issue of change in administrative structures is A.F.C. Wallace. According to Wallace (1971: 1) administrative forms of social organization depend on "large, conspicuous, and permanent institutions" whose membership is defined by contract, and which depend on a hierarchical system of super-and subordination to channel communication. An administrative structure is composed of three groups: owners (those on whose behalf or under whose auspices work is done), clientele (those for whom or to whom the work is done), and the administrative organization itself. The latter is usually the "action" group charged with the implementation of policy, which generally flows from the "owners."

An action group may develop into a bureaucracy, first by a process which Wallace (1971: 5) calls "insulation":

> The system ideally requires that the personnel comprising the management organization proper carry out the institutionally assigned tasks according to abstract rules. Personal considerations which would divert information or contradict the chain of command may reduce the effectiveness of the management structure; thus only personal relationships that enhance these ties can be tolerated.

Such structures can survive only if they strive to eliminate "sentiment." The more nearly they can operate on the basis of "objective" rules and regulations, the more efficient they are believed to be. Conflict arises when adherence to such rules and; regulations shuts off the humanitarian concerns which generated the system in the first place.

Moreover, management structures tend to assimilate the prevailing authority structures in the society around them — even those which, like the community mental health system, were set up at least partly to protest those authority models. In our society, disabled people in general are held in low regard because of a very strong value which we place on economic productivity. No disabled people are more socially disvalued than those with mental impairments, because of the intellectual demands of a highly literate, technologically oriented way of life. To the extent that the community service bureaucracy reflects the values of the culture at large, there develops a kind of class/caste bias against the mentally disabled. This bias is not usually expressed in terms of obvious disapproval on the part of service providers, but in terms of a patronizing belief that the clients are simply not capable of making their own decisions. And that point of view works effectively to the same end — that of shutting the clients out of processes of decision-making, even when it comes to decisions that affect their own lives, and even when the system was designed to promote the dignity of the individual client.

Wallace (1971: 6) notes that although administrative structures are "at least as long-lived as other forms of social organization," they are nonetheless superficially unstable, subject to a process of "decay and reorganization" reminiscent of his more familiar "revitalization'" movement. Bureaucracies tend to engage in almost constant self-tinkering, featuring periodic new organizational charts. This tinkering serves the obvious purpose of responding to the complaints, apprehensions, and bickering that arise when people are allocating power over others' lives. But it is basically a "conservative" process because such shifts are usually purely cosmetic, and serve to preserve the "essential structure" (Wallace 1971: 6).

This exercise seems to be necessitated by the inevitable tendency of the administrative structure to become "corrupt," not in the pecuniary sense, but in the sense of a "kind of emotional or social entropy" (Wallace 1971: 7). As Wallace (1971: 7) describes the situation:

> Personal antipathies, for instance, become ingrained, creating blockades in the communication process. Personal friendships and sympathies become so entrenched that personnel changes cannot be made. Cliques of factions become polarized and diverted from the organization's proper goals to the goal of institutional ascendancy.... A kind of institutional unconscious develops, the repository of unconscionable ambitions and practices which cannot be admitted to open communication in the structure but which remain nonetheless to poison the milieu.

Human service workers cannot readily admit to feelings of resentment against their own institution, and so tend to project their frustrations onto either the government which finances the institution, or the clients, who are charged with being either ungrateful or uncooperative. More importantly, the work of the bureaucracy can come to be seen as obsolete and unsatisfactory to both clients and governments. The impulse to preserve the organization even when it has become an anachronism is a form of "corruption" in Wallace's terminology. The organization is set up to achieve the goals of the government and its clients, but while those goals may change, the organization solidifies around its original plans. Its major goal becomes to preserve itself. There is an assumption that if it does so, it can adapt and serve the reformulated needs of its clients and those who finance it, but its preoccupation is in maintaining its own status.

In the case of the mental health system, the community treatment network now finds itself at the wrong end of the political system: the federal and state governments which have supported the expansion of that network for the past two decades now are disinclined to spend for the human services at levels that characterized the 1960s and 70s. The system is also being criticized for its increasing insensitivity in dealing with the changed demographics and other needs of its clients.

We must therefore view the evolution of a state's mental health policy not as the caprice of deal-cutting politicians, but as a general process that creates administrative structures as agents of policy. Those agents then grow up to contend with their creators for control of access to service. As the commodity becomes scarcer (as funding for mental health services currently is), only a critical rethinking of the policy will serve to redress the imbalance in the conflict — allowing the system to tinker with its own internal organization will no longer serve the purpose.

We will now look at the ways in which the Florida Mental Health Act has been involved in a process of self-definition and change, to illustrate Wallace's discussion of this evolution.

SYSTEMIC REORGANIZATION: AMENDMENTS TO THE BAKER ACT

The Baker Act established a new system of mental health delivery in Florida, one presided over by localized administrative boards, with service agencies situated in communities around the state, and based on a strongly anti-institutional philosophy of treatment. The new mental health system set about to secure its position by almost constant tinkering with definitions of services and target populations, and with organizational features of the system itself. The decade following the passage of the Act saw a virtually annual process of legislative amendment in response to the discrepancies the system saw in its operation. Philosophically these amendments continued to refine the sphere of client rights, and could thus be defined as constituting a liberalizing trend. In fact, the amendment procedure might better be thought of as a conservative one, in Wallace's terms, because the ultimate result was the entrenchment of the new system which acted to preserve itself and its founding ideals even though the perceived needs and expressed desires of its governmental "owners" and its citizen clients moved steadily in other directions. Client advocates began complaining that the community-based treatment network had become an "institution without walls" because of the top-heavy bureaucracy that retarded communication and referral. Legislators began to worry about the increasingly autonomous system and the lack of sufficient government oversight — even though that system had been created originally because the Legislature was concerned about *too much* central control. And the community-at-large began to feel threatened by the overemphasis on client rights, to the perceived detriment of the "rights of the community." This latter shift again mirrors larger sociopolitical trends. Just as deinstitutionalization was made acceptable because it harmonized with the then-fashionable movements for minority rights, the more recent interest in the rights of the community to be "protected" from the mentally ill parallels the return to a law-and-order orientation typical of the current Administration.

Since clients, owners, and the community-at-large could no longer depend on the system itself to make its tinkering sufficiently radical to respond to a very different set of social and political expectations, there is increasing evidence that both the structure of the mental health system and the philosophy that underscores the original Baker Act will shortly be challenged by substantially new policy directions.

Let us review the history of amendments to the Baker Act to see how this evolutionary process grew. The first amendments were passed in 1974. They involved the right to individual dignity, and procedures for hearings to determine the need for hospitalization. Jails were firmly ruled out as holding areas for mental patients.

Amendments in 1975, 1977, 1978, 1979, 1980, and 1981 all further extended the rights of clients and refined the concept of "individual dignity." They also expanded the definition of "mental health professional," and made it possible for those other than psychiatrists or clinical psychologists to work with clients in the system; this shift indicated a move away from a "medical model" of treatment to a "developmental model."

The 1982 amendments may be seen, in retrospect, as the high water mark of the patients' rights philosophy. Perhaps the most far-reaching of these amendments was one mandating the Department of Health & Rehabilitative Services to provide for the publication and distribution of an information handbook to facilitate understanding of the Florida Mental Health Act. This handbook was designed to educate the public, mental health professionals, and law enforcement professionals as to the policies, procedures, implementation strategies, and ongoing responsibilities of service providers under the Baker Act. The Mental Health Associations sponsored a series of statewide training workshops for these target groups after the handbook was prepared.

Moreover, under the 1982 amendments, each patient was to be given the opportunity to participate in his or her own treatment and discharge planning. Each patient was to be notified in writing of his or her own right, upon discharge or release, to seek treatment from the professional of his or her choice. According to the 1982 amendments, a person could be involuntarily placed only when: 1) found by the court, with "clear and convincing evidence," that he or she suffers from apparent or manifest mental illness, 2) voluntary treatment and placement are rejected, 3) he or she is unable to determine for him- or herself whether placement is needed, 4) all possible less restrictive treatments have been determined inappropriate, and 5) the client is incapable of surviving without attention and care. The recommendation for placement had to be made primarily by a psychiatrist, and secondarily by a clinical psychologist. Both professionals must have examined the patient within five days of the hearing. All criteria for involuntary placement had to be met. One of the professionals who originally executed the involuntary placement certificate had to be a witness at the placement hearing.

The 1982 amendments also attempted a redefinition of mental illness. According to these guidelines, mental illness was defined as "an impairment of emotional processes, of the ability to exercise conscious control of one's actions, or of the ability to perceive reality or to understand, which impairment substantially interferes with a person's ability to meet the ordinary demands of living." This definition explicitly excluded mental retardation, developmental disability, substance abuse/dependency, or antisocial behavior.

Although these sweeping public educational, procedural, and definitional amendments seem to deal almost exclusively with the hospitalized patient, in fact they represent the culmination of the philosophy of deinstitutionalization, since they made it exceedingly difficult to place any but the most intractable patients in institutional care. Moreover, by defining out so many populations previously lumped into the mental health service system, the emphasis was placed on the provision of *appropriate* services, a definite blow for client rights.

It should be noted that Maxine Baker now feels that the original, rather general wording of the Act was preferable to the very specific language that has developed over the past decade. Although greater specificity has been attempted so as to protect clients, the main outcome, from the point of view of clients themselves, has been to weave an ever more complex web of red tape over the process of accessing services. From the point of view of our analysis, however, such a direction was an almost inevitable outcome as the system sought to define its own area of operation — in other words, to establish its own turf in no uncertain terms.

1984

By 1984 it was becoming clear that the Florida mental health system was growing out of touch with its constituencies, and that its landmark 1982 amendments were essentially reflections of battles that significant groups no longer wanted to see fought.

Some of the discomfort surfaced in a very public way at one of the seminars, held in early 1984, at which the new handbook was presented to concerned groups, in this case one composed of law enforcement officers, mental health officials, social workers, and other direct service providers. The participants found that even with the greater specificity in language, there were many "gray areas" in the wording of the amended Act. By this phrase, the participants meant not that procedures were unclear, but that they were uncertain as to whether the mandated procedures were really in everyone's best interests.

There was particular concern expressed about the ways in which the regulations seemed to trap law enforcement personnel in a "no-win situation." Police officers complained that the new regulations forced them to act as a combination of psychologist, social worker, and "taxi service." In fact, so deep was the resentment over the use of law officers in this uncomfortable variety of roles that the state agreed to allow each receiving facility to make its own transportation arrangements; the local police department or county sheriff's office had the right to refuse to become involved unless it was absolutely clear that a crime was being committed.

Late in 1983, the Governor appointed a task force to study the community mental health system, with particular emphasis on the problems of civil commitment and access to services. The outside, "blue ribbon" task force was a vehicle for expressing alternative views and thus for stimulating reform. One irony in its creation, however, was that it was chaired by an ex-Senator de la Parte, who had been one of Maxine Baker's principal allies in the early days of her fight to create the Mental Health Act.

Meanwhile, public concern was heightened in the summer of 1983 when Billy Ferry, a man who lived alone in the woods outside Tampa, and who frequently harassed people from surrounding communities, showed up at a suburban supermarket. Complaining that he had been cheated over some bad soda pop, he sprayed gasoline on a crowd at a checkout counter, igniting a blaze that killed five persons and injured thirteen. Ferry's distraught family later claimed that they had been trying unsuccessfully to have him committed because he was so dangerous; they insisted that the system could not provide adequate "community" treatment for Billy, nor was there any way they could complete the procedures necessary to take more drastic action on his behalf.

No single case, no matter how horrifying, could be sufficient to turn public opinion around all by itself. However, by the time of the Ferry case, the community was already quite prepared for a thoroughgoing criticism of the mental health system and its philosophy of patients' rights and community-based care. There was extensive media coverage of Ferry's arrest and incarceration, much of it with a distinct editorial tone hostile to the mental health system. To many citizens, that system had gotten out of hand because decent, innocent people could no longer be protected from dangerous "crazies." The state, they implied, was more concerned with the "individual dignity" of a man like Ferry than it was with the plight of his victims. The jury ultimately disregarded the insanity plea, and Ferry was found guilty on five counts of murder in September 1985. Ignoring the jury's recommendation of a life sentence, the judge sentenced Ferry to death.

It should be no surprise, then, that the 1984 legislative session, meeting in the wake of the Ferry case and the Governor's Task Force, hastily passed provisions to broaden the criteria for release of information (to "warn" relevant community members about "dangerous" people in their midst), and for involuntary examinations. There was a strong expression of a desire to make the mental health system *accountable* — not so much in the financial, as in the moral sense.

Prospects

The 1985 legislature adjourned with the promise to address further the issues raised by the 1984 mental health amendments. That session, however, was overwhelmingly preoccupied with other matters (as was the 1986 session, which took place in the midst of frenzied gubernatorial primary contests in both parties), and no substantive revisions in existing mental health policy have been forthcoming. However, it is significant that the matter of much of the legislature's attention was that of "growth management." Florida's leaders are beginning to confront the problems raised by decades of unrestrained development and population growth. Politicians in the state do not yet question that growth has brought many positive benefits to Florida, and yet they are now espousing the notion that further growth must not compromise the "quality of life." It seems likely that, if current trends hold, the desire to "get the crazies off the streets" will be translated into the rhetoric about "quality of life" rather than into the harsher, more punitive language of the older "law and order" debate. In either case, the system created by the Baker Act is not likely to survive without major reform.

In 1985, a proposal to close one of the state mental hospitals completely was tabled, and a plan to convert that hospital into the nucleus of an "integrated regional service network" is now being seriously considered. Since nationally prominent deinstitutionalization advocates are now openly discussing the need to maintain hospitals as legitimate anchors of a "continuity of care" system (Bachrach 1983; Muzekari, Knudsen, and Meyer 1981), it seems that once again the larger social and political context will support a major conceptual and structural reorientation in the delivery of state services. One evident problem in the mental health policy world as of this writing is "the lack of confidence among mental health professionals in changing course" (Mechanic 1985: 86). That being the case, reform will almost certainly come about at the instigation of government and clients, not as a result of further tinkering from within the system.

SUMMARY AND CONCLUSIONS

This case study has described the way in which mental health policy came to be established in Florida. That policy, while reflecting national trends, developed in the specific context of Florida's emerging demographic, political, and economic system. It has been our intention to utilize some of the methods of ethnographic data collection to describe the cyclical process of policy evolution. While we have not been much concerned here with more traditional anthropological concerns (such as the life ways of chronically mentally ill people who have been affected by the Baker Act over the years), we believe that it is important for medical anthropologists to understand the ways in which policies that shape the lives of "their" people come about, and that it is possible to study that phenomenon in ways consonant with the holistic perspective of our discipline.

This study interpreted the descriptive data about the policy by means of Wallace's concepts about administrative structure, and Jones' delineation of the policy cycle. This analysis should help integrate the Florida data in a comprehensive manner by demonstrating them to be examples of more general types of process.

ACKNOWLEDGEMENTS

This study was carried out under the auspices of the University of South Florida's Human Resources Institute (Center for Applied Anthropology), and with the cooperation of the Hillsborough County Mental Health Association. Students assisting in the data collection were: Marie-Anne Johnson, Dorle Kind, Linda Miller, George Root, and Annabelle Winch.

NOTES

1. See Marsella (1984) for a recent, comprehensive overview of this literature.
2. See Mechanic (1980: 80–6) and Ozarin (1982: 36–7) for more information on the history and accomplishments of the JCMH.
   In 1955, Congress passed the Mental Health Study Act, which allocated funds to NIMH to study the national needs and available resources in mental health. NIMH used the funds in part to create the Joint Commission on Mental Health and Illness. Its membership was drawn from thirty-six participating professional

and lay advocacy organizations (with a permanent, professional staff based at NIMH). Under NIMH contract, the Commission published several interim studies and, in 1961, its major report, *Action for Mental Health*. The report's main recommendations were for an increased program of services and more funds for basic, long-term mental health research. It expressed the growing bias against institutional care and sounded the first official note of approval for the community mental health center concept. Although the Joint Commission is no longer in existence per se, it has been succeeded by various interim commissions with much the same charge. The latest was the President's Commission on Mental Health, appointed by President Carter in 1977 under the honorary chairpersonship of Mrs. Carter. Its final report led to the drafting of sweeping reforms embodied in the 1980 Mental Health Systems Act — one of the first pieces of legislation repealed when the Reagan Administration took office.
3. Kiesler, *et al*. (1983) is a useful brief summary of the history of national mental health policy. See Wagenfeld and Jacobs (1982) and Lemkau (1982) for more detailed surveys.
4. See Dauer (1982) for an extended analysis of the demographic, political, and economic trends which are summarized in this section.
5. This trend is described and analyzed by Mechanic (1980: 82–3).

REFERENCES

Bachrach, Leona L., 1976. *Deinstitutionalization: An Analytic Review and Sociological Perspective* (Mental Health Statistics Serices D, No. 4. DHEW No. [ADM] 79–351), Washington, DC: Government Printing Office.
Bachrach, Leona L., 1982. Young Adult and Chronic Patients: an Analytical Review of the Literature, *Hospital and Community Psychiatry* 33: 189–197.
Bachrach, Leona L., 1983. Planning Services for Chronically Mentally Ill Patients, *Bulletin of the Menninger Clinic* 47: 163–188.
Curella, Gene, 1966. Snake Pit 66, *Broward-Palm Beach Sun Sentinel* (July 18–22).
Dauer, Maning J., 1982. Introduction. In *Florida's Politics and Government*, (ed.) M.J. Dauer, 3–12. Gainesville: University of Florida Press.
Dye, Thomas, 1972. *Understanding Public Policy*, Englewood Cliffs, NJ: Prentice-Hall.
Edgerton, Robert B., 1967. *The Cloak of Competence*. Berkeley: University of California Press.
Estroff, Sue E., 1981. *Making it Crazy*. Berkeley: University of California Press.
Flaschner, Franklin N., 1972. Florida's New Mental Health Law, *Florida Bar Journal* 46: 344–350.
Halpern, J., *et al.*, 1980. *The Myths of Deinstitutionalization: Policies for the Mentally Disabled*. Boulder, CO: Westview Press.
Hays, Paula, 1982. *Baker Act Handbook and Facilitator's Guide*, Tampa: Florida Department of Health and Rehabilitative Services.
Jones, Charles O., 1984. *An Introduction to the Study of Public Policy*. Third Edition, Monterey, CA: Brooks/Cole.
Kiesler, Charles A., *et al.*, 1983. Federal Mental Health Policymaking: an Assessment of Deinstitutionalization, *American Psychologist* (Dec.): 1292–1297.
Landy, David, 1983. Visions of the Future and Lessons of the Past, *Medical Anthropology Quarterly* 14: 3ff.
Lemkau, Paul V., 1982. The Historical Background. In *Public Mental Health: Perspectives and prospects*, (eds.) M.O. Wagenfeld, P.V. Lemkau, and B. Justice, 16–29. Beverly Hills, CA: Sage Publications.
Marsella, Anthony J., 1984. Culture and Mental Health: An Overview. In *Cultural*

Conceptions of Mental Health and Therapy, (eds.) A.J. Marsella & G.M. White, 359–388. Dordrecht, Holland: D. Reidel.

Mechanic, David, 1980. *Mental Health and Social Policy*, 2nd ed., Englewood Cliffs, NJ: Prentice-Hall.

Mechanic, David, 1985. Mental Health and Social Policy: Initiatives for the 1980s, *Health Affairs* 4: 77–88.

Miller, Kent, 1976. *Managing Madness: The Case Against Civil Commitment*. New York: Free Press.

Miller, Robert D., 1982. The Least Restrictive Alternative: Hidden Meanings and Agendas, *Community Mental Health Journal* 18: 46–55.

Muzekari, Louis H., Harold Knudsen, and Emily Meyer, 1981. The Interlocking Treatment System: A Model for the Delivery of State Hospital-Community Mental Health Center Services, *Hospital and Community Psychiatry* 32: 273–276.

Ozarin, Lucy D., 1982. Mental Health in Public Health: the Federal Perspective. In *Public Mental Health: Perspectives and Prospects*, (eds.) M.O. Wagenfeld, P.V. Lemkau, and B. Justice, 30–45. Beverly Hills, CA: Sage Publications.

Scheper-Hughes, Nancy, 1983. A Proposal for After-Care of Chronic Psychiatric Patients, *Medical Anthropology Quarterly* 14: 3ff.

Wagenfeld, Morton O., and Judith H. Jacobs, 1982. The Community Mental Health Movement: Its Origins and Growth. In *Public Mental Health: Perspectives and Prospects*, (eds.) M.O. Wagenfeld, P.V. Lemkau, and B. Justice, 46–89. Beverly Hills, CA: Sage Publications.

Wallace, Anthony F.C., 1971. *Administrative Forms of Social Organization*. Reading, MA: Addison-Wesley Modular Publications.

Weaver, Thomas, 1985a. Anthropology as a Policy Science: Part I, A Critique, *Human Organization* 44: 97–105.

Weaver, Thomas, 1985b. Anthropology as a Policy Science: Part II, Development and Training, *Human Organization* 44: 197–205.

Williams, Donald H., Elizabeth C. Bellis and Shiela W. Wellington, 1980. Deinstitutionalization and Social Policy: Historical Perspectives and Present Dilemmas, *American Journal of Orthopsychiatry* 50: 54–64.

International visitors: Coping with American Society and its Health System

On Being Sick Away From Home: Medical Problems and Health Care Needs of International Students

MARY K. SANDFORD

The University of Southwestern Louisiana

INTRODUCTION

The number of international students attending Western institutions of higher education has increased dramatically since the second World War. While fewer than 10,000 international students were enrolled in the United States in 1930, their numbers increased to well over 100,000 during the 1960's (Miller and Harwell 1983). On a global scale the growth rates of students studying abroad averaged 7.5% between 1960 and 1975 (Zwingmann and Gunn 1983). If present growth trends continue, approximately 1,000,000 international students will be attending American colleges and universities by 1990 (Miller and Harwell 1983).

To a large extent, the influx of international students reflects the intense desire of many developing nations to enhance their techno-economic productivity and self-sufficiency. In many cases, laboratory facilities and educational programs in highly technical fields are inadequate in such countries and students must be sent abroad for formal training. For example, the majority of students studying in the United Kingdom are majoring in technology and engineering, while many others are pursuing studies in science, business, and social administration (Zwingmann and Gunn 1983). In other instances, the students wish to obtain graduate or post-graduate degrees in disciplines for which advanced training cannot be found in their home country. For still other students, the opportunity to study abroad is viewed as a way in which to enhance personal and familial prestige (Zwingmann and Gunn 1983).

Over the past two decades, increases in international student enrollments have been accompanied by a growing awareness of their unique medical problems and health care needs (Ward 1962; Maha 1964; Ray 1967; Huang 1977; Miller and Harwell 1983). In this essay, case histories are used to illuminate and provide anthropological perspectives on two aspects of international student health care. The initial case histories present the students' perceptions of and reactions to various physical symptoms which they have experienced during their stay in the United States. Most importantly, these case histories demonstrate why students are reluctant to seek or to comply with medical assistance. The second set of case histories illustrates interactional difficulties which often occur when international students consult American physicians. Such case histories indicate that even subtle cultural differences can create conflict and misunderstandings between health care providers and their international patients.

By focusing on the students' perspectives, the analysis presented in this essay differs from most of the previous studies concerning international student health. Earlier studies were conducted largely by medical personnel for purposes of familiarizing other professionals with the stresses of international student life and the health care utilization patterns of these students. For example, the special medical problems of international students first came under the scrutiny of several campus physicians during the 1960's (Ward 1962; Maha 1964; Ray 1967). At that time, studies conducted at the University of Illinois (Maha 1964) and Northwestern University (Ray 1967) revealed that international students have higher visitation rates to campus clinics and higher admission rates to university hospitals than did their domestic counterparts. At Northwestern Univesity, for example, the average annual visitation rate to the university health center was 7.3 visits per international student as compared to a rate of 4.6 visits for the student population as a whole.

This phenomenon has been attributed to several factors. First, Maha's health survey demonstrated that some international students enter college with such pre-existing health problems as parasitic infections, skin disorders, refractive errors, and dental disease (Maha 1964). Thus, in some instances, incoming international students may be suffering from poorer health than the average American student.

Most observers argue, however, that international student health problems are more indicative of the stresses inherent in adjusting to both campus life and a new cultural environment. Academic pressures, stemming from difficulties in verbal communication and/ or reading comprehension, may be directly related to health problems as students may neglect their health needs in order to spend long hours struggling with assignments (Akka 1967; Huang 1977; Miller and Harwell 1983). Concurrently, the student often experiences additional stress in attempting to re-establish a social network. Under these circumstances, health problems may arise if students exercise their new freedom by overindulging in social activities (Huang 1977). Superimposed on these difficulties are the challenges of adjusting to a new culture, so that health problems may be precipitated or exacerbated as the student adjusts to dietary or climatic changes (Williamson 1982; Miller and Harwell 1983).

While many medical disorders experienced by international students may be the direct outcome of cultural, social, and/or academic stresses, there are other instances in which the student may subconsciously somaticize an emotional problem. This is particularly true when the student perceives psychological problems as signs of failure or weakness on his part (Ichikawa 1966; Akka 1967; Huang 1977). In such cases, physical symptoms may seem to the student to be a far more acceptable reaction to stress than would be the admission of an underlying emotional problem.

Thus, many international students present a complicated array of physiological and emotional symptoms when seen by an American physician. Ward (1962) first characterized this phenomenon as the "foreign student syndrome," in which somatic problems occur in conjuction with such symptoms as a withdrawn attitude, a reluctance to engage in conversation, and feelings of resentment toward those upon whom the student has grown dependent.

More recently, Zwingmann and Gunn (1983) have subsumed the "foreign student syndrome" under their detailed description of the "uprooting disorder." According to their analysis, uprooting disorders develop in those students who are unable to regain their normal psycho-social, physiological, and cognitive functioning, after leaving home. The symptoms of uprooting disorder include feelings of isolation, powerlessness, alienation, and disorientation as well as hypochondriachal reactions. In addition, Zwingmann and Gunn have found "nostalgic-depressive" reactions to be a distinctive feature of uprooting disorders, which occur when difficult circumstances in the present are viewed against idealized memories of the home country. In the most severe cases, the individual may fixate on his life back home, abandoning all attempts to function in his new environment. Some degree of hostile, paranoid, and/or aggressive behavior is also typical of uprooting crises, with self-destructive acts or violent outbursts occurring in more severely affected individuals. Mild and severe forms of uprooting disorders are covered by the descriptions of "adjustment reactions" and "non-organic psychoses", respectively, as outlined in the International Classification of Mental Disorders (Zwingmann and Gunn 1983: 178–18).

The nature and severity of uprooting disorders are influenced by a number of predisposing factors, including the state of the individual's physical and mental health. Additionally, uprooting problems are most likely to develop in students who communicate poorly, behave ego-or ethnocentrically, demonstrate an overdependency on parents, or suffer from motivational difficulties. While such factors serve to lower an individual's resistance to an uprooting problem, the disorder, itself, is often triggered or exacerbated by specific stress factors. In general, these stress factors are derived from cultural and environmental dissimilarities between an individual's host and home. Thus, differences in values, religious beliefs, political ideology, diet, or interactional customs may serve as catalysts which ignite or intensify an uprooting crisis (Zwingmann and Gunn 1983: 18).

Studies such as these suggest that health problems are inextricably linked to the adjustment difficulties of international students. Medical problems can in fact be both a precursor to and a result of uprooting crises. The association between health and uprooting was most recently indicated by an extensive study in which the diagnoses of foreign and domestic students were compared for a three-year period. Not surprisingly, a higher incidence of stress-related medical problems was documented among members of the former group (Ebbin and Blankenship 1986).

Awareness concerning international student health has prompted researchers on some college campuses to evaluate the adequacy of existing health care services in meeting the needs of this special student population (Faniran-Odenkunle 1978; Miller and Harwell 1983; Thomas 1984; Bowen 1985). In general, these studies indicate that many international students are reluctant to use the health care facilities of either the campus or the surrounding community. Many students strongly prefer self-treatment, relying heavily on the advice of friends and family when they become ill (Torrey 1970; Faniran-

Odenkunle 1978; Miller and Harwell 1983). Most observers feel that greater attempts should be made to educate international students in both preventive health care and existing health care services.

METHODS

The case histories presented in this essay were collected in conjunction with a research project designed to assess the medical needs and problems of international students at the University of Southwestern Louisiana. International students comprise over 12% of the total student population of approximately 16,000 in attendance at the university.

During the course of the project, international students were randomly selected for interview purposes. The demographic information collected from each student included age, sex, country of origin, ethnic/tribal affiliation, marital status, and the number of years they have resided in the United States. The students were then asked a number or open-ended questions regarding their past and present medical problems, their reactions to those problems, and their previous contacts with American physicians. Students who had consulted an American doctor were then asked to describe their experiences in detail and to informally compare their treatment here with that which they would expect to receive in their own country.

This essay focuses on information obtained from African and Latin American students. Case histories were collected from a total of 46 African students, representing such countries as Nigeria, Ghana, Cameroon, and Ethiopia. Interviews and case histories were also provided by 24 Latin American students, representing Honduras, Colombia, Venezuela, and Guatemala. Pseudonyms are used in the following case histories in order to insure the students' confidentiality.

In order to facilitate comparisons between Latin American and African students, two smaller groups of interviews were reviewed intensively and the responses to specific questions were tabulated. The two groups consisted of interviews with 18 Nigerian Igbo and 13 Latin American students respectively. Portions of the informaiton obtained through this phase of the research are integrated into the discussion of the case histories which follows.

RESULTS AND DISCUSSION

The results of the interviews further substantiate the existence of a link between cultural adjustment difficulties and the development of health problems among international students. Conversely, the two groups of international students demonstrated different symptomologies which appear to be largely culture-specific and triggered by different external stress factors. Moreover, Latin American and African students also differed with respect to their experiences with and responses to the American health care system.

African Students

The African students often displayed symptoms which were consistent with previous descriptions of the "foreign student syndrome" (Ward 1962). Of particular interest were the symptoms recounted by the Nigerian Igbo students, shown on Table I. Only one individual in this group reported that he had not experienced physical or emotional symptoms since arriving in the United States. In contrast, over half of these students admitted suffering from feelings of stress, stemming from a variety of sources, often accompanied by such somatic symptoms as headaches and fever. A typical description of these symptoms is provided in the following case history.

> Joshua, a 28 year old Igbo, has been studying in the United States for two years. Soon after his arrival, he became very worried about his future and his school work. He began to suffer from insomnia, fatigue, restlessness, and loss of appetite. The political situation in Nigeria also worried him and contributed to his problems. Eventually, he found it difficult to function socially or academically and he secluded himself from others.
>
> When he began to run a fever, he visited a specialist in a local medical group. The doctor ran a series of tests which all proved to be negative. The doctor told him that while there was nothing physically wrong, he needed to relax and socialize more with others. The doctor reassured him that he would eventually feel better again. The student followed the doctor's advice and found that after 4–6 months he started to feel like himself again.
>
> Joshua had high praise for the medical system in the United States, calling it "fantastic." In particular, he noted that the hospitals are well equipped and sophisticated and the doctors are able to take proper care of their patients.
>
> He now believes that his health has improved since coming to the United States because he used to suffer from chronic malaria. He no longer has this problem and is glad that it is gone.

Although Joshua's case history presents a classic example of the relationship between physical symptoms, emotional problems, and uprooting crises, it is a typical in that he had consulted a physician concerning these symptoms. Although most of the Igbo students had, as shown in Table I, contacted an American physician, the

Table I Comparisons between Latin American and Nigerian Students: Medical Symptoms and Reasons for consulting American Phyicians

	Latin American N = 13	Igbo N = 18
Average Age of Respondants	23 years	27 years
Average Length of Stay in U.S.	2½ years	4 years
Marital Status: Single	12	13
Married	1	5
Consultation with American Physician:		
Have seen American doctor	10 (77%)	14 (78%)
Have not seen American doctor	3 (23%)	4 (22%)
Symptoms Experienced in the U.S.	N = 13	N = 18
Stress/Emotional problems	1 (7%)	9 (50%)
Upper respiratory infections	6 (46%)	5 (28%)
Headache	0	10 (55%)
Fever	0	4 (22%)
Fatigue	2 (15%)	3 (17%)
Visual problems	3 (23%)	0
Stomach problems	1 (7%)	4 (22%)
Influenza	1 (7%)	0
Urinary tract infections	1 (7%)	0
Bone pain	1 (7%)	0
Dental problems	2 (15%)	0
Constipation	1 (7%)	1 (6%)
Insomnia	0	2 (11%)
Vertigo	0	2 (11%)
Loss of appetite	0	2 (11%)
Venereal disease	0	1 (6%)
Weight gain	7 (54%)	0
Reasons for Consulting American Doctor	N = 10	N = 14
Upper respiratory infection	5 (50%)	2 (14%)
Stomach problems	1 (10%)	2 (14%)
Urinary tract infection	1 (10%)	0
Visual problem	3 (30%)	0
Injury	2 (20%)	3 (21%)
Bone pain	1 (10%)	0
Constipation	1 (10%)	0
Routine physical	0	4 (29%)
Influenza	1 (10%)	0
Fatigue	1 (10%)	0
Fever	0	2 (14%)
Headache	0	2 (14%)
Food Poisoning	0	1 (7%)
Vertigo	0	2 (14%)
Venereal disease	0	1 (7%)

presence of such somatic complaints as headache and fever were infrequently their reasons for doing so. Typically, Igbo students consulted American physicians to obtain routine physical examinations or to receive treatment for an injury. The characteristic response shown by Igbo students to their physical and/or emotional symptoms is seen in the following case history.

> Joseph is a 24 year old Igbo who has been studying in the United States for three years. He reported that he often has bouts of "migraine headaches" every two weeks or so. Although he had occasionally experienced headaches in Nigeria, they have greatly increased in frequency since his move to the United States. His headaches seem to bother him the most when he is under the most stress. The major sources of his stress are financial and academic problems. Whenever he is more relaxed, he has less trouble with his headaches, but they return promptly whenever the stress reoccurs.
> Although he has suffered from this problem for over three years, he sees no reason to consult an American doctor since he knows the cause of his problem. Whenever his headaches occur, he takes asprin which provides some relief. Despite the fact that he has never seen an American doctor, he is convinced that medical care is better in the United States than in Nigeria because of "higher technology." The only problem he sees with American medical care is the expense involved.

Joseph's case history illustrates why many Igbo students are often unwilling to consult an American physician for somatic complaints. From their perspective, the physician's role is that of a diagnostician who is contacted when the individual is unable to discern the cause, or alleviate the symptoms, of his illness. Because such symptoms as headache and fatigue are readily attributed to stress, a visit to an American doctor is deemed unnecessary. In addition, many Igbo students regard such symptoms as headaches as being minor and insignificant because they often pale in comparison with more serious medical conditions, such as malaria, which they have previously experienced. Over half of the Igbo interviewed believe that their health has improved since they moved to the United States. And, a majority of these students attribute this improvement to the fact that they no longer suffer from malaria.

Many Igbo students also express a strong preference for self-treatment which does not appear, in most instances, to be a reaction against the American medical system. Over half of the Igbo students were, as shown on Table II, completely satisfied with the treatment they had received. The preference for self-treatment seems to be firmly rooted in their cultural traditions, which places great emphasis on individual initiative and achievement (Uchendu 1965). From this cultural context, self-help may be viewed not only as a proper course of action, but also as an individual's responsibility. Several students told us that they were accustomed to self-treatment in their own country even for such serious illnesses as malaria.

Many Nigerian students, like Joshua and Joseph, have very favorable impressions of the American health care system. Because many students have had only limited contact with American doctors, their feelings are directed toward the "macro" level of American health care, rather than the "micro" or more interpersonal level. Such

Table II Comparisons between Latin American and Nigerian Igbo Students:
Attitudes Concerning Medical and Interpersonal Treatment
By American Physicians

	Latin American N = 10	Nigerian Igbo N = 14
Feelings Concerning Medical Treatment:		
Completely Satisfied	3 (30%)	8 (57%)
Some Dissatisfaction	7 (70%)	6 (43%)
Complaints About American Physicians:		
Impersonal Treatment	6 (60%)	0
Not informative to patients	2 (20%)	0
Keep patients waiting	1 (10%)	5 (36%)
Spend too little time w/patients	1 (10%)	0

impressions are often based on informal comparisons which they
have made between health care in the United States and that of
their own country. During the course of the interviews, many students spoke highly of such things as the level of technological
sophistocation and sanitation, as well as the availability of qualified
medical personnel, while citing instances from their own country
where facilities, doctors, or medication are in short supply. In
short, the American medical system, represents a level of technological achievement that they would like to see in their own country.
Their views are congruent with traditional Igbo attitudes toward
change which one anthropologist has characterized as, "Whatever
improves the individual's and community's status is acceptable to
the Igbo (Uchendu 1965: 104)."

Latin American Students
The health related experiences and attitudes of African students are
not, however, characteristic of all international students. In marked
contrast, Latin American students typically reported different health
problems, reactions to those problems, and opinions of the American medical system.

As shown in Table I, few Latin American students reported
symptoms such as headaches, insomnia, and stress which were often
described by African individuals. This difference is not, however,
entirely surprising, as the uprooting process is often less traumatic
for these students than their African counterparts. In general, Latin
American students are confronting cultural differences of less magnitude than those from African nations. In addition, many Latin
American students have had some exposure to the United States

through either personal contact or the experiences of relatives or friends. Moreover, because these students are studying in closer proximity to their home, they are able to rely more heavily on pre-existing support networks. Most of these students are able to return home at least once a year, while most African students are unable to see their home again until their college career has been completed.

While the overall uprooting process is often less severe among Latin American students, they are not immune to specific cultural adjustment difficulties. In particular, problems in establishing new social networks and in adjusting to dietary changes are often sources of stress for these students. The following case history illustrates both stress factors and their relationship to health-related problems.

Juan is a 23 year old Guatemalan who has been a student in the United States for almost three years. He commented that his health became worse when he first moved to the United States. He attributed this to difficulties he encountered in adjusting to college life. Here, he noted, he has more freedom to stay out late and for the first eight months after his arrival he stayed out late around four nights per week. He also had experienced problems adjusting to the food served in the cafeteria. At one point, he became constipated for 15 days.

His constipation problem led him to visit a physician at a local clinic. At the same time, he was suffering from a throat infection which he had contracted in Guatemala. The doctor prescribed a fiber remedy for the constipation, which proved to be successful. The doctor also took a throat culture which later proved negative and prescribed a cold syrup for his throat. Juan was convinced, however, that he needed antibiotics and when the doctor failed to prescribe any, he called his family at home to send the medication to him.

Juan also experienced homesickness soon after his arrival which was affecting his performance in school. He went to see a counselor who, he noted, had given him good advice and had helped him to learn to deal with his homesickness.

At the time of the interview, Juan was suffering from urethritis and had recently consulted a specialist. Although he was satisfied with the medical treatment he had received, he was unhappy with the way the physician had acted toward him. The doctor, he explained, had acted as if he didn't want to tell Juan what was wrong with him. Juan said it was like the doctor wanted to keep his diagnosis a "secret." Following the examination, the doctor had simply written a prescription and given him no explanation about his condition. Juan commented that he had noticed the same thing about the first doctor he had visited. Medical treatment in the United States, he feels, is too "automatized." In Guatemala, he said, "Doctors get more involoved with patients . . . They talk more to you."

Juan's pattern of overindulgence during his first months in the United States is not uncommon among international students. In many instances, the student is attempting to form a new social network (Huang 1977). His difficulty in doing so may also be evident in his tendency to rely on his family back home for help with medical problems. Ideally, physicians and counselors could form an ancillary, but important, part of such networks during the initial period away from home. The counselor that Juan had contacted had clearly suceeded in this respect. He felt, however, that the first physician he contacted had not responded appropriately to his needs and he was compelled to call home to obtain antibiotics. Similarly, other Latin American students reported calling home for medical advice or delaying visits to medical doctors until they could arrange to see one in their own country.

Juan, like many of his peers, associated dietary changes with the development of specific somatic symptoms. The food served in the United States, and particularly that available in the dormitories, was variously described by these students as being too "greasy," "spicy," or "heavy." In additon, seven students felt that the food was responsible for increases in their body weights. Such increases, which were almost always viewed quite negatively, ranged in amounts from nine to fifty-five pounds.

It is possible that the association between dietary changes and somatic problems among Latin American students is partially founded in the traditional disease causation concepts of Latin American cultures. In this context, illness is thought to be caused by the introduction of excessive heat or cold into the body. Thus, the ingestion of "hot" or "cold" foods can sometimes cause an imbalance which must be countered by an appropriate remedy designed to restore the normal, internal balance (Foster and Anderson 1978: 59). While we cannot determine whether such concepts are responsible for the association drawn by Latin American students between food and physical symptoms, it is clear that dietary differences were believed by some to have caused or exacerbated medical problems, as shown below.

Marco, a 23 year old Venezuelan, had been studying in the United States for three years when he developed symptoms of pneumonia. The student called his father, a worker in a Venezuelan hospital, who advised his son to rest, eat only mild foods, and avoid abrupt changes in temperature. Because Marco was a dorm resident, he was unable to obtain anything to eat but "greasy" and "heavy" foods. His attempts to avoid abrupt changes in temperature were also thwarted because it was summer and he had to walk in and out of air conditioned buildings to attend his classes. Consequently, his condition grew worse and he was forced to seek help at a medical clinic. The doctor at the clinic ran some tests but failed to prescribe antibiotics for another four to five days until the lab results were returned. In the meantime, the student was given an over-the-counter drug for his symptoms. When the test results came in, Marco was readily admitted to the hospital. He was released from the hospital after one week, but was advised to spend the next month resting. Because the semester was almost over, he decided to return to Venezuela, where he was again admitted to the hospital.

As shown in Table II, almost all Latin American students, like Juan and Marco, expressed some dissatisfaction toward the American medical profession, in general, and American doctors, in particular. Unlike the African students, their comments concerning the American medical system were directed toward an interpersonal level, as much of their displeasure centered around difficulties they had experienced in interacting with American physicians. As Table II illustrates, over half of the Latin American students who had contacted an American doctor felt that they had been treated in an impersonal manner.

As King (1962: 207) has observed, social interaction is inherent in the treatment of disease. Consequently, in a cross-cultural setting, incongruencies in social interaction may create misunderstandings between patients and health-care providers. During a therapeutic interview, for example, each party is acting in accordance with culturally prescribed role expectations that are deemed approporiate to the situation. Interactional difficulties are minimized, if not avoided altogether, if their respective role behaviors are congruent. If, however, the parties have different role expectations, dissatisfaction will occur. In a cross-cultural context, the failure to recognize even subtle differences in role expectations and to adapt one's behavior accordingly can result in a mutually unsatisfactory encounter between patient and physician (Foster and Anderson 1978: 117; Mumford 1983: 215).

The displeasure which Juan felt toward his American doctors was largely the result of such disparate expectations. Based upon his remarks, he was accustomed to a more informal and open exchange with physicians. He was particularly discouraged that his encounters with American physicians had been so "automatized." Clearly, he had expected more out of his visits with physicians than simply a prescription for medication.

Interactional problems may also arise from larger, underlying areas of cultural dissimilarity. In particular, many cross-cultural conflicts between Latin American students and American physicians may stem from the different ways in which time is perceived and managed in the two cultures. Hall (1973) notes, for example, that American culture is distinctly monochronic in that it emphasizes punctuality, scheduling, and conducting one activity at a time. In contrast, Latin American cultures use time in a more informal and flexible manner. In the Latin American business world, several activities often taken place simultaneously while clients engage in friendly, personal conversations with one another.

Perhaps nowhere in American culture is the emphasis on monochronism more marked than in the physician's examination room where attempts are made to diagnose and treat patients as quickly and efficiently as possible. Largely because of his cultural background, the Latin American student perceives such expedient treatment as a lack of caring or concern on the physician's part, as shown in the following case history.

> Rene, a 23 year old student from Guatemala, consulted two American doctors a year ago when he contracted a sore throat. He believes that inadequate nutrition caused his illness by making his "defenses" poor. After visiting the first doctor, who had prescribed some medication, he awoke the next morning unable to talk. He felt as if the doctor had not recognized the seriousness of his condition, so he consulted a specialist. The medicine the specialist gave him seemed to work better, but he felt as if he still had "poor defenses." Consequently, he later visited a doctor in Guatemala who was able to supply him with some medication to restore his resistance to infection.
>
> He was most unhappy with the care he had received from the first doctor he visited. He commented that there had been too many people in the waiting room and that it had seemed as though the medical personnel were attempting to "get rid of me." He felt that the situation would have been much different in his own country. He commented, "In Guatemala the doctor would treat you as if it was a special case. You can tell the difference in the way they talk to you." He also said that his doctors at home would have encouraged him to call if he developed any problems, possibly giving him their private numbers so that he could call in case of emergency. He also noted that the Guatemalan doctors "... give you more confidence in them ... more closeness."

Many Latin American students, like Rene, perceived American doctors as having no personal interest in them, and in their eyes, this is a serious matter, as a physician's demonstration of concern is essential in developing trust and/or confidence in the doctor. This conflict is not, however, insurmountable. As the following case history demonstrates, the problem can be avoided entirely by doctors who are willing to spend a little additional time expressing some personal interest in their patients.

> Ernesto, a 24 year old from Honduras, has visited three different doctors since his arrival in the United States two years ago. On two occasions, he had contacted different doctors for a persistent throat infection. Shortly before the interview, he had seen a third doctor for a cough. He was satisfied with the medical treatment he had received and felt that it was not significantly different from that which he had received for similar problems in his own country.
>
> On an interpersonal level, he was happy with two out of the three doctors. The first two doctors he had seen had known something about his country and had asked him about it during his visits. The third doctor was not, however, "... like the others. He went straight into business."

In short, subtle cultural differences surrounding the use of time can profoundly influence the quality of a cross-cultural encounter. To the Latin American student, a doctor who goes "straight into business" will often be regarded as being cold, unfriendly, and unworthy of trust, regardless of the physician's actual attitude or intentions. In the same fashion, the way in which a physician uses personal distance or "interaction space" can also have a marked affect on an intercultural consultation (Hall 1979). For example, Latin Americans normally interact in closer proximity to one another than is customary in North America (Hall 1973). A doctor who responds to this difference by moving further away from his Latin American patient will be perceived in the same manner as a doctor who goes "straight into business." The following example illustates the importance of interaction space in successful cross-cultural situations.

> Jose is a 28 year old student from Honduras who has been studying in the United States for three years. Unlike most international students, he has family living in the United States. His ability to find medical care is enhanced by the fact that his father and brother are medical doctors in another state. When he gets sick, they usually supply him with the medicine he needs. On one occasion, however, he had run out of some medicine which he regularly takes. He visited an American doctor and explained the situation. The doctor understood the situation and issued a prescription without question. Jose was very satisfied with the way in which he was treated. He was most impressed with the fact that the doctor had seated him beside him at his desk instead of across the desk. Jose found that this made him feel like he had a closer relationship with the doctor.

Although cross-cultural clashes between physicians and Latin American students often arise over seemingly minor cultural differences, the consequences of such encounters are potentially dangerous. Some students, for example, reacted to negative experiences by strictly avoiding further contact with American physicians, relying instead on self-treatment coupled with the medical advice of family and friends. The student described in the following case history became so proficient as self-diagnosis and treatment that he gained the reputation as a quasi-doctor among his peers.

> Daniel, a 23 year old student from Guatemala, has a fear of American doctors. The reason for his fear was that a good friend of his was misdiagnosed in the United States and became very ill as a result. His friend apparently had malaria but had been told by an American physician that he had "homesickness" and a minor infection. Knowing that he had malaria, his friend flew home to Guatemala and developed an attack as soon as he arrived at the airport. He was rushed to the hospital where they immediately diagnosed and began treatment for his condition.

Because of his fear of American doctors, Daniel has avoided seeking medical care in the United States since his arrival four years ago. The secret to his success lies in his ability to obtain medicine from home. He told us, "If you have a mild illness such as a cold or the flu or trouble with the stomach, well then you bring the medications from home." He also noted that if he gets a more serious infection he always has a supply of antibiotics on hand. His mother is a pharmacist and sees that he stays well-supplied. He was also well aware of the various over-the-counter brands of medication which are available in this country for minor disorders. His friends know of his ability to treat illness and some of them will come to him for help when they become sick.

For other students, unpleasant experiences with American physicians trigger feelings of alienation, powerlessness, and disorientation as well as nostalgic-depressive reactions, which often occur in conjunction with uprooting disorders. Because these reactions cause the student to dwell on the past, rather than to realistically cope with the present, their occurrence can greatly impede the cultural adjustment process. The following case history illustrates the characteristic features of a nostalgic-depressive type reaction which was exacerbated by a negative experience with the American medical system.

Julio, an 18 year old from Honduras, had been living in the United States for only a few months when he sought medical attention for pain in his left ankle. Following an inconclusive x-ray, the doctor ordered a bone scan to rule out the possibility of a tumor. Although the bone scan revealed a minor problem, the student was told that he did not have a tumor. At the time of the interview, Julio was still experiencing some pain, but it was diminishing.

Julio was distressed, however, about the way in which the doctors had acted toward him. He felt that his doctors back home would have behaved differently. He told us, "At home it would have been much different. In my country the doctors would have been more worried. They would have seemed to care more. It would have been better back home. The doctors would have been more concerned for my state of health. They would have taken more time. They would have spoken more with me about my problem. I would have known more (about) what was going on and felt better, more informed. The doctors here focus on the essentials and don't leave time for details."

The case histories of Julio and Daniel demonstrate an urgent need to familiarize health care providers with the problems of international student health care. Whether a student reacts negatively to a physician by internalizing his feelings or by administering his own treatment, the student is made more vulnerable to further physical or emotional problems. It is doubtful that most doctors are aware of how negatively they can be perceived by international students or of the potential consequences of these perceptions.

SUMMARY AND CONCLUSIONS

To summarize, the case histories discussed throughout this essay underscore the close relationship between medical problems and cultural adjustment difficulties of international students. Largely because of diverse cultural backgrounds, however, the nature and symptoms of uprooting disorders appear to vary widely among students. In particular, the somatic problems associated with cultural adjustment problems are often sparked by different stress factors including dietary changes, climatic differences, financial problems, and academic concerns. Similarly, the students' reactions to both their physical conditions and to American physicians differ in a manner which is founded in their cultural backgrounds. Thus, comparisons between different cultural groups are essential for understanding why some students are hesitant to comply with medical treatment or seek the assistance of an American doctor.

The interviews also suggest that programs are urgently needed in order to make the American health care system more familiar, accessible, and attractive to these students. Ideally, educators, foreign student advisors, and representatives of the local medical commmunity should work together in achieving these goals.

A program designed to meet the needs of international students should begin by familiarizing the students with the organization and procedures of the health care system. Some students are, for example, unaware that many medications, which they purchased over-the-counter in their own country, are available only by prescription in the United States. Others, who are accustomed to seeking medical care in hosptials, will go to emergency rooms for minor problems only to encounter a long wait and great expense. More importantly, adequate preparation will allow students to frame more realistic expectations of the American health care system and be less likely to experience unpleasant surprises when they attempt to find medical help.

International students should also be granted the opportunity to attend seminars in preventive health care, stress management, and nutrition, at which time they should be reassured that it is normal for them to experience stress when undergoing "culture shock." It is essential, however, that they be given suggestions as to how they can constructively cope with these stresses.

A number of American universities have recently instituted programs which address the health care needs of international students, with some universities sponsoring health care orientation sessions, while others are providing written information on local medical facilities. Other schools are using peer assistants or health advocates to give personal, sympathetic attention and advice to students with specific health problems (Thomas 1984).

At the University of Southwestern Louisiana, three projects, designed to facilitate health care delivery to international students, were recently undertaken on an experimental basis. First, all new international students were furnished with a brochure which provides information on local medical facilities and outlines the procedures to be used in seeking medical treatment on campus and in the community. Anthropological perspectives were used in writing the brochure, pointing to ways in which a visit to an American doctor may differ from a similar experience in the students' own culture. In addition, a special clinic for international students was sponsored by the school's nursing department on a biweekly basis. The clinic personnel provided routine physical exams, some laboratory testing, and advice on specific medical problems. Lastly, a volunteer program of health care assistants was established to provide personal attention to students with health problems. The health care assistants helped students to make appointments with physicians, provided transportation to the doctor's office, and facilitated communication between students and physicians.

Ultimately, however, the improvement of international student health care requires the presence of a sensitive medical community. What is most urgently needed are training seminars aimed at familiarizing medical professionals with the special needs and problems of this student group. Such professionals need to be acquainted with some of the basic skills involved in intercultural communication and interaction as well as the various ways in which culture can influence the students' perceptions of and reactions to medical disorders.

The problems of international student health care are inherently anthropological. And, because of our unique, biocultural perspective, anthropologists are ideally suited to address these complex and sensitive issues.

ACKNOWLEDGMENTS

The author would like to thank Jordi Sales and Benson Nwogu who served as Research Assistants during this project and who provided valuable assistance in the data collection phase of this research. Thanks are also due to Edward Kibbe and Mary Ellen Colon for providing advice and support. The author is also grateful for the enthusiastic support given by the International Student Office at U.S.L., under the leadership of Bruno Masotti and Kathy Steiner, and the Dean of Student

Personnel, Mary Olive McPhaul. Finally, this research would have been impossible without the cooperation of the many international students who graciously consented to interviews.

REFERENCES

Akka, Reuben I., 1967. The Middle Eastern Student on the American College Campus, *Journal of the American College Health Association* 15: 251–254.

Bowen, Pamela, 1985. Promoting your Student Health Service to International Students, Paper Presented at the Sixty-Third Annual Meeting of the American College Health Association, Washington, D.C., May 29-June 1.

Ebbin, Allan J., and Edward S. Blankenship, 1986. A Longitudinal Health Care Study: International Versus Domestic Students, *Journal of the American College Health Association* 34: 177–182.

Faniran-Odenkunle, F., 1978. *Health and Illness Behavior of Nigerian Students in the United States*. Doctoral Dissertation, Bryn Mawr College.

Foster, George M., and Barbara G. Anderson, 1978. *Medical Anthropology*. New York: John Wiley and Sons.

Hall, Edward T., 1973. *The Silent Language*. Gardern City: Anchor Books.

Hall, Edward, T., 1979. Proxemics: The Study of Man's Spatial Relations. In *Culture, Curers, and Contagion*, ed. Norman Klein, 22–31. Novato, California: Chandler and Sharp.

Huang, Ken, 1977. Campus Mental Health: The Foreigner at Your Desk. *Journal of the American College Health Association* 25: 216–219.

Ichikawa, Alice, 1966. Foreign Students in Crisis: Clinical Observations. *Journal of the American College Health Association* 15: 182–185.

King, Stanley H., 1962. *Perceptions of Illness and Medical Practice*. New York: Russell Sage Foundation.

Maha, George E., 1964. Health Survey of New Asian and African Students at the University of Illinois, *Journal of the American College Health Association* 12: 303–310.

Miller, Dean F., and Deanna J. Harwell, 1983. International Students at an American University: Health Problems and Status, *Journal of School Health* 53: 45–49.

Mumford, Emily, 1983. *Medical Sociology: Patients, Providers, and Policies*. New York: Random House.

Ray, Mary M., 1967. Health and Disease among International Students in the United States, *Journal of the American College Health Association* 15: 361–364.

Thomas, Kay A., 1984. Meeting the Health Care Needs of International Students: NAFSA's Role, *National Association for Foreign Student Affairs Newsletter* 35: 111.

Torrey, E.F., 1970. Problems of Foreign Students: An Overview, *Journal of the American College Health Association* 19: 80–86.

Uchendu, Victor C., 1965. *The Igbo of Southeast Nigeria*. New York: Holt, Rinehart, and Winston.

Ward, L.E., 1962. Some Observations of the Underlying Dynamics of Conflict in Foreign Students, *Journal of the American College Health Association* 10: 430–440.

Williamson, Geraldine, 1982. Impediments to Health Care for the Foreign Student, *Journal of the American College Health Association* 30: 189–190.

Zwingmann, Charles A., and Alexander D.G. Gunn, 1983. *Uprooting and Health: Psycho-social Problems of Students from Abroad*. Geneva: World Health Organization.

Pregnancy and Motherhood Among Micronesian Students in the United States

University of Arkansas at Little Rock

The increasing numbers of young Micronesians attending college in the United States face a host of difficulties in coping with the demands of a new cultural environment. Migration as well as beginning a new school are both commonly considered stressful situations, with potential health consequences (e.g., Dohrenwend and Dohrenwend 1974, 1984; Elliott and Eisdorfer 1982). Migration has been identified as a risk factor, although no reliable, direct relationship exists between migration and illness (Hull 1979; Kasl and Berkman 1983). Furthermore, migration, like other life events, need not result in mental breakdown. Migrants have many ways of coping and of making use of social supports, varying from informally turning to kin to joining organized voluntary associations (Graves and Graves 1975). Studies of the health consequences of migration among Pacific Islanders, however, have focused almost exclusively on risk factors for cardiovascular disease (e.g., Beaglehole et al. 1977; Hanna and Baker 1979; Hornick and Hanna 1982; Labarthe et al. 1973; McGarvey and Baker 1979; McGarvey, Schendel, and Baker 1980; Reed, Labarthe, and Stallones 1970; Ward and Prior 1980).

One study of the experiences and problems of Micronesian students in the United States describes excessive drinking among male students and its impact on their behavior and academic performance (Larson 1979). It is not clear from the analysis the extent to which their drinking may be in response to stressful situations, or an attempt to cope with them, since possible adaptive elements of their drinking may involve reinforcing or creating social ties. It does appear that both drinking and the students' behavior when drunk relate to their cultural conceptions of manliness and the appropriate expression of aggression (Larson 1979:48; Marshall 1979b). One consequence of their behavior, however, is that negative stereotypes of Micronesians are thriving in the communities where they are concentrated.

Whereas drinking appears to be confined largely to males, women, too, have their own difficulties. Many are becoming pregnant and bearing children out-of-wedlock, and typically they drop out of school. Their behavior contributes to being stereotyped by Americans, at times exacerbating an already difficult situation, yet it has quite a different meaning to the women themselves and to their families back home. This meaning can be understood only when their behavior is placed in the context of their own beliefs surrounding pregnancy and motherhood, and their experiences coping with problems in the United States. In fact, getting pregnant appears to be quite an effective coping strategy for these women and a way of adapting to a stressful situation. They take on aspects of the "sick role" (Parsons 1951:428–479), since they are relieved from the role expectations associated with being students.

Josepha is an example of one of these young women.[1] She grew up on an atoll in the Western Islands of Truk State, one of the most traditional areas in all of Micronesia. She lived on an islet about a third of a square mile in area and inhabited by about four hundred people, where women's lives are oriented around taro gardening and child rearing, and where they live in simple thatch houses and dress in wraparound lavalavas. In the space of four years Josepha went from this tiny, traditional islet to school first on a neighboring atoll, then to an urbanizing port town, and finally to a community college in the southeastern United States. One of the brightest of Truk High School's students, she, like many other young Micronesians in the same situation, experienced difficulties coping with the new environment she faced in the United States. She soon had to cope with the additional problems of unwed pregnancy and childbirth and the consequent stigma of being stereotyped by Americans as a "loose woman" and disgraced in the eyes of the host community. After the birth of her child, Josepha's relatives eventually sent her money to return home with her child.

Carmen, another woman from the same islet, left for college a few years before Josepha, and Sylvia left a year later. All three selected the same school. These two women, like Josepha, soon found themselves pregnant and unmarried, left school, and moved in with other Micronesians in a trailer park in a nearby town where Josepha had been living. They both expected their relatives to ask them to return home but meanwhile remained with the other young people, caring for their infants.

Maria attended school with Josepha throughout her elementary and secondary school years and was another of the brightest students, perhaps even more so than Josepha. Her older sister, Susie, had left for college a few years before. In fact, Susie was the first woman from her island to go off to college and chose the school Josepha, Sylvia, and Carmen later attended. Maria, however, was not allowed to attend college. When she graduated from high school, her uncle (her mother's brother, the senior man in her descent group) insisted she return to the atoll and her descent group homesite.

Linda's brothers came very close to forbidding her to attend college as well, even though she had received academic awards in high school. Especially in the wake of pregnancies by other Western Island women in the United States, her brothers were reluctant to take such risks with their sister, despite their perception that a college education is valuable, even for women. These islanders see education as the key to a well-paying and prestigious government position in Truk, and they realize that the material and political benefits of such a job extend to one's kin and, at times, to the island as a whole. Nonetheless, they are becoming increasingly reluctant to allow women to leave for the States.

The behavior of the women already in the United States relates in part to their adjustment to college life. In attempting to cope with their many problems, Micronesian college students prefer to avoid confrontations. In addition, they frequently turn to other Micronesians, either taking advantage of existing ties or creating new ones, following a model of kinship transactions practised both on their home island and in the port town. These ties can provide emotional as well as practical support and can buffer negative stereotypes and attitudes held by Americans. The young Micronesian woman who becomes pregnant in the United States, however, is faced with the medicalization of pregnancy and childbirth, much of which is quite alien to her, and many aspects of the process obviously cannot be avoided. Furthermore, due to hospital rules, most of labor, delivery, and the first days of motherhood have to be faced alone, without the support of close kin.

In order to understand the motivations, attitudes, and experiences of these women concerning unwed pregnancy and childbirth, it is necessary to understand their own belief systems surrounding femaleness, the traditional role of young women, the position of women in the kinship system, and their attitudes and practices surrounding birth control, marriage, pregnancy, childbirth, and maternity. These young women seek the perceived advantages and benefits of a college education, but even traveling to the United States is alien to their notion of womanhood. They are caught up in the "education explosion" in Truk, but education, particularly beyond the secondary level, presents new opportunities and roles which conflict with traditional ones for women far more than they do for men. In addition, their notions of womanhood, motherhood, and pregnancy are not congruent with American ones. Having a child — even out of wedlock — allows them to become adult women in the eyes of Pulapese. Moreover, having borne a child and being called home, they can return without admitting failure in school and without closing off the option of eventually obtaining a degree. They believe that in a year or so, they may return to college and continue their education, so that at least for a time, they can retain aspects of both sets of roles and opportunities without having to abandon one or the other.

Their pregnancies, however, are having an impact on decisions being made about other prospective college students. On the surface, this appears to involve a moral concern about pregnancy and unwed motherhood but has a good deal more to do with fears about losing the women themselves and their children. Such a loss poses a severe threat to the kinship and economic systems, since women are responsible for land, subsistence horticulture, and children, which are all essential to the well-being and perpetuation of the matrilineal descent groups. Considering the current high population increase, however, "losing" some of these women and children may have a long-term advantageous effect.

THE ATOLL SETTING

The young women described in this study come from an islet of Pulap Atoll, located in the Caroline Islands of Micronesia. The atoll is one of three that comprise the Western Islands (*Nomwon Páttiw*) of Truk State about 130 miles west of Moen, the administrative center of the area. The atoll economy is primarily a subsistence one, with women responsible for taro cultivation and men for fishing. Islanders can earn small amounts of cash from selling copra, but the only Pulap residents with full-time incomes are the elementary school teachers, who engage in subsistence activities as well as teaching.

The Western Islands are all low, coral atolls, in contrast to the high, basalt islands of Truk Lagoon, centrally located in the state. These include Moen, the administrative and commercial center of Truk State, where the port town is located and the site of the government offices, high schools, hospital, post office, airport, air-conditioned stores, and major harbor. The outer islands, lying to the north, west, and south, are all low, coral atolls, including the three atolls of the Westerns. These outer islands are serviced by government field trip ships, allowing for the movement of cargo, passengers, and administrative services in and out of Moen. Most of Truk's population is concentrated on the high islands: in 1980, out of a total population of 37,383 (United States Department of State 1980), 76 percent lived in Truk Lagoon and only 24 percent in the outer islands. The population of the Western Islands in 1980 was 1,329 (United States Department of State 1980). The entire area has been part of the United States Trust Territory of the Pacific Islands and in 1980 joined several other districts in ratifying the Constitution of the Federated States of Micronesia.

A system of matrilineal clans links the Westerns with other islands in Truk and with the atolls of Yap State to the west. Members of the same clan are expected to offer each other hospitality, regardless of whether or not the genealogical links can be traced.[2] Ideally, clans are also exogamous; a fellow clan member is conceptualized as a 'sibling,' never a potential 'spouse.' These ties can prove quite valuable when visiting another island, and students in the secondary schools and in college often choose to recognize and activate clan ties with students from other islands and thus convert strangers to kin. This practice is a common way of establishing social ties with other Trukese and outer island Yapese in the United States.

To understand the situation of the college students in the United States, it is necessary to understand the relative importance of siblingship and marriage and the various kin roles a woman may play. Siblingship underlies the clan and descent system, and the strongest cross-sex ties are those between siblings, not spouses. Relations among descent group members are viewed as sibling relations, and sibling sets consisting of complementary "brothers" and 'sisters' have been described as the building blocks of Trukese social structure (Marshall 1981). Moreover, notions of gender are intimately associated with notions of siblingship, and ideal male-female relations are modeled on ideal cross sibling relations (Flinn 1985b). The strength and importance of siblingship is in marked contrast to marriage and conjugal ties. Marriage in a sense is only secondary to childbirth and motherhood, and a woman has value as 'sister' and 'mother' rather 'wife.'

The importance of siblingship is reflected in certain marriage rules, including clan exogamy, the sororate, and the levirate. Marriage to a clan member is considered marriage to a 'sibling' and tantamount to incest. Marriage to anyone of the father's descent line (a 'parent' in their Crow-type terminology) or the offspring of any man of the father's descent line (a 'sibling') is also forbidden. Ideally this rule applies not only to the father's descent line but to his entire clan and the offspring of all its men. Marriage to the son or daughter of a man in one's father's clan is considered more reprehensible, however, than to someone in the father's clan itself because it entails a "sibling" relationship. It nonetheless occasionally occurs, but such couples are considered rather short-sighted and even a bit stupid, converting sibling ties into marriage and affinal bonds.

Divorce was once fairly frequent and easy, but since conversion to Catholicism in the early 1950s, this is no longer the case. Once a church wedding has taken place, a husband and wife may separate but not remarry or take up permanent residence with anyone else. All the islanders are Catholic, but many of the other areas in Truk are Protestant, and a Protestant man who marries a Pulap woman is expected to convert to Catholicism and at least outwardly follow church dictates.

This situation has been arising more frequently than in the past because of increasing numbers of inter-island marriages. Inter-island marriage used to be discouraged, but today fully one-third of the marriages involve a spouse from another island. Most of these marriages are between young people who met each other through the contemporary educational system. One factor which has influenced the acceptance of inter-island marriages, especially with a man from another island, is wage labor and its cash income, because parents are much more likely to accept an off-island man as a husband for their daughter if he brings money into the family.

When planning to marry, it is customary for the boy or a close relative of his to ask the girl's parents for permission once he has asked the girl herself. If she has been adopted, both sets of kin take part in the decision, and they will consult with the girl's adult descent line 'brothers.' The ceremony is a Roman Catholic one and is followed by a feast attended by the whole community. Since the priest does not usually reside on the island, the couple must either wait until he visits or travel to his current residence. This entire procedure is obviously difficult for students who meet in the United States, and as yet they have no new precedent or model to follow.

At marriage men and women receive land and trees from their parents, but what a husband brings to the marriage he gives to his wife in order to provide for their children. Thus land does not stay in the hands of any one descent group but comes into the group through its women and goes out through its men. In other words, women acquire land for their descent group and subsequently care for it to sustain their children and in so doing nurture and strengthen the whole descent group. Again, a woman's importance is as descent group 'sister' and 'mother,' not 'wife.'

Even affinal terminology highights siblingship. The term for 'my spouse' is simply *fóónimwey*, literally 'my person-of-the-house'. In the past, two other categories of kin were also referred to by the same term: the same-sex sibling of one's spouse and the spouse of one's own same-sex sibling. As the term implies, either relationship entitled the parties to sexual access under certain circumstances. Since conversion to Christianity, though, many Pulapese prefer to avoid the term.

Once married, a woman hopes for children. She typically gives birth in her own home in the company of her female kin with a trained midwife. A celebration follows the birth: the mother's male relatives provide fish and the female relatives prepare vegetable staples for *mwéngén upwutiw* 'birth food.' Then for about six months following the birth, the mother does very little work aside from tending her child. She and the father are expected to refrain from sexual intercourse for about the same period of time. In fact, before resuming intercourse with the mother, the father must first administer medicine to his child. The medicine is kept secret, so that a man must acquire his own recipe from a parent or other close kin. He may even receive the information from a deceased relative through a dream. Pulapese believe that if a child becomes sick before administration of the medicine, the father may be to blame. Some people claim a child can also become ill if the mother is worried or jealous, or if she harbors anger towards her husband, and children are particularly susceptible to ghosts prowling at night.

Despite conversion to Christianity, ghosts and sorcery retain an active role in Pulap life. Ghosts can still cause illness, eat souls, and possess selected victims, although at times, holy water and a crucifix may be used to cure such a victim. A woman who dies in childbirth is believed to experience the sort of death that makes her soul become an evil ghost, because her life has been prematurely cut short. Sorcery on the part of other islanders (but not other Pulapese) is another fear. Women are reluctant to deliver in Truk Hospital on Moen because none of the nurses or other attendants come from islands that can be trusted. Pulapese are even apt to attribute any mishap or later illness of a child to sorcery on the part of someone attending the birth at the hospital.

TRUK'S "EDUCATION EXPLOSION"

The experiences of these women relate to what has been labeled an "education explosion" in Truk, a phenomenon that has been particularly marked since 1965 (Hezel 1978). For example, the total number of high school graduates from Truk in all the years prior to 1965 is exceeded today by the number who graduate in a single year. Although formal education existed before that time, far fewer students, particularly Western Islanders, attended the schools. The "education explosion" initially occurred at the elementary school level, but in the 1960s began affecting secondary education and then in the 1970s post-secondary education. Shifts in United States policy, designed at least in part to foster a permanent political relationship with Micronesia, established increasingly higher levels of education as universal rights of Micronesians. At the same time, the orientation became increasingly more academic.

After World War II the United States Navy established a system of elementary schools throughout the district of Truk to provide six years of education for all children, both male and female (Singleton 1974: 79). Although the Navy sponsored the system, the schools remained largely under local commmunity control. The administration even sought consent of local magistrates before assigning new teachers to their schools (Nagao and Nakayama 1969). The military government established a public secondary school in 1946 on Moen and staffed it with American teachers; in 1947 it became Truk Intermediate School and continued as such until 1962. An entrance exam determined admittance, and only a limited number of students attended. Even fewer continued their education at Pacific Islands Central School (PICS), the only public high school in the entire Trust Territory until 1962.

The educational system underwent a fundamental change in 1962 when the United States budget ceiling for Trust Territory appropriations more than doubled. One of the consequences was a far heavier

emphasis on education and a policy of providing not six but twelve
years of free and universal education (Smith 1968: 75; Pearse and
Bezanson 1970: 29). Education was to be the key to Micronesia's
development and was seen by some as means of irrevocably binding
Micronesia to the United States in a dependent relationship (Gale
1979; Nevin 1977). The intent was to develop social, political, and
economic ties through rapid development such that Micronesia
would establish a permanent political affiliation with the United
States rather than eventually become a politically independent nation. Results of these attempts include over-populated port towns,
unemployment, and higher crime rates.

In the 1960s, the administration took away from the local community most of their responsibility for the elementary schools
(Nagao and Nakayama 1969), and a high school in each district
replaced PICS, the single inter-district school. Academically
oriented secondary education was to be available for all young
people rather than remain a privilege of a select few. Truk High
School soon opened on Moen, and secondary school enrollment
increased dramatically at that time and then again in 1970 with the
establishment of academic junior high schools.

The forerunners of the junior high schools were post-elementary
vocational schools set up in 1967, one of them on Ulul in the
Namonuitos, north of the Western Islands, which Pulapese could
attend. Until 1970, the Ulul school was a vocational alternative for
those who failed the entrance test required for the academic secondary schools, although graduates could later continue their education at Truk High School. It was with the establishment in 1967 of
these post-elementary schools in the outer islands, rather than the
earlier opening of Truk High School, that enrollment of Western
Islanders in secondary schools began its sharp increase. Pursuit of a
secondary education has become the norm for all Pulap young
people who can maintain the necessary grade point average. Since
the opening of the school on Ulul, only a small handful of Pulap's
elementary school graduates have failed to pursue post-elementary
education. They are all girls, and they have remained home because
of marriage, illness, or failure to pass the entrance test. Then once
in secondary school, students tend to remain unless compelled to
leave for academic reasons, illness, or marriage.

The "education explosion" at the college level is more recent in
Truk than at the secondary level. Not only are more high school
graduates attending college, but a higher percentage are selecting
United States mainland colleges and pursuing academic programs.

During the 1950s and 1960s, most Trukese college students attended the College of Guam, and these young people were the most intellectually gifted of the high school graduates, because their Trust Territory scholarships were awarded by merit and given only to a relatively small number of students (Hezel 1978: 26). In the early 1970s, however, many more high school graduates continued into post-elementary education. Although part of the explanation lies in the establishment of post-elementary schools within the Trust Territory (the Micronesian Occupational Center in 1970 and the Community College of Micronesia in 1971), a major reason is the eligibility of Micronesians, beginning in 1972, for federal education grants, such as Basic Education Opportunity Grants (BEOG). Not only could virtually any high school graduate find an American college willing to accept her, but she could obtain money for college from the United States government. Both in sheer numbers and in percentage of total high school graduates, more students began attending college, and they tended to choose mainland schools. Moreover, since obtaining funds was no longer based on merit, they constituted a far less select group of students than in the past.

The first college graduate returned to Truk in 1967 (Singleton 1974: 81), but by 1977 about two hundred had returned with degrees (many from junior colleges). The first student from Pulap to attend a mainland school, however, did not leave until 1974. From then on, almost every Pulap high school graduate has at least considered attending college. Attitudes among high school seniors towards attending college are approaching those towards secondary education:

> It seems that overseas education has also become something of a rite of passage, and that many Micronesians go overseas simply because they feel it is the thing to do at their age or because they don't want to be left behind (Thompson 1981: 127).

Even if they return without a degree, having gone abroad and come back with tales of adventure provides them with some status. Most simply assume that appropriate jobs will be available, despite the fact that the government positions most of them expect are fast becoming scarce (Hezel 1982: 110–111).

Almost all Pulapese choose to attend college with at least one other student they know, preferably another Pulap student or someone related through clan or created sibling ties from another island, and Pulap students already in college have encouraged later high school graduates to join them. In his study of Trukese college students, Larson (1979) found the same tendency for students to choose schools with the advice and prompting of friends or relatives, although he mentioned that a small number of males preferred to attend a school alone or with only a few other Trukese. No Pulap girl expressed similar feelings, and even those who had only applied to college but did not subsequently attend had also chosen to go with or to join another relative in college.

While in the United States, Micronesian students have a number of problems to contend with, ranging from finding transportation and housing to budgeting money and passing courses (Flinn 1982: 158–163; Morikawa 1975; Shmull 1978). Micronesian students often do not know where to go for help or how to do so appropriately; nor are they used to taking on the responsibility and initiative themselves of seeking help (Naughton 1975: 9). Many also feel they have to contend with racism and negative stereotypes on the part of Americans (Morikawa 1975), contributing to feelings of isolation and insecurity. Drinking is a problem among males, and both sexes have some difficulties relating to Americans of the opposite sex, though females a bit more so than males (Larson 1979). Drinking and a lack of familiarity with American laws has led in some cases to serious legal and financial consequences (del Sobral 1977).

Male drinking is related in part to the role of drinking in Trukese culture (Larson 1979: 45–51; Marshall 1979b). Most of those who drink in the United States also did so in Truk, where drinking is associated with masculinity (Marshall 1979b: 85). Three valued aspects of Trukese character are bravery, respectfulness, and strong thought (Caughey 1977), but in the absence of warfare, drunken comportment is one of the few avenues available to men for exhibiting some of these traits. Trukese society prohibits the open display of anger and aggression, yet young men have to contend with problems of anxiety, little control over their lives, and dependency (Marshall 1979b). Drinking and expressing aggression while drunk are sanctioned outlets for aggression in Truk, and men are not held accountable for their actions. In the United States, however, people are held accountable for drunken behavior, presenting additional problems to these young men. In fact, when describing ideal character traits, the young men tend to stress aggressiveness as opposed to respectfulness (Larson 1979: 50). Even if an individual would prefer not to drink and concentrate instead on studying, the social pressures and value placed on group activities almost invariably prevail. A young man will drink in order to maintain social relations and to retain a good reputation not only as a male but also as someone who cooperates and shares.

Aside from drinking, financial problems are probably the most common. Many students have little conception of the costs of living in the United States, they have no experience with budgeting money, and they receive inadequate advice on how to do so. Unfamiliar with the notion of saving money, they fail to dole out a stipend or paycheck over a period of time. Wages in Truk are spent fairly quickly and shared with others, not saved. In the United States, students continue to share their money, which can leave someone with insufficient funds for rent and food. In some cases, the result may be an inadequate diet, especially during cold winters (Naughton n.d.).

Academic problems are also common because students arrive poorly prepared. Their education at Truk High school does not adequately prepare them for college in the United States, and their study skills are minimal. Even though they are taught English in Truk, language is a major problem for almost all of them. Nor do they receive ample counseling about appropriate schools to attend. One young man, for instance, was interested in a maritime major and selected a college on that basis, only to discover it dealt only with navigating the Great Lakes.

In addition, students are unfamiliar with many of the rudiments of American culture, although they leave Truk feeling fairly confident in their knowledge, especially because of movies they have seen. Yet even electricity and running water may be new, much less escalators and elevators, city buses and traffic lights, telephones and stoves. Registration lines, American food, and winter are all uncomfortable hurdles for them, and life in dormitories can ease only a few of these problems.

Valued behavioral patterns and character traits can pose problems for Micronesian students in American culture. Their own values stress cooperation, compliance, respect, accommodation, and acquiescence.[3] They avoid confrontation and expressing potentially contentious ideas, opinions, or attitudes, but say and do what they think is expected of them. Approval of peers, and cooperation and sharing with others are valued, which can inhibit academic success, especially when pressure is exerted to join a drinking group.

In a study of Micronesians in Hawaii, Severance (1983) has described how feelings of shame and embarrassment when confronted with American assertiveness can cause students to withdraw from interaction, resulting in a maladaptive pattern whereby they fail to receive help, support, or information they require. In general, rather than seek help, Micronesian students tend to wait for an offer of assistance; ashamed of failure, they prefer to withdraw and remain non-confrontational (Naughton 1975). Micronesian values can hinder or interfere with successful integration into American college life, creating stress for students, but other Micronesian students who have been able to adjust can act as "culture brokers" and serve as models for new students.

In fact, one crucial strategy of these students is to form relationships with other Micronesians, including those from outside their own cultural group. Seeking companionship and assistance from co-nationals is a common strategy among foreign students in general, providing them with emotional and social support as well as practical, tangible assistance (Coelho 1982; Pedersen 1980; Spaulding and Coelho 1980). Social supports can also mediate or buffer the impact of stress. For Pulapese, relationships are established with other Micronesians through the idiom of kinship. In Truk they can establish ties with other islanders by activating and recognizing distant or putative kin ties or by creating sibling ties, and friendship is interpreted as kinship (cf. Marshall 1977).

PULAP WOMEN IN THE UNITED STATES

The Pulap women attending college in the United States all selected the same community college in the South, and when they left school, they moved to a nearby town to live in a trailer park with other Micronesians. Carmen and Maria's older sister Susie were the first women to leave the island for college, although they left a few years later than the first young man to do so. They attended college together with some other Truk High School students from the western part of Truk Lagoon. Josepha arrived a few years later with a friend from the Hall Islands (atolls north of Truk Lagoon), followed by Laura, Sylvia, and a friend from the Namonuito Atoll north of the Westerns. At least three other Pulap women, including Maria, had planned to attend the same school the year that Josepha left; they had all gone through the secondary schools together, but only Josepha was allowed to leave for college.

At the time of the study, Susie had returned to Truk and was living on Moen while her relatives made plans for her to marry a Trukese man she had met in the United States. The initial plans, primarily on the part of her mother's brother (her 'brother'), involved arrangements for the man to convert to Catholicism. She was hoping to continue her education at the University of Guam some time in the future. Josepha had been called home by her relatives, who were also in the process of planning her marriage to the Trukese man who had fathered her child in the United States.

The others were all out of school but still living in the United States, Carmen and Sylvia with their babies, and Laura helping the two mothers and planning to transfer to another school in a few months. They formed part of a small Micronesian community, which in addition to the three Pulapese included a woman from the Halls, one from the Namonuitos, three men from Truk Lagoon, and half a dozed others from Kosrae, the Marshalls, and the outer islands of Yap. Only one, however, was attending school at the time, in a nearby town, and he visited the others in the trailer park on weekends. The students had arrived in town to join the community at different times, usually directly from a college they had been attending, activating a kin tie with one of those already resident. The girls had all befriended each other (by activating or creating kin ties) at one of the secondary schools in Truk and had previously attended college with other relatives. Most of the other relationships had been established when the students met at college in the United States.

In the eyes of the Pulap students, each relationship among them was one of kinship. The ties were based on membership in the same clan, making them 'siblings;' membership in another's father's clan, making them 'parent' and 'child', created sibling relationships; or, in the case of couples living together, 'spouse' relationships. None of the ties remained dyadic, however, because each individual drawn into the network through a relationship with a single person became related to them all through the existing ties. Even Americans drawn in as friend or 'spouse' were treated as friends or affines by the others.

Although most of the students were not in school and therefore not supported by educational grants or loans, they managed to survive by sharing what little they could earn. Turning to kin and sharing resources are common strategies among migrants in general. Just as in Truk, students in the United States share because they are kin, and they are kin because they share. In the trailer park they behaved as members of one household, though living in three separate trailers. A few of the young men had jobs and helped support the rest, and all of them made use of any government aid they discovered they were eligible for. For example, while pregnant and nursing, the mothers could receive food such as cheese, eggs, and bread through a government program. The supplies were not reserved for their use, however, but were shared and distributed among all the members of the group, as would be the case among the members of a household on Pulap. In their minds, it would be an abrogation of kinship not to do so. In the same way, other resources such as clothing, cars, shelter, labor, and information were also shared and passed on as some members of the group left and others came to join them. Josepha, the first to become pregnant, for instance, learned from another Micronesian friend of a free clinic they could use, and this information was passed on to each new person.

Various government benefits and free or low cost medical care based on their poverty status are resources the Micronesians take for granted because of their experiences in the Trust Territory as virtual wards of the United States. Micronesians became quite familiar with a welfare system as they grew increasingly dependent on appropriations from the federal government for their budget. They are also used to the United States government providing education, hospitals, and medical care and including them in many welfare programs. In the wake of a typhoon or tropical storm, for instance, Micronesians receive food from the United States Department of Agriculture through the Needy Family Feeding Program.

Nevertheless, these young people encountered difficulties. For example, the heat had been turned off in one trailer because the gas bill had not been paid for several months, and the electric bill was three months behind. The male students spent a good deal of their earnings on alcohol and drank as often as their money allowed. Moreover, most had had very little experience in managing money before arriving in the United States and thus had virtually no conception of budgeting. Even when living in dormitories, with food and housing paid in advance, they experienced problems with handling finances.

Turning to kin provides both emotional as well as practical support, and for Micronesians kin ties can be created when they do not already exist. Strong male-female ties that develop among Trukese students in the United States are created sibling relations. In English they call each other 'promise brother' and 'promise sister,' and they pay particular attention to the well-being of the other. A woman's "promise brother" is the first she would turn to for transportation, for instance, and she ensures that he is fed and provided with clean clothes. The other cross-sex relationships are sexual ones, but especially with pregnancy and childbirth, the ties are not casual or transient. Before conversion to Catholicism, premarital affairs were not uncommon, and despite the efforts of the Catholic Church, that remains the case today. Discreetness is essential, however, and these young women are not promiscuous, either in Trukese or in American terms. Especially once the students have become pregnant or delivered babies, the couples act as if married, in many ways following the pre-Christian, traditional pattern. The early part of a marriage at that time was more or less a trial period, with divorce fairly common, but the relationship typically became more stable with the birth of children.

One problem for these couples in the United States, alluded to earlier, pertains to religion, since the men the Pulap women became involved with were Protestant. In Truk, a couple in this dilemma can readily talk with a priest, who can arrange for the spouse to convert, but in the United States the procedures remain mysterious to the young people. As previously mentioned, these students generally have difficulties seeking assistance and tend to avoid uncomfortable situations or confrontations whenever possible as a way of coping. In addition, they have not yet obtained permission from abroad to marry which is traditional on Pulap. It was not until Josepha returned to Truk together with Susie that they were able to secure permission for their marriages and begin the procedures for the two men to convert. The women moved in with relatives living on Moen, who were able to begin arranging the details while the two of them waited for the young men to return from the United States.

Not only do these women face practical difficulties arranging to marry in the United States, but they also encounter a different set of cultural meanings surrounding marriage and motherhood. Micronesians who are unmarried and pregnant contribute to an image among some Americans of their being "loose," "promiscuous," and of "low morality." Most Americans in their community have little or no idea of where Micronesia is and may view the women as South Sea Islanders, with implications of free and easy sex. Such would not be the case on Pulap, however, and the same sort of stigma would not be attached to their behavior. Having a child, regardless of whether or not a woman has been married in the church, adds to her status. By becoming a mother she produces a new member for her descent group and thus fulfills one of her obligations as a 'sister.' Being a good 'sister' is essential to being a woman on Pulap. Moreover, a child born out of wedlock is considered a full member of his or her mother's descent group, with rights in descent group assets.

Young women back home on Pulap have already begun to bear children. They are productive women in two senses, because they are producing both food and children for the descent group. Attending college in the United States accomplishes neither one, and as yet, these students have no other model to follow. If they were to succeed in school, they would presumably then be able to contribute to the well-being of their descent group through increased status and income, assuming the women obtained employment. Or they could contribute in other ways. Several of the women want to become nurses, for instance, in order to care for Western Islanders at Truk Hospital and thus ease fears about sorcery. Yet academic success is difficult for them to achieve, and being a 'mother' at their age has far more meaning and relevance than any other role, whether it be student or nurse or teacher.

Although a few Pulap women have secured employment, they cannot serve as adequate models for the college students. Three women, all high school graduates, work at the elementary school on Pulap, one as a teacher and two as teacher aides, but no more positions are likely to become available. The only other employment opportunities are on Moen. The women at the elementary school on Pulap have been able to combine teaching with motherhood, marriage, and subsistence obligations with minimal conflict because their sisters and mothers can care for their children while they teach, as is the case whenever any descent line woman works in the taro gardens. The only conflict appears to arise from their own expectations of an appropriate period for maternity leave. A teacher complained that she was allowed only four months, whereas women typically spend closer to six months at home with their infants, relying on other descent line women to tend to any remaining work.

Another factor contributing to the relative unconcern of these women about marriage, as opposed to motherhood, is that marriage on Pulap does not perform important alliance functions. Members of descent groups are linked not by marriage or affinal ties but by father-child ties. In other words, in addition to duties and privileges in one's own descent group, a person has important obligations to members of his or her father's descent group, who are all referred to as 'parents.' They, in turn, refer to the offspring of descent group men as 'children.' The relationship exists not because the child's mother is married to the father, but because the man fathered the child. A man not a woman, is believed to give substance to child, providing the basis for the paternal tie (cf. Thomas 1977).

When faced with the possibility or reality of pregnancy, these young women do not seriously consider the choices most American women would, in part because they do not attach the same meaning to the situation. They do not have the same 'problem.' First of all, the women do not choose to use birth control to avoid pregnancy. Although they do not seek to become pregnant, they have relatively little concern with or fear of pregnancy; if anything, bearing a child will enhance their status, and they place a high value on having not just one child but many. These attitudes dovetail neatly with and are reinforced by their priest's emphasis on avoiding birth control. It would be difficult for them to go against both sets of beliefs, especially when it would also entail actively seeking assistance from someone in the American medical system. These students prefer to avoid such potentially uncomfortable situations.

Once they find themselves pregnant, the women do not contemplate the two options of abortion and adoption commonly considered — and chosen — by American women. Again, the Catholic Church's stance on abortion is consistent with their own attitudes concerning the value of children and relative lack of stigma attached to being unmarried. Adoption, at least in the American sense of the word, is not deemed a solution either. Pulap women never "put up" their children for adoption, even when they are born out of wedlock. Nor would a woman consider transferring her parental rights to another person, allowing a complete stranger to adopt her child and then keep its identity and natural parents a secret. Adoption is nonetheless a common practice on Pulap, but it differs in fundamental ways from the American practice. First of all, a child is requested by a prospective adoptive parent, not "put up" by a mother who does not want her child. Only a relative has the right to request a child in adoption, and the child must, in fact, already be a classificatory 'child.' The preference is for a woman to adopt the child of a 'brother' (usually a male member of her descent group), thus strengthening the 'parent-child' tie between the descent group and the offspring of its men (Flinn 1985a). From the perspective of the natural mother, the adoptive mother is therefore commonly a woman of her husband's descent group, although other people can just as readily request the child, including the woman's own sisters, mother, and mother's sisters. Another difference from the American pattern is that adoption does not involve substituting one set of parents or one mother for another; rather than transferring parental rights, adoption more accurately results in the sharing of such rights. If anything, adoption on Pulap amounts to adding another set of parents or activating latent rights in the child, a pattern fairly typical of adoption in Oceania (Brady 1976). Children, like other resources, are shared among kin (cf. Marshall 1976). A woman's sisters and other descent line women, in particular, will share in child care even in the absence of explicit adoption. An adopted child does not even have to give up his or her descent group identity to take on that of the adoptive parent. Thus in many ways, the American concept of adoption is quite foreign to the Pulap student.

Because of adoption and the sharing of responsibility for children that is expected among kin, the unwed Pulap mother does not face the same financial or emotional stress confronting an American woman. She sees no need to rid herself of the burden of a child, since the burden is always shared and can easily be temporarily transferred. Nor is she expected to perform as the child's sole caretaker. For months after the child is born, she is responsible for attending to the infant's physical needs, but she is released from responsibility for subsistence production and other female tasks. These are taken on by other descent line women. Later, as the child grows older, the mother can leave the child with others at home so that she can work elsewhere, and child care in general is shared among household members. A woman can even have a child stay for a time with female relatives while she leaves the island, or she may take a relative with her to help care for the child. In other words, many options are available, allowing a woman to keep her child but share the burden of raising it.

These young women can deal with some of the practical problems of pregnancy through taking advantage of government welfare programs and medical care. They do not seek out information from the approporiate agencies but learn of them from advisors and other students, especially other Micronesians. In addition, they have the small community of Micronesians, which includes other Pulap women, to retreat to, through whom they can receive the emotional support they need in order to cope with the host community's negative attitudes towards their situation.

Much of labor, delivery, and childbirth, however, is entirely another matter because American expectations differ from their own. Although many American women are becoming increasingly assertive regarding their desires about childbirth and hospital procedures, the Pulap women simply comply with whatever procedures and regulations they encounter. In general, these islanders avoid

confrontation and at least outwardly say and do what they perceive
to be expected of them, especially in the presence of authority
figures. On Pulap, childbirth ideally takes place with a midwife and
other feamle kin in attendance. Even when on Moen, a woman
prefers to give birth with a midwife in a home in the Pulap migrant
community rather than deliver in Truk Hospital because she fears
sorcery on the part of nurses or other personnel.

On Pulap when people are either sick or in labor, relatives are
expected to attend them, keep them company, cool them with fans,
and massage them. A patient should never be left alone. The initial
states of labor are comparable for the young women in the United
States since the other women living in the trailer park, including the
non-Pulapese treated as kin, can remain with them through the first
hours of labor at home. None have training in midwifery, however,
and would not consider giving birth outside the hospital in the
United States. They do not hold the same fear of sorcery as they do
in Truk, and they feel more comfortable complying with the expectations of medical personnel than they would asserting their own
wishes and preferences. Being assertive or confrontational is labeled
lamalam tekiyah — 'conceited, arrogant' (literally 'high thoughts'),
an extremely negative character trait and the opposite of *méhónó-
hón* — 'quiet, modest, unassuming' (Elbert 1972: 89).

Furthermore, the Pulap midwives were trained by American personnel after World War II, and this is an area in which Pulapese
have great faith in American medicine. One Pulap woman is particularly popular as a midwife, in part because she is a senior female
of the chiefly clan. All members of the chiefly clan share at least a
measure of the chief's responsibility for the island as a whole. Such
a woman is thus eminently trustworthy, not just in the eyes of
Americans because of her training, but also in the eyes of Pulapese
because of her clan status. The number of live births on the island
began increasing during the post-war period, a rise that Pulapese
attribute primarily to the impact of American midwifery training. A
number of other changes were introduced during the post-war years,
however, including sanitation measures, treatment for venereal diseases, and medical care that reduced infant mortality and deaths
due to infectious diseases, but the conventional wisdom among
Pulapese holds that their midwives, trained by Americans, brought
about the change.

Once the young women arrive at the hospital in the United
States, the process begins to differ significantly from the Pulap
situation. Most critical is that the women are suddenly and com-

pletely isolated from their kin and have to experience the rest of labor and delivery in the company of strangers. They have neither the emotional support of kin nor the option of avoidance to cope with the situation but must simply comply with hospital rules and regulations. Compounding the problem, the infant is separated from the mother after delivery and has to remain in the nursery except for brief feeding periods every four hours. If the option of having the infant remain in the mother's room is available at the hospital these women delivered in, they had neither heard of nor requested it. Consistent with Pulap behavioral style and values, they meekly do as they are told and at least outwardly accept the situation they find themselves in.

The other Micronesians come to visit the mother and baby during designated visiting hours, but otherwise the young mothers are left alone, which they consider uncomfortable under any circumstances but a hardship during a crisis. Separation from their kin is one problem, but separation from the infant they find even more trying. The women are particularly incensed at the way hospital personnel ignore the crying of infants in the nursery. Infants on Pulap are not put on any sort of schedule for sleeping or eating, and are nursed, held, cuddled, or rocked whenever they cry. Once released from the hospital in the United States, however, the women are able to return to the trailer park, live in the company of relatives again, and care for the infant as they are more accustomed to doing. If possible, other Pulap women, like Laura, move from elsewhere in the United States to stay with the new mother.

At the time of the study, Carmen and Sylvia, two of the women who had borne children, were still in the United States, but Josepha had returned to Moen. She had been asked to return by her kin, who had sent her money for the air fare. The other two were complacently expecting similar requests. None of the women attempted to keep the pregnancies or births a secret from relatives in Micronesia. Such situations would not be secret for long on Pulap, and the women in the United States assume their relatives will hear about them through letters other students write home. As a rule, students keep in touch with other Pulapese and with relatives from elsewhere in Truk who are living in the United States, and they expect news and gossip of their activities to reach Pulap eventually.

By returning to Truk, these young women are not closing off the option of returning to school, especially on Guam, where the environment and culture are not as alien. Josepha, for instance, was considering attending the University of Guam in a few years to finish her degree. She could take the child with her, counting on the assistance of Pulap women and perhaps other relatives going to the University to help care for the child. Another option would be to leave the child with women of her descent line or even with the father's kin for a time.

Although interviews with these young women did not reveal that they deliberately seek pregnancy and childbirth as a way to leave school relatively honorably, without admitting failure, they nonetheless expect their relatives to ask or even insist that they return home. Thus they do not have to admit to failure in school or an inability to cope. By becoming pregnant, these young women are released from responsibilities required of students, typical of someone taking on the "sick role." Thus they effectively escape an uncomfortable and stressful situation.

Pregnancy is not a disease, but the situation is not unlike that of *susto* or other diseases of adaptation (Klein 1978, Rubel 1964, Uzzell 1974). These women experience role stress, and like victims of *susto*, they cannot directly confront the sources of stress. Pregnancy provides them with a culturally appropriate alternative role, one that is more rewarding for them than the role they seek release from. Being a student is problematic and unrewarding; pregnancy creates an escape without having to admit defeat. Becoming pregnant may well not be a deliberate and conscious act on the part of women, but the role provides them with certain benefits compared with the role of student. Their families expect them to be students, but for many, living up to those expectations can be difficult, probably more so for women than for men. Men are socialized to be mobile and adventurous, to travel and meet other people. Women are socialized to be nurturing and to care for family, children, and land. Pregnancy not only releases them from an onerous role but offers them a positive alternative, which, like *susto*, brings some benefits. The role also obliges others to respond in predictable and valued ways, especially in urging a return home and providing attention, care, and emotional support. Becoming pregnant provides a measure of status as well. Granted, there are costs to the women, physiological, financial, social, and emotional costs, especially in the face of American attitudes. But in their own cultural system, pregnancy carries value and provides relief from a stressful role.

Continuing in school not only appears difficult but promises them very little, especially since they, unlike the young men, have no model or example other than the traditional one of motherhood. As mothers they can return home feeling valued; as failures they have nothing to offer their kin compared to their peers who remained in Truk. Not only do they escape a difficult, unrewarding, even alien situation, without having to admit to failure or close off the option of eventually obtaining a degree, but they can fulfill traditional, valued roles and be welcomed home.

CONCERN WITH THE FUTURE

Pulapese are becoming increasingly concerned with the impact of allowing their young women to attend college abroad, in part because of these pregnancies. Their attitude has less to do with morality, however, than with concern that the women, together with their children, will remain abroad or in some other way be lost to the descent group. Many Pulapese parents and older brothers are growing increasingly reluctant to allow young women to leave for the mainland. At least for a time, a compromise has developed of allowing the women to attend the University of Guam, because it is much closer, and Pulapese feel they can more easily monitor the activities of the students. Older Pulapese have even gone for a time to live on Guam with the students. Guam is only about an hour's flight from Moen, and flights are available about every other day. From Moen, where a number of Pulapese reside in a small migrant community, Guam is actually more accessible than Pulap.

Another concern lies with allowing too many women from one descent group to leave. Maria, for instance, was not permitted to attend college despite her academic promise. Two of her brothers and her older sister had left for college, but she was told to remain on Pulap to care for her mother and to attend to her descent group responsibilities. The next sister was about four years younger, just finishing elementary school, and soon to leave for high school. In very real terms, then, Maria was needed at home. No man could take over for her and care for the land and taro gardens, and no other young woman was available. Considering the female role as caretaker, a descent group cannot afford to lose many of its women. Furthermore, women are taught, beginning in childhood, to respect and obey their brothers, and they would not choose to leave for college in direct violation of a brother's expressed wishes.

From another perspective, however, "losing" some of these women and children could be advantageous. Certainly the fact that the women going off to college are marrying and having their first children later than women remaining on Pulap may prove beneficial through a reduction in overall fertility. The island's population has been growing rapidly, with the current rate about 3.3 percent. The population in 1909 was only 60 (Krämer 1935), although this low figure may have been due to a near-massacre in the nineteenth century. The population was stable between 1925 and 1949, varying only from a low of 153 to a high of 159 (Fischer 1949; United States Navy Department 1948). Since that time, however, the population has steadily increased, and the official census figure for 1980 was up to 432 (United States Department of State 1980), about half of whom were under the age of fifteen. At the moment, Pulapese perceive no problem, but they are aware of population pressures on other atolls in Truk and realize it could happen to them eventually. At least currently they would not accept birth control as a potential solution, an attitude that is reinforced by the Catholic Church. Children are also still perceived as resources, valued for labor, affection, food, and care in later life. Without some sort of slowing of growth, however, the island will eventually experience difficulties. Migration is currently siphoning off some permanent residents, easing any immediate pressure on resources, because migrants usually do not exercise their rights to Pulap land while they are absent.

Data from Namoluk Atoll, south of Truk Lagoon, where the "education explosion" began much earlier than in the Western Islands, indicate that the atoll is experiencing depopulation due to emigration of young people, most of whom originally leave to pursue secondary and then post-secondary education (Marshall 1979a). Many then remain away because of employment, marriage, or simply the excitement and activities unavailable at home. Most of the migrants reside on Moen, which contributes to its large growth rate and increase in social problems. In addition, a higher percentage of women are leaving for school than in the past, and the more highly educated women are tending to marry later and to have fewer children (Marshall and Marshall 1982), a pattern likely to emerge for Pulap as well.

Pulapese are leaving their atoll for reasons similar to those among the Namoluk people. Employment is not available on Pulap, since the positions at the elementary school have already been filled. The initial motive for leaving is to attend school, but most of those who finish high school look for jobs on Moen after graduation if they are not going on to college. For the most part, these young people have returned home after a few years if they have been unsuccessful at obtaining employment, but returning college students may not be as likely to do so:

> However intrinsically valuable education may be, 16 years of formal schooling is bound to foster in many young Micronesians expectations that can not be fulfilled in years to come. Given the underdeveloped state of Micronesia's economy at present, it is impossible to believe that the 3,000 Micronesian students away at college can all hope to obtain government jobs when they return from school. Will they leave Micronesia for good to seek employment elsewhere? If they remain, will scarcity of jobs bring upon the educated young widespread frustration at not being able to enjoy the lifestyle to which they aspire (Hezel 1982: 111)?

The population problem is simply shifting, then, to the port town. From 1967 to 1973 the annual growth rate for all of Truk was 3.6 percent, whereas during the same period Moen grew at an annual rate of 8.3 percent (Kay 1974) because of migration, primarily of young people, from outlying islands (Marshall 1979b: 7). In 1980 the population of Moen was up to 10,374, with a density of 1,421 per square mile (United States Department of State 1980).

Migration to the port town does not solve a potential population problem. The classic solution is a reduction in the birth rate, and with a rise in the number of educated women in Truk may come reduced fertility. Already the college students are having children at a later age than before. If some of the Pulap women finish school and return to Truk to find jobs, and if the new students are more adequately prepared for what they face in the United States, the women may wait even longer before bearing children and have a smaller completed family size. Thus the actions and decisions of these women have consequences for the future well-being of their descent groups and the island as a whole.

NOTES

1. The names of the women and some minor details have been changed in order to disguise and protect their identities.
2. The descent group most relevant to daily life on Pulap is a descent line (*tettel*) associated with a named homesite (*yiimw*). The members of each *tettel* can trace their descent from a common ancestress a few generations back. Since postmarital residence tends to be uxorilocal, those residing at a homesite are usually the females of the descent line, pre-pubertal boys, and in-marrying men.
3. For discussions of Trukese personality, see Fischer and Swartz (1960), Gladwin (1953, 1959), Gladwin and Sarason (1953), Marshall (1979b), and Swartz (1958, 1961, 1965). For an analysis of ideal Trukese character traits, see Caughey (1977).

In general, the material concerning respectfulness is applicable to Pulap, but the problem of aggression does not seem to be as acute as described for Truk.

REFERENCES

Beaglehole, Robert, *et al.*, 1977. Blood Pressure and Social Interaction in Tokelauan Migrants in New Zealand, *Journal of Chronic Diseases* 30: 803–812.
Brady, Ivan, 1976. Problems of Description and Explanation in the Study of Adoption. In *Transactions in Kinship: Adoption and Fosterage in Oceania*, ed. Ivan Brady, 3–27. ASAO Monograph No. 4. Honolulu: University Press of Hawaii.
Caughey, John Lyon, 1977. *Fáánakkar: Cultural Values in a Micronesian Society*. University of Pennsylvania Publications in Anthropology, No. 2. Philadelphia: Department of Anthropology, University of Pennsylvania.
Coelho, George V., 1982. The Foreign Student's Sojourn as a High Risk Situation: The "Culture-Shock" Phenomenon Re-examined. In *Uprooting and Surviving: Adaptation and Resettlement of Migrant Families and Children*, ed. Richard C. Nann, Dordrecht, Holland: D. Reidel Publishing Company.
Del Sobral, Sr. Maria M., 1977. Trust Territory Students Adjustment to the Complexities of the United States Legal System, *Justice in Micronesia* 1(1): 16–20.
Dohrenwend, Barbara Snell, and Bruce P. Dohrenwend, 1974. *Stressful Life Events: Their Nature and Effects*. New York: John Wiley and Sons.
Dohrenwend, Barbara Snell, and Bruce P. Dohrenwend, 1984. *Stressful Life Events and Their Contexts*. New Brunswick, New Jersey: Rutgers University Press.
Elbert, Samuel H., 1972. *Puluwat Dictionary*. Pacific Linguistics, Series C, No. 24. Canberra: Linguistic Circle of Canberra.
Elliott, Glen R., and Carl Eisdorfer, 1982. *Stress and Human Health*. Institute of Medicine, National Academy of Sciences. New York: Springer Publishing Company.
Fischer, John L., 1949. Western Field Trip Notes. Manuscript, Archives of the Bernice P. Bishop Museum, Honolulu, Hawaii.
Fischer, John L., and Marc J. Swartz, 1960. Socio-Psychological Aspects of Some Trukese and Ponapean Love Songs, *Journal of American Folklore* 73: 218–224.
Flinn, Juliana, 1982. Migration and Inter-Island Ties: A Case Study of Pulap, Caroline Islands. Ph.D. Dissertation, Stanford University.
Flinn, Juliana, 1985a. Adoption and Migration from Pulap, Caroline Islands, *Ethnology* 24(2): 95–104.
Flinn, Juliana, 1985b. Kinship, Aging, and Dying on Pulap, Caroline Islands. In *Aging and Its Transformations: Moving Towards Death in Pacific Societies*, eds. Dorothy Ayers Counts and David R. Counts, 65–82. ASAO Monograph No. 10. Lanham, MD: University of America Press.
Gale, Roger W., 1979. *The Americanization of Micronesia: A Study of the Consolidation of U.S. Rule in the Pacific*. Washington, D.C.: University Press of America.
Gladwin, Thomas, 1953. The Role of Man and Woman on Truk: A Problem in Personality and Culture, *Transactions of the New York Academy of Sciences* Series II, 15(8): 305–309.
Gladwin, Thomas, and Seymour B. Sarason, 1953. *Truk: Man in Paradise*. Viking Fund Publications in Anthropology, No. 20. New York: Wenner-Gren Foundation for Anthropological Research.
Gladwin, Thomas, and Seymour B. Sarason, 1959. Culture and Individual Personality Integration on Truk. In *Culture and Mental Health*, ed. Morris Opler, 173–210. New York: Macmillan Company.
Graves, Nancy B., and Theodore D. Graves, 1974. Adaptive Strategies in Urban

Migration. *Annual Review of Anthropology*, Volume 3, eds. Bernard J. Siegel, Alan R. Beals, and Stephen A. Tyler, 117–151. Palo Alto, CA: Annual Reviews, Inc.

Hanna, Joel M., and Paul T. Baker, 1979. Biocultural Correlates to the Blood Pressure of Samoan Migrants in Hawaii, *Human Biology* 51: 481–497.

Hezel, Francis X., 1978. The Education Explosion in Truk, *Micronesian Reporter* 26(4): 24–33.

Hezel, Francis X., 1982. *Reflections on Micronesia*. Working Paper Series, Pacific Islands Studies. Honolulu, Hawaii: Center for Asian and Pacific Studies in collaboration with the Social Science Research Institute, University of Hawaii at Manoa.

Hornick, Conrad A., and Joel M. Hanna, 1982. Indicators of Coronary Risk in a Migrating Samoan Population, *Medical Anthropology* 6: 71–77.

Hull, Diana, 1979. Migration, Adaptation, and Illness: A Review, *Social Science and Medicine* 13A: 25–36.

Kasl, Stanislav, and Lisa Berkman, 1983. Health Consequences of the Experience of Migration. In *Annual Review of Public Health*, Volume 4, eds. Lester Breslow, Jonathan E. Fielding, Lester B. Lave, 69–90. Palo Alto, CA: Annual Reviews, Inc.

Kay, Alan, 1974. Population Growth in Micronesia, *Micronesian Reporter* 22(2): 13–22.

Klein, Janice, 1978. *Susto*: The Anthropological Study of Diseases of Adaptation, *Social Science and Medicine* 12: 23–28.

Krämer, Augustin, 1935. *Inseln um Truk*. Ergebnisse der Sudsee Expedition 1908–1910. II.B.6, Subvolume 1. ed. G. Thilenius, Hamburg: Friederichsen, de Gruyter & Co.

Labarthe, Darwin, et al., 1973. Health Effects of Modernization in Palau, *American Journal of Epidemiology* 98: 161–174.

Larson, Bruce, 1979. Between Two Cultures: Trukese College Students in the United States. M.A. Thesis, University of Iowa.

Marshall, Leslie B., and Mac Marshall, 1982. Education of Women and Family Size in Two Micronesian Communities, *Micronesica* 18(1): 1–21.

Marshall, Mac, 1976. Solidarity or Sterility? Adoption and Fosterage on Namoluk Atoll. In *Transactions in Kinship: Adoption and Fosterage in Oceania*, ed. Ivan Brady, 28–50. ASAO Monograph No. 4. Honolulu: University Press of Hawaii.

Marshall, Mac, 1977. The Nature of Nurture, *American Ethnologist* 4(4): 643–662.

Marshal, Mac, 1979a. Education and Depopulation on a Micronesian Atoll, *Micronesica* 15: 1–11.

Marshall, Mac, 1979b. *Weekend Warriors: Alcohol in a Micronesian Culture*. Palo Alto, CA: Mayfield Publishing Company.

Marshall, Mac, 1981. Sibling Sets as Building Blocks in Greater Trukese Society. In *Siblingship in Oceania*, ed. Mac Marshall, 201–224. ASAO Monograph No. 8. Ann Arbor: University of Michigan Press.

McGarvey, Stephen T., and Paul T. Baker, 1979. The Effects of Modernization and Migration on Samoan Blood Pressures, *Human Biology* 51: 461–479.

McGarvey, Stephen T., Diana E. Schendel, and Paul T. Baker, 1980. Modernization Effects on Familial Aggregation of Samoan Blood Pressure: A Preliminary Report, *Medical Anthropology* 4: 321–338.

Morikawa, Susan, 1975. College Life: Micronesian Students in America, *Micronesian Reporter* 23(2): 21–26.

Nagao, Clarence M., and Masao Nakayama, 1969. A Study of School-Community Relations in Truk. In *The Truk Report*, ed. Stephen Boggs, Honolulu: University of Hawaii.

Naughton, June, Advising Micronesian Students. Manuscript, International Students Office, University of Hawaii at Manoa, Honolulu, Hawaii.

Naughton, June, 1975. A Case of the Normal Micronesian Student. Manuscript,

International Students Office, University of Hawaii at Manoa, Honolulu, Hawaii.

Nevin, David, 1977. *The American Touch in Micronesia*. New York: Norton.

Parsons, Talcott, 1951. *The Social System*. Glencoe: The Free Press.

Pearse, Richard, and Keith A. Bezanson, 1970. *Education and Modernization in Micronesia: A Case Study in Development and Development Planning*. Stanford, California: Stanford International Development Education Center, School of Education, Stanford University.

Pedersen, Paul B., 1980. Role Learning as a Coping Strategy for Uprooted Foreign Students. In *Uprooting and Development: Dilemmas of Coping with Modernization*, eds. George V. Coelho and Paul I. Ahmed, New York: Plenum Press.

Reed, Dwayne, Darwin Labarthe, and Reuel Stallones, 1970. Health Effects of Westernization and Migration Among Chamorros, *American Journal of Epidemiology* 92: 94–112.

Rubel, Arthur J., 1964. The Epidemiology of a Folk Illness: *Susto* in Hispanic America, *Ethnology* 3: 268–283.

Severance, Craig, 1983. Shame, Restraint and Adaptation to College Expectations: Some Micronesian Experiences in Hawaii. Paper presented at the 15th Pacific Science Congress, Dunedin, February 1–11.

Shmull, Temmy Lee, 1978. Micronesian Students in Western Schools. In *New Neighbors: Islanders in Adaptation*, eds. Cluny Macpherson, Bradd Shore, and Robert Franco, Santa Cruz, California: Center for South Pacific Studies, University of California at Santa Cruz.

Singleton, John, 1974. Education, Planning and Political Development in Micronesia. In *Political Development in Micronesia*, eds. Daniel T. Hughes and Sherwood G. Lingenfelter, 72–92. Columbus: Ohio State University Press.

Smith, Donald F., 1968. Education of the Micronesian with Emphasis on the Historical Development. Ed.D. Dissertation, American University, Washington, D.C.

Spaulding, Seth, and George V. Coelho, 1980. Research on Students from Abroad: The Neglected Policy Implications. In *Uprooting and Development: Dilemmas of Coping with Modernization*, eds. George V. Coelho and Paul I. Ahmed, New York: Plenum Press.

Swartz, Marc J., 1958. Sexuality and Aggression on Romonum, Truk, *American Anthropologist* 60: 467–486.

Swartz, Marc J., 1961. Negative Ethnocentrism, *Journal of Conflict Resolution* 5: 75–81.

Swartz, Marc J., 1965. Personality and Structure: Political Acquiescence in Truk. In *Induced Political Change in the Pacific: A Symposium*, ed. Roland W. Force, 17–39. Honolulu: Bishop Museum Press.

Thomas, John Byron, 1977. "Consanguinity" and Filiation on Namonuito Atoll, *Journal of the Polynesian Society* 86(4): 513–519.

Thompson, David M., 1981. The Social Adjustment of Overseas-Educated Micronesians. M.Ed. Thesis, University of Hawaii.

United States Department of State, 1980. *Annual Report to the United Nations on the Administration of the Trust Territory of the Pacific Islands*.

United States Navy Department, 1948. *Handbook of the Trust Territory of the Pacific Islands*. Office of the Chief of Naval Operations. Prepared at the School of Naval Administration, Hoover Institute, Stanford University.

Uzzell, Douglas, 1974. *Susto* Revisited: Illness as Strategic Role, *American Ethnologist* 1: 369–378.

Ward, Ryk, and Ian Prior, 1980. Genetic and Sociocultural Factors in the Response of Blood Pressure to Migration of the Tokelau Population, *Medical Anthropology* 4: 339–366.

Prevailing Over Adversity: The Story of a Vietnamese Physician's Internship in an American Community Hospital[1]

WILLIAM RITTENBERG

Michigan State University

"He's such a youthful man." "He has such intelligent eyes." "I've heard so many good things about him." "He's such a nice man." Such was the response to Dr. Thieu, a 38-year-old Vietnamese refugee physician.[2] When I knew him Dr. Thieu indeed seemed youthful for his years. Despite what he had seen, his face had no lines, no signs of fear. His step was light. His manner was spontaneous, active, gentle. When he moved, he moved lightly with a bit of rustling which suggested a certain happiness and ease.

One of the first things I learned about Dr. Thieu was he wrote poetry in Vietnamese. In high school he composed a poem about the moon. More recently he wrote, about his own circumstances,

> In ending there's beginning.
> In misfortune, there is fortune
> Out of each change, something new arises.

In Vietnam Dr. Thieu had been a physician and nationalist. After Saigon fell he escaped as one of the boat people, then came to the United States, and set out to re-establish himself in his profession. This case study will tell the story of how he met and overcame the adversity of an internship in a new culture.

In the last twenty years large numbers of foreign doctors like Dr. Thieu entered the United States for advanced study and/or permanent residence (Feldstein et. al. 1978; Haug et. al. 1971; Stevens et. al. 1978; Stimmel et. al. 1984). These physicians are known as "foreign

147

medical graduates" or "FMGs." FMGs are typically persons of elite origins in their home country, highly educated, from professional families and ambitious to gain advanced training abroad (Brody 1974, Stevens ibid). In the United States, however, they must meet and overcome many barriers before obtaining American training and licensure. First the FMGs must get certification of their foreign medical training from the Educational Commission for Foreign Medical Graduates (ECFMG), a non-profit organization supported by the AMA, and US hospitals and medical schools. Next, they must pass the rigorous ECFMG medical and English examinations. Finally, FMGs must enter the crowded medical labor market to compete with US physicians for internship positons. An unknown but substantial number of FMGs fail to find positions despite years of effort (Mick et. al. 1980); those who succeed are typically accepted only in low status training programs in which American physicians are unwilling to serve (i.e. inner city hospitals, state psychiatric hospitals, or poor Southern states [Goodman et. al. 1981, Inglehart 1985]).

Once accepted for US training, FMGs then face multiple problems which compound the normal stresses of internship. At first they know little about the organization of American medicine or the routines of American hospitals, and they are unfamiliar with the class, ethnic, and family patterns of the patients they treat (Brody 1971, Gavira 1975, Gelb 1972). Not surprisingly they experience problems with the new social patterns. Rather than being welcomed and appreciated, the FMGs find themselves treated with ambivalence by patients and supervisors (Char 1974, Miller 1971, 1974). Accustomed to treating their home instructors with respect, deference, and reserve, they reportedly have difficulty with the aggressive give and take of American clinical pedagogy (e.g. Bruce 1974, Gelb 1972, Lassers 1975). Accustomed to more subordination among women than is normal for Americans, the female FMGs often have difficulty asserting themselves and the males are said to find American women, including nurses, "aggressive, domineering, and threatening" (e.g. Ananth 1979; Char 1971; Fikre 1974; Tarnower 1981). Even FMGs educated in English must learn new varieties of American colloquial and technical speech, and they have language problems (Ananth 1979; Candlin 1980; Shuy 1975; Van Naerssen 1975; 1978).

In response to their new situation, the foreign physicians show familiar signs of culture shock — tendencies toward withdrawal and isolation, ambivalence toward new social patterns, caution and reticence with supervisors (Brody 1971; 1974; Gelb 1972; Miller 1974;

Stevens 1978, Tarnower 1981). They also adapt through a massive, successful process of sociocultural learning. Through daily participation in the US medical system, FMGs gradually acquire both the background knowledge about institutions and the new habits of interaction that are needed to work effectively in a new culture. Ultimately, despite struggle and stress, they successfully obtain licensure and enter US medical practice in large numbers (Stevens 1978).

I knew Dr. Thieu from my participation in a project to help FMGs with the difficult process of second culture learning. The project was designed to ease and deepen the FMGs' culture learning by intensifying their attention to their new social environment. Each participant was assigned a series of ethnographic exercises (e.g. home visits with patients, biographical dialogues with coworkers, analysis of video-taped clinic visits) to study aspects of his or her everyday training situation. After the assignments, the FMG met individually with an anthropologist preceptor to reflect on observations and draw lessons about American culture and his own process of second culture learning.

I served as Dr. Thieu's preceptor for a year in this project. In our regular meetings he told me about his past life and shared the ongoing events of his training. He allowed me to observe and videotape his interaction with patients and supervisors. I also was able to interview many of his coworkers and supervisors about his performance. My record of his internship comprises 350 pages of notes and tapes.

As I will describe, Dr. Thieu encountered and overcame serious trouble in his internship which, for a while, put his professional career in danger. His story illustrates the process of social control by which the medical profession responds to "problem" residents and interns.

PROFESSIONAL SOCIALIZATION AND SOCIAL CONTROL

Historically the American medical profession has been largely independent of state regulation, but internally the profession has not used its power to develop strong controls over its members (Bosk 1981; Freidson 1970; Starr 1982). Formal professional mechanisms for sanctioning unethical or incompetent physicians tend to be weak (Annas 1981). Informally, physicians are reluctant to criticize each others' practice in public, and the boycott is the most important sanction against errant colleagues (Freidson 1970; Freidson and

Rhea 1972). Physicians boycotted from practicing in one setting, however, are usually able to continue practice elsewhere. To a large degree, then, the profession has valued the autonomy of its individual practitioners (Bosk 1981, Brown 1979, Freidson 1970), and has left the maintenance of adequate standards of practice to individual self-regulation.

As one might expect, the most important exception to this pattern occurs among interns and residents. Their medical practice is subject to more extensive control than established physicians (Bosk 1981, Freidson 1970, Goss 1964). As apprentices, interns and residents work under the supervision of more experienced clinical instructors who guide their professional development. The instructors monitor, evaluate, and correct the interns' care of patients, and may impose severe sanctions (such as probation or expulsion from training) in case of serious departures from professional standards. This process of supervision and control over medical apprentices has a gatekeeping as well as a training function — to prevent entry of unsuitable persons into the profession. High ethical standards are strictly enforced because interns and residents must be self-regulating when training is complete (Bosk 1981).

Causes for failure or major trouble among interns and residents are cited in the literature — unethical conduct, emotional disturbance, drug addiction, deficient medical knowledge or technical incompetence, cultural or language problems, physical disability and others (Bosk 1981, Garetz 1976, Nadelson 1979, Russell 1975, 1977). However, rather than focus on such causes of serious trouble and failure, research on the professional socialization of physicians has focused on the normal development of successful trainees (Becker 1961, Bosk 1981, Bucher 1977, Haas in press, Johnson 1983, Light 1980, Merton 1957, Mumford 1970). As a result relatively little is known about the occurrence and response to the above mentioned problems in internship and residency programs. Except for one study in psychiatry (Russell 1975, 1977), the prevalence of the problems has not been explored. The proportion of cases in which the problems are present without seriously disrupting training has also not been defined (Garetz 1976). Nor has the process by which the problems are detected and managed in particular training programs been described.

Dr. Thieu's story, then, provides a example of this little investigated process of social control in the medical profession. His trouble arose from a common problem, estimated to interfere with training among 30% of FMGs (Stevens 1978: 213–14), namely difficulty with

English. His story does not represent the expericence of all FMGs who get in major trouble during training. Yet, as I suggest in the conclusion, it does provide clues about possible commonalities in the experience of FMGs whose training is disrupted by serious language problems.

Writing on deviance, Emerson and others distinguish between an individual's "problems" and "troubles" (Emerson 1977, Pollner 1974, Rudington 1964). "Problems" are difficulties in a person's behavior. "Troubles" on the other hand involve the social response to such problems. In this usage, a person may have problems, but if the problems go unnoticed by others and do not elicit a response, they do not cause trouble. The emergence of trouble is a social process, which depends on others' perception and response to some party's real or presumed problems.

This paper about Dr. Thieu, then, is a microethnography of trouble (see the discussion in Emerson 1977) which traces the social process by which his trouble emerged and was dealt with in his residency program. My story will describe the conditions of medical training and work in which his language problems first appeared. It will relate how and why his coworkers and supervisors came to perceive those problems as troublesome. And it will examine how his trouble was interpreted and dealt with once it became public.

Overall, the narrative presents the social interactional process by which professional control over a "problem" resident was effected. It is also a tribute to Dr. Thieu's personal dignity and strength of character under conditions of great stress.

PAST, VALUES, CHARACTER

Dr. Thieu grew up amidst conditions of war and revolution in Vietnam. Born in 1945 — the year that Ho Chi Minh seized power and declared Vietnam independent from France — he came from an elite Vietnamese Buddhist family. His father had been educated in the West and was active in anti-French politics. His mother was from a wealthy landowning family from what Thieu described as a traditional center of Vietnamese patriotism.

The family was both nationalist and anti-communist. The communists killed many of Thieu's uncles and also imprisoned his father, who escaped execution only because Thieu's mother bribed the authorites. Nevertheless, after his release Thieu's father joined the nationalist-communist alliance (the Vietminh) and became an important commander in the struggle for independence. For nine years he fought the French separated from his family. Even as this happened, his communist allies imprisoned his wife to the South without his knowing it. At this time while his father was away fighting and his mother was imprisoned, Thieu saw the communists take one of his mother's friends, bury her up to her neck and cut off her head with a furrow.

With the defeat of the French at Dienbienphu in 1954, Vietnam was partitioned. Thieu's father returned from fighting, his mother was released from prison, and the family moved to the South where Thieu's father held a high post in the South Vietnamese government. However, when Thieu's father sheltered some nationalist comrades from persecution by the secret police, he came under suspicion of ties to the Viet Cong. In 1961 he was imprisoned again, this time by the South Vietnamese government.

Thieu said his father never discussed his prison experiences, so his family would not feel sad. In this connection, however, Thieu mentioned the prison poetry of a famous Vietnamese nationalist leader. He said these beautiful, realistic poems (published in Paris) tell the truth about prison life and reading them brought tears to his eyes.

After a change of regime in South Vietnam, Thieu's father was released from prison in 1964. By that time Thieu was married and studying medicine. While still a student he worked to clear his father of reputed sympathy for the Vietcong. Making friendships at the highest level of the state security police, he obtained a hearing and won recognition of his father's loyalty.

Thieu graduated in 1971 and served as a physician in the South Vietnamese air force until 1975 when Saigon fell to the communists. He said conditions were harsh under communist rule.

In 1979 Thieu decided to escape, following one of his brothers to the United States. He went by boat with his eldest son, leaving his wife and younger son behind. The boat, however, capsized at sea. Two hundred passengers drowned, including Thieu's son. Ten persons managed to cling to a large inner tube, floating on the open sea. It was a terrible ordeal, Thieu said, of freezing cold and blazing sun, nothing to eat and nothing to drink. The blisters from the sun broke and each wave of salt water caused pain. One by one, over three days, the remaining survivors dropped off the inner tube and died. Finally on the third day, a Norwegian freighter sighted the inner tube and picked up Thieu and the other person left.

"How could anyone survive that?" I asked Thieu. "You must

have been very strong." I asked if he had trained physically. No, he responded, he did meditation, yoga. It wasn't outer strength that saved him but inner strength. "My wish to survive was very strong. I thought of my parents. Vietnamese think a child has a great debt to his parents, and I wanted to live to repay it. I thought of my wife and other son (4 years). I did not want to disappear leaving them with a void, a doubt."

Vietnamese communists on the Norwegian freighter took Thieu back to Vietnam where he was imprisoned. Then his wife bribed the communists for his release, and for six months he lived as a fugitive, moving from house to house to escape detention. Finally, in 1980, with his wife again pregnant, he left by boat a second time, alone.

Thieu's boat successfully reached Malaysia after nine days, beginning four years separation from his family. After a year in the Malay refugee camp, he came to the United States to live with his brother in Los Angeles. Immediately Thieu began to prepare for the medical and English examination (the "ECFMG") for an American internship. Despite lack of money for preparatory courses and inadequate textbooks, he passed the medical part of the ECFMG a year later. Six months later he passed the English examination and began seeking a residency program. In Winter 1982 he was accepted as an intern in the family practice residency at Canyonville Medical Center, and in July 1983, only two years after reaching the United States, Thieu arrived in Canyonville to begin his training.

Given the losses and traumas Dr. Thieu was able to overcome in his past life, it is probably not surprising he was also able to overcome the adversity of his internship. It was in fact the very values instilled by his Vietnamese background — family unity, nationalistic loyalty, and Buddist serenity — that helped sustain him in that trying period.

Thieu said it was painful to be separated from his family, their correspondence limited, remittances effectively prevented, and reunion uncertain. Even amid separation, his Vietnamese family bonds remained "very close, very strong". Family loyalty gave his wife and mother courage to free their husbands from prison. This same loyalty prompted his dangerous effort to clear his father's name. The thought of his family helped him survive at sea. Similarly, I think, his wish to bring his family to the United States and support them helps explain the vigor of his efforts in obtaining an internship and his strength in withstanding its adversity.

By his own account, Dr. Thieu was also a nationalist, a man

deeply identified with the fate and well-being of his country. In Canyonville, he told coworkers about his family's history in war and revolution. His story struck a chord. As the coworkers learned of his struggle under communism, how he had lost his son at sea, how he had a daughter born after his escape whom he had never seen, they responded with respect and fellowship that helped support him during internship.

Finally Dr. Thieu was Buddhist. Vietnamese Buddhism embodies a deep aspiration for the wisdom that culminates in compassion. There was indeed a kindness inherent in Thieu's character that was spontaneously recognized by his coworkers. In Vietnam, he had treated many patients free of charge. He sought to be vegetarian out of respect for life. In Malaysia he befriended an American with medical aid. When he reached the United States his father wrote admonishing him to have compassion toward all persons he met. When he received a salary he began sending money to the Christian Aid Society for the hungry in the African Horn. He sent money and letters to three Vietnamese siblings, orphaned at sea and living miserably in a Thai refugee camp. When he reached Canyonville, he offered a place in his apartment to a friend in need. His kindness tempered his other values too, so when he spoke of Vietnam's national suffering, and his own family's portion of it, and when he described communist oppression, his manner and voice did not suggest hatred or bitterness.

In Canyonville, despite adversity, Dr. Thieu seemed basically at home, open to his new surroundings, not fundamentally threatened or isolated. As we shall see, he met adversity not with hatred or anger, but gently, and energetically set about doing what needed to be done.

CANYONVILLE RESIDENCY

Canyonville Medical Center, where Dr. Thieu trained, is the major public hospital in a small city. With 700 beds it serves a predominantly poor and ethnically diverse patient population, many of them unemployed or on relief. It has residency programs in nine specialties (including family practice) and 80 residents, most of them FMGs. These FMGs are respected for the service they provide, yet they are also considered a liability to the hospital's public reputation.

The family practice residency at the medical center is relatively small, with a full-time director, an assistant director, and twelve residents in training. The residency's decision making body, the "Training Committee," bears responsibility for educational policy, for hiring, evaluating, firing, and certifying residents, and for recruiting residency staff. As an accredited training program, the residency must meet nationally established curriculum requirements. Three years of training are required, and in each year residents must have supervised work experience in a number of clinical settings, such as a primary care clinic, a family medicine clinic, and a neonatal intensive care unit (NICU).

Residents are appointed for a year at a time. Formal reappointment is required for continuation in the second year and again in the third year. Successful completion of training entitles students to take the Family Practice Board examinations. Passing, they become licensed, board-certified family practitioners.

The residency year starts in July, and as it unfolds four institutionally required processes occur that affect the experience of interns like Dr. Thieu. First is the process of scheduling. Many institutional pressures exist for scheduling to be done on a long-term rather than a month-by-month basis. Thus, in Dr. Thieu's program, the Residency Director drew up the entire year's schedule for residents at the beginning of the residency year. In this schedule, each resident received a particular sequence of rotations: for example, a month in the NICU, a month on the family medicine ward, a month in clinic, and so on.

A second yearly process is for residents to carry out the work of the scheduled rotations. Each month as they change to new assignments they must adapt to new people, work organization, and medical problems. Every rotation has its own monthly and daily schedule of routine events each of which involves standard types of interaction with patients and fellow professionals.

As the interns proceed through their scheduled rotations, the third required process is an ongoing evaluation of their performance. Evaluation must determine how much responsiblility can be entrusted to the resident in caring for patients and whether the resident is making adequate progress in training. In accord with national requirements, every resident is evaluated on a monthly basis at the end of each rotation by a supervisor who must fill out a standard evaluation form about the resident's performance. These evaluations are shown to the residents and kept in their file. Also, each resident undergoes a biannual evaluation by the Training Committee when all the monthly evaluations together with other information, are discussed to decide the resident's overall status in the program — whether the resident should be dismissed, promoted to the next training level, and so on.

Linked to the evaluation of residents is the residency's fourth yearly process, recruitment. At the end of the training year individual residents move out of their positions at one training level, and new individuals must be recruited to fill the positions at that level for the following year. To fill its first year slots with suitable interns each program competes for recruits in a national labor market, through a process called the National Residency Matching Program. To fill second and third year positions, however, a program will seek recruits from among its own residents, promoting individuals who have finished training at one level to fill open slots at the next. The decisions about promotion and offers of contracts are made nationally in January or February. This is normally late enough in the training year for programs to judge whether residents are qualified for promotion, and yet it is still early enough to minimize departures of qualified residents from the program and to avoid the problems of last minute recruitment when suitable candidates have disappeared from the market.

In Canyonville then, Dr. Thieu entered a training system based on nationally established curricular requirements and having an established yearly rhythm of activity. At the beginning of the training year, residents are scheduled for a string of monthly rotations in which they work under supervision in a series of clinical settings. In each new clinical setting the intern must adapt to a new set of persons and new expectations about authority, cooperation, and care for patients. As an apprentice the intern's performance is under continuous formal and informal evaluation as the training proceeds. Toward the middle of the training year, as part of the yearly process of promotion and recruitment, a comprehensive review and evaluation is made of the resident's performance in order to decide whether the intern should be terminated at the end of the year, offered a contract to continue at the next training level, or whether some other option such as probation and delay should be taken.

Figure 1 outlines the particular form which this general process took in Thieu's internship. As it shows, his first six months comprised a kind of "honeymoon period" without significant trouble, when his standing as an intern was intact. In his seventh month, however, after the transfer to the NICU, a crisis occurred and he was put on probation.

FIGURE 1: Dr. Thieu's Internship Year

July-Dec.	The Honeymoon	Clinic, Nursery, Sports Medicine
January	The Crisis	NICU
Feb.–April	Probation	Family Medicine Ward, Clinic
May–June	Leave of Absence	Remedial Work
July	Probation Lifted	Family Medicine Ward

It appeared he might be terminated from the program. However, by force of character and with the program's support, Dr. Thieu was able to weather probation and eventually was promoted to the second year training level. It is to this story I now turn.

THE HONEYMOON PERIOD

When Dr. Thieu arrived to begin his internship in July 1983, his contact with Americans had been relatively limited. He knew no one in Canyonville which had only one Vietnamese family. He was faced with strangers, and strangers from a culture different from his own.

Dr. Thieu told me by nature he was an "active, outgoing person". He wished to have good social relations with Americans, yet admitted, "I hesitate," and shied away from many invitations to start new friendships.

In this regard Dr. Thieu cited weakness in his English. Sometimes the English language made him feel helpless, and he said he became tongue-tied. Dr. Thieu gave an image of mortal danger to describe this experience. For him being tongue-tied was like being "surrounded, circled by enemies with spears, no way out."

Vocabulary was one of Dr. Thieu's self-identified language problems, something he worked on deliberately long before reaching Canyonville. Part of being tongue-tied was not having the right words available at the right time to express his thoughts.

Also Dr. Thieu identified "a strong accent" as another of his problems. Again this was something he had worked to improve before coming to Canyonville. He had taught himself the International Phonetic Alphabet, was familiar with technical descriptions of English intonation and had analyzed his own phonological habits. When I had an ESL specialist do an evaluation of his English accent, he immediately understood the summary of her findings — a one page description in phonetic symbols of his typical phonological errors and their distribution within syllabic and morphological structure.

Making casual English conversation was the third problem he identified, especially finding topics to talk about. Dr. Thieu liked warm, lively, flowing conversation but found himself unable to find the right topics when becoming acquainted with American strangers. He mentioned with approval that his brother's children were receiving instruction in American conversation in the Los Angeles public schools. This problem with conversation was also something he had thought about and worked on before coming to Canyonville. He had obtained a self-help book on methods of casual conversation from a friend, which he copied and studied. He showed it to me with enthusiasm and explained the author's (very sensible) principles which he sought to apply. He told me he actually planned topics for conversation to avoid becoming tongue-tied.

Dr. Thieu's strong feelings about the weakness in his English, his technical ideas about his difficulty (in grammar, phonology, conversation), and his habit of self-instruction and improvement were all part of his makeup before he actually began the process of adapting to new people and work in Canyonville.

Purely by chance, when the residency director made up the yearly schedule for the program, Dr. Thieu was given a statistically unusual sequence of training assignments. In the first six months of his internship he was assigned only to easy rotations — at the hospital's family practice clinic, the well baby nursery and a nearby freestanding clinic and a sports medicine rotation. Conversely, in the second six months Dr. Thieu was assigned only to difficult inpatient rotations — in the NICU, ICU, and family medicine ward. Because the schedule gave him only easy work assignments at first, it contributed to his first six months being a kind of honeymoon. Because the schedule delayed all of his most difficult work to the second six months, it postponed the time at which his ability as an intern could be truly tested and evaluated. As the Assistant Residency Director explained, a resident's real weaknesses become apparent only under stressful inpatient rotations such as the ICU and NICU.

During the honeymoon period no serious questions were raised about Dr. Thieu's performance. There were no questions about his intelligence, his commitment and motivation, or his judgment, and there was no significant criticism of his medical knowledge. From the standpoint of the program's official evaluation system, his performance was considered sound and his reputation as an intern was intact.

Against this background of normal progress, however, there were signs of difficulty in Dr. Thieu's routine communication — in patient visits, case presentations and group discussions. Though ignored or smoothed over at this stage, these difficulties were precursors to the communication problems that led to major trouble later in his internship.

In the honeymoon period, Dr Thieu told me about three trouble-some incidents with his patients. He recognized his difficulty in communicating with them and wanted to correct it. I was also able to observe four of his patient encounters directly, of which two were videotaped.

The most systematic risk factor in Dr. Thieu's interaction with patients was his tendency to discourage the expression of patients' perceptions. Discouraging expression of patient views and worries is a thorny problem for FMGs operating in American culture (Erickson & Rittenberg 1985) and a classic source of frustration and misunderstanding in medical visits. It led in Dr. Thieu's case, to a mother's crying in one visit and to a misunderstanding which wasted 25 minutes of a mother's time in another. In the four clinic visits I observed directly Dr. Thieu omitted any invitations for patients to tell about their perceptions — for instance, why they came for care, how they interpreted their symptoms, or what sort of therapy they preferred. When patients themselves brought up their perceptions by asking questions or mentioning a new topic, he tended to close off discussion rather than explore the matter. In medical histories he restricted discussion almost entirely to medical points of his choos-ing. He did this by limiting his own utterances to specific, directive questions on medical points and by using listening and turn-taking behavior that limited patients to giving brief answers and prevented them from changing the subject. In closing the visits, Dr. Thieu kept the explanation of his findings to a minimum and didn't check to see if patients understood the explanations or had additional questions.

Counterbalancing his first risk factor, was a positive factor in his interaction with patients — one of friendliness. "Friendly" was Dr. Thieu's term for the qualities of interaction he valued. His friendli-ness came out in response to conflict and trouble. Thus in the three stories he told me about problems with patients, he recounted how he responded to patients' criticism not with antagonism, but with an open, kindly effort to allay the patients' fear and calm their distress. His friendliness was manifest under more normal conditions as well, as in the four clinic visits I observed directly. As those visits began, Dr. Thieu would pay special attention to names, asking when pronouncing them, "Is that right?", and repeating them with satisfaction. He massaged the name, as it were, showing respect for the person's self. Also as the visits opened, he commented good naturedly on the setting and made the child comfortable (with a blanket or through reassuring touches). Later in the visits he complimented the other's person — "Such a strong boy!", "What a young grandmother!" This latter remark elicited a flattered and pleased aside — "He says all the right things" — from a attractive middle-aged grandmother. Finally he expressed friendliness at the end of the visit as well, by lightly touching caretakers and parents, something he did in a gentle way to nearly everyone.

It seems Dr. Thieu pleased many patients. When trouble arose, it was contained by his own kindly, non-defensive efforts at repair and by the nurses who liked him and may have helped smooth things over. As a result, in the honeymoon period no serious patient complaints about Dr. Thieu reached his supervisors' attention. No supervisor, peer, or nurse mentioned any complaints about him to me, nor were any patient complaints noted in his written evaluations.[3] Even supervisors, who stated in evaluations that Dr. Thieu had some "language problems", also wrote that he cared about and had good rapport with his patients.

In contrast to Dr. Thieu's stated concern about communication with patients, it is not clear at this stage whether he recognized the difficulties in his case presentations. In the seven presentations I observed, however, he had difficulty in four. Indirect evidence suggests difficulty was probably present in his other presentations as well.

In addition to nervousness and a thick accent, a repeated problem was not providing needed background information to orient his listeners to the presentations. For example, in one case presentation, given to a clinic supervisor, Dr. Thieu omitted any mention of the patient's chief complaint. It is conventionally expected that case presentations should begin with a statement of this complaint. In the absence of such expected information, the clinic supervisor said she became confused, and eventually she interrupted the presentation to ask, "But why is he (the patient) here?" Dr. Thieu didn't know. When the supervisor later asked the patient's mother, it turned out she had told Dr. Thieu the complaint but he "missed hearing it".[4]

Another problem appeared in a presentation to a second clinic supervisor. As Dr. Thieu presented the patient's case; rather than listen, the supervisor read from the patient's medical record. When the supervisor and Dr. Thieu went to see the patient together, the supervisor again ignored Dr. Thieu's effort to volunteer information and concentrated on examining the patient. The difficulty here was in holding his listener's attention.[5]

A final area of communication difficulty in the honeymoon period was participation in group discussion. In the three discussions observed, Dr. Thieu's level of participation was quite low. For example, at a "core curriculum conference" he approached the teacher privately to ask a question both before and after the formal group discussion, but during the thirty minute discussion itself he made only two attempts to speak. In the first, his utterance began clearly and succeeded in taking the floor, but then he paused momentarily and a more articulate intern with flawless English started up and drowned him out. In the second, he tried to speak but began in overlap with another speaker and yielded the floor. Not participating, being drowned out, and being bypassed because of a combination of shyness about expression, uncertainty about understanding and deference to authority is a well recognized pattern in the speech of newly acculturating foreign physicians (Bruce et al., 1974, Gelb et al., 1972). At this stage, however, neither Dr. Thieu nor his supervisors made his relatively low level of participation in group discussion an explicit issue.

Dr. Thieu received only one significant warning about his communication in the honeymoon period. This came in September when his supervisor filed an evaluation stating that Dr. Thieu was "severely handicapped by problems of communication". The residency director called Dr. Thieu to discuss this evaluation and told him he should work to improve his English.

To make improvements, Dr. Thieu started a night class in English, bought a tape-recorded course in medical English, and reviewed videotapes of his patient encounters with me. Dr. Thieu held himself to high standards of expression. He approached reviewing the videotapes like a man determined to face an unpleasant truth, asking me to be frank about his "mistakes," and himself finding a variety of real or supposed errors of pronunciation, grammar, politeness, and fluency that other viewers had entirely overlooked. Often, he said he would find himself unable to remember the right English word or phrase to express his thoughts. This resulted in his hesitation and search to find some approximate expression (for instance, an English circumlocution, a borrowed French word, or some invention by analogy). Sometimes the very vigor and inventiveness of his effort to find a suitable expression produced bizarre sounding errors (through hypercorrection), and as he pointed out, sometimes the intensity of his effort to speak correctly made his speech even more choppy and hard to understand, and distracted his attention from other important practical features of the speech situation.

Though communication problems were a concern for Dr. Thieu himself in the honeymoon period, at this stage most of his supervisors did not give the difficulties much attention. The supervisors made generalized passing note of some "language problems" in his evaluations. However, they did not describe the problems as significant or serious. Nor, as far as I could tell, did the supervisors talk about the problems together. In the honeymoon period, his trouble had an incipient status only. It grew to the point where individual supervisors privately perceived Dr. Thieu had some language difficulties, but it did not reach the point where there was public agreement that he had a major problem.

One factor that contributed to the slow emergence of Dr. Thieu's language trouble and that later influenced how it was dealt with once it did emerge was his friendly character. Despite the "hesitation", he acknowledged feeling initially with Americans; he seemed to reach easily across cultural boundaries to establish good relations with his coworkers. He did not push people away. He consistently drew them forward. Ship captains, patients, businessmen, and casual acquaintances befriended him. Their expressions of generosity were part of a pattern not marred by one expression of personal animosity.

Among his coworkers it seemed Dr. Thieu's most successful relationships were with females. These women were of all ages, statuses, ethnic groups, and nationalities. Unlike some of the male foreign physicians in the program, who had antagonized the nurses with perceived overbearing and sexist attitudes, Dr. Thieu won the nurses' respect. He expressed kind feeling toward them, for instance, through his habit of touching, which was natural and friendly. Recognizing their wealth of professional experience, he requested their help in his clinic and nursery work. They were pleased to teach him. Also I believe his story of separation from his family and the death of his son at sea helped arouse the nurses' generosity.

In July and August, at the beginning of his internship, the nurses helped him shop and get his apartment furnished.

In September, at the end of his rotation at a free standing clinic, a special party was organized by the female clerk, nursing aids, and clinic nurse (who were black, Norwegian, and middle American respectively) with cake, cookies, and other food to tell him goodbye. At this time (I was invited) the male attending physician, who had supervised Dr. Thieu's work at the clinic (and who had, ten days earlier, made the damaging evaluations of his English communication) said, "You're an easy man to get along with. You can see from this party how people like you. This party is special, not for everybody. You should come back."

A month later in October, Dr. Thieu announced his wife and children had finally received clearance to leave Vietnam and rejoin him after four years separation. The nurses at the hospital family practice clinic and freestanding clinic had earlier helped him with household supplies but his needs were very modest. With the prospect of his family arriving, they rallied to collect further furniture, clothing, and household goods to welcome the family, and a day before the arrival had a housewarming party for him to prepare his apartment.

In the first six months of internship, then, Dr. Thieu by chance had received an unusual schedule that gave him only easy work assignments. There were some difficulties in his communication, but these weren't perceived as serious by his supervisors. He established good relations and won the good will and respect of his coworkers. His performance was considered to be adequate.

TROUBLE

In January Dr. Thieu went to the NICU, his first inpatient rotation and, by general agreement, the residency's most intense training experience. This was the setting where Dr. Thieu's incipient communication troubles were transformed into full blown, publicly recognized trouble, and his standing in the program came in danger. The NICU cares for premature, severely ill infants, most of them extremely fragile and dependent on sophisticated life support systems. Their caretakers must be able to respond to their needs quickly and correctly or they may die. With a staff of 57–60, the NICU is the hospital's largest unit and one of its prime sources of revenue. It can accommodate up to 44 infants. The lights are always on and the unit is noisy. The number of patients and workload can oscillate wildly, from a few stable infants who need only routine monitoring to sudden multiple crises when several infants are simultaneously in life-threatening emergencies requiring immediate, intensive care. Practitioners refer to the unit as "crazy," "a zoo," "a battlefield." "Often we just try to survive to get through the night without anyone dying," said the male head nurse.

The NICU director is a Singapore Chinese, Dr. Wu, a veteran of power struggles in the hospital, who had forced others out and entrenched himself in control of the unit. In the hospital administration I was told he is referred to as "Chinese Mafia". He has a history of conflict with residents. His nurses in the unit and colleagues in the residency describe him as being "extremely demanding," "having a low threshold for problems," "having no patience for repeated mistakes," and very outspoken. Dr. Wu has two physician associates, who share the responsiblity for supervising patient care and night call in the unit.

Beneath these physicians in the NICU are the nurses, many of whom have worked in the unit for over ten years, some since its inception. The NICU nurses have highly specialized training and are accustomed to considerable decision making power, more than most nurses. Formerly, said the head nurse, they were "the keepers of the keys" and made all decisions about admissions, discharge, settings of life support systems, and so on. Like Dr. Wu, "They are a very outspoken group of people", said the current head nurse, explaining "you have to be aggressive here to survive".

Of all the settings where interns work, they have perhaps the least status and authority within the NICU. The unit is not organized as a teaching service, which means it lacks a senior resident. On all other inpatient rotations, there is a senior who buffers relationships between the attending physician and the interns. The senior is responsible for the basic decision making and supervision of interns' work. The seniors take night call along side the interns and may help them with unfamiliar tasks in working up new patients. The senior can lend his or her authority to an intern in dealing with nurse or disagreeing with an attending. No such shielding authority, experienced assistance, or insider's tips, however, are available to a new intern in the NICU. They are on their own in working out their relations with Dr. Wu and the nurses.

In the NICU, nurses are chronically in conflict with interns. Moreover, when discord develops between them, Dr. Wu sides with the nurses. "He can't have 'em bitching and moaning" said the residency director. From special training and experience the nurses know how to do the work of the NICU. Legally, however, before they can do anything for their patients, the interns must first write the orders in the medical record. The interns begin the NICU completely unfamiliar even with the simplest routine procedures and orders. Each month the nurses must suffer their inexperience and

errors. Waiting on and explaining "obvious" things to "green interns" becomes especially irksome in the high stress situation which
abound in the unit where the well being of acutely sick infants
requires quick, effective action. Not surprisingly, under such conditions, the nurses become impatient and problems occur repeatedly.

When Dr. Thieu started in the NICU on January 1, he knew
nothing of this. Because of his unusual schedule, he had had *no*
prior inpatient experience elsewhere in the hosptial. He hadn't
prepared by visiting the unit, learning of its routine procedures,
introducing himself to the director and nurses, or discussing the unit
with his peers or the residency staff. He knew nothing about Dr.
Wu's reputation, the unit's organization, the special status of the
nurses, or their chronic problems with interns. To complicate matters further, six of the seven interns on Dr. Thieu's rotation had
never been in the NICU before. Also, the entire unit was on edge
when his rotation began because shortly before a baby had been lost
in the unit, with the intimation that irregularities in its care had
contributed to its death.

Not knowing the special characteristics of the NICU, Dr. Thieu
approached it as he had successfully approached his other easier and
differently organized outpatient rotations in the honeymoon period.
With his friendly, kind disposition he expected the NICU nurses
would help him as the other nurses had done elsewhere in Canyonville Medical Center. In fact, Dr. Thieu's trusting approach was
almost exactly the contrary of the more wary, adversarial approach
interns need to adapt to the unit. Under these conditions he was
quickly in trouble.

On the morning of January 1, arriving in the NICU, he received a
booklet ("Dr. Wu's Bible") about routine fluid and electrolyte
orders for the NICU babies. Later that morning Dr. Wu met the
interns to explain how to write each order. Dr. Thieu said he
understood. By the afternoon he had begun caring for several infants and had written their routine fluid and electrolyte orders.
When implementing the orders, however, the nurses found Dr.
Thieu had omitted a critical 40 cc portion. Dr. Thieu didn't understand why the nurses asked him to add the 40 ccs. He told me he felt
"burdened" about changing the fluid orders without first being sure
the change was correct. He didn't want to do something that might
anger Dr. Wu. So before making the change he tried to clarify the
nurses' reasons for it.

The nurses thought Dr. Thieu was arguing against their suggestion.
They took considerable time to persuade him. Eventually Dr. Thieu

did add an extra 40 cc portion, but by then it was too late. The nurses had already complained several times to Dr. Wu.

Dr. Wu had an angry, frustrated talk with Dr. Thieu and called the Residency Director, Dr. Smith, to complain. Dr. Smith in turn called Dr. Thieu to his office to discuss the problem. Dr. Thieu explained he hadn't sought to argue with the nurses but only to clarify the orders. Both Dr. Wu and Dr. Smith admonished Dr. Thieu in the future he should check if he didn't understand.

In subsequent days Dr. Thieu's problems in the NICU continued. The nurse said he had great difficulty presenting patients at morning rounds, led by Dr. Wu or his associates. The impression from the nurses' description was that Dr. Thieu became tongue-tied (the nurses said he was intimidated by Dr. Wu). When asked for information about patients or a question, he often answered slowly, followed by long silences. He stuttered and sometimes gave answers that had no relation to the question. Yet the nurses said, he never said he didn't understand.

Dr. Wu felt that Dr. Thieu was making repeated elementary mistakes because of an inability to understand Englaish. On three successive mornings Dr. Wu said he explained how to write fluid orders and gave the interns the brochure explaining the orders. But Dr. Wu told me, impatiently, that by the third or fourth day Dr. Thieu was still unable to do this properly.

On January 4 Dr. Wu brought the situation to a head by again calling the Residency Director, this time requesting Dr. Thieu be removed from the NICU. He attributed the request to problems of communication. Dr. Smith reluctantly took Dr. Thieu off the NICU and in effect put him on probation. He told Dr. Thieu if he wasn't able to improve his English he might not be able to continue in the program.

However, Dr. Smith had by no means turned against Dr. Thieu. "I want to be fair to him" he said. "It's only one service where he has had this serious problem." He said it was unfair to have started Dr. Thieu in the NICU with no other inpatient experience. Dr. Smith told Dr. Thieu he wanted to support him in improving his English and proving himself. He added other residents also have trouble with the NICU nurses. "If it's not their English, it's something else."

Nevertheless Dr. Thieu was now publicly identified as a "problem resident" and his career was threatened. Dr. Smith and the residency Training Committee had to decide whether to dismiss him or let him continue. For the residency, Dr. Thieu's problem had emerged at an ackward time. January was the month when decisions were normally made whether to promote residents and offer them contracts for the following year. But in Dr. Thieu's case, given his unusual schedule of rotations, as of January there was insufficient information available about his performance to make the decision. There was a need to give him more time, both so his performance on the important, more difficult inpatient rotations could be evaluated and so he would have the chance to demonstrate improvement in his English. Conversely, because of the institutional pressure to complete recruitment for the following year, Dr. Smith and the Training Committee were not in a position to delay the decision for long. At most Dr. Thieu had two or three months to prove himself.

AFTER THE CRISIS: RESPONSE AND RESOLUTION

When other residents' professional future and family livelihood is threatened, as was Dr. Thieu's, they manifest strong emotional reactions — intense anger, depression, anxiety (Rittenberg 1985, Rittenberg et al 1986). In response to the crisis, however, Dr. Thieu's behavior did not suggest such inner turmoil. We were friends and met frequently for confidential talks about his situation. Yet I did not once hear Dr. Thieu express anger toward Dr. Wu or Dr. Smith for pulling him off the NICU, nor did I hear him state he had been treated unfairly (he said it was his responsiblilty to adapt to work in the NICU, and he didn't want to criticize the authorities there). Nor in the time of greatest urgency in his situation did I have one meeting with him when he seemed agitated or depressed. At each of our meetings in that period he had something good to say about somebody involved in his drama, and he pretty regularly had some good news to report. He did not seem to be straining to put a good face on things. During his probation, Dr. Thieu worked late at night, reading long after midnight, and going to the hospital at seven a.m. For the first time he said he began drinking coffee to wake up. But when we met, he seemed as alert and fresh as he had before the crisis developed. When I expressed admiration that he could work so hard and seem so rested, he said, "I don't sleep long, but I sleep very deeply."

A story Dr. Thieu told about a painful experience with Dr. Wu illustrates the absence of anger in his response to trouble. It seems Dr. Thieu took the initiative to stay beyond normal NICU work hours in order to ask for Dr. Wu's instructions on how to do an exchange blood transfusion needed by one of his patients. Dr. Thieu had never performed such an exchange transfusion before. It seems Dr. Wu started the transfusion and abruptly told Dr. Thieu to continue. Dr. Thieu said:

> But I didn't know how to four stop, how to operate the fourstop [the fourway stopcock]. Dr. Wu explain very fast very fast. I didn't know how to do. He explain too fast. Finally [he] said, "You have confused thinking."

Dr. Wu then had to take a phone call, so his colleague Dr. Lamb took over the teaching. Dr. Thieu continued:

> I work [with] Dr. Lamb very nicely. No problem. After that I know how to function [the fourway stopcock]. Very simple but [Dr. Wu] explain very fast. Want [me] to do quickly. Dr. Wu first — He's nice. But in this case I was almost started [startled]. First Dr. Wu explain. Then asked [me] to do it. [I was] confused, worried about danger to baby. Confused put the dirty blood back to baby. Felt danger to baby.
>   Dr. Wu a nice guy. Wants to teach. But high expectations. Wants residents to do a lot quickly. Very active. Haste. Thinks stopcock very simple. Thinks resident can handle very quickly. To me this [has] to be learned. Dr. Wu very active attending physician. No want to give me trouble, difficulty, I'm sure of that. He think resident must have very quick. But for me in first days I need to adjust, acquainted with new facility. I am slow to him.

This story is a criticism of Dr. Wu, but in the most gentle possible form, which avoids any suggestion of a personal attack on Dr. Wu. It identifies Dr. Wu as a "nice guy" and explicitly denies attributing ill intent to him. Though it indicates a *difference* of view between Thieu and Wu, it avoids stating Dr. Wu was wrong, and it omits mentioning Dr. Wu's thick Chinese accent as a source of trouble.

Dr. Thieu did not burden others with anger, hurt, or recrimination about the crisis. He did not pressure them to take sides but left them free. Then something interesting happened. Out of the freedom allowed them, Dr. Thieu's coworkers stepped forward spontaneously to take his side, to express their view he had been mistreated in the NICU, and to offer him their support.

For example, Dr. Lamb (Dr. Wu's associate in the NICU) approached Dr. Thieu privately to apologize for Dr. Wu and offer help. She said Dr. Wu is too rushed, impatient, talks too fast, and confuses residents. She said Dr. Thieu should change his schedule to do the NICU rotation with her as attending.

Similarly, the NICU head nurse and former head nurse suggested Dr. Thieu was not a troublemaker, and hadn't been given a chance to show he could adapt and succeed. They too advised he should come back to the NICU when Dr. Wu wasn't attending. Other persons offered help as well.

In January, after Dr. Thieu was pulled off the NICU, he worked for the remainder of the month in clinic. During January he and I made a comprehensive assessment of the causes for his trouble, based on extensive interviews and data from the honeymoon period. First was the obvious need for improvement in pronunciation, grammar, and vocabulary. To work on this, Dr. Thieu began studying English three nights per week at a local International Institute. Second was a need for better orientation to the organization, personalities, and routines of new hospital units. Lack of orientation to the NICU, and especially to the special role of the nurses there vis-a-vis residents, contributed to Dr. Thieu's trouble. To be better oriented for his February rotation on the family medicine ward, Dr. Thieu went in January to spend time at night on the ward with the resident on call. After returning from his English classes, he also read late at night to review the most common medical problems he would meet on the ward. A third problem area identified was that of "interaction" or Dr. Thieu's difficulty with certain sociolinguistic patterns of language use such as checking and repairing understanding, constructing explanations for a particular audience, and others. He and I used role playing and review of tape recordings to work on these problems.

In February Dr. Thieu was assigned for the first time to the family medicine ward. It was at this point especially that his supervisors began evaluating his trouble to determine its seriousness, causes and prospects for remediation. The ward team included an attending physician, a senior resident and two other interns. During the day the interns cared for the ward's patients supervised by the senior. At night one of the interns would stay on call in the hospital along with a senior. Then in the morning the entire team would meet at rounds with the attending to review the situation of all patients, including any newly admitted patients from the night before. Dr. Thieu was pleased with the organization of the ward rotation. He mentioned, unlike the NICU, the ward had a senior resident. He said he and the senior were on call together; she reviewed what he did and helped by "correcting anything inappropriate."

After the first week of the rotation, I asked the Residency Director, Dr. Smith, about Dr. Thieu's performance. He said Dr. Thieu was very hard to understand at morning rounds, even for someone accustomed to foreign accents. The director's first impression seemed to support the criticism from the NICU.

The next day the Assistant Residency Director, Dr. Jonas, stopped me to ask about Dr. Thieu's problems. When I described Dr. Thieu's efforts to correct his problems, Dr. Jonas was impressed. He said he had not realized Dr. Thieu was studying English at the International Institute or reading medicine late into the night. Dr. Jonas said Dr. Thieu wasn't *showing* his reading properly at rounds. "He's in danger", Dr. Jonas said. "The Training Committee has to decide soon whether he should continue. It's urgent for him to show his hard work now. If he's really motivated, he can learn. If I knew he's really motivated, I wouldn't vote against him."

Hearing the urgency of Dr. Thieu's situation and seeing Dr. Jonas' willingness to help, I asked if he would meet with Dr. Thieu to tell him how to show his reading at rounds and perform successfully on the ward. Dr. Jonas said he couldn't promise results but he would try. Dr. Jonas and I agreed the English lessons at the International Institute probably were not meeting Dr. Thieu's needs. He had to find a truly expert tutor to work on his accent. Also I mentioned that Dr. Thieu's efforts to correct his English were so self-critical and intense, they might actually be increasing his mistakes, and I suggested it might best to give him a six months leave of absence to concentrate on language study under less pressure.

A week later Dr. Jonas met with Dr. Thieu to give his advice. By Dr. Thieu's report, Dr. Jonas made all the points made in our discussion — that a decision on Dr. Thieu's contract was imminent, that Dr. Thieu had to demonstrate at rounds he had been reading, and that he should get an expert private tutor work on his English. As of mid-February, then, Dr. Thieu was well appraised of his situation, what he had to do, and he was working hard to do it.

As February passed, however, evidence of Dr. Thieu's communication problems continued coming in. Dr. Smith and Dr. Jonas noted the difficulty medical students had in understanding him. It was remarked he was saying "yes" or nodding rather than acknowledging when he didn't understand. Also senior residents and attendings reported he was not implementing some of the orders about patient care which they gave to him by telephone. Over the phone, Dr. Jonas said, "He led you to believe he understood [the orders]" but then later didn't carry them out. Because the supervisors were confident in Dr. Thieu's character, they all attributed this to a language problem, not to personal irresponsibility. Also in February the senior resident appeared to bypass Dr. Thieu by not explaining some routine ward procedures, which he performed incorrectly until they were corrected by his Senior in March. February, then, seems to have ended with Dr. Thieu's performance demonstrating his good character while also supporting continuing concerns about his communication.

In March Dr. Thieu was assigned again to the family medicine ward. From March 1st through 9th Dr. Jonas was scheduled to be the ward attending supervising the interns' work, including Dr. Thieu. Then starting March 10th Dr. Smith would return from vacation and be the supervisor for the remainder of the month. For the first time they would get the kind of direct experience of Dr. Thieu's performance they needed to evaluate him and decide what to do about his situation.

When the first nine days of the March rotation was over, Dr. Jonas stopped to talk with me about Dr. Thieu's performance. He had a favorable report, which showed the analysis and interpretation he had made of Dr. Thieu's trouble.

First Dr. Jonas said Dr. Thieu was very highly motivated and hard working. Unlike certain other residents, his character was definitely not a problem. When a resident is smart and strongly motivated like Dr. Thieu, Dr. Jonas said, the residency should support his development.

Second, Dr. Jonas stated his evaluation that Dr. Thieu's medical knowledge was below par, but he added that was not serious because Dr. Thieu was learning and improving. Before Dr. Thieu was reading but not showing it. Now he was showing it. His care for patients was adequate. His writeups were acceptable and showed he could communicate effectively with patients to get accurate information. No patients had complained about him.

Finally, Dr. Jonas said he thought he had seen some improvement in Dr. Thieu's English. However, he added others were still having problems communicating with Dr. Thieu. The medical students still had puzzled expressions when listening to him. The senior residents mentioned he was not following through on some orders given over the phone, presumably from lack of understanding, and some attendings were possibly avoiding discussions with him because of his language difficulties.

Dr. Jonas suggested Dr. Thieu must be quite apprehensive about the impending decision whether he would continue in the residency. Personally, he said, he felt Dr. Thieu should be allowed to continue. But he probably needed to do an extra six months as an intern before advancing to the second year level. Dr. Jonas and I decided to meet Dr. Thieu that afternoon to give encouragement on his progress and urge him to work intently on his accent. On that upbeat note, at noon, Dr. Jonas left to attend the Patient Management Conference where Dr. Thieu was scheduled to present a patient. We felt good Dr. Thieu seemed to be overcoming his problems.

At 1:30 Dr. Jonas called to delay the meeting with Dr. Thieu and came back to see me privately. He seemed shaken because Dr. Thieu's case presentation to the Patient Management Conference had been a communicational disaster. This conference is a residency-wide event, attended by all faculty, residents, and medical students in the program, and devoted to discussion of a single patient case from the ward. A respected senior family practitioner led the discussion after Dr. Thieu presented the case. This physician's English is good, Dr. Jonas said. He spoke slowly, clearly. He asked Dr. Thieu several straightforward questions. Dr. Thieu answered but the answers were obviously to a different question than the one intended by the speaker or heard by others. Dr. Thieu did not realize he had misunderstood what was said. The family practitioner repeated the questions, but before Dr. Thieu responded others answered. Dr. Thieu's expression was very prolonged. The medical students looked puzzled and didn't understand him. It was a difficult experience. The twelve or fourteen persons attending had wasted their time, Dr. Jonas said, using an hour for a topic that could have been dealt with quickly with better English. The senior family practitioner (a voting member of the Training Committee) commented that Dr. Thieu's English was weak. Dr. Jonas added his English might adversely influence others' views of the program. Discouraged, Dr. Jonas told me maybe Dr. Thieu might have to go into pathology where there is less need for good English.

Dr. Jonas and I were acutely aware that Dr. Thieu would soon come to meet with us. We decided not to mention the conference to him at all, to stay with our original plan of being as encouraging as possible. When he came, Dr. Jonas told him he had been doing good work. He emphasized the importance of getting expert tutorial assistance to improve his English.

On March 10th, the following day, Dr. Smith returned from vacation to take over supervision of the ward from Dr. Jonas. Dr. Jonas had the difficult task of deciding what to say to Dr. Smith about Dr. Thieu's performance. The decision about Dr. Thieu had to be made soon, and Dr. Jonas with his substantial experience of Dr. Thieu's work and his trusted relationship with Dr. Smith could influence what it would be. I didn't know what balance Dr. Jonas would strike between his favorable impression of Dr. Thieu's progress, mentioned to me on the morning of the 9th, or his much more pessimistic feeling, expressed after the debacle at the Patient Management Conference.

Apparently Dr. Jonas gave a basically favorable report to Dr. Smith. According to Dr. Thieu, when Dr. Smith started supervising on the ward, he told Dr. Thieu, "You're doing good work." He was "Very friendly in discussion" Dr. Thieu said. Then Dr. Smith and Dr. Jonas together emphasized to Dr. Thieu he should follow my advice and get special English instruction at the university. Two weeks later Dr. gave me his view of Dr. Thieu's communication. He estimated Dr. Thieu understood about 25% of what's going on at rounds. This is "dangerous for patients." We decided Dr. Thieu should go for a comprehensive English assessment at the university.

Two days afterward I called Dr. Thieu and he announced good news. He was excited and pleased. The Training Committee had made a favorable decision for him.

> Dr. Smith made arrangements at English Language Center. Yesterday [I] went there. The Training Committee [met to] evaluate me. Hardworking, conscientious, reading good. Dr. Jonas very important evaluation. [The] problem was English. Give me three months leave of absence to study. When I return, [they'll evaluate my English], then continue if good.
> Try for full benefits, ask [hospital] for free housing for three months for family.... [I met] Director of English Language Center yesterday. He is *optimistic*. Evaluation [was] 1) writing test 2) reading 3) writing and speaking. [He] knows main problem. Will assign language expert. Twenty to twenty-five hours a week. Fifteen or twenty hours with him. Live with an American.
> When [I] arrived in United States, wanted $900 to attend intensive English in Los Angeles. Couldn't have. No money.... No [this wouldn't happen] elsewhere. The financial official of hospital, give official rental deferment, benefits, insurance. No other place that's so nice. Kindness, [use their] power. All nice to me.

This expression of gratitude was typical of Dr. Thieu.

Later Dr. Smith told me he had given the Training Committee three options about Dr. Thieu — either immediate termination, termination after completing the internship year, or a chance to correct the language problems and continue in the second year. Playing the devil's advocate, Dr. Smith acknowledged Dr. Thieu's communication problems were "quite major." However, Dr. Smith argued "we hired him, we owe him the chance" and the committee agreed to Dr. Thieu's leave of absence. While studying English, Dr. Thieu worked three nights a week and all day Saturday at the pediatric emergency clinic for half salary. Also to help him support his family, his rent would be deferred and benefits continued.

Two months later I met Dr. Smith who said Dr. Thieu was back from language training. His comments make a fitting end for this narrative:

> Dr. Smith said Dr. Thieu is back from the university. "It's like night and day. He makes himself understood. He understands what's happening. When he doesn't he says 'pardon me' to check. This month he is on the family medicine floor where I'm attending, and I've been with him fifteen days seeing his work."
>
> Dr. Smith said "He worked like a dog six to eight hours a day at the Univesity. Then came back at night for the emergency clinic — twelve hours per day. He gave it his all, real improvement in his English. Gives everything his all, a very determined man. The language training was a success. Now it's much easier to know what he knows than before. Before the language got in the way — left uncertainty. Now it's clear, he knows a lot, a lot of basic medicine. He's bright. As far as I'm concerned, he's over his period of probation. Confident he's going to succeed. The upshot is, his training will be extended for three months. But next month he's going to have a real text — he's on the NICU with Dr. Wu. He says with training he's much more confident — gets less nervous than before, helps him speak. I'm pushing him too. The NICU might not be such a challenge as before."
>
> "He went through hell. He knew the danger he was in."

DISCUSSION

One theme of Dr. Thieu's story might be called "the power of compassion." Much evidence points toward the kindness in his character: his generosity toward persons in his past life, patients in Vietnam he treated for free or the Vietnamese orphans he was supporting in the Thai refugee camp; the absence of hatred in his manner of speaking about the suffering inflicted on him and his family by Vietnamese communism; again the absence of anger in his response to criticism from patients in Canyonville and more significantly the absence of anger toward supervisors (such as Dr. Wu) whose actions threatened his career; the friendliness in his way of interaction with co-workers and patients, including the gentle touches that he habitually gave to others; and his own recognition and spontaneous expression of gratitude for kindness toward him.

Dr. Thieu's gentle response to adversity, without anger, should not be taken as a sign he did not suffer. "He went through hell", said the residency director. He was upset when pulled off the NICU. Getting tongue-tied was painful for him. He experienced a severe threat to his professional future and his family's livelihood. He must have suffered.

Why then did Dr. Thieu not respond to his painful experience with outward hurt and anger, as other residents often do in his circumstances. One hypothesis is that his absence of anger was based on internal denial and repression. This hypothesis assumes he did react internally to the crisis with anger but bottled up the anger inside. In this view Dr. Thieu's outward kindness and gentleness would have been the opposite of the repressed forces within. However, there were too many signs that this was not Dr. Thieu's way of coping — he slept well, was alert and fresh, friendly and gentle during the crisis. He was too easily able to maintain genuinely friendly relations with critical authorities to be struggling, consciously or unconsciously, to restrain inner antagonism toward them.

Instead of the defense mechanisms, I suggest there is an alternative explanation for Dr. Thieu's gentle response to adversity. This was the way supported by his own religious tradition and recommended by his own father — the response of compassion. Compassion, as understood in Dr. Thieu's Buddhist tradition, is above all a way of relating to suffering (threat, pain, discomfort, unpleasantness, unsatisfactoryness), in which the presence of suffering in others and the self is accepted openly rather than ignored, feared, hated or pushed away. The examplars of compassion are not overwhelmed by suffering or defensive toward it. When it occurs they are able to be present for it. This relationship toward suffering differs from fear, anger, and sorrow.

Along with Dr. Thieu's habit of friendliness and kindness toward others it seems he had this inner relation of compassion toward himself. That is, it seems he was able internally to accept the unavoidable painfulness of what he underwent to be present for it without aversion. Rather than use of repression or denial, I suggest it was this inner acceptance of difficulty that helped free him from anger and opened the way for the friendly and energetic practical response he made to his stressful situation.

We have seen numerous ways in which Dr. Thieu's inner habit of compassion affected his outer situation. Because his relationship to his difficult past experience was not dominated by anger or self-pity, he was able to tell his remarkable story with dignity, in a way which won him friends and respect from his coworkers, especially from many of the female coworkers during the honeymoon period. Through his friendliness too, his spontaneous expression of appreciation for assistance, his good relations also were strengthened. During the crisis proper in the NICU, when treated unkindly and threatened professionally, his absence of anger and continued expression of friendliness again helped motivate others to take his side and offer him their support. Compassion — the ability to be truly present for suffering — was indeed a power in his situation.

As well as suggesting the inner strength of a man, Dr. Thieu's story also illustrates the process of social control by which the medical profession responds to major language problems among foreign residents. Reflecting on Dr. Thieu's story I believe we can discern a progression of four phases which may occur in other cases where language problems disrupt an FMG's training. Naturally these phases must be considered tentative, since they are extrapolated from a single case. They represent moments in the process by which an individual's problems are transformed into full blown, socially recognized trouble.

The process begins with a "pre-trouble phase" — a time before significant difficulty is perceived in the FMG's communication. When a residency accepts an FMG, it adopts the hope that the FMG's English will prove adequate for training. The "pretrouble phase" is the initial period when supervisors and coworkers are not yet willing to abandon this hope. It occurred at the very beginning of Dr. Thieu's training. At this stage difficulties in the FMG's English either are overlooked or, if noticed, allowances are made they are not significant. For instance, as comments about Dr. Thieu suggested, allowances may be made that "the resident's English should improve with time" or "his English will be clearer once I get accustomed to it," or "It's OK, with a little effort and patience we can understand each other."

In the next phase of "incipient trouble" the FMG's communication difficulties begin to become more noticeable and significant to supervisors and coworkers. Many factors may contribute to supervisors' and coworkers' noticing the difficulties: increased time with the resident, increased work dependence on the resident or the program director's periodic inquiries about the resident's performance. At this stage, however, no serious damage occurs to the FMG's reputation in the residency. Supervisors and coworkers may keep private their judgment that the FMG has "language problems" or begin to mention the problems to others. If mentioned, however, the problems will not be described as a serious threat to the resident's performance. For some residents, this phase of "incipient trouble" may be very brief. For Dr. Thieu it lasted most of the honeymoon period. Throughout this time his supervisors noticed and were making brief comments about "language problems" in his written evaluations. However, the comments were phrased in a way which suggested the problems were not serious.

In the next phase trouble becomes public and the resident acquires a reputation for having a severe problem. The resident's communication difficulties begin to be perceived as a cause of significant inconvenience for supervisors and coworkers — e.g. as a threat to patients or cause for extra work, wasted time, or embarrassment. Sometimes a dramatic incident (like Dr. Thieu's "misunderstanding fluid orders and arguing with nurses") will cause this to happen, sometimes a chronic pattern of difficulty. As supervisors or coworkers decide the resident's difficulty may be serious, they begin communicating this to others. A critical step is informing residency authorities. If coworkers or supervisors take initiative to tell the residency director about trouble, there seems to be an expectation they should also directly warn the resident about their concerns, but if the residency director solicits their views on the resident, the need for such warning is obviated. As private perceptions of difficulty are communicated, the resident's purported "serious communication problems" become a publicly recognized condition. The resident's status changes from a "trainee making normal progress" to "a resident in trouble". In Dr. Thieu's case, though the residency director had initially tried to prevent this from happening (by keeping serious criticism of his communication confidential in September), in January when Dr. Wu demanded Dr. Thieu be removed from the NICU because of "intolerable" communication problems, the director was forced to make the trouble public by removing Dr. Thieu from the unit.

The final phase in the process, once the resident's status is changed into "someone in serious trouble," is to work out the consequences of this change. A first development that occurs is that expectations of the resident as a communicator will change. The resident's communication will be subject to increased scrutiny. Because of a heightened attentiveness to the possibility of problems, supervisors and coworkers are apt to notice difficulties in the resident's communication that would be overlooked in "normal communicators". The resident also will become more explicitly accountable for repairing his communication problems, being told, for example, "If you don't understand, ask," and being held responsible as Dr. Thieu was, for not asking, and even worse for disguising lack of understanding when it ought to have been repaired. With the communication of the sanctioned advice "be open, ask when you don't understand," the resident beomes subject to many risks: others' misinterpretation of efforts at clarification as "arguing," others' impatience with the clarifications as a waste of time, others' judgment that the attempted clarification reveals subminimal language skills or doubtful medical knowledge, and so on. Thus, although the resident is told to be open about lack of understanding, at this phase he or she may be even more inclined to conceal it than "normal" communicators.

Along with such changed expectations about communication, the other major development occurring after a resident's trouble becomes public is work by supervisors and coworkers to interpret the trouble's cause and practical significance. In Dr. Thieu's case, a limited set of alternative explanations (ranked according to seriousness) were repeatedly invoked by supervisors and coworkers when interpreting his trouble (see Fig. 2). As illustrated in Dr. Jonas' commentary about Dr. Thieu, the work of interpretation seems to involve collection of data and reasoning to determine which among these standard alternative explanations do or do not apply to the resident's problem. Though with Dr. Thieu the explanation of "mental disability" did come up indirectly (e.g. "You have confused thoughts", "He has smarts"), it was not seriously entertained. It would have been the most damaging possible interpretation of his difficulties, since a person with mental disability obviously has no place training as a physician. On the other hand, the possibility of Dr. Thieu having a "bad attitude" (or character defect) was explicitly discussed and ruled out by everyone except one NICU nurse. All agreed, for example, that his character was sound and did not contribute to difficulties like not implementing orders. As to "deficiencies of medical knowledge," there was uncertainty. Supervisors complained they could not judge how far Dr. Thieu's difficulties reflected language problems or a lack of medical knowledge, and this left them uncertain about how much supervision he needed and how much independence he could be trusted with in caring for patients. As regards the possibility of "physical disability" or hearing loss, it was explicitly entertained and ruled out by direct questions about Dr. Thieu's hearing tests. Hearing loss was potentially the least serious explanation for his problems, since it might be easily corrected with a hearing aid.

In Dr. Thieu's case, of course, "communication problems" was

FIGURE 2: Causes for Trouble

1) Mental Disability (subnormal IQ, thought disorder, flawed judgment)
2) Bad Attitude (motivation, commitment, ethics)
3) Medical Knowledge (grossly insufficient for training level)
4) Bad English ("communication problems")
5) Physical Disability (bad hearing)

the primary hypothesis entertained to explain his trouble from the start, and the primary explanation accepted in the end. However, the hypothesis was not definitively accepted until his supervisors had checked and were largely convinced of his "smarts," his medical knowledge, his motivation and sound character, and his sound hearing. It is a tribute to Dr. Thieu that the interpretation of his difficulty was definitely narrowed to "language problems". Had the initial interpretation of "communication problems" widened to include findings of laziness and bad attitude, his situation would have been much more serious. This was prevented from happening, however, by Dr. Thieu's compassionate character and vigorous work.

Two years after the events reported here Dr. Thieu was successfully completing his third and final year of pediatric residency. His family was prospering. He said — half joking, half seriously — this story of his internship was "a terrible truth." He said he had been through a lot.

NOTES

1. The research reported in this paper was supported by a grant from the Educational Commission for Foreign Medical Graduates. For additional information about the adaptation of foreign physicians in the United States and the case discussed in this paper see Rittenberg and Erickson (1986). I am grateful to David Kallen, Ronald Simons, and Frederick Erickson for helpful criticism of earlier drafts of this paper.
2. All names used for persons, places, and institutions are pseudonyms.
3. Repeated patient complaints can be extremely damaging to an FMG's reputation and play a major role in transforming the FMG's status to that of resident having serious troubles (for such a case, see Rittenberg 1985). Dr. Thieu's success, despite risks, in preventing such complaints from reaching his supervisors made an important contribution to prolonging his time of good standing in the residency.
4. If repeated often enough such difficulties with case presentations could lead a supervisor to conclude an FMG has "communication problems." More seriously, difficulties with case presentations may even lead to inferences an FMG has a "thought disorder" (cf. Rittenberg 1985).
5. In an apprenticeship relationship, where a less experienced trainee learns by interacting with more experienced teacher-supervisors, the inability to hold a supervisor's attention during case discussions can limit an FMGs opportunities to learn and seriously dilute the quality of the FMG's training (see Stevens 1978).

REFERENCES

Annas, G., L., Glantz, and B., Katz, 1981. *The Rights of Doctors, Nurses and Allied Health Professionals*. Cambridge, MA: Ballinger.
Becker, H.S., B., Geer, E.C., Hughes, and A.L., Strauss, 1961. *Boys in White*. Chicago: University of Chicago Press.

Bosk, C.L., 1981. *Forgive and Remember*. Chicago: University of Chicago Press.

Brody, E., 1974. A Preventive Approach to the "Problem" of Foreign Medical Graduates: Toward International Standards for Psychiatric Education, *Bulletin of the Menninger Clinic* March, 159–162.

Brody, E., T. Modarressi, M. Penna, R. Jegede, and R.L. Menges, 1971. Intellectual and Emotional Problems of Foreign Residents Learning Psychiatric Theory and Practice, *Psychiatry* 34: 238–247.

Brown, E.R., 1979. *Rockefeller Medicine Men*. Berkeley: University of California Press.

Bruce, D.L., E.A. Brunner, J.M. Breihan, and R.L. Menges, 1974. A Public Speaking Course for Foreign Medical Graduates, *Anesthesiology* 41(4): 380–388.

Bucher, R., and J.G., Stelling, 1977. *Becoming Professional*. Beverly Hills: Sage.

Candlin, C., *et al.*, 1980. *Doctor-patient communication skills: Working papers 1–4 and appendices*. Lancaster, England: Department of Linguistics and Modern English Language, Lancaster University.

Char, W.F., 1971. The Foreign Resident: An Ambivalently Valued Object, *Psychiatry* 34: 234–238.

Emerson, R., and S. Messinger, 1977. The Micro-Politics of Trouble, *Social Problems* 25(2): 121–134.

Erickson, F., and W. Rittenberg, 1985. Topic Control and Person Control: A Thorny Problem for Foreign Physicians Interaction with American Patients. Presented to the American Anthropological Association, Washington, DC.

Feldstein, P., and I. Butter, 1978. The Foreign Medical Graduate and Public Policy: A Discussion of the Issues and Options, *International Journal of Health Services* 8(3): 541–558.

Fikre, W., M. Klein, M. Miller, A. Alexander, and K.H. Tseng, 1974. The Alienated Minority of Psychiatry, *Bulletin of the Menninger Clinic* 157–159.

Freidson, E., 1970. *Profession of Medicine*. New York: Harper & Row.

Freidson, E. and B., Rhea, 1972. Processes of Control in a Company of Equals. In *Medical Men and Their Work*. eds. E. Freidson and J. Lorber, 185–189. Chicago: Aldine-Atherton.

Garetz, F., O., Raths, and R., Morse, 1976. The disturbed and disturbing psychiatric resident, *Arch. Gen. Psychiatry* 33: 446–50.

Gaviria, M., and R. Wintrob, 1975. Foreign Medical Graduates who Return Home after U.S. Residency Training: The Peruvian Case, *Journal of Medical Education* 50(2): 167–175.

Gelb, A.M., and E. Cassell, 1972. Approaches to the Training of Foreign Medical Graduates, *Journal of Medical Education* 47(6): 429–433.

Goodman, L., and L. Wunderman, 1981. Foreign Medical Graduates and Graduate Medical Education, *JAMA* 246: 854–858.

Goss, M., 1961. Influence and authority among physicians in an outpatient clinic, *American Sociological Review* 26: 39–50.

Haas, J., and W. Shaffor, In press. *Becoming Doctors: Adoption of the Cloak of Competence* JAI Press.

Haug, J.N., and B.E. Martin, 1971. *Foreign Medical Graduates in the United States, 1970* (Special Statistical Series). Chicago: Center for Health Services Research and Development, American Medical Association.

Inglehart J., 1985. Reducing Residency Opportunities for Graduates of Foreign Medical Schools, *NEJM* 313(13): 831–836.

Johnson, J.G., 1983. *Physicians in the Making*. San Francisco: Jossey-Bass.

Lassers, E., and R. Nordon, 1975. Difficulties in Postgraduate Training of Foreign Paediatric Residents and Interns in Child Psychiatry, *British Journal of Medical Education* 9(4): 286–290.

Light, D., 1980. *Becoming Psychiatrists*. New York: W.W. Norton.

Merton, R.K., G.G., Reader, and Kendall, 1957. *The Student Physician*. Cambridge, MA: Harvard University Press.

Mick, S., and J. Worobey, 1984. Foreign Medical Graduates in the 1980's: Trends in Specialization, *AJPH* 7(7): 698–703.

Miller, H.M., and T. Lin, 1974. Even Psychiatry Isn't Perfect, *Bulletin of the Menninger Clinic* 155–157.

Miller, M.N., 1971. The Foreign Resident as a Disappointed Person, *Psychiatry* 34: 252–256.

Mumford, E., 1970. *Interns: From Students to Physicians*. Cambridge, MA: Harvard University Press.

Nadelson, C., and Notman, M., 1979. Adaptation to Stress in Physicians. In *Becoming a Physician*. eds. E. Shapero and L. Lowenstein, 201–215. Cambridge, MA: Ballinger.

Pollner, M., 1974. Sociological and common-sense models of the labelling process. In *Ethno Methodology*, ed. R. Turner 27–40. Middlesex: Pargin Books.

Rittenberg, W., 1985. Trouble and Change: The Story of an Indian Resident's Internship in an American Community Hospital.

Rittenberg, W., and F. Erickson, 1986. Guided Self-Study: An Approach to Facilitating the Second-Culture Learning of Foreign Medical Graduates. Final Report to the Educational Commission for Foreign Medical Graduates. Philadelphia, PA

Rubington, E., and M. Weinberg, 1964. *Deviance: The Interactionist Perspective*. London: MacMillan.

Russell, A.T., R.O., Pasnau, and F.C., Taintor, 1975. Emotional Problems of Residents in Psychiatry, *Am. J. Psychiatry* 132(3): 263–67.

Russell, A.T., R.O., Pasnau, and F.C., Taintor, 1977. The Emotionally Disturbed Psychiatric Resident, *Am. J. Psychiatry* 134(1): 59–62.

Shuy, R. *Problems of Communication in the Cross Cultural Medical Interview*. (Working Papers in Sociolinguistics, No. 19). Austin, Texas: Southwest Education Research Laboratory.

Starr, P., 1982. *The Social Transformation of American Medicine*. New York: Basic Books.

Stevens, R., L.W. Goodman and S.S. Mick, 1978. *The Alien Doctors: Foreign Medical Graduates in American Hospitals*. New York: John Wiley & Sons.

Tarnower, W., 1981. Foreign Medical Graduates: The Stress of Psychiatric Residency. In *Foreign Medical Graduates in Psychiatry: Issues and Problems*. eds. R. Chen & A.G. Mazaraki, New York: Human Science Press.

Van Naerssen, M., 1975. ESL in Medicine: A Matter of Life or Death, *TESOL Quarterly* 12(2).

Van Naerssen, M., 1978. *Improving English Medical Recordings by Foreign Medical Graduates*. Paper presented at the Conference of the Association Internationale de Linguistique Applique. Montreal, Quebec, Canada.

Medical Encounters: The On-Going Saga of the Physician-Patient Relationship

A Close Encounter with a Court- Ordered Cesarean Section: A Case of Differing Realities

BRIGITTE JORDAN
SUSAN IRWIN
Michigan State University

INTRODUCTION

Early in 1984, a staff member from the Medical Humanities Prog- ram at Michigan State University asked one of us (Jordan) if she would be interested in participating in an upcoming Medical Ethics Case Conference which was to take place under the auspices of Obstetrics and Gynecology Grand Rounds at a local hospital. The conference would concern the case of a West African woman who had refused to undergo a Cesarean section after a physician had advised her that her baby was in danger. A judge had been con- tacted who declared himself willing to order the section, but before procedures could be formalized, the woman gave birth to a healthy baby.

The conference would be moderated by a well-know physician/ philosopher from the University. The judge who had been asked to issue the order would speak and Jordan was to provide a commen- tary on the case from an anthropological point of view. It was expected that many of the obstetric practitioners in the community would attend.

FACTS, DATA, AND STORIES

Jordan, a medical anthropologist specializing in crosscultural ob- stetrics, was indeed interested. Shortly after the phone call, she re-

ceived an announcement for the conference in the mail. It contained
meager data.

Grand Rounds Announcement

"An African patient, wife of a foreign student, had difficulty prog-
ressing through labor. Internal fetal monitoring at 5–6 cm dilatation revealed
repetitive late decelerations. A c/section was recommended but the patient, with
the approval of her husband, refused to consent. It was their view that upon
their return to Africa, facilities for repeat c/sections would not be available and
above all else, they wished to maintain the patient's fertility. If necessary, they
were willing to sacrifice the life of this infant to insure future vaginal deliveries.
Hospital adminstration contacted Judge ... and he indicated his willingness to
order a c/section. However, the patient suddenly progressed rapidly to the
second stage of labor and delivered vaginally."

Jordan's first thought was: I wonder what it was like for this woman
to give birth in such a foreign environment, hooked up to machinery, with all sorts of people making suggestions and demands she
didn't understand. Or did she? How could the necessity (if that is
what it was) of a section be explained to her or, even more problematic, the implications of a court order? In what sense was her
refusal to consent to the section an informed refusal? What was this
woman's understanding of what was happening to her and her baby?
During the phone call, the difficulties of crosscultural communication had been mentioned. But perhaps there was more to this case
than communication problems with a woman in the throes of labor
who didn't speak English. Or did she? And anyway, how would one
do a section on a woman against her will? Would they tie her down?
And where was her husband? Would he throw himself over his
wife? Attack the doctors? Would they have to subdue him, too?
Would hospital personnel be willing to engage in such struggles? Or
would they call the police?

Other questions occurred to her. What exactly had happened
during this birth? What were the facts of this case? On second
thought, she realized that this would not be a question of facts to be
recovered. Facts are always constructions, always suspect, and in
fact there may be no facts here. It might be better to think in terms
of stories, or different versions of stories. There must be a number
of stories floating around and so far she had only one, the story
contained in the announcement for Grand Rounds. Who else might
have a story to tell?

Interviews

Making some phone calls within the local birthing community, Jordan learned that some staff members at the hospital were willing to speak to her informally. One of them gave her a run-down of the patient's chart entries over the phone, thereby providing some background information and at least one version of the time frame for the events of that day.

The woman is a student at a local junior college; her husband is a student at the university. This is the couple's second baby. The first pregnancy was essentially normal with the baby weighing 6 lbs 13 ozs or 7 lbs 14 ozs (there are two entries on the chart).

3:00am: The couple comes to the hospital shortly after spontaneous rupture of membranes (with clear fluid) and onset of contractions. Contractions are 3–5 minutes apart. 〈These are normal events.〉

4:00am: Dr. A., the staff family physician, sees her between 4 and 5 am. External monitor shows late decelerations to 90. 〈An external monitor is a device, strapped to the woman's abdomen, which plots fetal heart tones against uterine contractions. Certain patterns are considered indicative of fetal distress. Normal fetal heart tones during labor range between 120 and 160 beats per minute.〉 Vaginal examination done by Dr. A. shows 5 cm dilatation. 〈Dilatation refers to the opening up of the cervix which needs to reach 10 cm before the baby can be born. Though there is wide variation among individuals, this process usually takes about 8 hours for a woman who has had children before.〉

7:00am: Vaginal examination by Dr. B., the consulting obstetrician, shows 5 cm dilatation.

7:30am: Internal monitor is attached and fetal heart tones look better. Variable decelerations as low as 120, generally fetal heart tones are around 150. Better pattern when sitting up. Dr. B. notes on chart: "repetitive late decelerations with good beat-to-beat variablility. Good quality contractions lasting 30–40 seconds. Secondary arrest with failure to progress." Dr. B. recommends section. Parents refuse.

9:00am: Vaginal examination done by a resident between contractions: 5 cm dilatation. Contraction are of good quality but irregular. The possibility of administering oxytocin is discussed. 〈Oxytocin is a drug which stimulates uterine contractions〉.

10:45am: Nurse suggests nipple stimulation to produce natural oxytocin. Deceleration of fetal heart tones to 60 for about 10 minutes. During one contraction a vaginal check by a resident shows 7–8 cm dilatation.

12:30pm: Dilatation complete. Patient transferred to delivery room.

13:26pm: Baby born with Apgars of 8 and 9. 〈An Apgar score is a measure of the physical state of the newborn. A perfect Apgar score is 10, with anything below 7 considered indicative of fetal distress.〉

What kind of a story is being told in the chart? A section is recommended as early as 7:30am, after only four and a half hours of labor, because of "late decelerations" and "secondary arrest." What about the slowing down of the fetal heart tones? There are three different pieces of information, three separate events here.

First, low heart tones are ascertained by the external monitor at 4am. This looks "ominous" (as the medical jargon goes) if the monitor accurately reflects the condition of the baby. However, it is well known that external monitors often indicate that there is something wrong even when there isn't. Second, when the more accurate internal monitor is attached at 7:30am, the fetal heart tones are much better than before. They now range between 120 and 150 ⟨a range of 120 to 160 beats per minute is considered normal⟩. Later, at 10:45am, after nipple stimulation, there appears to be a real drop in fetal heart tones, but this was long after the recommendation for a section had been made.

How, then, did the consulting obstetrician come to recommend a section some time between 7 and 8am? His decision seems to have had less to do with the fetal heart tones than with the "arrest of labor," the failure to show documentable progress, the view that dilatation had stopped at 5 cm. But had it? There are some fine points buried in the chart. For example, it matters whether one checks for dilatation during or between contractions. Between contractions the examination tends to be less painful but also gives a lower reading, so that 5 cm measured *between* contractions at 9am might well have been progress over 5 cm measured *during* a contraction at 7am. Whether the obstetrician took other criteria for judging progress into account as well, such as thinning of the cervix and descent of the fetus, is not evident from the chart.

The chart, interestingly, also says nothing about the drama that must have developed meanwhile in hospital corridors and over telephone lines. Who called whom concerned about what? To suggest what? The chart is silent on how this labor, which under different circumstances might have been characterized as normal, was transformed into a life-threatening situation requiring the intervention of a court.

Another thing that is not clear from the chart (nor does it ever become clear) is what information the person who called the judge drew on. Was it the low fetal heart tones (down to 60) that coincided with the nipple stimulation, which was tried, presumably, in an effort to get this birth moving? But then who knows why the fetal heart tones dropped. By this time the couple must have been under considerable pressure to agree to the section, exactly the kind of psychological stress that tends to disturb labor (Sosa et al. 1980).

One wonders what other information was available or was sought by the staff. How had the labor gone with this woman's first child? This might be important because of individual variation in labor patterns. Had fetal scalp blood sampling been done? ⟨This is a procedure which increases the predictive power of electronic fetal monitoring data by checking the acidity level, indicative of oxygen saturation, of the fetal blood.⟩

Within the next few days, further interviews yielded some additional information as well as a number of assessments and opinions:

Fetal scalp blood sampling is not done at this hospital. The couple's first birth had taken a similar course. A section had been recommended but the woman had resisted and had given birth normally.

One staff member was impressed with the woman's firm conviction that she did not want to have a section. Ever. Her husband, who was present throughout the labor, was in full agreement. This staff member had talked to the woman alone as well as with her husband present. Neither of them had trouble communicating in English. Neither ever wavered in their conviction. However, they became increasingly upset under the pressure. This staff member's view was that the woman had progressed slowly but steadily throughout the morning. The section was discussed at the shift change at 8am. Neither the primary physician in charge nor the resident on the floor nor the parents knew anything about contemplated legal intervention.

One pediatric resident took it upon himself to talk to the parents at least twice, trying to change their minds. He assured them that they would be consumed with guilt later if they did not consent to the section. Other staff members told him to lay off. At least some staff members believed that all that disturbance and the anxiety it generated may have contributed to the irregularities in the fetal heart tones.

It appears that the nurses reported the parents' refusal to the hospital administration who set the legal machinery in motion. Staff speculated whether the parents ever knew anything about the court order (or about their case being the topic of Grand Rounds, for that matter.) They also wondered if any of the surgeons (other than Dr. B., presumably) would have done the section on an objecting mother. Could reluctant physicians be subject to a court order as well? For nurses, this situation contained further troublesome elements. Would they be called upon to restrain the mother? And if they were unwilling to do so, to what extent would this impair their working relationship with physicians?

Hospital administration was very concerned about getting adequate documentation in case of subsequent legal trouble. They wanted the obstetrician to get the woman and her husband to sign a document stating that their refusal of a section could lead to a brain-damaged child or even the child's death. The husband asked if brain damage and death were not also possible with a section; when the obstetrician replied yes, the husband said he would only sign if that information were added to the document. The obstetrician said he would do that. This was very upsetting to the couple since it occurred at the time the woman had completed dilatation and was in the process of being transferred to the delivery room. In the end, neither signed anything. The baby weighed 8 lbs 6 ozs and was in good condition.

If we compare the "story" obtained from interviews with the "story" contained in the announcement for Grand Rounds, we note some inconsistencies. The announcement indicates that the patient was "in trouble." From reading it, it is easy to assume that the section was recommended after some period of internal monitoring. This conflict with interview information suggests that a section was discussed with the parents at or before the time the internal monitor was attached. Similarly, the formulation "the patient suddenly progressed rapidly" is not supported by the interview and chart data. After 9 o'clock, there is steady progress, from 5 cm to 7–8 cm at 10:45 and to 10 cm at 12:30. There is also no indication in the interviews that the couple were willing to "sacrifice the life of this infant to insure future vaginal deliveries." Rather, it appears that the couple's experience during their first birth played a major role in their decision. We have, then, two accounts of the same event which differ not only in the "facts" but also in the interpretation which these facts suggest.

Grand Rounds

Grand Rounds was a breakfast meeting. The room was buzzing with nurses, doctors, medical social workers and other staff, seated around a U-shaped arrangement of tables, catching up on news while attacking their breakfasts. A physician who specializes in medical ethics opened the meeting.

> He pointed out that Cesarean sections have been ordered by courts elsewhere in the country and are rumored to be increasing in Michigan. He speculated about parallels between the present case and others which involve surgical procedures for the benefit of the unborn child. For example, should a woman have to undergo an operation so that fetal surgery can be performed to correct fetal defects known through amniocentesis? Going one step further he asked, suppose that a woman has a 12-year-old child who needs a kdney transplant to survive and the mother provides the best tissue match. If she refuses, would it be proper to order her to "donate" a kidney against her will? And extending this line of reasoning, he asked if the court should have the right to incarcerate a woman who drinks, smokes, uses drugs or otherwise engages in behavior which is known to adversely affect the fetus. He challenged those who would argue that it is the mother's obligation to undergo increased risk to her own health in order to produce the best possible health outcome for her child, to state clearly where they would draw the limits of that line of argument.

These comments broaden the picture by pointing to the significance of this particular case within the ongoing debate about fetal versus maternal rights. This debate is typically conducted in medicalized language, (i.e. in terms of mortality and morbidity), and we note in the moderator's remarks the emphasis on physical risk for the woman versus physical risk for the fetus. Other concens or decision criteria which might be relevant, such as women's knowledge about the functioning of their bodies during birth, their concern for bodily integrity, their religious beliefs, the risk of this surgery versus the need to care for existing children, and the like, are not considered.

Then the judge spoke:

He prefaced his remarks by making two observations. First, due to the nature of this case, the time for reflection, analytical thought and consultation both with research attorneys and legal treatises was lacking. As a matter of fact, when his office was contacted at 12:05pm, he was out to lunch. His assistant found him at the local Big Boy, and negotiations were conducted over the phone, with short-order cooks yelling in the background. Second, a court order per se was never issued. Rather, there was a conversation with a particular doctor in which the doctor described circumstances which then existed. The judge questioned him as to whether the facts he had at his disposal were sufficient to ensure that the only method for saving the life of the fetus was a C-section.

In the view of the judge, the issue of nonconsensual operative procedures initially raises the question whether the health professional has committed assault and battery; that is, can the patient claim an unconsented bodily invasion? He thought that the clearest illustration of this issue occurs if the surgeon, while operating, encounters an additional or different situation than originally anticipated. Certainly, he said, common sense and medical wisdom would dictate that the surgeon not sew up the patient, secure a new consent and reoperate. The initial consent for the specific operative procedure implies consent for any other necessary procedures encountered in the surgery. Thus non-consent is not necessarily equated with assault and battery.

Procedurally, the judge continued, a patient entrusts himself or herself to the health care professional for a specific medical result. For example, in a hernia operation the patient wants the hernia repaired and doesn't care about the specific method the surgeon uses for sewing up the abdominal wall. The choice of method is up to the health professional. In the present case, too, we must focus on the desired result. Is it the delivery of a medically healthy baby? If so, the method for delivering that baby should be left to the health care professional.

The judge also pointed out that in this case it was not speculation but hard data from obstetric technology which formed the basis of the medical decision. He indicated that this weighed heavily in his decision.

If the patient retains the right to dictate his or her own care, including the method or procedure of care, what happens when it conflicts with the judgment of the health care professional? In order to avoid malpractice, the judge indicated, the physician must exercise the same degree of skill and learning ordinarily possessed and exercised under similar circumstances by other members of the profession. He argued that the doctor's legal duty should prevail over the patient's right to self-determination — particularly where the patient's demands are medically unthinkable, unreasonable or irrational.

What, then, asked the judge, are the woman's rights to dictate a procedure which may jeopardize the life of a full-term fetus? The United States Supreme Court, in Roe vs. Wade, ruled that in the last trimester of pregnancy the state has a strong and compelling interest in protecting a viable fetus. Therefore, he argued, the mother's right of decision must be weighed against the rights of the unborn. He drew an analogy with court orders for blood transfusions for children of Jehovah's Witnesses, where the state's interest in preserving the life of a child overrides the rights of non-consenting parents. Just as in the blood transfusion cases, the full-term fetus has a right to life which the state must fully accord.

Furthermore, he observed, the present case becomes even more complicated when we realize that while the risk to fetal life was lessened by cesarean surgery, the risk to the life or health of the mother was increased by the same surgical procedure. Thus, relief of stress on the child increased stress on the mother. He emphasized that it is incumbent upon the health care professional to examine as much data from the various personnel, monitoring devices and patient history as is possible in the short amount of time available. This documented information and the health care professional's good judgement will dictate whether the cesarean should be performed. Although he recognized that the result may appear to be shockingly invasive to many, he emphasized that the law would look at the medical decision in light of what was known at the time the decision was made — not what happened after the fact.

He then turned to the "cultural question," i.e. what to do with persons whose cultural values differ from those of the dominant Western culture. The judge thinks that this is a non-issue. A double standard cannot exist, either in medical or in legal pactice. We apply our standards, he said; we don't care where people are from; we don't care what they believe. An alien who commits a crime in this country is treated according to American legal standards. Similarly, the specter of havoc, malpractice suits and tragic medical results dictates that only one medical standard of care can be employed. He suggested that we should instead extend sympathy to the individual and concern ourselves with securing better informed consent in these situations.

Lastly, he asked, is there a universal ethic which has ready application to the health care professional faced with a situation similar, legally and ethically, to the one under discussion? He argued that we, in our Western culture, believe that our paramount concern must be the preservation of life. This should be our guiding principle to be weighed against cultural differences, religious differences and seemingly unreasonable and illogical refusal to follow a health care professional's advice.

Anthropologists are often concerned with culture-specific beliefs and knowledge. Within any society, a people's way of doing things appears natural; indeed, it appears to be the only way to do things. What is striking about the judge's remarks is his uncritical acceptance of his own society's views. He subscribes to some culture-specific notions about the nature of birth which are widely shared in the United States, though not necessarily in other countries (Jordan 1983). In this society, birth is generally defined as a medical event. As a consequence, relevant, authoritative knowledge is seen as owned by medical specialists. It follows then that birth is most appropriately managed by recourse to medical technology and surgery.

The judge fully subscribes to this view and sees it as the only reasonable, if not the only possible one. In contemplating the court order, he relied on the judgment of the obstetrician. Furthermore, he considered this judgment unproblematic. According to his testimony, he asked the physician whether, in his best professional opinion, a section was necessary to save the life of the infant; and when he received an affirmative answer he agreed to order the section. That he saw this single opinion as definitive of the situation has much to do with cultural notions about the nature of birth and about the allocation of management decisions. The judge saw this particular physician as a representative of the profession whose members know about such things and had no reason to question the adequacy of the medical assessment, especially since he believed that this assessment was based on fetal monitor data (though we have seen earlier that it was probably failure to progress that was the primary reason for the section recommendation). In some sense, the judge simply followed doctor's orders, something that is culturally appropriate in situations defined as medical. We note, however, that the obstetrician's assessment was not necessarily the only possible one. At least some of the medical staff had considered the labor as within normal limits ("slow but steady progress throughout the morning").

Given the weight accorded to obstetric technology, one might want the judge to be better informed about the degree to which fetal monitor data reflect the true state of the fetus. Minimally, he might have questioned the physician as to the reliability of the data. There exists a body of biomedical research which shows that fetal monitoring in routine labor does not provide data which lead to improved outcomes, particularly if not supplemented by fetal scalp blood sampling (Banta and Thacker 1979).

Congruent with the cultural definition of birth as a medical event, the judge equates the situation of a woman in labor with that of a patient, specifically that of an unconscious surgical patient who has put herself into the hands of a physician and cares only to awake from surgery delivered of her problem. His analogy breaks down when we ask if a fully conscious woman can be equated with a surgical patient under anesthesia. In the latter case, the physician is to make the decision which he thinks the patient would make if she were conscious and had all the facts at her or his disposal. This scenario does not apply in the present case.

While the judge argues that the initial consent to surgery implies consent to any other procedure that might become advisable, there are certainly countervailing opinions, viz. the idea, gaining prominence, that a surgeon cannot remove a breast when doing exploratory surgery, or a uterus during an appendectomy without the woman's specific consent. Such procedures are only permitted when the woman's life is at stake.

The judge asserts that the choice of method is up to the physician. While in surgery such details as the type of suture used may be of no interest to the patient, for a woman in labor method does matter. For many women, childbirth is a process, something they do, not something that is done to them; thus the argument that women should only be interested in the outcome, "a medically healthy baby," seems inappropriate. While it may be necessary for an unconscious surgical patient to delegate responsibility, the case is different with a woman in childbirth who may want to, and more importantly, may well be able to retain a major portion of the decision-making power. The question here is whether a woman should "give birth" or "be delivered." In this society there is a common notion that childbirth should be delivery and that delegation of responsibilities to medical practitioners is appropriate. For those who subscribe to this construction, any resistance to medical judgment appears illegitimate, indeed "unthinkable, unreasonable, or irrational." The judge holds this notion, as do the medical professionals.

Regarding the judge's argument as to the state's "strong and compelling interest" in the fetus during the third trimester, one might consider that the Roe vs. Wade decision does not sanction bodily invasion. It merely requires maintenance of the status quo, that is, the pregnancy. An alternative argument might proceed from the fact that courts have been generally unwilling to order bodily invasion. For example, the Massachusetts Supreme Court refused to order a cerclage ⟨a comparatively minor procedure involving putting stitches into the cervix to maintain a pregnancy⟩ against a woman's objections (Taft vs. Taft 1983). Courts have consistently refused to order parents to undergo surgery for the benefit of living children as, for example, in bone marrow transplants or organ donations (Annas 1982). If such orders are not legal for the benefit of a living child, they certainly should not be legal for an unborn fetus.

The judge mentions that the risk to the life and health of the mother must be balanced by the risk to the fetus. Yet, while he ascertains the medical opinion that the fetus will perish unless the section is performed, there appears to be no equivalent exploration of the risks to the mother. Though maternal death in childbirth is rare, death in section is between 2 and 30 times more frequent than in vaginal birth. There is also substantial maternal morbidity in sections. Particularly, infection occurs in up to 50% of cases when preceded, as here, by internal fetal monitoring (Banta and Thacker 1979, Marieskind 1979).

The question of what rights patients have in medical interactions is usually covered under the concept of informed consent. The informed consent doctrine is based on two principles. The first is the concept of the "fiduciary relationship," which occurs when one person places a special trust in others by virtue of their office. A fiduciary relationship requires acting in the best interest of the person who places the trust. The second principle is "patient self-determination." Legally competent persons have the right to decide what is to be done to their bodies and cannot to compelled to accept treatment that they do not wish (Miller 1980). Both principles suggest that the woman's wishes must be taken seriously.

One might also ask what moral, if not legal, jurisdiction one society has over members of another. The judge's position on this question is clear. For him, there are no legal double standards. Would we subscribe to his argument so easily if this principle were applied to an American woman traveling in China, pregnant with her third child, and the Chinese tried to force her to have an abortion (something that is sanctioned for citizens of that country)? In particular, if this woman had no intentions of living in China, just as the African couple had no intentions of staying in the United States, would we consider the application of Chinese law morally defensible?

CULTURES AND SOCIAL REALITIES

This case, of course, raises a large number of issues. Some of these are related to the particulars of the case and the circumstances of the woman, of the couple, who found themselves in the predicament we have described. During Grand Rounds, Jordan addressed primarily those. However, there are also larger questions which a medical anthropologist would want to consider. We will include two of these in our discussion: the question of different cultural meaning systems and the issue of the social construction of reality.

Interaction across linguistic and cultural lines quite commonly involves not only language difficulties (which apparently were not a problem in this case) but also the larger issue of cultural differences in the meanings imputed to objects, persons and events. While we have no information about the belief system of the African couple, we should nevertheless consider that their beliefs may not be the same as ours. There are societies in Africa, Australia and the Far

East where the fetus is in some sense immortal. It existed as a spirit before it took up residence in the woman's womb and if it should "die" it will return to the spirit realm from which it came (Ford 1964). The woman's pregnancy is a way for the spirit to find out if it wants to be born as a human being. It may well decide that conditions are not right, and in that case it will simply try again some other time. Now an ancestor spirit ready to be incarnated is something quite different from a baby whose existence can be terminated. And for parents who subscribe to this sort of belief, what we call "a fetal death" is not the same sort of event as it would be for us. It is not that an individual has died but rather that a spirit has made an unsuccessful try. There is no death in the sense of terminating existence. Communication that speaks about the potential death of the fetus has a different meaning depending on what the fetus is believed to be. In the light of such considerations, the characterization of the parents' refusal as a willingness to "sacrifice" their baby appears inappropriate and ethnocentric. It may be that there is nothing for them to sacrifice.

But even assuming that the fetus has the same status as it does for us, what does it mean to have a section? In our society, though there are certainly some negative aspects, a section is not a dreadful disaster. After all, one in five babies is now born by surgery in this country. On the other hand, we have no idea what such surgery may mean to an African woman and her family. Not being able to fulfill her normal function as a woman may certify her, for all to know, as not properly female, not an appropriate mother, not an acceptable wife. Her husband may divorce her or take another wife. While we can only speculate about this particular woman, it is quite possible that such an event could have a powerful influence on her status within her family and community when she returns to her native country. Considerations of this sort may be more important to individuals from other cultures than the unavailability of facilities for repeat sections.

One might also want to consider what death in childbirth might mean — an event so rare in the Western world as to be almost irrelevant. For this woman, however, coming from a country where death in childbirth is still quite common, it might represent more than a remote possibility. Furthermore, death during childbirth may be specially marked. Among some West African people, it is considered a terrible, shameful disgrace, one that causes the woman to be ridiculed even in death and to be ritually expelled from the community of the living and the dead (Ford 1964). This prospect, which is certainly more in the fore with surgery than with a normal vaginal delivery, could have contributed to the couple's adamant refusal of a section.

What is striking about all of the accounts we have discussed is that the woman's story is absent. There is hardly any information about how this woman, and her husband, saw the situation: they are officially silent. They are not in the medical record; they are not heard by the judge; they only appear as nay-sayers with no apparent rationality and little power to act. From official sources we have no sense of this couple's experience and very little understanding of their choice. Did they, indeed, have different notions of the fetus? What did surgery mean to them? To what extent did their prior experience play a role? Were their views really irreconcilable with those of the medical care providers? The fact that the woman's story does not figure in the official account is in itself relevant. It indicates who is entitled to construct the authoritative version.

In high-technology obstetrics, specialized instruments and machinery provide a kind of knowledge about the state of the event which is privileged (Jordan 1987). Whatever information, knowledge, or wisdom the woman may bring to the situation becomes irrelevant. The crucial information comes from a set of technical procedures, examinations and machine output interpreted by medical practitioners. Inherent in the definition of childbirth as a medical event is the assumption that physicians (the users and owners of the technology) are uniquely and exclusively qualified to pronounce on the state of the woman and the fetus.

Other cases of court-ordered sections that we have examined show a similar pattern. The woman's definition of reality is systematically disallowed (Irwin and Jordan 1987). Yet in all cases where medical staff believed the fetus would not survive unless a section was performed, a normal infant was born, sometimes after many hours of "fetal stress." In none of the cases where we have information about the outcome did the outcome justify a section (ibid.). A judge who knew that the predictive value of medical diagnoses in such situations has not been very high, might be less willing to disregard the woman's point of view. But neither medicine nor law has a tradition of negotiating with non-consenting participants; both have a language, a structure and a social status that demand that recommendations and judgments be followed.

Anthropologists have again and again emphasized the usefulness of eliciting the woman's story, the patient's "explanatory model" (cf. Kleinman et al. 1979, Helman 1985). By giving this unspoken but nevertheless pervasively present account a legitimate place in the negotiations about the management of birth, an adversarial interaction could be transformed into a collaborative form of decision-making.

Our discussion of different "stories" could easily lead to the inference that some evaluation must be made of the adequacy of the stories. This is the wrong conclusion — it is not that the doctor, the judge and the woman are right or wrong in any simple way; it is that they have different perspectives and different information with which to work. The problem is that these individul perspectives are embedded in an institutional framework which legitimizes some and disallows others. Women (and couples) who do not subscribe to the authoritative version, are essentially without support. While family members may be present, they find themselves in an institutional setting which is unfamiliar and over which they have little control. Physicians are at home in the hospital; they are in charge. The institutional setting, with its formalized system of allowable knowledge, where decision-making is relegated to a few, is no guarantor of individual choice, no respector of individual experience. This structural arrangement leads to an outcome which ratifies and enforces the official version of reality and contributes to the voicelessness of women giving birth.

Anthropologists have pointed out that the ethical principles and theories which have developed in Western civilization are expressed in language and concepts based on Western understandings of human natue, the environment and the cosmos (Hahn 1982, 1986). Recognition that other societies (and diverse subgroups within the dominant culture) maintain very different concepts, understandings, and values challenges monolithic ethics and leads us to ask whether "the ethical principles and theories evolved in Western society minister to, foster, or tolerate these differences or ignore, homogenize and destroy them" (Hahn 1986).

What, then, is the role of the anthropologist in situations where conflicting constructions of reality do battle with one another over life, health, and integrity of human beings? Anthropologists may become involved in such cases either as they arise in clinical settings, or, as was the case here, later on, as practitioners try to understand what happened. In either case, the anthropologist's primary concern must be with understanding, communicating, and possibly moderating between, the differing constructions of reality to which participants subscribe. Such efforts are often futile; but in the long run they may contribute to a broadening of medical and legal thinking which may yet lead to a more humane and respectful way of treating other human beings.

ACKNOWLEDGEMENTS

We thank Mary Alfano, Robert Irwin and Ronald C. Simons for critical readings of the manuscript.

REFERENCES

Annas, George J., 1982. Forced Cesareans: The Most Unkindest Cut of All, *The Hastings Center Report* 12(3): 16–17, 45.

Banta, David and Stephen Thacker, 1979. *The Premature Delivery of Medical Technology: A Case Report*. Washington, DC: National Center for Health Services Research, Department of Health, Education and Welfare.

Ford, Clellan Stearns, 1964. *A Study of Human Reproduction*. New Haven: Human Relations Area Files Press.

Hahn, Robert A., 1982. Culture and Informed Consent: An Anthropological Perspective. In *Making Health Care Decisions*. Washington, DC: President's Commission for the Study of Ethical Problems in Medicine and Biomedical and Behavioral Research. Volume III.

Hahn, Robert A., 1986. Perinatal Ethics in Anthropological Perspective. Forthcoming In *Ethical Issues at the Outset of Life*, eds. William Weil and Martin Benjamin, Boston: Blackwell Scientific Publications, Inc.

Helman, Cecil G., 1985. Communication in Primary Care: The Role of Patient and Practitioner Explanatory Models, *Social Science and Medicine* 20(9): 923–931.

Irwin, Susan and Brigitte Jordan, 1987. Knowledge, Practice and Power: Court-Ordered Cesarean Sections. *Medical Anthropology Quarterly*, 1(3) (in Press).

Jordan, Brigitte, 1983. *Birth in Four Cultures: A Crosscultural Investigation of Childbirth in Yucatan, Holland, Sweden and the United States*. 3rd Edition. Montreal: Eden Press.

Jordan, Brigitte, 1987. The Hut and the Hospital: Information, Power and Symbolism in the Artifacts of Birth. *Birth: Issues in Perinatal Care and Education* 14(1) 36–40.

Kleinman, Arthur, Leon Eisenberg and Byron Good, 1979. Culture, Illness, and Care: Clinical Lessons from Anthropologic and Cross-Cultural Research, *Annals of Internal Medicine* 88(2): 251–258.

Marieskind, Helen, 1979. *An Evaluation of Caesarean Section in the United States*. Washington, DC: Department of Health, Education and Welfare.

Miller, Leslie J., 1980. Informed Consent: I–IV. JAMA 244(18): 2100–2103; 244(20): 2347–2350; 244(22): 2556–2558; 244(23): 2661–2662.

Sosa, Roberto, John Kennell, Marshall Klaus, Steven Robertson and Juan Urrutia, 1980. The Effect of a Supportive Companion on Perinatal Problems, Length of Labor, and Mother-Infant Interaction, *New England Journal of Medicine* 303(11): 598–600.

Taft, Lawrence v. Susan Taft, 1983. 446 N.E.2d 395 (Mass.).

The Militarization of Cancer Treatment in American Society

DEBORAH OATES ERWIN

Arkansas Cancer Research Center
University of Arkansas for Medical Sciences

INTRODUCTION

Cancer is unequivocally a threatening, aggressive and widespread sickness in the United States. Currently, it strikes approximately 965,000 Americans yearly and the combined five-year cure rate is less than 40 percent (American Cancer Society estimate for 1987). The American population, which generally expects to be cured of most illnesses and diseases, is forced to find a suitable approach to cancer because it has not been easily managed within the traditional "cure" model of the biomedical system. This disease illustrates a failure for American society by posing problems unaddressed by the health care system and fearful to the public. Utilizing anthropological analyses, this chapter will attempt to identify some of the cultural mechanisms that society and the involved individuals are using to confront a medical and social enigma.

Cancer is a mysterious and terrifying disease because its etiology is bewildering, and often it behaves in an insidious and aggressive manner in spite of biomedicine's best efforts. Susan Sontag (1979) has described the myths and metaphors which surrounded tuberculosis in the nineteenth century and cancer in the twentieth century because they were imbued with these dreaded attributes. There is a persistent military and bellicose flavor in the metaphors and terminology regarding cancer. Sontag (1979: 63–64) indicates that because the body's "defenses" are not "vigorous enough to obliterate a tumor that has established its own blood supply and consists of billions of destructive cells," more aggressive, radical warfare is ordered. Radiotherapy and chemotherapy are compared to aerial and chemical warfare, respectively.

Arthur Kleinman (1980:107) also has discussed the prevalence of these war metaphors in the West. The cultural patterning for battle metaphors and imaging is evident in the Hippocratic corpus and filters through the Gallenic tradition to the present. This specific case study of cancer in the United States indicates that the symbolic use of these metaphors in treatment and coping strategies is a very functional and deliberate effort to manage the social and medical liminality of this threatening disease and illness.

When America declared "war on cancer," in the National Cancer Act of 1971, all areas of the cancer experience were affected and an archetypal avenue for coping with an inauspicious situation was erected; in effect a medical militarization occurred. That is, American culture is using military strategy, philosophy, and aggressiveness in the symbols, behaviors and language encompassing the clinical and ritual management of cancer. The cancer patient is not required to "get well," he is only required to fight the sickness. A "good" fight can provide the sick person with the glories of a war hero, and as much self-esteem as any "cured" patient. Medical militarization — portraying cancer as the enemy and developing a host of militaristic symbols and methodologies — is a conventional management technique for society and the sick person in America.

The reification of illness in this manner isolates cancer from other sicknesses and addresses it in the context of a socio-political enemy. This is not necessarily confined to the cancer experience. Researchers may find applications of medical militarization for other life-threatening and chronic illnesses. On the other hand, other industrialized cultures may not address cancer in such an aggressive fashion. Recent research on Japanese illness behavior indicates that there is a defensive aversion to discussing cancer, or even telling a patient of the diagnosis (Ohnuki-Tierney 1984; Long and Long 1982). The medical militarization strategies used in the United States to "fight" cancer are indicative of American cultural views toward other "evils" in the world. On several geopolitical levels — War on Poverty, Vietnam, Central America — the United States has preferred an aggressive, military-like approach. Therefore, the attitudes toward health and illness in the cancer experience are a reflection and extension of basic cultural orientations regarding problems in the world at large.

METHODOLOGY

In order to accommodate the maximum number of cultural influences and varied perspectives of patients, family members, and physicians, numerous tools and methods were used for collecting data over approximately two years.

The research involved over 60 households, 75 cancer conferences, in excess of 1800 hours in a radiation treatment center, 30 hours of "I Can Cope" classes, more than 24 hospital observation hours, the perusal of over 3,000 patient charts, and various other hours spent in doctor's offices, cancer organization meetings and projects. A set of open-ended interview questions and a structured questionnaire were used to illicit specific information from informants.

Patient and Physician Samples

The sample selected for scheduled interviews was drawn from a population composed of seven years of admission records of a radiation treatment center in Arkansas. Of this patient population, 47 percent were from urban central Arkansas, 51 percent were from more rural distant counties in the state. This population totalled approximately 10,000 patients of which 45 percent were expected to be living. It was decided to use a chronologically stratified random sample of cancer patients in order to have an equal opportunity to include patients recently diagnosed, with recurrent disease, recently treated, or diagnosed and treated several years ago.

The "lay sample" was composed of 35 patients plus 29 family members for a sum of 64. This sample was 58 percent female and 42 percent male. Approximately 55 percent of these respondents lived in a rural or small town environment, while 45 percent of the sample lived in an urban setting. The sampling process was intentionally limited to patients aged 18 to 65 years of age in order to avoid the variables intrinsic to pediatric and geriatric cancer and its treatment. The mean age of the lay sample was 45 years. Ninety percent of the patients had received combined treatment — surgery, radiation, and/or chemotherapy.

Questionnaires were also sent to a stratified random sample of physicians. Three strata of physicians were selected in order to prevent specific medical specialists from biasing the results: 1) physicians from the state population, including all specialties (55%); 2) medical, surgical, and radiation oncologists practicing in the central Arkansas area (20%); and 3) physicians who regularly attend cancer conferences (25%). Therefore, the physician sample was almost equally divided between physicians actively treating oncology patients, and those primarily treating non-oncology patients. Seventy-five percent of these physicians were located in an urban setting. Twenty different medical specialties were represented.

Research Methods

Questionnaire and interview results were the basis for one-tailed tests of the research hypotheses, and a *t* test was used to evaluate significant differences between the sample means. These statistical analyses were balanced with qualitative data obtained through the traditional participant-observation method. Biomedical decision-making and treatment-planning by physicians was monitored and evaluated through observation of cancer conferences. The cancer conference is an hour-long meeting once a week in which oncologists, surgeons, radiation therapists, pathologists, nurses, social workers, and other involved medical personnel present and discuss patient cases (and sometimes the patient), in an effort to formulate answers to diagnostic, treatment, and management problems.

Other research tools included evaluation of patient medical records in order to analyze physician-patient relations from the perspective of the physician. These records also illustrated the biomedical patterns of treatment and symbolism. The "I Can Cope" classes offered an observing experience to provide information regarding the concerns patients and family members voiced in a group experience, over an 8-week period. This served as a forum for examining how well the patients and family members accepted, utilized, agreed, or disagreed with the biomedical responses to their illness problems.

As in any field experience, anthropological research in a biomedical clinical setting in the United States requires the same total immersion into the culture. The researcher should be as objective as possible — through rigorous methodology — and also as broad as possible — through holistic sociocultural investigation. It is important to place the illness experience (cancer) within the social fabric of American culture and not simply to examine it as an isolated sickness episode.

Results

Statistical analysis of the research hypotheses indicate 1) that the treatment for cancer is often perceived to be worse than the disease, 2) that there is a significant amount of perceived stigma related to cancer and its treatment, 3) that rituals in the form of daily routines and normalization strategies, are perceived to be positive coping mechanisms, and 4) that patients and family members perceive a need for additional support services in addition to the physician. Although the patients and physicians are frustrated with the inability of current medical practices to cure more cancers, they generally perceive unorthodox treatments and unproven methods as fruit-less. Paradoxically, the research indicates that most cancer patients show continual optimism regarding their treatment and great faith in their physician.

On the basis of these results and analysis, it is evident that there are institutions or culturally accepted methods of aiding and abet-ting the ramifications of an illness and disease which is outside the biomedical capacities of health care systems. On the macroscopic level, American society is developing a chronic sick role which sym-bolically addresses cancer with military-like strategy in order to cope with the stigma and difficulties of this widespread and dreaded disease. Physicians and the patients under their guidance are attri-buting the meaning of enemy and aggressor to cancer and are following a model of knowledgeable commanding officer and heroic soldier, respectively.

THE AMERICAN SICK ROLE IN THE CANCER EXPERIENCE

In her critique of the Parsonian sick role, Linda Alexander (1982:354) asks a series of questions about chronic, interminable illnesses:

> What are the attributes and character of the new American sick role when it becomes a permanent, not a transient, assignment? What axiom can replace the medical caretaker's curative premise? How can the healer fail to cure with sanctity? How can the sick person fail to get well with grace? How can illnesses be maintained creatively and productively?

The attributes and character of Alexander's "new American sick role" require the medical community to maintain the patient and the physician-patient relationship over a long period of time, as opposed to the traditional sick role defined for acute illness. This chronic model for society and the sick individual necessitate exten-sive sacrifices of time, energy, and money. The curative premise so popular in earlier times has been replaced by "mean survival time." Increased survival time and increased response rates to treatment are the tools of measurement in the oncological discipline. The word "cure" is often considered too radical and unrealistic and dodged with some brief reference to a vague time when "we're farther out" from the research. Effective response rates or increased survival are relatively safe goals at which to aim because they are subjectively interpreted and compared to a phantom historical precedent for the specific disease. In battling an infamously feared and aggressive disease, which society has accepted as a "killer", oncologists are seen as tilting at windmills and praised for even small advances. No one expects them to cure every patient. They are only expected to *treat* every patient. The "sanctity" to which Alexander refers applies twofold when a patient is reported "in remission" or "cured." The oncologist is perceived as having single-handedly purloined the patient from the jaws of death — which may be an accurate perception. For those patients he does not cure, the lowered expectations in the face of cancer provide the oncologist a way to preserve his sacredness through a commanding authority of the facts of the disease, its prognosis, and ability to apply his mastery of the therapeutic techniques for pain and symptom relief.

This case study indicates that the physician-patient interactions in the cancer experience often are aggressive, hostile, or fearful, but the patient and physician seldom perceive this as a detriment to healing the disease. (Patients do perceive difficulties communicating with their physician as detrimental to managing the *illness* symptoms, however.) The patients and physicians continually attribute the meaning of enemy and aggressor to cancer. The vocabulary of patient interviews and cancer conferences is replete with references to attacking the cancer: "fight," "aggressive," "kill," "killer," "attack," "invasion," "defenses." At first, it appears that the patients might be fighting the physicians as well, but the data indicates just the opposite. The physicians are seen in a favorable light regardless of outcome. The patients and physicians are allies against cancer.

Cancer As the Enemy: Social Sanctions

Although each person responds in a unique manner to the experience of cancer, there are some attitudes and norms which are culturally sanctioned and encouraged. These responses relate to the meaning which people within a culture attribute to the sickness. In Lipowski's model of "Common Styles of Attributing Meaning to Illness" (1970), the two most common styles of attribution, and the two most sanctioned by the medical community and the public are "Illness as Challenge" and "Illness as Enemy." In 1971, the President of the United States exhorted Americans to accept cancer as the new challenge in his "State of the Union Address": "The time has come in America when the same kind of concentrated effort that split the atom and took man to the moon should be turned toward *conquer-*

ing this dread disease. Let us make a total commitment to achieve this goal" (emphasis added).

Cancer is an insidious enemy, perceived either as an intruder from a foreign source (chemicals, pollutants, etc.) or a traitorous rebel trying to lead some kind of insurgency against the normal cells and tissues within the body. A female patient with thyroid cancer refers to the cancer cells as, "black, greedy little things that eat up everything in reach." Patients say that the "cancer preys on the weakest part of your body," and could "just lay kind of dormant in your blood, then come back at you again." Thirty-five percent of the patients and family members mentioned chemicals or environmental pollutants as carcinogenic catalysts. Seventeen percent believed they inherited the potential for cancer. Fifteen percent thought it was trauma induced, and 13 percent believed stress helped cause their cancer. Other causes included smoking (6%), fate (6%), "don't know" (6%), and hospital tests (2%). In any case, cancer is the enemy which is to be bombarded, excised, and otherwise killed and removed from the rest of the healthy tissues, so the latter can try to repair the damage of the warfare and the pillage.

The medically militarized attitudes and norms which America sanctions for patients and families in this assault to counter the cancer adversary are those of a stoic, brave, loyal, and romantically optimistic soldier. Even if death is the final outcome, Americans illustrate that they want and expect dignity, and maybe even glory. One patient's criticism of another patient's attitude illustrates the expected and desired behavior:

> It was very uncomfortable for us and her husband. She didn't really want to accept the challenge to keep living. Maybe she wanted to die from the breast cancer. My husband and I are not used to losing. We're used to getting what we want and working for it, and that's the attitude we took with the cancer. I'm gonna fight like hell.

The patient and family members are involved in a continuous fight to approach a semblance of normality, to regain their former lifestyles, and to prevent as much disruption as possible; as a sarcoma patient lamented, "I just want to get on with my life ... I just want things to be normal again." This normalization battle is the therapeutic ritual which responds to the cultural meanings of the sickness in an emotionally satisfying way. In order to approach normal lifestyles and manage the distress, there are three basic psychosocial difficulties associated with cancer and warfare which need to be addressed: 1) fear, 2) loss, and 3) stigma.

Fear. Many patients express a desire to hide their fears from their spouses and children. Some patients even refuse hospital visits from family or friends in order to avoid confrontation of their death or diagnosis. One young woman addresses this issue following the death of her husband:

> We never really talked about death. We just tried to live one day at a time, and be satisfied with that and with doing it that way. I think he didn't talk about death around me because he didn't want to hurt my feelings. A lot of people told me that I coped so well. But inside I felt just terrible. I was trying to do so much for him and I couldn't just run out of the room, although that's what I felt like doing. I'd just think, "if he can stand it, I can."

Like the model American soldier, many cancer patients illustrate an unwillingness to show what others might perceive as cowardice and many patients even hesitate to admit that they ever felt fearful. Certainly, the data indicate that there is a general trend for patients not to admit that they cannot handle their problems by themselves and that they might need professional help.[1]

Many times when a patient seems flippant about his disease, or seems to ignore the seriousness of it, friends have a tendency to label this as "denial." It appears to be more realistic and useful to see this behavior as an adaptive use of ritual in which the patient is not denying the cancer, or the fear of the cancer, but rather placing higher priorities on maintaining duties, roles, and abilities as close to the normal lifestyle as possible: "I had to get it [cancer] off my mind or I would have gone nuts." The fear is there — cancer is a frightening experience, just as war is a frightening experience. But it serves no purpose for the patient to dwell on the fearful aspects of his situation, and survival response is to counter the fear with more mundane, daily tasks which allow the patient to have as few disruptions as possible and eventually draw praises from those around him.

One husband explains, "M. has been so strong. She never let on like she was really afraid. It made me feel stronger." Herein lies one of the major bulwarks of strength in patients: they do not want to let their families down, they do not want to frighten them, they want them to be hurt as little as possible. There is an extremely strong emotionalism within the family members when cancer is diagnosed, and the person most responsible, the patient, shoulders much of the burden of strength. Patients express their ideas regarding death, and illustrate how they achieve strength: "I never expected to die," "I knew I had an angel on my shoulder," "I'd just think, 'Someday, you're gonna get out of all of this.'"

This optimism in the face of danger and threat sometimes appears foolish to outside observers. But that is exactly what the family and friends of a cancer patient want and need. Especially in the beginning, the patient and family often face the war with cancer much like soldiers who marched off to the Civil War, World War I and II — with great romantic optimism of an almost mythical quality. As World War I historian, Paul Fussell, states, "No man in the prime of life knew what war was like. All imagined that it would be an affair of great marches and great battles, quickly decided" (1977: 21).

The more the patient behaves with strength, the more positive strokes and reinforcement he usually receives, and the more the patient believes in his own abilities. One male patient with testicular cancer tells of a woman at his oncologist's office who had a son and a daughter with Hodgkin's disease [cancer of the lymph system]. One child had died from the cancer and the other child is living with it and "doing a very good job." The patient says that it was inspiring to see how she handled her problems and how optimistic and friendly she was with the other patients. Another patient with cancer of the larynx says, "If you just go on about your business and don't keep mopin' and worrying over the cancer, people forget you have it and start treatin' ya' like a normal person again."

It is only later, for those patients who experience recurrences or whose disease progresses in spite of treatment, that the reality of the battlefield splits the rosy fog of optimism and the real fear of losing begins to grow. A spouse of a dying patient illustrates the frustrations of coping:

> With each setback we lost confidence in the idea that he would get well. And, with the recurrence, of course they told us it was even more serious and harder to cure. Before the cancer came back, we were encouraged by other patients and friends, and we tried to encourage other people we knew — about the treatments and stuff. Then we got a lot less optimistic as time went on and the recurrence showed up. I can't be too optimistic now because most of the people I knew with cancer are no longer living.

At this time, it is often what Fussell (1977: 21) refers to as the "quiet action of personal control and Christian self-abnegation," which prevails for the sake of "the others" (family and friends). Everyone wants to be able to say, "Even at the end, he still had his dignity; he never gave up."

Loss. Like war wounds, the scars of the battle against cancer take on a symbolic meaning for the patient, as in the case of a 45-year-old male patient undergoing chemotherapy:

The veins in my arms are just burnt up [from the chemotherapy]. But I don't care cause everytime I look at them, or a nurse tries to take blood out of my arm, it reminds me that I'm alive and beat that cancer.

Sometimes the loss of an organ or tissue is the most difficult aspect of the illness to counter, i.e., colostomy, limb amputations, and laryngectomies. One-third of the research sample indicated that physical problems from treatment were the most difficult episodes in their illness experience. The patient and family may spend the rest of their lives attempting to normalize the physical abnormality which the cancer has effected. Patients often carry these losses as a continual reminder of their fight with cancer, and it is a constant disruption of their lives. Some patients wear the loss proudly as a battle scar indicating their ability to successfully fight cancer and "carry on." The American Cancer Society is currently sponsoring a professional model for advertisements and public relations who had had a leg amputated due to cancer. She is portrayed as "walking" evidence of successful treatment and coping strategies.

Other war wounds are concealed and illustrate how well former patients can reintegrate into society. Organizations have been formed all over the United States to help ostomy patients cope with whatever their particular loss might be, and breast cancer patients are encouraged to have their breasts surgically rebuilt or use a prosthesis so that they can imitate their former appearances.

The most mutilating surgical procedures are generally those of the head and neck area. The results of surgery in this area sometimes produce gross abnormalities. One gentleman introduced to the cancer conference had no nose, one eye, and a skin flap from his scalp across his forehead and cheek that was growing long hair. Other patients endure extensive nerve and muscle loss, chronic irritations, and loss of speech. However, some studies on breast cancer patients indicate there is less psychosocial stress associated with the surgical loss of organs or tissues than there is with chemotherapy treatment regimens or the stigma and fear of cancer as an illness and disease (Peters-Golden 1982: 489; Bloom 1982; DeSantis 1979).

Stigma. One of the negative aspects of cancer for the American public is that it stands as a monument to biomedical failure. It is a prevalent disease which is fatal in the majority of cases. This incurability causes the cancer to be stigmatizing for the patient. The irony of a country that can put men in space, even on the moon, but cannot control something as basic as a cell, is difficult for Americans to understand and intimates some kind of moral failure. A patient's husband who works on agricultural research describes his frustration with what he considers less than optimal treatment options:

> If you'd given us ten billion dollars to work with, we'd give you a soybean plant
> that would fill the room and feed thousands of people. I can't understand why
> more of it [the research money] can't be seen in the results of the research.

There is a definite need for some kind of vehicle to transfer the struggle with cancer into a more positive light. Some of the unorthodox therapies attempt to utilize relaxation, positive mental attitude and imagery for this. Dr. Marcia Angell (1985), Editor for the *New England Journal of Medicine*, attacked these efforts to move the failures of cancer into a less biomedical sphere. Dr. Angell castigated those persons and methods which promote the curative use of imagery and positive mental attitudes in fighting cancer. These methods are used in an attempt to help patients feel less helpless and more powerful in the face of cancer. But Dr. Angell (1985: 1571) suggests that these theories are "folklore" and, "The myth serves as a form of mastery . . ." She goes on to say,

> The corrollary view of sickness and death as a personal failure is a particularly
> unfortunate form of blaming the victim. At a time when patients are already
> burdened by disease, they should not be further burdened by having to accept
> responsibility for the outcome (1985: 1572).

On the larger sociocultural level, the answer has been to couch the social and medical responses to cancer in aggressive militaristic terms and, therefore, attach some of the romanticism, challenge, and glory of warfare to a miserable enigma. In many ways, it has been fairly successful. But as time goes on, and the "mystique of death" continues to shroud the disease, cancer is, according to Sontag (1979: 65), fast becoming our new Vietnam.

Specific examples of the symbols of this medical warfare include the American Cancer Society crusade slogan: "Fight Cancer — We Want to Wipe Out Cancer in Your Lifetime".[2] Many articles in the public media use an aggressive, competitive vocabulary of "fighting," "battles," "warriors," and "veterans".[3] A popular advertisement for the American Cancer Society (*Cancer News* 1984) claims:

> More Americans have survived cancer than now live in the City of Los Angeles.
> We are winning. Please support the AMERICAN CANCER SOCIETY.

On the individual level, the stigma of cancer generally takes one of two forms: physical, visible stigmatizing effects; or emotionally stigmatizing effects. The visible effects include the red or white carfusion marks for radiotherapy, surgical mutilation, foul odors caused from the disease, loss of hair, skin reactions, etc. Thirty-five percent of the patient and family member informants perceive the cancer as "unclean." And even those persons who perceive their cancer as just a clinical abnormality ("cells going wild") without polluting properties, believe cancers that could be seen *outside* of the body (as opposed to internal organ sites) *were* "unclean," "dirty," and possibly even contagious.

With regard to the stigma of labeling, 65 percent of the patient and family respondents continue to label a person as "cancer patient" regardless of their physical health status. Most of these persons also struggle with the fear that the cancer is currently dormant, but will be lethal later. These concepts have the capacity to produce many emotional problems. The total illness episode causes a major disruption in the lives and plans of patients and family members.

The sanctioned position is to make a "career move" to being a full time soldier in the battle against cancer. This is the development of an attitude, an approach, a behavior, which friends and employers appreciate and support, and it is the closest a patient can get to achieving normality. He faces the cancer like a new occupational challenge and each battle won is an opportunity to achieve glory for himself and his family. Family members' comments illustrate this pride and heroism: "J. was able to go to work every day of his treatment;" "She never lets it get her down;" "She's a fighter." Coping seems to be measured by how closely one approximates life before the diagnosis. In order to do this, the patient is involved in a constant battle not to give up former roles and responsibilities. Goffman (1963) has shown that the more disruption in lifestyles, the more stigma is attached.

This stigma and fear of the illness and the possible demise of a cancer patient may cause friends and acquaintances to begin separating themselves from the patient's life. Often, people will begin severing even close relationships because they are afraid that *they* (not the patient) will be unable to handle the relationship if, or when, the patient reaches a terminal stage. Statements and questions people make to patients are often intended as antennae. They want to test the patient's attitude and coping skills in order to fashion their own management approach. People may initially expect the worst. But those patients who illustrate a strong, forceful, less fearful approach encourage friends, family, and acquaintances to feel more comfortable with them and to begin reintegrating them into previous roles and responsibilities. Those patients who face the challenge and approach their former appearances feel that they have proved themselves, are proud of their accomplishment, and talk about their cancer experiences like "war stories." Although people might *expect* a patient to look extremely ill and die from cancer, they *want* the patient to look healthy and recover.[4]

Therefore, the therapeutic ritual of medical militarization is a cultural adaptation for patients and family members to manage the cancer experience, to become a part of the courageous army fighting the enemy cancer, maintaining as many normal roles as possible, and becoming an "inspiration" for other patients and people in the community. The patient is encouraged to fly in the face of doom; to say "yes, I am not denying the cancer or its seriousness, but I am not going to give in to it, and I am not going to 'stop living' because of it." That is the culturally sanctioned way of facing the enemy in the United States, and therefore death — in war and in cancer. Dying bravely can become a victory. A courageous fight is what is needed because it makes defeat easier if it can be said that "he fought bravely in spite of the odds." Cancer is made emotionally easier for others if the patient assumes the fighting soldier approach rather than the pitiful pessimistic sick person. One oncologist recognized this issue when he told an "I Can Cope" class of patients:

There are only so many miles in your body — kind of like a car. And some people choose to spend the entire remaining moments worrying and fearing the cancer and its recurrence. Then, the cancer becomes the focal point of their life. I have patients who literally *live* to get their cancer treated. It's a terrible psychological burden — knowing you have a terminal illness. And no one can tell you how to cope. But life's easier if you take a positive approach. There's no reward for being sad and unhappy.

Not only is there "no reward," but there is a feeling of helplessness. If the cancer is approached in a militaristic manner, attributing the meaning of challenge to the experience, the patient, family, and physician can develop strategies, maneuvers, management skills, and rituals which give them the perceptions of control and power. The physician, patient, and family are a team organized to fight and obliterate the cancer. This medical militarization is an excellent Western example of Geertz's (1979: 81) "models of" and "models for" reality. These symbolic structures both depict and shape the experience.

Physician, Patient, Family: Roles and Relationships

The results of the research in Arkansas indicate some very basic differences in responses and perceptions between the lay (patient and family member) sample and the physician sample. Placing the physician, family, and patient roles within the military framework offers some explanations of how and why these clinical relationships function. The patient and the doctor are facing the cancer experience from different parapets, with diverse risks, and varying goals and objectives.

In the attack on cancer, the physician is the equivalent of a staff officer — "the man with the plan" — as one patient with Hodgkin's disease explains it. When asked, "What is the role of a physician?" almost ninety percent of the initial responses from the patients and family members mention taking action or playing a supervisory role. Almost half of the respondents state that the doctor was primarily responsible for a patient's care. The physician has the responsibility of weighing the factors involved and planning the ways and means of achieving his goal. This goal is to defeat the cancer cells within the patient's body and also achieve better methods of treating all cancers.

Ironically, in an attempt to treat the *patient*, many physicians are forced to concentrate on treating the *cancer*, with less regard for the patient. The ultimate responsibility for the consequences of the battle lies with the staff officer, so it is with the physician. Improper diagnosis or failure to treat the disease can mean death to the patient and a malpractice suit against the doctor. Often, even when the right decisions are made, the enemy still wins, bringing criticism on those responsible.

One very important aspect of the physician/officer role is his leadership ability. The majority of patients state that they have great confidence in their physician and his abilities. They would "do whatever that man said." One female patient with cancer of the kidney said, "He plays the part of God and Santa Claus all rolled up together." All training and preparation for war relies upon the soldier responding to and obeying his commanding officer in the heat and crisis of battle. The same situation applies in the cancer life crisis. Physicians must be able to lead patients, like officers lead soldiers. A patient cannot be forced to accept treatment, just like a soldier cannot be forced to fight. This requires almost blind trust on the part of the patient/soldier. Even if the patient is frustrated with the system and the medical options, usually at least one physician is regarded higly and completely trusted. This is essential because the physician, like the officer, is responsible for offering hope and dispelling fears.

One of the primary reasons the patient accepts the judgment of his physician and places his life in the hands of the physician is that the latter is recognized as a highly trained specialist with greater knowledge and facts at his command. Both medical and military leadership positions demand that the individual become skilled and knowledgeable in two areas: the technical knowledge, and the emotional de-sensitization. The technical skills required in oncology are recognized as very extensive, detailed, variable, and controversial. The information available to a trained oncologist is thought to be beyond the capacities of most lay persons, and therefore, allows the physician to dominate treatment decisions. Additionally, this controlled information permits the patient to relinquish much responsiblity when he gives informed consent for treatment. Because the physician assumes so much responsibility, however, he must be able to make quick, objective decisions under extremely adverse and critical conditions. This is why the emotional de-sensitization is required. John-Henry Pfifferling (Ferguson 1980:7) draws a comparison between physicians' medical training and the military organization:

> The medical system is patterned along military lines. After all, doctors are "at war" against disease. Like the military, there's an enormous reliance on hierarchical authority structures, which are the very opposite of coordination and teamwork. ... There's a whole mysterious set of rules, procedures and ceremonies in a hospital, none of which are discussed openly. The patient's input is not particularly valued.

From the military perspective, formalizing a crisis permits the officer to respond in a more deliberate and objective manner than an emotional response would effect. Ironically, the historian, John Keegan (1977:20), sees military education as analogous to medical education:

> ...the deliberate injection of emotion into an already highly emotive subject will seriously hinder, if not indeed altogether defeat, the aim of officer-training. That aim, which Western armies have achieved with remarkably consistent success during the two hundred years in which formal military education has been carried on, is to reduce the conduct of war to a set of rules and a system of procedures — and thereby to make orderly and rational what is essentially chaotic and instinctive. It is an aim analogous to that — though I would not wish to push the analogy too far — pursued by medical schools in their fostering among students of a detached attitude to pain and distress in their patients, particularly victims of accidents.

The basis of these obvious similarities between military and medical education emphasize what Comaroff (1978: 253) has explained as a shared feature of all healers — to provide patients with a "fundamental therapeutic tool". This tool is a "set of codes for ordering disrupted perceptions and for restoring the discontinuity between physical and social state, which is implied by illness." So, the American physician, especially the oncologist, is trained in medical school and residency programs to respond on the cancer battlefield with objectivity, specialized rhetoric, hopefulness, and leadership. And in turn, the physician symbolically restructures the chaos of the patient's illness experience with the aid of biomedical technology.

The physician's goals and objectives center around winning the battle and winning the war. The physician is making the decisions (sometimes life and death) and taking responsibility for hundreds of patients' lives and disease courses. He tries to maintain an objective perspective and total approach to the treatment of cancer as a disease. An oncology surgeon urges physicians to be objective in a cancer conference saying, "Don't let this patient's age and attractiveness influence your treatment plan." For the medical doctor, the long range goal is to determine which treatment protocols produce the best statistical survival curves — that, in his opinion, is the way to win the war. The war is his career. Fighting a single battle is the concern of the individual patient/soldier.

The cancer patient is like the soldier in the trench. He responds to orders and does what he is told. Several patients comment about their position with the physician: "I don't do nothing 'less the doctor says 'okay';" "If the doctor thinks I need the treatments, I guess I do ... he's supposed to know." A male patient with prostate cancer indicates how his sights are limited to that day's battle:

> I want to live each day as if it were my last.... I can't worry about next week, it's better if I just kind of live each day at a time, like an alcoholic. Especially while I'm taking treatments [chemotherapy]. I can't think about the next one or it just makes me want to give up.

The patient is fighting death hand to hand. His problems are immediate.

According to Keegan (1977: 131), the soldier is faced with three options: 1) attack, 2) defend, or 3) attrition. In general, patients and physicians prefer attack. Defense is acceptable in the later stages, but even then, it should be done with vigor. A breast cancer patient reported that at one treatment institution she saw patients and employees wearing t-shirts that said, "Cancer is a hard fight." Using military symbols, an oncologist explains this aggressiveness at a cancer conference:

> If you're going to treat a patient, you need to really give them all the guns the first time around ... that's your best shot at cure. When it [the cancer] comes back, your chances are next to nothing for cure. But if a patient wants to keep fighting, and wants me to keep treating him, I'll do it.

The third choice, attrition, could also be called Absent Without Leave (AWOL), and refers to those patients who decide to abandon the prescribed treatments or seek unorthodox treatments.

The diagnosis of cancer changes the individual's perspective of life and reorganizes priorities. Virtually all of the patients and family members interviewed in this study said that they appreciated their life, their family, and their health in a new way. Especially during therapy, there is a simplification of living, much like that of a soldier. Although there are tumultuous emotional changes and increased life stresses, daily routines, work, duties and familial obligations take on a magnified image. The patient's perspective of what is really important — family relations, eating, sleeping, and perhaps career obligations — seem to cause other, less important things in life to fade. The soldier and the cancer patient, at least for some days or moments, share these consequences of facing and fighting a life threatening attack on their person.

The sanctioned approach for family members and close friends is to sustain the patient's hope and faith in treatment, trust in his physician, and not raise too many questions which might undermine the attack. At the same time, many family members must suffer severe stress attempting to respond to the patient's needs and fulfill all of the familial roles and duties. In the beginning, sometimes the drama of the experience sustains individuals, but later there is less excitement, less glory, and the family is struck by the same disenchantment and loss that affects the patient. A wife of a lymphoma patient, and mother of four young children describes her struggle between supporting her husband and her children:

> It was so hard, especially since we lived so far from [the hospital]. I just couldn't keep up with everything. And I felt so torn between staying with C. at the hospital, and being a Mother and Daddy to the kids — they really needed me with him sick.

This is when the patient and family members rely upon their relationships and inner strength to sustain them.

Just as so many individuals have romanticized war before the battle, often the cancer experience is referred to euphemistically, even glamorously, especially with regard to the dignity of dying, and the percentages of survival or responses to treatment. Examples of the American image of cancer, as it is romantically portayed, in the news media and movies, include "baldheaded little kids twirling around in Disneyland teacups," "Brian's Song," "Love Story," "Terms of Endearment," and "Promises in the Dark" (Konte 1984: 13). In American culture, suffering is close to sacrifice, and individual effort is seen to end in heroism. So, approaching cancer with a romantic image sustains the patient and family.

Often, only during the very worst of times does the patient or kin really realize the true depths of pain, depression, and anguish that the cancer has created. For most families, only those persons most intimately involved with them ever know that they have reached these depths. Quite often it is a nurse or other outsider who is the support for a patient or family member during this time. The individual does not want the other family members to know his fears, weakened resolve, or deep depression. An experienced oncology nurse says, "The patients really need somebody to hold onto. And sometimes a stranger can be better." She goes on to say that the patients often want to release emotions and feelings with a stranger because when they leave the hospital, they can leave those frailties behind them also.

The physician, patient and family have been depicted as the commanding officer and individual fighting unit, respectively. In this way, the variance in expectations, goals, and individual concerns are integrated into a single system. The fact that the physician does not focus and respond to the patient's psychosocial problems, and perhaps, does not empathize with the patient and family members, does not preclude a successful therapeutic relationship; the cultural context of the disease allows them to assume very different roles. The patients and family members in this study indicate that they expect their oncologist to diagnose, treat, and analyze their condition as a "well paid professional" from the commanding officer's quarters with the most recent technology possible, rather than assume a direct supportive role in the trenches. The patient and family member recognize that often personal support is achieved from someone other than their oncologist. Three patients discuss their solutions for problems unaddressed by the oncologist:

The doctor's so busy, and doesn't really have time for me to discuss all my problems. I always forget something anyway. But his nurse has just been wonderful to me.

I learned a lot more about stuff [rehabilitation services] from that little [physical] therapist than I ever got out of the doctor.

These doctors are just too specialized to be able to treat your every symptom. Unless he thinks it's from the chemotherapy, he doesn't pay any attention to it. So, I keep seeing my family doctor.

The patient-physician roles primarily integrate in the narrowly defined area of treatment.

Healing Activities

The period of active treatment is usually the major period of "combat" that a cancer patient encounters. This can last for weeks or months, and sometimes it is prolonged for years. It is during this period that the patient and family members have the closest contact with the oncologist(s) and generally experience the most disruption in their lives. If the disease recurs, it is like being called back for "active duty" and sometimes repeating the entire process again. For example, one "veteran" patient was hospitalized over two dozen times for at least seven separate surgeries, two separate courses of chemotherapy, and a complete five week course of radiotherapy for a series of soft tissue sarcomas that recurred in different sites in her body over a three year period. In this kind of situation, it is almost as if the few months between battles were just "R and R" rather than any form of true "discharge." For the more fortunate patients, one or two hospitalizations, with one or two surgeries, followed by out-patient radiotherapy, and perhaps a year of chemotherapy might be the total combat period for a Stage I or Stage II disease. Then, they might be in the "reserves" for many years before they are "retired" (considered "cured" or in remission) or called back to "active duty" (experience a recurrence).

In the cancer experience, as in military organizations, the fighting unit often assumes the personality of its commander. Some of the oncologists in this study were portrayed by patients, families, and hospital personnel with qualities which are characterized as Dr. Continually-Optimistic-Never-Stop-Treatment, Dr. Egotistical-Highly-Competent, Dr. Down-to-Earth-Easy-to-Work-With, and Dr. No-Communication-2 a.m. Rounds. This physician/officer motivates and socializes the patient/soldier in the cancer experience and promotes the attitudes and spirit necessary for treatment within the American clinical reality.

The patient brings with him the vastly differing cultural and social realities of his life experiences, just like a new recruit. But, in an amazingly short time, a commanding officer/physician can reeducate and socialize that "new recruit" into a soldier prepared to endure some of the most rigorous and painful experiences of his life. With specialized medical facts, statistics, and advanced technologies, all presented in terms of glowing expectations and past victories, patients who were adamant against a particular treatment are somehow encouraged and impelled to "fight this thing to the bitter end" — with any and all treatment modalities. Even when the outlook is less than optimistic, that one chance in a thousand still exists, and the patient is encouraged to think he can be that one.

An important factor in treating cancer with highly technical biomedical armaments is that it requires cooperation and aid from an entire army and social organization. Usually, cancer in the United States is not successfully fought by the patient by himself. There are probably only a small percentage of people in the United States who, when the time to choose actually occurs, choose not to seek biomedical care. Many people say that they would never take chemotherapy or radiotherapy, that they would rather die with the disease. Many patients interviewed state that they felt that way before they were diagnosed. However, when actually facing the enemy eye to eye, most people are socialized within their cultural fabric enough to take up arms and at least begin the fight as a member of the socially sanctioned medical "army". The specter of cancer is frightening and the reassurances and sincere promises of that physician seem to offter more hope and promise for success than any solitary attempts an individual or family could stage.

Like traditional healers in other cultures, the biomedical physician is at least a symbolic intervenor in the fight with the amorphous, silent, almost spirit-like cancer. A patient with lung cancer describes his faith in his biomedical healer: "I can't fight this devil alone — that's why those doctors go to school so long. If they don't know what to do, nobody does." The patient is not expected to be able to fight cancer without medical help because the disease is perceived to be on a level above any simple treatment; it requires the use of magical tests, skills, and technology of the modern biomedical rituals. Paradoxically, all of these symbols which mediate the disorders caused by the illness and positively affect the therapeutic process are also the causes of discord when a seemingly healthy, asymptomatic patient is found to have cancer.

There are popular myths surrounding the treatments for cancer like "the sicker she gets with chemotherapy, the better the drugs are working," or "radiotherapy makes you lose all of your hair" or "makes you radioactive." Sometimes patients continue to believe in these myths of treatment even after cognitive explanations are presented. One patient with cervical cancer insists that the radiotherapy to her pelvis has caused the hair on her head to thin. Another woman says it turned her blood to "tar." These beliefs function to help glorify the combat experience and provide additional heroics and stories for the veteran. For over 90 percent of the respondents, the experiences of treatment are perceived as the most difficult and painful, and require the most fortitude of any of the cancer experiences. What happens, however, when the treatments are ineffective? When the oncologist cannot seem to control the cancer? When the battle plan is scrapped and the commanding officer can no longer make bold promises and provide assertive answers?

Most patients continue to have faith in their physician because that is what they have been "trained" to do, and they are too fearful to strike out in a new direction. A woman with lung cancer says, "I put myself in his [the doctor's] hands. I'll live or die by him." The continuing promises by the physician for relief from pain provide at least a little shelter from the driving fears that the cancer will become agonizingly painful. A small percentage of patients take the AWOL road to unorthodox treatment and possible miraculous cure. A few of these patients are interested in unorthodox treatments from the beginning of their sickness and have spent much time and energy discovering the various options available. This requires a lot of effort because the information on unorthodox treatments is not readily available. Many physicians consider the use of unproven, unprescribed treatment to be behavior deserving "dishonorable discharge" and will refer the patient elsewhere. One oncologist said, "I'd just as soon refer her to someone else, she doesn't want me to treat her," in response to a patient's use of unorthodox therapies. Other physicians, recognizing the patient's personal need to exhaust all efforts or take more control in the treatment, will continue to supervise the biomedical therapy while the patient is involved in his own "guerilla warfare" on a more remote battlefield.

Approximately 17 percent of the patients interviewed discussed some aspect of suicide — why they would not commit suicide, or why they considered it. Seeing death as a positive alternative may be perceived in the United States as a negative coping strategy.[5] But, it did help some people get through difficulties. In fact, some patients wanted some form of narcotic on hand; as one women with breast cancer said, "Just to know that it was there if things got too unbearable."

What seems more amazing than almost any aspect of the cancer experience is that so many patients willingly endure so much discomfort during a treatment, which they consider to be worse than the disease itself, for uncertain results. Physicians state that the results of no treatment are always a poor prognosis with increasing complications and obstruction. Once patients enter the "ranks", accept the information from the physicians, and integrate that into their own life experiences and prior knowledge of other cancer experiences, they feel obligated to continue fighting and following the doctor's orders. That is, desertion is perceived as too dishonorable for the individual and his family, and the thought of isolation from the oncologist is too fearful. Many patients would rather stay and fight than admit defeat so easily as to stop treatments in which their oncologist exhibits so much faith and which offers even a slight glimmer of hope for cure.

Even though the war with cancer is not yet won, the symbolic structures of medical militarization are creating an atmosphere of containment. There is an elan of productivity and resourcesfulness in the biomedical community today. However, while treatments are developing to attack the enemy, there also is a growing awareness of the gross denial of the underlying causes of cancer. In the 1980's, biomedicine is beginning to increase support of prevention activities. Historically, however, the general response for American society (and its biomedical culture) is to attack a resulting problem rather than address the source. As economic pressures of DRG's, prospective payment plans, and greater competition increasingly affect the biomedical spheres of influence, American society will be forced to do one of two things: 1) decrease costs, possibly through rationing of technological health care (as Britain has done), or 2) intensify efforts to explore the social and economic origins of illness.

IMPLICATIONS AND COMMENTARY

This case study of cancer treatment in Arkansas carries implications for applicability to other chronic illnesses. As Kleinman (1985:69) observes, "Each illness episode and each clinical encounter presents the anthropologist who works in medical settings with an occasion to *interpret* how illness and clinical reality are organized in particular local cultural systems of meanings, norms and power." This case study indicates that there is a significant difference between interpretations by patients, family members and physicians of the meanings of cancer and also in treatment decisions. When this information is disseminated to medical professionals it can provide appropriate guidelines and better understanding of the social context of cancer treatment.

Study of American cancer behavior and treatment practices can be utilized in cross cultural comparisons for health education. Emiko Ohnuki-Tierney (1984) and Susan and Bruce Long (1982) discuss the contemporary Japanese approach to cancer and the lack of direct confrontation with the diagnosis. This defensive aversion is quite different from the candid, aggressive approach in the United States and should certainly be considered in any cancer education programs utilized in the Japanese culture. For example, the American Cancer Society has been frustrated in their inability to promote health education programs in Japan using the American models. This failure is directly related to the ignorance of specific cultural patterning in that country. The American approach toward cancer education and information is culturally specific and effective only in the United States because it is seen as part of the sanctioned approach to the disease for Americans.

This research data can be organized in such a way that a prospective model can be developed for use by physicians in order to predict which patients may be at greater risk for treatment problems (Erwin, 1985: 196–202). When certain variables of age, site of cancer, etc. are combined, some sick persons and/or their families perceive a greater need for additional aid in combating psychosocial issues. Being aware of the propensity for certain patients to experience more perceived problems, the physician or hospital staff may be able to prevent a patient from becoming a management problem to them by providing additional psychosocial support sources. These sources include trained social workers, psychologists, psychiatrists, clergy, group therapies, or other support systems.

The information from this case study also can be applied directly to health care planning: 1) There is a need for increased development of health education programs for patients, families, physicians and the public regarding cancer. Most importantly these programs need to be broadened regionally to include populations in areas outside major medical centers. 2) There are indicators of popular support for more equal distribution of funds among clinical research, psychosocial research and concrete services for patients/families. This applies to government funding and especially funds available from private organizations and the American Cancer Society. 3) Physicians should be encouraged to be more critical and economically astute in considering, utilizing, and supporting technological gadgetry. Is the new advance in treatment or machinery really going to change the outcome of diagnostic processes or significantly influence survival rates? What is the cost to the patient?

These results indicate that cancer is as much a social issue as it is a medical vexation. What at first impression looks to be a hopeless situation in which patients and physicians recognize the insufficiencies of the current medical care system, the stigmatizing effects of the disease and treatments, and the lack of appropriate support systems to manage these problems is screened through a cultural filter. The resulting picture is one of hope, control, and effectiveness. The cancer patient who appears to be in a liminal position between life and death, disease and cure, is socialized into a new role as heroic soldier.

From the high expectations of the 1960's the American goal of cure (unequivocal winning) seems to have been amended to increased survival time (postponement of losing). This provides for the reporting of all the small victories against certain cancers: increased cure and survival in Hodgkin's Disease, increased survival in some pediatric tumors, effective treatment for certain leukemias, and increased cure and survival due to earlier diagnosis. This adjustment in perspective is another cultural buffer for managing the difficulties of a fearful enemy. Discussing and portraying cancer in terms of technological and political advancements is an optimistic camouflage for an otherwise debilitating social and medical situation.

On the other hand, there are some negative aspects to medical militarization and its resulting optimism. It encourages Americans to fight the disease rather than affect the necessary changes to prevent it. For example, smoking cessation programs are not as effective as they could be, partially because many Americans mistakenly believe that the medical community is able to cure most lung cancers ("Public Attitudes Toward Cancer and Cancer Tests," 1980). Secondly, sanctioning a "Never Say Die" approach to therapy has allowed health care costs to skyrocket as physicians continue to aggressively treat patients beyond any hope of actual cure. This medical militarization also places some patients at a disadvantage: those persons who cannot or do not choose to accept this philosophy may have more difficulty coping with their disease because people perceive them as having "given up." A fourth problem created through this approach to cancer is a continued dichotomy between healer and patient. Medical militarization develops the same kind of distance between physician and patient as the military creates for officers and enlisted men. The oncologists' responsibliities are strongly sanctioned toward technology and technical skill, but are reinforced less for empathetic care.

Additionally, American physicians traditionally have been liberated from responsibilities for the social and behavioral etiology of cancer. Biomedicine's emphasis in cancer reasearch has been cure, not prevention. But, as previously indicated by Sontag, the lack of total victory in the war with cancer has finally instigated a rising need for attention toward the social causes of this disease. Since 1980, the American Cancer Society and National Cancer Institute have increased media attention toward diet, behavior, and early diagnosis. Physicians' roles within growing health maintenance organizations also are intensifying preventive behaviors. However, the biomedical community, including physicians, has not waged a major campaign against large-scale chemical, tobacco or other environmental carcinogenic manufacturers for apparent economic reasons. Even though the overall medical cost for Americans with cancer was reported to be $10.8 billion in 1980, the American cultural response is to wage war with the monster, rather than alter the social and behavioral ills which help create it.[6] As these figures indicate, and as is true with most wars, the medical militarization of cancer treatment has propagated its own industry and technology which is rapidly expanding. This topic has additonal implications for further research and analysis outside the scope of this chapter.

The role of anthropology in this particular case study is to illustrate the theoretical perspective of the liminal position of cancer and the cancer patient in society, and also to apply interpretations of this illness and disease to strengths and weaknesses which are evident. The next step is to encourage development of those areas in the medical and social fabric which can combine the cultural meanings of the disease with practical policy in order to encompass and address the problems facing the professionals as well as the patients. One of the greatest roles applied anthroplogists can play in analyzing illness is to illustrate how the meanings and relationships within their interpretations effect the course of the sickness episode. In the case of cancer in the United States, battle metaphors are a trajectory of control and optimism for the patients, physicians, and the society in general. This increases technology and technological utilization, medical compliance, early detection, and in some cases, quality and years of survival for individual patients.

NOTES

1. Fifty-six percent of the lay sample considered themselves successful at managing their illness. Seventy-six percent of the lay sample indicated that they did not find it difficult to manage the stress and anxiety.
2. The American Cancer Society, reflecting on this expectation, has since changed to more of a service and rehabilitation orientation: "Share the Cost of Living" (1983), "Your Dollar will make the Difference" (1984).
3. Examples of media articles emphasizing these symbols and vocabulary includes "Mrs. Battle: Happy Warrior in Fight Against Cancer," *Arkansas Democrat*, 31 July 1983, p. 3B; "The Emotional Battle," *Newsweek*, 2 November 1981, p. 98; "Study Finds Cancer Victims Experience Discrimination at Work," *Dallas Times Herald*, 27 March 1980, p. 15B.
4. The research on Arkansans indicates that in order to limit stigma, it was important for patients to look as well as possible, and to closely approximate their pre-cancer appearance.
5. The option of suicide for cancer patients appears to be a much more acceptable strategy in other countries, especially Japan. See Ohnuki-Tierney(1984), Long and Long (1982). The topic of suicide was voluntarily introduced by those patients who mentioned it. Suicide was not a subject on the interview schedule or questionnaire.
6. This figure could be nearly double, since medical care costs have been rising at a rate of 20 percent or more per year. Source: National Center for Health Statistics.

REFERENCES

Alexander, Linda, 1982. Illness Maintenance and the New American Sick Role. In *Clinically Applied Anthropology*, eds, Noel J. Chrisman and Thomas W. Maretzki, 351–367. Dordrecht, Holland: D. Reidel Publishing Company.

Angell, Marcia, 1985. Disease As a Reflection of the Psyche, *The New England Journal of Medicine* 312: 1570–1572.

Bloom, Joan R., 1982. Social Support, Accommodation to Stress and Adjustment to Breast Cancer, *Social Science and Medicine* 16: 1329–1338.

Comaroff, J., 1978. Medicine and Culture: Some Anthropological Perspectives, *Social Science and Medicine* 12B: 247–254.

DeSantis, Lydia Ann, 1979. *"I Think I'm Going To Live" — An Ethnographic Account of Breast Cancer as an Illness Episode*, Ph.D. Dissertation, University of Washington.

Erwin, Deborah Oates, 1985. *Fighting Cancer, Dying to Win*, Ph.D. Dissertation, Southern Methodist University.

Ferguson, Tom, 1980. A Conversation with John-Henry Pfifferling, *Medical Self Care* 10: 4–9.

Fussell, Paul, 1977. *The Great War and Modern Memory*. London: Oxford University Press.

Geertz, Clifford, 1979. Religion as a Cultural System. In *Reader In Comparative Religion*, eds. William A. Lessa and Evon Z. Vogt, 78–89. New York: Harper and Row, Publishers.

Goffman, Erving, 1963. *Stigma*. Englewood Cliffs, New Jersey: Prentice-Hall.

Keegan, John, 1977. *The Face of Battle*. New York: Vintage Books.

Kleinman, Arthur, 1980. *Patients and Healers in the Context of Culture: An Exploration of the Borderland between Anthropology, Medicine and Psychiatry*. Berkeley and Los Angeles: University of California Press.

Kleinman, Arthur, 1985. Interpreting Illness Experience and Clinical Meanings: How I See Clinically Applied Anthropology, *Medical Anthropology Quarterly* 16: 69–71.

Konte, Sandra Hansen, 1984. I Will Get Well, If You Will Let Me, *Newsweek* May 21: 13.

Lipowski, Z. J., 1970. Physical Illness, the Individual and the Coping Process, *Psychiatry in Medicine* 1: 91–102.

Long, Susan and Bruce Long, 1982. Curable Cancers and Fatal Ulcers: Attitudes Toward Cancer in Japan, *Social Science and Medicine* 16: 2101–2108.

Ohnuki-Tierney, Emiko, 1984. *Illness and Culture in Contemporary Japan*. Cambridge: Cambridge University Press.

Peters-Golden, Holly, 1982. Breast Cancer: Varied Perceptions of Social Support in the Illness Experience, *Social Science and Medicine* 16: 483–491.

Public Attitudes Toward Cancer and Cancer Tests, 1980. *Ca-A Cancer Journal for Clinicians*, 30: 92–98.

Sontag, Susan, 1979. *Illness As Metaphor*. New York: Vintage Books.

Owning CF: Adaptive Noncompliance with Chest Physiotherapy in Cystic Fibrosis

ANNA BELLISARI

Wright State University

INTRODUCTION

The patient's point of view regarding compliance with medical advice has only recently been recognized as a legitimate concern of clinical practitioners and behavioral scientists. Rarely is there reference in the compliance literature to the impact of professional prescriptions for drug therapies or of medical recommendations for lifestyle changes upon patient quality of life. This chapter explores the issue of patient compliance from the "other side," as children with cystic fibrosis express their experiences and ideas regarding an aspect of their prescribed treatment regime.

Patient compliance has been defined as "the extent to which a person's behavior (in terms of taking medication, following diets, or executing lifestyle changes) coincides with medical advice" (Haynes 1979:2). Noncompliance, referring to failure to enter treatment, forgetting, erroneously or incompletely implementing, creatively substituting, prematurely terminating, refusing treatment altogether, or taking medication not prescribed by a physician (Blackwell 1976; Hulka, Cassel and Kupper 1976), is relatively common — it is estimated that one-third to one-half of all medical advice is not followed by patients (Cohen 1979; Haynes, Taylor and Sackett 1979).

Explanations for noncompliance are usually sought in such patient characteristics as demographic and personal traits, disease factors, and patient knowledge and beliefs. For example, adolescents are regarded as the least compliant of pediatric patients (Litt and Cuskey 1981; Shope 1981), and lower compliance rates have been noted in long-term, chronic illnesses (vs. acute, short-term conditions) (Cohen 1979; Haynes et al. 1979). Intervention strategies to improve compliance also focus on the patient by stressing patient education as the basis for changing compliance behavior (DiMatteo and DiNicola 1982).

Patient compliance is important to health care practitioners and clinical researchers. In the first place, compliance with therapies of well-established efficacy has a direct impact on illness outcome (Mayo 1978; Ruley 1978). Whether the patient takes the recommended doses of medication for the recommended length of time may determine whether a cure is effected. According to Addington (1979), for instance, the control of tuberculosis in the U.S. is limited only by patient noncompliance with therapeutic regimens.

Secondly, clinical trials of therapeutic regimes may be biased by patient noncompliance (Feinstein 1979; Goldsmith 1979), a problem of particular concern to pharmacologists (Lasagna 1976). Positive treatment outcome may be falsely attributed to a therapy the patient had actually failed to follow; a treatment may be judged ineffective when the patient was actually noncompliant (Feinstein and Ransohof 1976).

Clearly, professionals tend to view noncompliance as a problem that interferes with their efforts to provide adequate health care and to hold patients responsible, both for the high incidence of noncompliance and for efforts to improve compliance behavior. It is becoming apparent, however, that aspects of patients' sociocultural environment, including the health care system which serves them, affect patient behavior in response to medical advice; that the responsibility for reducing noncompliance belongs not only to the ones who are sick, but also to significant others and to those entrusted with their care (DiMatteo and DiNicola 1982; Janis 1983).

COMPLIANCE TERMINOLOGY

Another professional concern, that of maintaining medical dominance, is revealed in the lively debate surrounding use of the term *patient compliance*. Many alternative terms have been offered in order to describe more accurately the nature of the physician-patient relationship and patient action in response to professional advice. The main objection to the term *compliance* is its implication of a hierarchical relationship between physician and patient (Glanz 1980; Haynes 1979), with the physician in a position of authority over the patient, who simply accepts and carries out instructions. Proposed substitute terminology points up the importance of the patient's status and role in health-seeking decisions and behavior. Alternative terms such as *therapeutic alliance* (Zola 1981), *concordance* (Hulka, Cassel and Kupper 1976; DiMatteo and DiNicola 1982), and *congruity* (Hayes-Bautista 1976) connote agreement between equals, while *cooperation* (Twaddle 1981), *adherence* (Blackwell 1976; Stuart 1982), *negotiation* (Katon and Kleinman 1981; Zola 1981), *patient participation* (Barofsky 1978; Caplan 1979), and *implementation* (Blackwell 1976) are suggestive of patient autonomy in decision-making and action.

Claiming that the coercive connotation of *compliance* reflects the actual situation in medical practice, Barofsky (1978) offers a way of socializing patients into the health care system that develops their self-control and ultimately their self-care, and suggests that *alliance* should become the appropriate descriptive term. Haynes (1979: 2) maintains, however, that *compliance* is deeply rooted in the literature, that no really suitable alternative exists, and that the "unhealthy connotations of *compliance* keep the ethical and social issues . . . up front where they belong."

In line with the latter argument, it may be more useful to retain *compliance*, but it must be pointed out that, contrary to professional interests and concerns, patient compliance is not always the approporiate response to medical prescriptions and recommendations. Health care professionals generally assume that resolution of health problems depends on patient compliance with recommended therapeutic regimens. A regimen of antibiotics, taken as prescribed, is expected to cure a respiratory infection. However, there is often no direct relationship between patient compliance and illness outcome (Epstein and Cluss 1982). If a recommended treatment is ineffective, for example, even the strictest adherence will not improve the patient's condition.

In chronic illness patients can expect only amelioration of symptoms, or a delay of the inevitably fatal outcome. The small benefits of compliance may not justify the large costs of inconvenience and discomfort to the patient. Noncompliance may very well be the most logical, rational response to professional instructions in such cases. Weintraub (1976: 45) distinguishes between capricious compliance which involves "irregular therapeutic behavior based on false theory and misinformation" and intelligent noncompliance where patients have valid reasons for not complying, such as unpleasant side effects, confusion about dosage, or too much prescribed medicine.

In a study of pediatric asthma patients it was found that patient and parent noncompliance with medication schedules is actually a positive, adaptive response (Deaton 1985). Based on parental knowledge of their child's disease severity and seasonal variability in asthma symptoms, concern for limited effectiveness and potentially severe side effects of prescribed medications, and consideration of the impact of therapeutic costs on family quality of life, noncompliance decisions were part of the patient's strategy for coping with chronic illness. In this particular study adaptive noncompliance was found to be significantly correlated with better asthma control, while stricter adherence to the medical regimen was not. "A conscious decision which is based on adequate information about the regimen and on intimate knowledge of the child may in fact be superior to passive compliance with the regimen" (Deaton 1985: 12).

The case studies reported below illustrate the concept of adaptive noncompliance in cystic fibrosis (CF), the most common hereditary fatal disease among American children of European ancestry, considering not only the impact of the disease upon patients' lives, but also the influence of their social and cultural environment on their decisions to comply. Like their health care providers, these children and their families are primarily concerned with illness outcome, but they have the additional task of adapting to their illness — of adjusting to physical limitations and of coping with demands and restrictions imposed by therapeutic regimens upon their life styles, social interactions, value systems, and future hopes. *Why* noncompliance with medical advice is sometimes an adaptive response is not always obvious to clinical professionals and social scientists.

CYSTIC FIBROSIS

About 13,000 children and young adults in the U.S. have been diagnosed as CF patients (Cystic Fibrosis Foundation 1979; Wood 1982). Their disease is inherited from both parents, and their average survival age is 20. There is much about CF that is still unknown; as a disease entity it has been recognized for less than 50 years. The reason for its extremely high incidence (about 1:2000) in west-central Europeans and in populations descended from them is not understood, the mode of inheritance is not well known, and the basic biochemical defect of the CF genotype remains unidentified (Wood, Boat and Doershuk 1976).

CF symptoms are caused by faulty exocrine gland secretion.

Sweat glands secrete too much salt, sometimes causing dehydration, heat stroke, and cardiac arrest. Digestive organs secrete abnormally thick, sticky mucus that may block the bowel and plug the pancreatic duct, interfering with digestion of proteins, fats, and carbohydrates. As a result, CF patients often suffer from intestinal discomfort, pass loose, bulky, foul-smelling stools, and appear malnourished and thin for their height and age. Growth and maturation are usually delayed, and fertility is severely reduced in adulthood. Thick, sticky mucus is also secreted by cells lining the pulmonary bronchi and smaller airways, causing obstruction, air trapping, uneven ventilation, and permanent scarring of lung tissue. Chronic hypoxia ultimately stresses the cardiovascular system, often resulting in death by heart failure. Retention of the thick mucus leads to respiratory infection, another common cause of morbidity and mortality. Decreased exercise tolerance, barrel-chest deformity, digital clubbing (thickened fingertips), chronic shortness of breath, wheezing, and dry cough contribute to abnormal appearance and limited ability to carry out usual childhood activities. Although onset, number, and severity of symptoms varies greatly, all CF patients face the possibility of early death, most often due to respiratory complications.

CF cannot be cured. Treatment is symptomatic, and therefore complex. Most patients must take a number of medications — water-soluble vitamins and pancreatic enzymes to aid in digestion and absorption of nutrients, nebulized decongestants and mucolytic agents to break down thick mucus in the lungs, antibiotics to combat chronic infection, digitalis and diuretics in cases of cardiovascular complication. Regular and frequent appointments with CF clinic personnel are necessary. Often dietary restrictions on fat intake are recommended. And almost all patients are instructed in the use of daily chest physiotherapy (CPT) to loosen and remove the thick, tenacious mucus obstructing their lungs.

CPT must be conducted twice daily from the time of diagnosis. This form of therapy requires cooperation between patient and therapist (usually a parent). While the patient assumes various body positions, the therapist claps on the chest and back with cupped hand. After two minutes of percussion of each position (up to eleven in all) the patient exhales slowly several times while the therapist vibrates chest and back by stiffening arms and wrists and applying pressure with flat hands. Percussion and vibration are meant to loosen the sticky mucus adhering to bronchial walls, allowing the secretions to move into the larger bronchi from which they are expelled by coughing. The patient then either swallows the secretions or spits them into a tissue or cup. If done according to instructions, the entire CPT procedure, preceded by nebulization therapy, takes about one hour to complete (Children's Hosptial 1977).

Although CPT has long been advocated by the Cystic Fibrosis Foundation, physicians, and respiratory therapists (Cystic Fibrosis Foundation 1977; Doershuk, Matthews, Tucker, and Spector 1965; Lorin and Denning 1971; Motoyama 1973), medical literature documents considerable scientific skepticism about its effectiveness, particularly for improving long-term respiratory condition. At best, only CF patients whose lungs secrete large amounts of mucus seem to benefit from daily CPT (Hosclaw and Tecklin 1977; Kerribijn, Veentijer and Water 1982; Mellins 1974; Murray 1979; Rochester and Goldberg 1980; Sutton, Pavia, Bateman, and Clarke 1983; Wood et al 1976).

Few studies have reported on compliance with medical regimens in CF. Medication compliance seems to be relatively high, but many patients take antibiotics even though none are prescribed (Meyers, Doland and Mueller 1975). Dietary and CPT compliance rates are much lower, compliance with CPT in particular declining with increasing age regardless of disease severity (Passero, Remor and Salomon 1981).

CASE STUDIES

A group of 27 children and their parents, all of whom attended the same CF Clinic in a large midwestern city, utilized the same physician there, and received the same CPT recommendations and instructions, volunteered for a study of patient compliance with CPT (Bellisari 1984). I visited each family three times for direct observation of therapeutic behavior and for extensive interviewing. Volunteers were told only that I wished to learn how they cope with CF, not that the primary study focus was on compliance with CPT.

I found that overall compliance with CPT was low in this small group of CF patients, with somewhat higher compliance rates for therapy frequency (families completed an average of one CPT session per day) than for therapy quality (less than 25% of all CPT components were completed), suggesting that families attempted to carry out instructions, but did not do so proficiently or effectively. Because the study group consisted of volunteers, and also because of possible observer effect, I assumed that these findings actually overestimate compliance with CPT in the general CF patient population.

Three correlates of low compliance emerged from the observations and interviews — patient perception of CPT inefficacy, patient perception of mild respiratory involvement, and multiple CF patients with at least one death per family. In other words, it appeared that patients and families who believed that CPT was ineffective therapy, who felt that their respiratory symptoms were relatively mild, and who had the burden of caring for several children with CF, one or more of whom had died, were less likely to carry out physician's instructions for daily CPT. These findings suggest that patients weigh the advantages and disadvantages of therapeutic recommendations before deciding to implement them.

The following case studies, based on the research project described above and excerpted from interviews and observations of the children and their parents in their own homes, illustrate how some of these therapy decisions are made, and why noncomplicance with CPT recommendations is often a positive response to medical advice. Although events and experiences related here are real, all names have been changed.

Case 1: Susie

Susie is a pert, blond second-grader. She is very active and loves to rollerskate, ride horseback, and most of all swim in the pool her father has installed in the backyard of the tiny house shared by this family of three. She also takes gymnastic lessons and is an avid drum player. There is little indication that Susie has CF, because her height and weight are normal, she attends school regularly, and there are no apparent respiratory symptoms such as chronic cough, barrel-chest, digital clubbing, blue lips, and frequent respiratory infection.

When Susie was three years old, however, she was struck with a sudden attack of intestinal cramps and diarrhea while on a camping trip with her family. She still remembers the sharp pains in her stomach. The cramping and diarrhea persisted until they became a daily occurrence, but the family doctor found no reason for concern. Although a visit to a nearby pediatrician also revealed no cause, grandmother insisted that Susie's condition was not normal, so mother and child returned to the family physician. To mother's dismay, he declared that the problem was not with the child, but with the mother, that something she was doing gave Susie a nervous stomach, and that as a good mother, she ought to stay home from her job to take proper care of her daughter. Mother and grandmother, however, persisted in their search. Finally, when Susie was four years old, another pediatrician recognized Susie's symptoms and suggested that she might be a victim of cystic fibrosis. He had Susie hospitalized for a battery of tests, including upper and lower GI and finally a sweat test.

"I'll never understand," said mother, "why Susie was put through the pain and discomfort of all those tests when the simple and painless sweat test to measure salt content could have been done first. Why did we have to go through all those days of hospitalization and all those tests costing hundreds of dollars each if a simple $12 test could have been done first to confirm the CF diagnosis?"

The sweat test was repeated several times, but each result was positive; Susie had CF. A prescription for daily pancreatic enzymes immediately alleviated the intestinal complaints, and Susie's respiratory complications were only minor, appearing as infrequent flu-like respiratory infections for which powerful antibiotics were prescribed. Although her parents were relieved to find out what was wrong with Susie, they were shocked to learn about the implications of CF — that Susie had inherited the disease from them, that it was chronic and ultimately fatal, and that Susie would require medications and chest physiotherapy for the rest of her life.

"I was simply overwhelmed by the shock of her disease and could not imagine how I would accomplish all that was required to care for her. Everything was thrown at us at once while she was in the hospital, all the medications and the mist tent and nebulizer. We were taught how to do CPT in one short lesson and got only one chance to practice it with a nurse present. I am still not really sure whether we are doing it the way we are supposed to, but we do our best."

Susie is not the only family member with medical problems. Father recently injured his back in an accident, sustaining a permanent and painful disability. Both parents have jobs and share the household duties — cooking, cleaning, laundry — and regular, daily CPT which they conscientiously try to carry out. The back injury makes each CPT session a painful experience for father, so often his share of the therapy is abbreviated by reducing percussion time to one minute for each position.

Susie dislikes CPT very much, complaining of pain and discomfort during percussion, especially when she has to be tilted head downward on the therapy board and "when mom tells me to cough. I just can't bring up anything." Susie has become very skillful at minimizing CPT sessions. When dad lets her monitor percussion time with his watch, she manages to stop him after only 45 seconds. Sometimes, when she and dad are engrossed in a TV program during CPT, she is able to convince him to skip a position or two by reminding him that he had already done them. When these techniques don't work, Susie becomes "antsy," wiggling, complaining, and distracting until CPT is ended early.

Another reason that Susie resists CPT is that it interferes with her social life. Rarely is she permitted an overnight visit at her girlfriend's house, because that would interfere with the CPT schedule recommended to her parents. According to their instructions, CPT is to be conducted first thing in the morning and just before bedtime at night. Sometimes, however, friends come to visit around bedtime, and then CPT may be forgotten for the evening. "It's much more important for her to enjoy normal friendships than to be dragged away for CPT. Many friends don't understand what the CPT is for, so we do not insist on doing it in front of them," says father.

In spite of all the obstacles, Susie and her parents tried to maintain a regular CPT schedule in the hopes that it would keep her lungs clear of the sticky mucus associated with CF. Once, however, when Susie had a week-long bout of flu with chest pains and fever, they had to relent. And during their Florida vacation they stopped the treatments because "Susie was getting in enough exercise by swimming every day to keep her lungs clear." Although aerobic exercise is recommended by some physicians as an appropriate alternative to CPT, Susie's doctor is among those who accept no substitute for daily CPT.

Recently Susie and her parents moved to a new home in another town. The move disrupted their daily routine so much that they postponed resumption of regular CPT and finally dropped it altogether. "She has few of the respiratory symptoms typical of CF, she never brings up any mucus, and we don't think she needs it right now. The enzyme pills are essential — we can see a big difference when she forgets to take them. But Susie's lungs are just the same, whether we do the therapy or not. Of course, if she should get worse, we will start it again. Besides Susie is so active — she just goes form morning till bedtime, while some of her little friends are just exhausted after school and have to take a nap. She can do anything that normal children can do and she hardly misses school. Why make her feel like a patient when she is not really sick?"

Mother states that they have not informed the doctor at the CF clinic about their decision to stop CPT. She and father have been somewhat disappointed that they are never consulted about their daughter's condition and are not encouraged to make some of the decisions regarding therapeutic needs. The doctor at a clinic they attended previously had always shown them Susie's chest X-rays and given them detailed information about the condition of her lungs, heart, etc. He expected them to decide, on the basis of their day-to-day observations and experiences with Susie, when to reduce or increase CPT. "At this CF clinic we never see an X-ray, and we get the results of the throat culture tests on a postcard about three weeks afterwards. By that time Susie could have gotten very sick with whatever is causing her infection."

Case 2:   Ellen

When she was born Ellen appeared to be a perfectly normal baby. Her parents were full of joy and pride over their first child. Only gradually did they come to realize that something was wrong. Although she had a tremendous appetite, Ellen had not gained much over her birthweight by three months. When she was hospitalized with pneumonia at five months, her problem was identified as CF.

After diagnosis most of Ellen's digestive symptoms were effectively controlled with medications, and she actually began to gain weight. But, in spite of regular CPT, she suffered frequent bouts of pneumonia. Although she began to grow and develop, she wheezed and coughed constantly and often became tired. Almost every evening she fell asleep during CPT. When Ellen was ten years old, the doctors determined that the pulmonary complications had affected her heart, causing the right ventricle to enlarge in its efforts to pump enough blood to maintain adequate oxen levels. Ellen had to add digoxin for support of her weakened heart to her long list of medications.

Now that she is twelve years old, it is painfully clear that her disease has progressed rapidly and that Ellen will not survive to adulthood. She is extremely small and thin. Some of her classmates are beginning to show signs of maturity, but Ellen has not yet begun to menstruate and, to her distress, she does not yet have to wear a bra. Her chest protrudes, but that is due to the typical barrel-chest deformity related to CF. Her fingertips are so enlarged that she tries to keep her hands balled up into fists so that the other children cannot see them. Breathing is difficult for Ellen. Her lips are often a strange shade of blue, and in combination with her permanently stained teeth (a result of taking certain antibiotics in early childhood), her appearance evokes comments and jokes from her classmates. She is always short of breath, and when she talks, she cannot complete an entire sentence without gasping. Frequently she coughs up big, thick gobs of sticky mucus.

Although she is usually tired and weak, Ellen tries very hard to keep up with her friends. She forces herself to attend school regularly, missing only when she is down with the flu or is hospitalized. She understands that giving in to her illness would cause her parents a great deal of worry. So she tries to keep up the appearance of normality as much as possible.

Her mother struggles to persuade Ellen to cooperate with CPT. Ellen has full responsibility for taking her medications on schedule and for reminding her mother about refills, but she continues to resist CPT. "I wish there were a pill to thin mucus, or a CPT pill," she says. "I hate CPT — it hurts, and it takes too long. I always give my mother a hard time when it's time for CPT. It interferes with my sleep in the morning and with play or TV at night. I wish they'd let me make the decision whether I want it or not. It's my body, after all." But her mother, who bears the major burden of providing therapy since her husband is often away on business trips, manages to convince Ellen to submit to CPT almost daily, sometimes through persuasion, other times through more coercive measures.

"I just hate to beat on her poor thin chest and back. She has no fat padding to cushion the blows, and CPT really does hurt her. And sometimes she brings up so much mucus that she has to gag and vomit. When friends and visitors are here, we skip CPT. We don't like to have others watch, because they would think we are abusing our child. In fact, her grandmother refuses to do CPT for fear of hurting Ellen. But it's the only thing we can do to try to help her."

Her parents were quick to understand the implications of the CF diagnosis — there was a good chance that they could have other children with CF. So they decided to adopt a little brother for Ellen. Benny is a wonderful, healthy and active little boy, who is the delight of the entire family. Ellen watches over him and protects him. Once, when a bigger boy bullied her brother in school, Ellen confronted him and frightened him away. But Benny has come to resent all of the concern showered on Ellen, and works very hard to attract his parents' attention toward himself. Although it is difficult to believe, Benny wishes he could be sick and have CPT every day too.

Ellen's mother is very discouraged and often depressed because she feels so helpless. She has suffered several nervous breakdowns, and, along with Ellen, has sought psychiatric counselling for her feelings of hopelessness and grief. But Ellen is not satisfied. "Do you know, some kids won't play with me because I'm going to die. We all saw it on TV, on the Today Show. They said that kids with CF die by the age of 20. No one will talk to me about it. I want to know what will happen. Doctors should tell kids what to expect, so they can be prepared."

Case 3:   Tim

Tim is a high school senior, the youngest of five children. His family has suffered tragedy as a result of CF. An older brother died three years ago, and another older brother is near death now. After completing college and working as a park ranger for two years, Dick had collapsed and was forced to return home. He died in a nearby hospital at the age of 27. Jack is 28 now and confined to his bedroom. He is too weak to walk up and down the stairs, so he spends his days in his bed or easy chair. Although he has had CPT regularly since his diagnosis in infancy, his lungs have become progressively worse, and he receives continuous supplemental oxyen through a nasal tube. Jack will not be hospitalized when his crisis comes; his family plans to share in Jack's death and release at home. Tim's two sisters are normal. Both have completed college and are working. Tim enjoys their presence, for both live at home and bring some joy and laughter into the house.

Tim's parents are in their late fifties, and have to work very hard to maintain their emotional equilibrium. Both of them attend to Jack — he needs CPT three times a day in order to ease his efforts to breathe. They can see, however, that all the work will ultimately be useless. Jack will die, just like Dick. At one time Tim's parents tried to provide daily CPT for three children. It seemed as though they did CPT all day long, but even then it was just impossible to give each boy two treatments a day. They were forced to cut back to one session per child, unless one or the other of them had the flu or another infection.

Acutely aware of his family's burden because of CF, Tim worries about the medical bills that must be paid and all the work he and Dick make for his parents. Tim will not allow anyone to give him CPT, saying that he is old enough to do his own. The trouble is he never feels like doing it. Dick needs it to help him breathe, but *he* is not really sick enough. Besides he is old enough to make his own decisions about his health needs.

Tim is anxious to finish high school. He has always enjoyed history and social studies courses, but he despises math. The worst problem, though, and the main reason he is eager to graduate, is that he has no real friends and has always felt like an outsider at school. All of his troubles can be traced to CF. First, he is very thin and small compared to other boys in his class. He coughs a lot and is always short of breath. There was never any possibility of participating in sports to gain some recognition and impress the girls. Sometimes he gets so tired in school that he has trouble staying awake and attending to lectures and assigned work.

Then there is the problem of taking medicine at school. He has told only one classmate about his illness; no one else knows that he is not normal. Sure, they notice that he coughs a lot, and they can see that he is small and thin, but they don't know he has a disease. So he cannot let anyone know he has to take pancreatic enzymes with his lunch, and he swallows them, four at a time, while no one is looking. Recently he decided to leave the pills at home, but the lack of enzymes causes stomach cramps and necessitates frequent trips to the bathroom in the afternoon. There is nothing that irritates his teachers more than to sign bathroom passes during classes and study halls.

Tim longs to be with the other boys, horsing around or talking about girls. But he has never had a girlfriend or even a date, and he is afraid to approach a girl now, after several rejections. When someone asks about his chronic cough, Tim has found that the best thing to do is to deny there is anything seriously wrong. That way he doesn't have to go into any elaborate, embarrassing explanation. And, compared to his brother, he is pretty well and really doesn't need all the medications and therapy. Anyway, they did no good; Jack died, and Dick will follow Jack soon. There seems to be no way of stopping the disease progression, no matter how hard you try. His parents have both had to work to support the family, and there is never enough money for a vacation or for extras like an occasional restaurant dinner. "So what's the use of spending all the money and effort on treatment when it could be used to make life enjoyable? Doctors should pay more attention to the quality of life rather than the length of life. It's much more important."

Depression and misery often describe Tim's mood. At this point in his life he is worried about what will happen to him after graduation. Both of his brothers went to college, but one could not graduate. Should he really ask for his parents' financial support for something he might not be able to complete? What kind of work should he plan to do anyway? And how can he ever get a job if he has to indicate that he has CF on the application? How will he pay his medical bills after he is too old to be covered by his parents' insurance? What is the use of making future plans? The only thing left to do is to "forget the whole thing, to try to act normal, and to live every day as it comes, as well as possible. I've decided that I own CF — I don't allow it to own me."

DISCUSSION

These cases illustrate the correlates of noncompliance revealed by the study. All three of these patients, as well as some of their families, have come to perceive CPT as ineffective therapy for pulmonary symptoms. Susie's parents observe that omission of CPT seems to make no difference in her condition. Ellen and Tim are quite aware that CPT does not alter the ultimate prognosis of CF, and, through their own logical processes, tinged with adolescent rebellion, have decided against its use. Ellen, however, produces a large quantity of mucus with CPT, a fact which encourages her mother to continue with it.

Tim and Susie tend to minimize the seriousness of their respiratory condition. Although their X-ray reports contain evidence of some lung damage indicating pulmonary involvement common in CF, they and their parents are either unaware of these reports or are able to rationalize away their implications. Combined with the delay in receiving sputum culture results and corresponding antibiotic prescriptions to combat infections, this lack of information tends to leave patients with the impression that their respiratory complications are of minor importance, or, at least, require little urgency and regularity in carrying out CPT.

Patients' denial of pulmonary complications is not based only upon the lack of pertinent information regarding their clinical status, however. The social environment and cultural system play a role as well. Americans value strong, healthy, and active bodies and tolerate little deviation from the ideal. Healthy adolescents often experience a period when they are excruciatingly aware of their physical imperfection. How much more difficult is this realization for children with CF! The term "normal" was frequently cited by the children who participated in the study — they tried to look "normal," behave "normally," lead "normal" lives, hide the fact that they were not "normal." Susie's heavy schedule of physical activity may be an attempt to create the illusion of "normality," and Tim's case exemplifies the importance of feeling and looking "normal" in the development of social relationships. Doing CPT is an open admission of abnormal health status and must, therefore, be avoided.

Without exception, study participants admitted that CF is a fatal disease, but only those who had experienced the death of a child with CF seemed to be fully cognizant of the implications — the gradual deterioration of the child's condition, the feeling of helplessness, the futility of therapeutic efforts. Those who had had such an experience and had other children with CF almost invariably gave up CPT (as did Tim), sometimes due to a kind of lethargy related to depression, sometimes as the logical result of experiencing loss despite therapeutic efforts. The combined effect of caring for several children with CF and a poor illness outcome thus counters the motivation to comply with medical advice.

Other aspects of CF mitigate against compliance with CPT by Susie, Ellen, and Tim. For Susie's family, the earliest contact with the medical system, before and during the diagnosis, left a decidedly negative impression. At worst, the indecisiveness, lack of understanding, and criticism from medical professionals engendered skepticism about physicians' knowledge of CF and cynicism regarding their motives in ordering laboratory tests and prescribing medications and therapies. Not infrequently families' expectations of support from health care providers are disappointed, as in the case of Ellen's wish for understanding regarding her imminent death. Not surprisingly, medical advice is often rejected.

Families' perceptions of the CF regime's therapeutic value seem to fall into a hierarchy, with medications having priority over physical therapy and dietary restrictions, both in terms of convenience and effectiveness. Ellen's plea for a "CPT pill" is very probably more than just a preference for a quick and painless drug. It may well reflect the American orientation toward chemical and technological health care that precludes CPT as fully legitimate therapy.

In their interviews, parents and patients revealed another, rather unexpected interpretation of CPT that impinges on compliance with this aspect of the regimen. Several children, including Ellen, referred to the treatments as "beatings," intimating not only that CPT is painful, but also that it has the appearance of child abuse.

One family was actually observed to lock the doors to their home and draw the curtains before CPT "to keep the neighbors from looking." And more than one parent reported that other family members and friends thought that therapy was cruel and punitive, especially when the patient was a small infant.

CONCLUSION

These case studies have important implications for clinical practice on the one hand, and for medical anthropology on the other. Although it should certainly be replicated in other patient groups, and on a larger scale, this study provides significant insights into patient compliance.

Susie, Ellen and Tim offer a glimpse of the patient's point of view (the emic perspective). Clearly medical advice is not simply accepted and carried out as ordered by the children with CF and their parents. Rather, it is received in a specific psychosocial context, evaluated according to personal estimates of appropriateness and efficacy, and implemented in varying levels and degrees within a particular sociocultural setting. Many external factors impinge upon the original prescriptions and recommendations until they are adjusted to each child's individual needs and situations. In chronic illness such as CF, needs and situations change, psychosocial and sociocultural environments vary, and evaluations of therapy are altered as children grow and mature. It becomes essential that clinical professionals understand the meaning of their recommendations for their patients' lives if they are to promote compliance and improve patient care.

Anthropologists are well prepared to provide the necessary data for such understanding and to make recommendations that may contribute to patient care. In the case of the CF patients represented in the three examples above, it appears that a reevaluation of the therapeutic merits of CPT is in order, with tailoring of CPT recommendations for individual children. It would also seem that regularly sharing current details regarding each patient's clinical condition would improve compliance where warranted, as would repeated opportunities to review therapy technique with respiratory and physical therapists. Adolescents' growing needs for independence might well be met with instructions for self-therapy, available in both manual and mechanical form. Families' special financial and emotional concerns and parental health problems ought to be monitored and supported with appropriate services.

Anthropologists have had a great deal to say about the rejection of biomedicine in Third World countries and among U.S. ethnic minorities. Perhaps because of a mistaken assumption that "mainstream" Americans concur with the values and goals of the prevailing biomedical system, they have largely ignored the issue of patient compliance in their own society. The case studies described above indicate, however, that there are important divergences. Professional and patient definitions of health and illness in CF are very different, with a resulting impact on patient compliance with CPT. While clinicians apply a "structural" definition based on lung function parameters, lung tissue damage, and presence of infective microorganisms, basing their therapy recommendations on these findings, patients and their families use a "functional" measure of health based on school attendance, athletic participation, activity level, and presence of cough to decide whether CPT should be implemented or not. Medical anthropologists are most qualified to explore and appreciate the relationship between such cultural differences, physical variation, and patient behavior.

A hallmark of medical anthropology research is direct observation of patient behavior. The importance of including direct observation, which is admittedly a time-consuming, and often expensive endeavor, is borne out in the results of the compliance research referred to here, which combined extensive patient interviews with observation in patients' homes in the data collection phase. Interviews measured the quantitative dimension of CPT; that is, patients and their families reported during repeated interviews on how frequently they executed CPT, and their reports were found to be accurate when cross-checked by various other methods. The finding of average compliance with CPT frequency (51%) was based on the interviews. But, although patients claimed to be conducting CPT more or less exactly as they had been instructed, direct observation of therapy sessions revealed that CPT *quality* compliance was relatively low (23%). Because clinical professionals rank therapy quality above quantity for effectiveness, their subsequent overall compliance rating for this patient group was low. The validity of compliance level measurement was considerably enhanced by assessing both the quantitative and qualitative dimensions of CPT.

Medical anthropologists still have many contributions to make to medicine and health care. Their orientation toward the patient's perspective, holistic approach, and participant-observation techniques is unique and complementary to that of other social sciences studying behavioral aspects of health. Extending traditional anthropology to the study of those "at home" (Messerschmidt 1981) can only benefit everyone concerned, from clinical professionals to chronically ill patients. The problem of patient noncompliance in America clearly parallels that of biomedical underutilization in other societies and demands equal efforts at finding explanations and solutions. Results of such efforts could well mean that many more children with CF will be able to say, "I am in control — I own CF."

REFERENCES

Addington, W., 1979. Patient Compliance: the Most Serious Remaining Problem in the Control of Tuberculosis in the United States, *Chest* 76 (Supplement): 741–743.

Barofsky, I., 1978. Compliance, Adherence and the Therapeutic Alliance: Steps in the Development of Self-Care, *Social Science and Medicine* 12: 369–376.

Bellisari, A., 1984. *Beating CF: Patient Compliance with Chest Physiotherapy in Cystic Fibrosis*. Ann Arbor: University Microfilms International.

Blackwell, B., 1976. Treatment Adherence, *British Journal of Psychiatry* 129: 513–531.

Caplan, R., 1979. Patient, Provider and Organization: Hypothesized Determinants of Adherence. In *New Directions in Patient Compliance*, ed. S. Cohen, 75–110. Lexington, MA: Lexington Books.

Children's Hospital (Columbus, Ohio), 1977. *Postural Drainage*. Publication HH-11-20.

Cohen, S., 1979. New Metaphors for Old Problems. In *New Directions in Patient Compliance*, ed. S. Cohen, 153–163. Lexington, MA: Lexington Books.

Cystic Fibrosis Foundation, 1977. *Guide to Management of Cystic Fibrosis*. Atlanta: CF Foundation.

Cystic Fibrosis Foundation, 1979. *Report of the Patient Registry, 1977*. Rockville: CF Foundation.

Deaton, A., 1985. Adaptive Noncompliance in Pediatric Asthma: the Parent as Expert, *Journal of Pediatric Psychology* 10: 1–14.

DiMatteo, M., and D. DiNicola, 1982. *Achieving Patient Compliance: The Psychology of the Medical Practitioner's Role*. New York: Pergamon Press.

Doershuk, C., L. Matthews, A. Tucker, and S. Spector, 1965. Evaluation of a Prophylactic and Therapeutic Program for Patients with Cystic Fibrosis, *Pediatrics* 36: 675–687.

Epstein, H.H., and P.A. Cluss, 1982. A Behavioral Medicine Perspective on Adherence to Long-Term Medical Regimens, *Journal of Consulting and Clinical Psychology* 50: 950–971.

Feinstein, A., 1979. Compliance Bias and the Interpretation of Therapeutic Trials. In *Compliance in Health Care*, eds. R. Haynes, D. Taylor, and D. Sackett, 309–322. Baltimore: Johns Hopkins University Press.

Feinstein, A., and D. Ransohoff, 1976. Problems in Compliance as a Source of Bias in Data Analysis. In *Patient Compliance*, ed. L. Lasagna, 65–76. Mt. Kisco, NY: Future.

Glanz, K., 1980. Compliance with Dietary Regimens: its Magnitude, Measurement and Determinants, *Preventive Medicine* 9: 787–804.

Goldsmith, C., 1979. The Effect of Compliance Distributions on Therapeutic Trials. In *Compliance in Health Care*, eds. R. Haynes, D. Taylor, and D. Sackett, 297–308. Baltimore: Johns Hopkins University Press.

Hayes-Bautista, D., 1976. Modifying the Treatment: Patient Compliance, Patient Control and Medical Care, *Social Science and Medicine* 10: 233–238.

Haynes, R., 1979. Introduction in *Compliance and Health Care*, eds. R. Haynes, D. Taylor, and D. Sackett, 1–10. Baltimore: Johns Hopkins University Press.

Haynes, R., D. Taylor, and D. Sackett, 1979. *Compliance and Health Care*. Baltimore: Johns Hopkins Universty Press.

Hosclaw, D., and J. Tecklin, 1977. The Effectiveness of Bronchial Drainage and Aerosol Inhalation in Cystic Fibrosis. In *Chest Physical Therapy in Cystic Fibrosis and Chronic Obstructive Pulmonary Disease*, eds. D. Baran and E. Von Bogaert, 230–238. Ghent: European Press.

Hulka, B., J. Cassel, and L. Kupper, 1976. Disparities between Medications Prescribed and Consumed among Chronic Disease Patients. In *Patient Compliance*, ed., L. Lasagna, 123–152. Mt. Kisco, NY: Futura.

Janis, I., 1983. The Role of Social Support in Adherence to Stressful Decisions, *American Psychologist* 38: 143–160.

Katon, W., and A. Kleinman, 1981. Doctor-Patient Negotiation and other Social Science Strategies in Patient Care. In *The Relevance of Social Science for Medicine*, eds., L. Eisenberg and A. Kleinman, 253–279. Boston: Reidel.

Kerrebijn, K., R. Veentjer, and E. Water, 1982. The Immediate Effect of Physiotherapy and Aerosol Treatment on Pulmonary Function in Children with Cystic Fibrosis, *European Journal of Respiratory Diseases* 63: 35–42.

Lasagna, L., 1976. *Patient Compliance*. Mt. Kisco, NY: Futura.

Litt, I., and W. Cuskey, 1981. Compliance with Salicylate Therapy in Adolescents with Juvenile Rheumatoid Arthritis, American Journal of Diseases in Children 135: 434–436.

Lorin, M., and C. Denning, 1971. Evaluation of Postural Drainage by Measurement of Sputum Volume Consistency, *American Journal of Physical Medicine* 50: 215–219.

Mayo, N., 1978. Patient Compliance: Practical Implications for Physical Therapists: A Review of the Literature, *Physical Therapy* 58: 1083–1090.

Mellins, E., 1974. Pulmonary Physiotherapy in the Pediatric Age Group, *American Review of Respiratory Diseases* 110: 137–142.

Messerschmidt, D., 1981. *Anthropologists at Home in North America: Methods and Issues in the Study of One's Own Society*. Cambridge: Cambridge University Press.

Meyers, A., T. Dolan, Jr., and D. Mueller, 1975. Compliance and Self-Medication in Cystic Fibrosis, *American Journal of Diseases in Children* 129: 1011–1013.

Motoyama, E., 1973. Assessment of Lower Airway Obstruction in Cystic Fibrosis. In *Fundamental Problems of Cystic Fibrosis and Related Diseases*, eds. J. Mangos and R. Talamo, 335–343. New York: Intercontinental Medical Book Company.

Murray, J., 1979. The Ketchup-Bottle Method, *New England Journal of Medicine* 300: 1155–1157.

Passero, M., B. Remor, and J. Salomon, 1981. Patient-Reported Compliance with Cystic Fibrosis Therapy, *Clinical Pediatrics* 20: 264–268.

Rochester, D., and S. Goldberg, 1980. Techniques of Respiratory Physical Therapy, *American Review of Respiratory Disease* 122: 133–146.

Ruley, E., 1978. Compliance in Young Hypertensive Patients, *Pediatric Clinics of North America* 25: 175–182.

Shope, J., 1981. Medication Compliance, *Pediatric Clinics of North America* 28: 5–21.

Stuart, R., 1982. *Adherence, Compliance and Generalization in Behavioral Medicine*. New York: Brunner/Mazel.

248

Sutton, P., D. Pavia, J. Bateman, and S. Clarke, 1983. Chest Physiotherapy: A Review, *European Journal of Respiratory Diseases* 63: 188–201.

Twaddle, A., 1981. Sickness and the Sickness Career. In *The Relevance of Social Science for Medicine*, eds., L. Eisenberg and A. Kleinman, 111–133. Boston: Reidel.

Weintraub, M., 1976. Intelligent Noncompliance and Capricious Compliance. In *Patient Compliance*, ed., L. Lasagna, 39–47. Mt. Kisco, NY: Futura.

Wood, R., 1982. Personal Communication.

Wood, R., T. Boat, and C. Doershuk, 1976. Cystic Fibrosis, *American Review of Respiratory Disease* 113: 833–878.

Zola, I., 1981. Structural Constraints in the Doctor-Patient Relationship: The Case of Non-Compliance. In *The Relevance of Social Science for Medicine*, eds., L. Eisenberg and A. Kleinman, 241–252. Boston: Reidel.

Cure, Care and Control: An Ectopic Encounter with Biomedical Obstetrics

MERRILL SINGER

University of Connecticut Medical School
Hispanic Health Council

The title of this paper is intended to suggest a double meaning for the word *ectopic*[1]. On the one hand, I have in mind its technical meaning in biomedical obstetrics, namely the pathological development of a fertilized ovum outside of the uterus, most commonly in the fallopian tube. Ectopic pregnancy is a major health problem accounting for a quarter of all maternal deaths in the U.S. (Laing and Jeffrey 1982). Significantly, several studies indicate that the rate of ectopic pregnancy is increasing, yet recognition of this life-threatening condition is commonly missed by physicians (Helvacioglu, Long and Yang 1979; Hallat 1974; Breen 1970). Undiagnosed, the mortality rate for ectopic pregnancy is over 60% (Patrick 1982). In this sense, ectopic pregnancy encompasses a dual problem: a problem of health and a problem of medicine, a health problem in need of medical treatment and a medical treatment that is itself a health problem.

On the other hand, I refer to the more general dictionary definition of ectopic, namely as a label for something that is out-of-place. In the present context, I focus on what Jordan (1980:49) has termed the "grossly visible incongruity between [pregnant] women's attitudes and expectations on the one hand and those of their [biomedical] attendants on the other," as illustrated below in the medical handling of a woman with a possible ectopic diagnosis. Herein is found a third sense in which ectopic pregnancy is a problem, a problem in the health care provider/patient relationship; that is, a social problem, which places all of the other problematic issues previously enumerated in their appropriate context: the relational character of health and medical care.

The frame for the following discussion of a concrete ethnographic case is an ongoing discourse in the medical social sciences about social relations in the clinical encounter. One party to this discourse is physicians and physician-helpers concerned about "problem patients." Thus, a literature has developed directed at assisting physicians to better understand so as to better control difficult patients (Taussig 1980). For example, in a popular medical school and allied health textbook, Alvin Burstein analyzes the varieties of the clinical entity known as the "angry patient." One varient of relevance to the case discussed here, which he calls the "controlling patient, "is typified ... by his struggle to stay in charge of his own treatment. Hence he may attempt to anticipate his doctor's diagnosis, press for his physician's working hypothesis and then challenge it, quarrel about the appropriateness of the treatment regimen, etc." (Burstein 1979:54). Why would a patient act, or, to stay within the idiom, "act out" in such a fashion? Burstein (1979:59) tells us, or more importantly tells future physicians, nurses and other health care professionals: "this form of antagonism often reflects a lifelong characteristic pattern of relating to potential helpers, and it springs from a basic distrust of parental figures and their surrogates."

In allegiance with this perspective, a major sector of the medical social sciences, what might be called the "service sector," has taken as its mission the understanding of patients of diverse cultural, ethnic, or class backgrounds so as to arm physicians with a culturally relative bedside manner (Baer and Singer 1982). Proponents of this approach argue that to be socially relevant the social science of medicine must be clinically relevant. While in most cases the service literature consists of simple solicitation for greater sympathy and sensitivity on the part of physicians for the meaning systems and illness behavior patterns of particular populations (e.g. Harwood 1981; Davis 1984), there also exist calls for the utilization of cultural information to facilitate patient management and increase patient compliance (e.g. Kleinman 1978).

Counterpoised to this stance and as such another party to the clinical encounter discourse are those who bemoan the medical monopolization of modern life. In the perspective of this group, biomedicine functions as a crippler of personal autonomy, rendering people impotent to handle their affairs without the aid of a medical crutch. In the words of Ivan Illich (1975:41), a leading exponent of this view, biomedicine "creates ill-health by increasing stress, by multiplying disabling dependence, by generating new painful needs, by lowering the levels of tolerance for discomfort or pain, by reducing the leeway that people are wont to concede to an individual when he suffers, and by abolishing even the right to self-care."

In short, while one set of observers of the clinical encounter, what might be termed the "pro-physician group," is concerned about the dominating patient, the other, the "pro-patient group," focuses its attention on the dominating physician. Each side recognizes that a key determinant of the medical encounter is power, but who has it and more significantly who *should* have it, are the issues under dispute.

Finally, there is a third camp in this debate, the camp in which this paper, so to speak, pitches its tent. It too views power as a key, if not the key, issue, but not just power relations in the microcosm of the clinical setting or medicine generally. Adherents of the inherently critical perspective espoused here seek to locate the clinical relationship and the whole medical complex within its encompassing political-economic framework so as to remind us that physicians and patients alike are but two layers in a larger social dynamic characterized by inequality, dominance, and, most importantly for the case at hand, *struggle* (Baer, Singer and Johnsen 1986). As Michael Taussig (1980:9) maintains, the clinical encounter is not merely an arena for the further enfeeblement of people as patients, but also has become a "combat zone of disputes over power and over definitions." These disputes are not best explained, as the pro-physician group would have it, by limiting attention to patient or even physician psychology. To limit analysis of social dynamics to the examination of individual psyches is the social scientific equivalent of executing foot soldiers for major war crimes as if foot soldiers begin and direct their own wars. Similarly, doctor-patient disputes are not insignificant, as the position of the pro-patient group might imply, just because, as cannot and should not be denied, the physician has the upper hand. To attend solely to the power of the powerful and thereby lose sight of resistance and struggle by the oppressed is itself an act of unintended expropriation and enfeeblement, and an act of social distortion as well.

The doctor-patient relationship in obstetrics is a fertile arena for the investigation of the issues noted above because of the sweeping changes that have occurred in this specialty over the past several years. As Wertz and Wertz (1979) have shown, early in its history obstetrics adopted a mechanical model of childbirth, viewing the process as a dangerous procedure regularly necessitating medical intervention. This perspective gained widespread acceptance as male obstetricians came to be the dominant caretakers during maturnity and delivery and female midwives were relegated to ever more subordinate and marginal roles. Increasingly, the hospital came to be seen as the appropriate site for delivery and, because of the prevalence of hospital infection, "[d]octors had to regard each women as diseased" (Wertz and Wertz 1979:128). By the 1930s, delivery routines were fixed in accordance with the needs of doctors and hospitals. Women were automatically placed in the lithotomy position and their arms strapped down. Anesthetics and analgesics were administered to control the woman's experience. Episiotomies were standard and forceps were employed in 50% of all deliveries. In short, birth became "the processing of a machine by machines and skilled technicians" (Wertz and Wertz 1979:165).

In recent years, the mechanical routinization of obstetric practice has faced widening challenges. As summarized by DeVries (1984:89):

> It appears as if the trend toward the "medicalization" of birth, marked by increasing numbers of surgical deliveries and new technological capabilities for intervening and controlling the birth process, has been slowed — if not halted — by a desire on the part of both consumers and professionals to "humanize" the care given to childbearing women and their families. There has been a flurry of professional and consumer activity based on a concern for "humanized" or "family centered" care in birthing.... The changes made in the medical treatment of childbirth ... [include] the creation of alternative birth centers which provide "homey" birthing environments and the establishment of programs to limit the separation of families during birth ...

Has the purported "humanization" of obstetrics pacified the so-called controlling patient? Or, conversely, has it cured the structural iatrogenesis of doctor/patient interactions? These questions are addressed by examining the case history of a recent obstetrics patient.

THE CASE

The case examined here is that of a 31-year old, college-educated Caucasian women who in July of 1983 sought medical attention for what she feared might be an ectopic pregnancy. I interviewed her for a total of eight hours over the course of five occasions during the course of her entrance and treatment in a prepaid health maintenance organization (HMO) with a recently expanded OB/GYN department.

The woman, five years previous, had suffered a tubal pregnancy and rupture. At the time, she was newly wed and unaware of being pregnant. One evening, after experiencing acute abdominal discomfort, she suddenly collapsed and was rushed by ambulance to a local hospital where her right fallopian tube was removed in emergency surgery. During recuperation, she was told that she was at-risk for a second ectopic pregnancy, and that the chances this would occur increased with time because of the postoperative internal scarring commonly associated with abdominal surgery. In her view, the most traumatic aspect of the entire episode was that up until that point she had taken her fertility for granted and suddenly it was in question.

In need of a fuller understanding of her situation, the woman began exploring the popular literature on tubal pregnancy. Contacting the Boston Women's Health Book Collective, the feminist organization that produced the widely read women's health manual entitled *Our Bodies, Ourselves*, she learned that "IUD-associated infections may cause tubal blockage resulting in tubal pregnancy." This particularly angered her because for seven years before the tubal rupture she had worn a Lippe's Loop IUD. As she indignantly commented, "When they gave me the IUD, that was a form of butchery. They knew damn well that I'd never had kids before. They knew that my generation of women was a bunch of guinea pigs ... They ... put this device in me that they knew nothing about and then for seven years never took the thing out of me. I asked them about taking it out, but they never did. As far as I'm concerned, they didn't even care whether I could have kids."

A desire to have children, first sparked while helping to raise her younger brother, now took on new urgency. But the woman's husband was not ready and continued to refuse for the next three years. As a result of this and other conflicts, their marriage deteriorated and finally dissolved in 1981. Her efforts to conceive resumed two years later shortly after she was remarried. Not wanting to have children after age 35 because of the increased risk, she felt that her "biological clock" was running out. Her second husband shared her concern, and they began trying to conceive. At about this time, through his work, her husband joined a health maintenace organization, a prepaid comprehensive health care program which operates its own health center.

The woman's first interaction with the OB/GYN department of the health center initiated a string of frustrating experiences which might be best characterized as an *ectopic encounter*. The incongruity between patient and provider attitudes, expectations, and behaviors in this encounter, as we shall see, were centered on issues of *cure* (i.e. adherence to the safest and most effective procedures to ensure the health of the patient), *care* (i.e. sympathetic treatment of the patient), and *control* (i.e. allowing the patient to both participate in and understand her treatment). The woman's expectations in this encounter were shaped by a variety of factors, including: (1) her socialization into the lay biomedical worldview and her familiarity with the technology and procedures of modern medicine; (2) her exposure to the feminist critique of male-dominated medicine; (3) her fears generated by the previous ectopic pregnancy; (4) her strong desire to have children; and (5) her sense that as a client in a prepaid program she had a contractual right to satisfying health care. When she contacted the OB/GYN department, the woman already (and as it turned out correctly) suspected that she was pregnant. Consequently, she expected to be given an appointment to meet the medical staff, discuss her obstetric and medical history with them, receive answers to her numerous questions about her condition, and be given a preliminary examination and routine blood workup.

Her initial telephone call to the OB/GYN department was handled by an "advice nurse," an RN whose job is to "answer questions, provide advice and arrange appropriate care of urgent OB/GYN problems" (Snyder 1984:2).[2] To the woman's surprise, "they wouldn't let me talk to a doctor. They didn't ask me to come in for an appointment. They said, our policy is prevention and unless there is something wrong with you, there is no need for you to see the doctor. As if there was nothing wrong with me!" The woman was particularly upset by the advice nurse's instruction to come in for a pregnancy blood test two weeks after missing her period, to be followed, if necessary, three weeks later by an ultrasound evaluation of the location of the developing gestational sac. Adherence to this schedule would have meant that the occurence of an ectopic pregnancy would not have been detected until about the seventh week after conception, a week later than the woman had ruptured during her previous ectopic pregnancy.

Consequently, the woman rejected the nurse's counsel and asked again to speak to a doctor. Instead her call was returned by an OB/GYN nurse practitioner, the occupier of the next rung in the institutional hierarchy, who, after reviewing the medical records the woman had had sent to the center, instructed her to come in for a blood test as soon as she missed her period. The woman reported that she felt "satisfied with what they said, but I still didn't understand why they didn't ask me to come in for an appointment to do a check-up and meet face-to-face."

One day after missing her period, the woman went to the the center's lab for an HCG (human chorionic gonadotrophin) blood test. The next day she called the advise nurse and learned that her score was 55, a borderline reading on a scale on which figures under 10 are negative for pregnancy and those above 100 are positive. A second blood test was scheduled for three days later. When the woman called back at the appointed time to get her second score, it was unavailable. Several hours later she was told that her first score had been misread and was actually 95 and that her second score was over 200. The misreading of the score reinforced the woman's apprehension about the HMO and that they still did not want her to come in for an examination even though her pregnancy was now confirmed magnified her distrust. The subsequent ultrasound was unable to locate the gestational sac and the radiologist informed the woman that it was still too early in the pregnancy for successful sonographic visualization. He instructed her to return in a week to ten days. Then, to the woman's dismay, he quickly departed, leaving her with an array of unanswered questions about sonographic efficacy and side effects.

At this juncture, the woman began to feel quite distressed. She had banked on the ultrasound providing her with a definitive answer and instead she went home empty handed. She stated, "I didn't feel that they knew what they were doing ... It was a complete bureaucracy. I go into the lab for a blood test and ... the guy in the lab doesn't even know when the results will be back ... this place doesn't know its arm from its leg. Not only do they not know what they are doing, they don't care about me as a patient. I wanted the doctor to give me a full plan of what he intended to do to monitor me. He also should give me his point of view of what should be done ... but these people didn't even want to talk to me about it."

In response to her dissatisfaction with the medical treatment she was receiving and the mounting anquish she was experiencing as a result, the woman activated her social support network. Although she did not know any health care professionals personally, she had friends and relatives who did. The woman's sister's boyfriend (a second year medical student), a friend engaged in pregnancy research, and a nurse contacted by another friend all supplied her with information about the signs and symptoms of ectopic pregancy. Moreover, the woman's sister conducted a computer search in the Harvard Medical School library and provided the woman with a number of current medical articles on the subject. Armed with this information, she called the HMO and insisted on an appointment with the obstetrician. At the same time, she suggested that they begin regular HCG monitoring, a recommended procedure because in intrauterine pregnancy HCG levels double every few days while in extrauterine pregnancy scores begin to fall off. The nurse practitioner agreed with this suggestion and scheduled the appropriate tests.

At the appointment with the obstetrician, the woman was handled by a new nurse practitioner, who wanted a full account of why she had come. The woman objected because she already had detailed her history to the first nurse practitioner and expected momentarily to retell her tale to the obstetrician. In fact, the obstetrician did not arrive until 45 minutes after the scheduled time for the appointment (a replication of the radiologist's tardiness) and then, according to the woman, walked into the examining room and said, "So what's your traumatic story, why are you here?" The woman reported, "I felt like punching him. He had a very smart alecky attitude, as if there was nothing wrong with me and why should I be so concerned. He sat down in a chair and didn't ask to examine me, didn't examine me the whole time. He said, I don't know why you're so upset and think you're going to have an ectopic." As it was eventually revealed, the obstetrician did not know that the woman had suffered a previous tubal rupture because he had been sent only a brief and somewhat inaccurate summary of her medical records. Even after she told him her full obstetric history, however, the woman felt that the doctor was still unconcerned and retained a condescending tone.

The woman's next HCG score was lost, but a subsequent test revealed that her plasma HCG levels were rising normally. Finally, during the fifth week of her pregnancy, a second ultrasound showed a normal intrauterine implantation, and the woman's first internal examination was scheduled. This encounter continued the previous pattern. According to the woman, "This physician hardly talked to me. He came in and didn't introduce himself. I was feeling lousy because of morning sickness and he never even asked me how I was. I was treated like an object. He rushed through it. When he did the exam, he didn't tell me why he was doing what he was doing, he just did it. I had to push him to tell me. Every piece of information I got out of him, I had to push for."

Following this examination, the woman was instructed to return for check-ups once a month. By approximately the thirtieth week of her pregnancy, the woman began to be concerned because she recorded no weight gain in between two visits to the HMO. Explained the woman, "I read that I should be gaining but nobody said anything to me about the fact that I wasn't gaining. So I asked and the nurses said I should be gaining. So I asked why they didn't seem concerned that I wasn't gaining weight. They decided I should come back in two weeks so they could check my weight again. This time I put on some weight but my uterus didn't grow. So they said come back in a week. That time my uterus had grown, but I hadn't gained any weight. The next time I gained weight, but my uterus didn't grow. When I pressed and asked the obstetrician who examined me that time, she casually said, "Oh, you might have interuterine growth retardation" and she began to leave the examining room. Alarmed, I asked what that was and she said, "I'm sorry, we only have seven minutes per patient." Then she paused a moment and left. I was shocked. I thought she was saying my baby might be retarded because of insufficient nutrition and she would stay to explain it. I went back to work in tears. I called my childbirth educator from the Lamaze classes and she explained what interuterine growth retardation meant."

Ultimately, it was determined that the fetus was developing normally, although the woman was informed that she would probably have a small baby. In fact, she delivered a full-term, healthy, baby with above average length and weight.

Asked to evaluate her experience, the woman replied, "I've had to push and push and push for every single response I've gotten out of the health care system. If it hadn't been that I told them I was concerned, that I wanted to be monitored, they would never have done anything. I don't trust the health care system at all. I feel I have to constantly be on top of the situation, reading as much as I can, pushing them to see me. I feel I can't stop for a single moment being on top of the situation. It occurred to me that the word patient must come from the word patience, because that's what patients are expected to have."

DISCUSSION

While the details of this case are particular, and have special reference to patients who share this woman's social class and educational background, there is sufficient literature on the subject of provider/patient interaction to suggest that the overall pattern is general

(Matthews 1983; Weaver and Garrett 1978; Friedson 1980; Schoepf 1975; Singer et al. 1984). From the narrow pro-physician perspective, the woman described here is a typical "controlling patient," and was seen as such by her obstetricians as disclosed by the question: "So what's your traumatic story?" This remark is not surprising given the medical view which "locates the authority to speak about birth truly and authoritatively in the medical profession" (Jordan 1980:39). Bound up in this physician's initial reaction to the woman is an apparent resentment of her effort to self-diagnose ("I don't know why you're so upset and think you're going to have an ectopic").

Among other things, this reaction reflects medicine's disregard for women's ability to diagnose their own pregnancies (Jordan 1977). Consequently, in established medical practice, the variety of signs and symptoms of pregnancy that are open to women's immediate experience, so-called presumptive indications such as breast changes, headaches, nausea, alteration of the mucous membranes, are assigned a low ranking as medical diagnostic criteria. As summed up in the *Handbook of Obstetrics and Gynecology*, "there is no subjective evidence of pregnancy which can be accepted as diagnostic" (Benson 1971:45). Evidence that requires the utilization of medical instruments, and is therefore accessible to the physician but outside the patient's control, by contrast, is accorded a high ranking. As Jordan (1977:8) found in her telephone survey of obstetricians and gynecologists while posing as a patient seeking an abortion:

> The policy of each and every physician was to require a positive pregnancy test before any further action would be considered. Moreover, the test turned out to be a nonnegotiable requirement, even if I insisted that I knew I was pregnant, citing the classic (presumptive) symptoms and pointing to my experience with previous pregnancies.

Empirical investigation by Jordan (1977), however, found that women's competence in diagnosing their own pregnancy is quite good. This research finding notwithstanding, physicians respond very strongly to self-diagnosis because "it threatens the very foundation of their authority. This dimension of the doctor-patient relationship is, for most physicians, an absolutely 'nonnegotiable' item" (Steward and Sullivan 1982:1401).

Physicians report having their greatest difficulty in this area with women patients. In a recent survey, over 450 general practitioners described their most troubling and time consuming patients as distrustful and demanding women (Stimpson 1982). As Kahan and Gaskill (1978:261) comment:

> As women begin to take a more active role in influencing the type of care they receive, they ask questions. Sometimes the caretaker perceives these questions and the emotions behind them as challenging his/her competence and authority when, in fact, the patient is requesting information. This distortion or misperception reverberates within the relationship sometimes resulting in the caretakers labeling the patient as "difficult."

That physicians are taught during their medical school training to view women's health problems as uninteresting, their history relating skills as underdeveloped, their personalities as highly emotional, and their symptoms as commonly reflecting nondisease has been suggested by several health care researchers and medical school textbook evaluators (Weaver and Garrett 1978).

In the liberal critique of biomedicine formulated by the pro-patient group, we have in the case presented above a clear-cut example of a "high-tech," irrationally bureaucratic, objectifying, infantilizing, expert-controlling medical system acting insensitively to the care-needs of an oppressed woman patient. Professional control over medicine, in fact, is seen from this perspective as the central defect of the medical system. This control is described as having "reached the proportions of an epidemic" and as having become "a major threat to health" (Illich 1975:3). The most socially pernicious consequence of professional dominance is that patients become addicted to dependency and are transformed thereby from independent actors and decision-makers into passive medical consumers. Especially affected by the onerous aspects of professionalization are women. In the homocentric understanding of health and health care developed by adherents of the pro-patient view "men act while women suffer" (Stark 1982:448).

Yet the words and actions of the woman described here reveal that an image of an active, aggressive male physician in control of health care, and a female patient that is a passive victim, manipulated and dominated, is faulty. On the one hand, it is clear that whatever her criticisms of biomedicine, a central concern of the woman is a demand for more and better expert attention and not for emancipation from biomedical enslavement. Like most of us, this woman is caught up in the biomedicalization of modern life. No less than the physicians and nurses, she is swayed by the power and cultural hegemony of biomedicine. Thus, hers is a protest over "what physicians do [or fail to do], not what medicine is" (Stark 1982:426).

But, most assuredly, she is not as a consequence passive and impotent. She is active and resourceful and prepared to do battle for her just rights and self-protection. Thus, her tale is not one of a powerless pawn, pushed, probed, and prodded by domineering physicians. Instead, we have accounts of the gathering of intelligence, the mobilizing of allies, the formulating of strategies, and the pressing of demands; in short, a narrative of struggle and combat in the very heart of physician-controlled territory. The lesson is clear: until we fully realize that social process in the medical arena is shaped not by the unrestrained will and might of potent oppressors but by an ongoing clash between those best served and those least served by existing medical institutions, and between those most in control of and those least in control of medical knowledge, procedures, and technology, we will misunderstand cases like the one presented here.

Additionally, and in conclusion, we will not understand this case by analyzing it merely in terms of the immediate setting of the events described. The behavior of all participants was in no small way shaped by what McKinlay (1976) has labeled the "changing political and economic context of the patient-physician encounter." Seen in this light, everything from the seemingly indifferent attitude of the physicians, the bureaucratic and assembly line character of treatment, the increasingly complex division of labor in health care, the labeling of concerned and questioning patients as demanding or controlling, the use of the telephone as a protective barrier, the transformation of prevention into a cost-cutting gimmick, the revolt of the patient, the demystification of medical knowledge, and the blossoming of the health maintenance organization itself are all products of the expansion of the logic and structure of corporate capitalism into the medical arena. As aptly summarized by Navarro (1976:119):

> We find then that the major conflict in the health sector replicates the conflict in the overall system. And that conflict is primarily not between the providers and the consumers, but between those that have a dominant influence in the health system (the corporate class and upper middle class) who represent less than 20 percent of our population and control most of the health institutions, and the majority of our population (lower-middle class and working class) ... who have no control whatsoever over either the production or consumption of those health services.

An examination of the HMO clearly reveals the way in which the health care industry, to use Navarro's phrase (1976:118), "is administered but not controlled by the medical profession." The HMO is a product of the often-described but still unresolved financial crisis in health care, created as a market-oriented approach to self-regulation and cost-cutting, and designed to forestall government-imposed national health insurance. In the words of the leading physician advocate of HMOs:

> The emergence of a free-market economy could stimulate a course of change in the health industry that would have some of the classical aspects of the industrial revolution — conversion to larger units of production, technological innovation, division of labor, substitution of capital for labor, vigorous competition, and profitability as the mandatory condition of survival (Ellwood et al 1976:350).

An added rationale for the prepaid health maintenance strategy was the emergence of an alleged alliance of interests between providers and consumers. Explain Ellwood et al. (1976:351), "Since the economic incentive of the contracting parties are identical ⟨i.e., cutting costs⟩, both would have an interest in maintaining health." Seemingly, the HMO then is not only a solution to skyrocketing health costs (based on the assumption that maintaining "health" is cheaper than restoring it), but also a corrective to professional dominance and patient pacification. Both are joined by the dollar in a prevention-partnership.

But things have not worked out quite so harmoniously. Patient complaints about HMOs are legion: physicians are inaccessible, waiting periods for appointments are protracted, and treatment is rushed, impersonal, and fragmented (Carnoy, Coffee and Koo 1976). In the evaluation of the Health Policy Advisory Center, HMOs take the profit motivation of fee-for-service medicine and turn it on its head: "Whereas fee-for-service doctors and hosptials make more money by seeing more patients, performing more operations and hospitalizing people longer. HMOs increase their net income by doing less" (Carnoy, Coffee and Koo 1976:361). What fee-for-service and HMO medicine have in common, however, is that service provision in both cases is ultimately determined by profit-making rather than patient need.

Importantly, HMO doctors and other care takers have their complaints too, and these are not just about increasingly demanding patients. At Kaiser-Permanente, a growing HMO program founded and largely controlled by a multinational industrial corporation, physicians lament management's emphasis on quantity of subscribers over quality of treatment: "Some doctors feel their schedules are so rushed and inflexible as to preclude delivering adequate, humane care" (Carnoy, Coffee, and Koos 1976:379). Thus, one of the nurse practitioners involved in the patient case presented here confirmed that providers are instructed to limit routine clinical encounters to seven minutes per patient. This care taker complained that the seven minute rule was unfair for patients and stressful for doctors and nurses.

In short, the physician-patient encounter/confrontation is played out on a stage increasingly owned and operated by a medical-industrial complex of profit-seeking corporations (Starr 1981; Wohl 1984; Waitzkin 1983). Of the nine individuals sitting on the Advisory Council of the HMO described here, for example, at least six represent industrial corporations, retail conglomerates, insurance companies, and banks. As the logic of business and commodity production becomes dominant, patients and physicians are left to squabble like grocery clerks and customers over a mispriced can of corn. Here is the classic example of health and healing succumbing to the idiom of business, reaffirming Taussig's observation that "Ours is the culture of business which puts business as the goal of culture" (1980:11). In this sense, the key ideological issue for medical social science research is not "the cultural construction of clinical reality" as Kleinman (1978) suggests, nor even "the clinical construction of culture" as Taussing (1980) asserts, but the *hegemonic capitalist construction of medical and nonmedical reality*. It is this socially constructed reality, forged in the larger arena of capitalist production, reproduction, and bureaucratic control, that multiplies the conditions for ectopic encounters in the biomedical setting. Contradictions in this reality and the social relations that produce them set the parameters and define the issues of clinical combat.

Herein can be found a central distinction between the pro-patient critique of medicine and the larger, more encompassing, class-oriented critical perspective argued for in this paper. While the former is concerned with the *de-medicalization* of social life and experience, the latter takes as its objective the *re-socialization* of medical ideology and practice (Singer et al., 1984). The social importance of the doctor-patient relationship lies in the inherent asymmetry of the interaction. Automatically, the medical encounter reproduces and reinforces wider class, racial, and sexual stratification, while establishing the medical role as an agency for social control. But control in whose interest? As Waitzkin (1984: 342–343) observes:

From a position of relative dominance, doctors can make ideological statements that convey the symbolic trappings of science. These messages reinforce the hegmonic ideology that emanates from other institutions — the family, educational system, mass media, and so forth — and that pervade a society. The same messages tend to direct a client's behavior into safe, acceptable, and nondisruptive channels ... [and] ... thus may help legitimate and reproduce class structure and current relations of economic production ... Wanting to help but unable personally to change the social structure, the health professional typically seeks a solution within the existing institutional context. ... What can be done tends to encourage coping and accomodation. Conscious recognition of ... choices and possible alternatives seldom occurs. Thus in sincerely seeking to help patients, the health professional becomes a "helping agent" for the very structures which produce the social conditions responsible for much patient distress and illness.

So too with the medical social science professional. By seeking to limit analysis to the medical arena and thereby seeing the medical bureaucracy as the ultimate cause of most of the failures and contradictions of health care, the medical social science professional becomes a helping agent for the social structures and social classes which produce the social conditions responsible for many of the problems they seek to eliminate from the health care system. Thus, the obstetric reforms of recent years, reforms designed to "humanize" or "debureaucratize" childbirth, have, in fact, furthered professional (and thus corporate) dominance over the process. Argues DeVries (1984:99):

Although the alternative birth center provides a home-like environment for birth, its location in the hospital reduces client control. In the hospital the client is a guest of the practitioner and is less able to control or direct her care.... Patterns of interaction between hospital medical personnel and their clients remain essentially unchanged in the alternative birth center.... The ... important and relevant issue ... would seem to be how to facilitate home births, but because this alternative is incompatible with the ideology that sustains medical control of birth, it has been ignored by the medical professionals.

Because recent reforms have been directed at the proximal rather than the ultimate causes of ectopic encounters (Rothman 1981), because most concern has been focused on the power of delegated authorities rather than of delegating ones, and because the place of obstetrics within the wider political economy has not been thoroughly analyzed, the "humanization" of obstetrics has not eliminated nor perhaps even reduced the number of doctor-client conflicts accompanying childbirth, and may, in heightening patient expectations about humanized care, have exasperated them.

NOTES

1. An earlier version of this paper was delivered at the Critical Approaches to the Social Science of Medicine Section of the 24th Annual Meetings of the Northeastern Anthropological Association, Hartford, Connecticut. My thanks to Lani Davison for closely reading and commenting on this and the prior draft and to Hans Baer for similar assistance.
2. Prior to contacting the HMO, the woman was seen at a woman's health clinic and referred to a fertility clinic. Records from this clinic were forwarded to the HMO at the woman's initiative, but the clinic failed to include a complete record on her prior salpingectomy. Also, the woman stopped drinking coffee and alcoholic beverages in preparation for pregnancy, evidence of her inclination to play an active role in health maintenance.

REFERENCES

Baer, H., and M. Singer, 1982. Why Not Have a Critical Medical Anthropology? Paper delivered at the 82nd Annual Meeting of the American Anthropology Association, Washington, D.C.

Baer, H., M. Singer, and J. Johnsen, 1986. Toward a Critical Medical Anthropology. *Social Science and Medicine* 23(2): 95–98.

Benson, R., 1971. *Handbook of Obstetrics and Gynecology*. 4th Edition. Los Altos, CA: Lange Medical Publications.

Boston Women's Health Collective, 1979. *Our Bodies, Ourselves*. New York: Simon and Schuster.

Breen, J., 1970. A 21 Year Survey of 654 Ectopic Pregnancies, *American Journal of Obstetrics and Gynecology* 106: 1004–1018.

Burstein, A., 1979. The Angry Patient. In *Psychosocial Medical Basis of Medical Practice*. eds. G. Bowden and A. Burstein, 50–55. Baltimore: Williams and Williams.

Carnoy, J., L., Coffee, and Koos L. 1976. Corporate Medicine: The Kaiser Health Plan, In *Prognosis Negative*. ed. D. Kotelchuck, 363–386. New York: Vintage.

Davis, D., 1984. Medical Misinformation: Communication Between Outport Newfoundland Woman and their Physicians, *Social Science and Medicine* 18(3): 273–278.

DeVries, R., 1984. "Humanizing" Childbirth: The Discovery and Implementation of Bonding Theory, *International Journal of Health Services* 14(1): 89–104.

Ellwood, P., N. Anderson, J. Billings, R. Carlson, E. Hoagberg, and W. McClure, 1976. Health Maintenance Strategy, In *Prognosis Negative*. ed. D. Kotelchuck, 347–352. New York: Vintage.

Friedson, E., 1980. Prepaid Group Practice and the New "Demanding" Patient, In *Readings in Medical Sociology*. ed. D. Mechanic, 407–417. New York: Free Press.

Hallat, J., 1974. Repeat Ectopic Pregnancy: A Study of 123 Consecutive Cases, *Annual of Obstetrics and Gynecology* 122: 520–524.

Harwood, A., 1981. *Ethnicity and Medical Care*. Cambridge, A: Harvard. Helvacioglu, A., E. Long, and S. Yang. 1979. Ectopic Pregnancy: An Eight-Year Review, *Journal of Reproductive Medicine* 22: 87–92.

Illich, I., 1975. *Medical Nemesis: The Expropriation of Health*. London: Calder and Boyars.

Jordan, B., 1977. The Self-Diagnosis of Early Pregnancy: An Investigation of Lay Competence, *Medical Anthropology* 1(2): 1–38.

Jordan, B., 1980. *Birth in Four Cultures*. Montreal: Eden.

Kleinman, A., 1978. Concepts and a Model for the Comparison of Medical Systems as Cultural Systems, *Social Science and Medicine* 12: 85–93.

Kleinman, A., L. Eisenberg, and B. Good, 1978. Clinical Lessons from Anthropologic and Cross-Cultural Research, *Annals of Internal Medicine* 88(2): 251–258.

Laing, F., and R. Jeffrey, 1982. Ultrasound Evaluation of Ectopic Pregnancy, *Radiologic Clinics of North America* 20(2): 383–396.

Matthews, J., 1983. The Communication Process in Clinical Settings, *Social Science and Medicine* 17(18): 1371–   .

McKinlay, J., 1976. The Changing Political and Economic Context of the Physician-Patient Encounter, In *The Doctor-Patient Relationship in the Changing Health Scene*. ed. E. Gallagher, 155–188. Washington, D.C.: U.S. Department of H.E.W.

Navarro, V., 1976. *Medicine Under Capitalism*. New York: Prodist.

Rothman, B., 1981. Awake and Aware, or False Consciousness: The Cooption of Childbirth Reform in America, In *Alternatives to Medical Control of Childbirth*. ed. S. Romalis, 150–180. Austin: University of Texas Press.

Schoepf, B., 1975. Human Relations Versus Social Relations in Medical Care, In *Topias and Utopias in Health*. eds. S. Ingman and A. Thomas, 99–120. The Hague: Mouton.

Singer, M., A. Arnold, M. Fitzgerald, L. Madden, and C. Von Legat, 1984. Hypoglycemia: A Controversial Illness in U.S. Society, *Medical Anthropology* 8(1): 1–35.

Snyder, B., 1984. OB/GYN Department Provides Growing Number of Services, *Planning for Health* 3(1): 2.

Starr, P., 1981. *The Social Transformation of American Medicine*. New York: Basic Books.

Stark, E., 1982. Doctors in Spite of Themselves: The Limits of Radical Health Criticism, *International Journal of Health Services* 12(3): 419–457.

Stewart, D., and T. Sullivan, 1982. Illness Behavior and the Sick Role in Chronic Illness, *Social Science and Medicine* 16: 1401–1414.

Stimpson, G., 1982. General Practitioners, "Trouble" and Types of Patients, In *Sociology of National Health Service*. ed. M. Stacy, Keele, Great Britain: University of Keele.

Taussig, M., 1980. Reification and the Consciousness of the Patient, *Social Science and Medicine* 14B: 3–13.

Waitzkin, H., 1983. *The Second Sickness*. New York: Free Press.

Waitzkin, H., 1984. The Micropolitics of Medicine: A Contextual Analysis, *International Journal of Health Services* 14(3): 339–378.

Weaver, J. and S. Garrett, 1978. Sexism and Racism in the American Health Care Industry: A Comparative Analysis, *International Journal of Health Services* 8(4): 677–703.

Wertz, R. and D. Wertz, 1979. *Lying In: A Natural History of Childbirth in America*. New York: Schocken Books.

Wohl, S., 1984. *The Medical Industrial Complex*. New York: Harmony.

Applications and Research in Clinical Settings

Consultation Psychiatry as Applied Medical Anthropology

THOMAS M. JOHNSON

Southern Methodist University, University of Texas Health Science Center, Dallas

INTRODUCTION

Although there is a long history of collaboration between psychiatry and anthropology (Favazza and Faheem 1982; Favazza and Oman 1977), such work has been predominantly in the areas of transcultural psychiatry, community mental health, or in psychological anthropology. In these areas of collaboration, theoretical investigations have predominated over applied programs. Over the past several decades, however, anthropologists have become involved in medical school teaching, often within departments of psychiatry. Despite increasing involvement of anthropologists in medical education (Kennedy 1979), most teaching activities have been confined to the lecture hall or, occasionally, in community settings. Collaboration between psychiatrists and anthropologists in clinical teaching is not common. And yet, the hospital arena holds enormous potential for teaching future physicians about cultural influences on health care.

The purpose of this paper is to describe briefly how an anthropologist should prepare for such work in clinical medicine, to illustrate specific contributions an applied medical anthropologist might make to hospital psychiatric consultation through a case study,[1] and to discuss some generic anthropological lessons of utility for the practice of consultation-liaison psychiatry.

PREPARATION FOR APPLIED MEDICAL WORK

To prepare for work in clinical medicine, normal graduate anthropology coursework should be expanded to include medical sociology, psychology, and community health. Exposure to medical school departments through research grants is invaluable, but an anthropologist should also conduct protracted periods of observational research by "lurking" on specific hospital wards and by "shadowing" medical residents in their daily (and nightly) work routines.[2] If one's primary goal is to be a medical educator, it is most important to become intimately acquainted with the process of medical education, both by direct participation (e.g., spending a year or more in training with health professions students to study their professional socialization) and by a careful review of the literature on professional socialization in medicine.[3] By such careful "fieldwork" it is possible for an anthropologist to learn the "language" of medicine and to become comfortable in clinical settings, much as any ethnographer becomes acclimated to a more traditional field setting. There exist many self-instructional texts in medical terminology, the formal study of which also should be obligatory.

Such preparation is important for a medical anthropologist who wishes to teach medical students because the most powerful teaching in medicine takes place not in the lecture hall, but at the bedside or in the clinic. Just as there is a "mystique about field work" (Agar 1980: 2), and just as fieldwork is a potent right of passage into professional status for anthropologists, clinical "fieldwork" serves the same socializing function for the student of medicine. Indeed, the touchstone of medical education is the "clinical case": student physicians learn as much from clinical experience with patients as from journals or books. The importance of such clinical experience in medical education is underscored by the ubiquitous practice of telling "war stories" — a formal lecture-hall and informal cafeteria ritual in which clinicians tell students about especially difficult cases. Such stories not only teach medical facts and techniques, but also transmit attitudes and values. Moreover, the experience and ability to recount clinical vignettes gives one higher status as a medical educator (most basic science faculty, such as anatomists and biochemists, are devalued by students because they "have never really seen patients"). A medical anthropologist who has clinical experience will be more highly valued by students.

In short, effective medical school teaching by an applied medical anthropologist demands active clinical involvement, a sensitivity to the "culture" of clinical medicine, and a temperament which favors spontaneity and "risk taking" rather than careful lecture preparation and oratorical skills (Johnson 1981). It also demands an objective, nonthreatening approach to medicine, and an analytical rather than critical posture which must be communicated to medical professionals who have been under attack from some of our more reform-mongering, doctor-bashing, social science colleagues.[4]

WORK IN CONSULTATION-LIAISON PSYCHIATRY

Six years as the only anthropologist reported to be a member of a consultation-liaison psychiatry team (Tilley 1982: 267) have provided interesting opportunities for me both to work with medical students and psychiatry residents (who are taught on such consultation teams) and to contribute to patient care activities in the hospital. It is, indeed, a fascinating type of applied medical anthropology.[5] Consultation psychiatrists are hospital-based practitioners who respond to requests form other physician specialists for assistance in the care of patients felt to have psychosocial problems either resulting from, or contributing to, their medical problems. Liaison activities by psychiatrists are more intensive interactions with these same specialists including making "rounds," conducting collaborative research, or facilitating support groups and counseling with staff on general medical wards in a hospital (thereby having more direct, ongoing interaction with patients, staff, and students on another specialty service).[6]

My participation in clinical work involves daily "attending rounds" with a consultation-liaison psychiatry team for formal discussion of patients seen by residents and students, "bedside rounds" (actually going to see patients previously seen by residents), and participating in "work rounds" (seeing patients for initial evaluation after receiving a request for consultation). Additionally, I have cultivated ongoing liaison relationships with a high-risk obstetrics service and a burn unit. For three years, for example, I made rounds with the high-risk obstetrical team (residents, students, nurse specialists, social workers) at 7:00 each morning, in which there are opportunities to comment on psychosocial issues as they spontaneously occur in this setting, to deal with staff problems, and to establish collaborative research projects. Conducting a weekly staff support group for nurses in the burn unit, provides both and opportunity to better understand this highly stressful milieu, and a mandate to help staff better cope with problems which occur therein.

Over the years, the relevance of anthropological perspectives and the utility of anthropological techniques for consultation-liaison psychiatry have been demonstrated many times. Indeed, requests for psychiatric consultation on high-risk OB patients increased from one in the entire year before such activities, to nearly three per week after two years, and two major research projects have been completed.[7]

As a social scientist, one might expect to enter a department of psychiatry with an even more warm reception than from other medical specialties (after all, psychiatry is the one medical specialty which, until the recent emphasis on primary care, has been virtually the standardbearer of the psychosocial tradition within medicine [Johnson 1985]). Yet this is not necessarily the case. My early optimism about doing anthropological work in clinical psychiatry has been tempered over the years because my work in psychiatry has involved a constant and sometimes tedious process of role definition and redefinition revolving around the issue of "clinical" activities, as distinct from "research" or "teaching." Psychiatrists generally do not want nonphysicians working with patients, and are also reluctant to relinquish teaching responsibilities, feeling that only other physicians can properly "model" or teach appropriate medical care. On occasion, however, there have been explicit, contradictory requests to interview a patient or "take students on rounds."

Some psychiatry colleagues routinely accuse other medical specialists of "using" me (more accurately, they accuse me of allowing myself to be "used") to avoid having to deal with psychiatry, thereby having to "admit" that psychiatry is important in medicine. As these sporadic conflicts about anthropological roles in psychiatry occur, and as I have monitored their occurrence, an important pattern has emerged: questioning of my role is more directly related to psychiatric colleagues' perception of their relationship to their physician colleagues than to the nature of any specific activities I am engaged in. Indeed, the same behavior on my part might be welcomed one week, ignored the next, and condemned the following.

The real impetus to my thinking about the role of anthropology in consultation-liaison psychiatry, however, relates to a key event on the high-risk obstetrics service. A medical anthropology graduate student working as a research assistant on that unit, and who had become friends with members of the team with which I routinely worked, informed me that one of the team members had said, "Dr. Johnson is the best psychiatrist we have ... and he's not even a psychiatrist!". When this was reported to me, I was both flattered and disturbed, wondering what I had done to act "like a psychiatrist" when I thought I had been acting like an anthropologist, and worrying that my psychiatry colleagues would again be taking issue with my role in the setting. Upon further reflection, however, I started toying with the heretical notion that, in fact, I had been doing anthropology and not psychiatry, but that anthropological practice has characteristics which are critical to good consultation-liaison psychiatry. I have explored this idea for the past year, and now believe that an effective consultant psychiatrist needs to be a good ethnographer, and that traditional anthropological perspectives can make significant contributions to patient care in consultation psychiatry.

PROCESS: CONSULTATION PSYCHIATRY AS ETHNOGRAPHIC "FIELDWORK"

At the most elementary level, anthropologists are taught to view human behavior as a function of the system demands (family, neighborhood, community) in which individuals live and work. This compels the anthropologist both to undertake periods of ethnographic research to understand the nature of such systems and to adopt the principle of "cultural relativity," a core concept which demands that any human behavior be evaluated only in the context of the cultural system in which it exists.[8] The "meaning" of patient or practitioner behavior in the hospital, then, must be sought not only at biological and psychological levels, but also at the sociocultural level. Patients must be seen to bring perspectives of the family and community systems into the hospital milieu, and individual subsystems within the hospital, such as a burn unit or postpartum ward, must be seen as "subcultures" with their own distinctive norms, attitudes, and values.

Historical trends in consultation-liaison psychiatry alone document a convergence in psychiatric and anthropological interest around the concept of cultural systems. Earliest psychiatric consultation activities, dating to the 1930s, were "patient oriented" (Henry 1929; Schiff and Pilot 1959). In this traditional model the consultant psychiatrist responds to requests for assistance by focusing on "what is wrong with the patient" through chart review, patient evaluation, and formal communication of impressions and treatment recommendations in a chart consultation note. Even today, some consultation requests are dealt with on this level, primarily dependent upon expertise in psychiatric diagnosis. Both historically and contemporarily, this approach to consultation has been noteworthy for poor "compliance" with psychiatric recommendations and inconsistency in requesting consultation by other specialists.

Problems with the "patient oriented" approach led psychiatrists to adopt a "physician-oriented" approach, in which the focus of consultation became the consultee-patient dyad. This approach reflects a conviction that a large proportion of consultation requests stem from difficulties in physician-patient relationships, which are revealed in the process of consultation requests (e.g., ambiguous or unclear purpose for requests or affective statements about the patient by the consultee). As I have noted elsewhere (Johnson 1985), this approach not only allows consultant psychiatrists to adopt a status-enhancing "therapeutic" posture toward consulting physicians ("what is wrong with the physician?"), but also expands the focus of consultation beyond the patient. The physician-oriented approach, however, shares with the patient-oriented approach a primary reliance on traditional psychiatric skills.

Historically, the expansion of focus in consultation psychiatry continued with the embrace of a "situation-oriented" approach (Schwab 1968), in which the consultant psychiatrist feels that consultation requests often stem as much from difficulties in the hospital milieu (nurses, hospital regulations, etc.) as from patient's psyche or the physician-patient dyad. In this aproach, the consultant attempts to "diagnose" difficulties in the ward milieu and to "treat" through group facilitation or environmental manipulation (Greenbert 1960; Meyer and Mendelson 1961). This focus has also led to a proliferation of liaison programs in which consultant psychiatrists begin to interact more intensively with ward staff and other physician colleagues in an attempt to better understand the clinical milieu generating consultation requests. Liaison activity is quite time consuming, however, and has been perceived by many psychiatrists as "unrewarding," "hopeless," "demoralizing" (Auerbach 1975), and "devalued by medical colleagues" (Meyer and Mendelson 1961). In fact, great debate has raged recently about the efficacy of liaison activities, with one prominent consultation-liaison psychiatrist advocating that it be abandoned in order to concentrate on more conventional consultation (Hackett 1982).

Despite this reticence to engage in "situation-oriented" consultation which demands increasing liaison activity, an even more "macro" approach has recently been advocated. "Systemic consultation" (Tarnow and Gutstein 1982) derives from the biopsychosocial model in medicine (Engel 1977; 1980) and general systems theory in the behavioral sciences (Buckley 1968). This approach takes an even more "social" view of psychiatric intervention, holding that the appropriate role for consultation-liaison psychiatrists is to help create "a psychologically healthy milieu for all individuals (parents, families, and staff) who come into contact with the hospital" (Tarnow and Gutstein 1982: 166), and advocating that psychiatrists develop intervention strategies which carry the potential of altering the structure and function of the hospital system.

Significantly, the consultation perspectives elaborated most recently involve greater deviation from the established biomedical emphasis on diagnosing the individual, and toward the more traditonal anthropological perspectives of working within social systems. Although not all consultation requests involve problems requiring systemic intervention, it is clear that many do, particularly in view of our increasingly complex health care delivery system. Yet, the very skills necessary for work at the systemic level are not the type of skills normally cultivated in the process of medical education. This may, in part, explain the ungratifying nature of such work for psychiatrists, who have increasing need to have "legitimacy" in medicine, and the appeal of biological psychiatric reductionism which allows psychiatry to conform to the major technological tradition of biomedicine.

My point is that, despite the obvious appropriateness of a systemic approach to many consultation requests, many psychiatrists are not prepared to diagnose problems in these complex social systems and find the obligatory intensive involvement in such systems to be professionally unrewarding. For an anthropologist, however, systemic approaches to consultation are compelling: they demand the very skills and knowledge resulting from traditional anthropological training. I am not suggesting that anthropology "take over" consultation psychiatry,[9] but rather, that some of the traditional elements of anthropological practice be incorporated into the repertoire of consultant psychiatrists, and that appropriately trained anthropologists be included as members of consultation-liaison psychiatry teams. In such teams, medical students and psychiatrists can be taught anthropological perspectives. I am suggesting that such medical anthropologists help psychiatrists be ethnographers, engaging in participant observation through liaison activities, becoming comfortable with the status/role ambiguity of the "inside-outsider," and learning some basic approaches to both patients and other practitioners which recognize the cultural basis for the construction of clinical "realities."

CONTENT: THE CULTURAL CONSTRUCTION OF CLINICAL REALITY

In systemic consultation, the entire hospital is seen as an arena in which a number of subsystems intersect. Anthropologically, any request for psychiatric consultation is an opportunity to investigate the plural constructions of "clinical reality" of nurses, physicians, patients, and family members, to assess the extent to which incongruities in perceptions may be contributing to an identified patient's problem, and to design interventions which can address problems at this level.

Indeed, my work would suggest that the clinical realities of the various "players" in the medical arena may be quite different: not all people involved in the care of a patient will see the situation alike. Physicians and nurses, despite having professional training and interests in common, have distinctly different "agendas" in terms of patient care priorities. In addition, a rivalrous relationship based on increasing role ambiguity (with expanding responsibility by nurses) and a history of sex role stereotyping (Stein 1967; Lynaugh and Bates 1979), often brings nurses and physicians into conflict. Such conflict, with resultant frustration and anger, may be displaced onto patients and result in a "psych consult." For example, I have seen requests for psychiatry to evaluate a patient for "depression and sleep disturbance," not because the patient was complaining to his or her physician, but because nurses were complaining that having the patient awake after the 11:00 p.m. shift change was disrupting their "normal ward routines." Nurses may also be more aware of, and more interested in, conflict between patients and family members, resulting in a request for a "psych consult" for family problems of which physicians may be unaware.

Indeed, family conflicts often result in requests for psychiatric intervention, as do conflicts between family members and medical staff. Patients bring with them into the hospital beliefs about symptoms which have come to be known as explanatory models (EMs) (Kleinman 1978). Family members also have EMs which may be more or less congruent with those of the patient, nurses, and physicians. It may not stop there: certain patients may also be cared for by clinical dieticians, occupational therapists, pastoral counselors, and a cadre of other specialist consultants (e.g. radiologists, plastic surgeons, orthopods, etc.) each of which can have views of the patient's sickness which are not only in conflict with the patient, but also with each other.

In this situation, a good consultant psychiatrist can benefit from the anthropological technique of explanatory model elicitation and negotiation betweeen any of these elements in the clinical milieu. Acting as a "translator" or "culture broker" (Weidman 1982), a psychiatrist employing the EM approach not only can bring lay and professional perspectives into congruence, but also can reveal and reduce intraprofessional incongruities which impede good patient care. Indeed, a major thrust in my day-to-day work on the psychiatry consult team has been to point out such instances of "systemic conflict" and to model approaches for negotiation.

In short, the hospital is a cultural system in which conflict is frequently displaced onto patients and results in requests for psychiatric consultation. In this setting, anthropological theory provides approaches for "diagnosis" of systemic dysfunction, while anthropological methods can enable practitioners to non-threateningly penetrate the various clinical subcultures to do "therapy."

SYSTEMIC CONSULTATION: A CASE EXAMPLE

M.D., a thirty-year-old native American woman was transferred to our teaching hospital hospital following a two-day hospitalization at another local hospital. Admitted with diagnoses of alcoholism, stage III alcoholic liver disease, and alcoholic peripheral neuropathy, the patient had a prognosis of marginal hepatic restorative potential. Upon admission, the patient had electrolyte disturbances and abnormal liver function tests. A liver biopsy revealed markedly invasive portal and reticular fibrosis with mixed inflammatory infiltrate and marked fatty metamorphosis: in short, an extremely diseased liver which was not likely to get much better. Although electrolyte problems were resolving by the second hospital day, the patient complained continuously of leg cramps, tender muscles, foot pain ("it feels like the nail of my big toe is being torn off!"), burning and numbness in her feet and legs ("like when we were kids frostbit [sic] by the snow", sleeplessness, and "vomiting from the pain".)

Our psychiatry service was consulted on the patient's fifth hospital day because of a "confusing personality," "hopeless attitude," "loneliness" and "depression." During this period the patient had been alternately tearful, withdrawn, anxious, and complaining. Our initial visit to evaluate the patient was made by a psychiatry resident and two medical students. They noted blunted affect, lack of eye contact, childlike whimpering, and psychomotor retardation in the patient, and made a tentative diagnosis of severe depression. Upon my arrival at attending rounds later the same morning, they commented that they "really had a good case for an anthropologist," told me "the patient is so depressed that she will hardly shake hands," and invited me to conduct an interview.

"Hardly willing to shake hands" should be a signifiant datum to any anthropologist. Native Americans traditionally do not shake hands or make eye contact, which are seen as aggressive acts, but rather "pass hands" with only a slight touch of the palms and fingers. I reported this ethnographic fact to the team as we passed into the patient's room.

As a "system diagnostician," the medical anthropologist's task in this case is to ascertain the extent to which cultural factors in the patient's background are being manifested in the hospital setting, to determine the degree of congruence of the patient's and staff's perceptions, and to gather as much pertinent life-history data as possible. The first assessment to be made on any patient from a distinctive ethnic background is the degree to which their health beliefs likely differ from those of the medical profession. Patients who are less acculturated usually have beliefs which are most divergent. The major predictors of less acculturation include recent arrival from another country, immigration later in life, frequent returns to the country of origin, less formal education, and lower socioeconomic status. In the case of this patient, all of the above proved to apply. She had lived in an isolated, rural community for most of her life, and had returned frequently to this community as an adult. But it was really only necessary to observe a "prayer feather" in a cup on the patient's bedside stand to make the tentative "diagnosis" of less acculturation. The presence of this prayer feather was a clear symbol of traditional beliefs, leading me to "pass hands" with the patient as I introduced myself, a greeting which elicited a quick upward glance by the patient followed by a willing response to questions carefully phrased to elicit the patient's explanatory model (EM) of her symptoms.

This patient interview allowed me to unequivocally demonstrate to medical sudents and residents how patients have beliefs about their symptoms which condition their illness behavior, including notions about etiology, pathophysiology, severity, prognosis, and treatment.

The patient saw her liver disease as a "punishment from her Indian spiritual god" for her alcohol dependence, which is contrary to "the red way" (the proper way for native Americans to behave). The patient also revealed that she underwent traditional curing rituals for her alcoholism on the reservation (including isolation in a teepee with a fire to induce sweating), and that she was wrapping herself in blankets in the hospital nightly to induce sweating. Upon direct but empathic questioning about self-medication, she also produced a bottle of "Indian tea" from the bedside stand, from which she drank each night.

Regarding her alcoholism and associated physical problems, the patient had several specific beliefs. She saw failure to stay with her own people on the reservation as the primary cause of repeated drinking episodes. In her mind, going away from the reservation to come to Texas always "got her into trouble." She also felt "unworthy" for not being able to "follow the red way," which demands harmony with nature and avoidance of excesses such as severe drinking. Failure to live up to traditional tribal values, resulting low self-esteem, and the serious physical complications of alcohol abuse all contributed to her depressive affect. Upon further questioning, she also confided that her traditional beliefs led her to eat dirt brought to the hospital by Indian friends (the dirt representing the earth as the "spiritual mother" in traditional tribal beliefs). Finally, although the patient acknowledged the relationship between her liver problems and her alcohol abuse, she was unwilling to accept the idea that her leg pains were also associated, maintaining that this represented a punishment. Her belief was that she would never be able to get well without traditional tribal healing (which would bring her back into harmony) and that in the hospital the nurses did not understand or want to help her.

From a psychiatric consultation standpoint, several problems needed to be addressed. First, how could we help medical staff better understand this patient's "confusing behavior?" Why did she seem unconcerned about her illness? Was the patient so depressed that she had "psychomotor retardation"? If so, should she be started on high doses of an antidepressant despite her impaired hepatic function? While the medical staff was primarily concerned about the patient's liver, why was she primarily concerned about the pain in her legs? Why was the nursing staff reacting with hostility toward the patient? How could long-term alcohol abuse treatment be arranged for discharge planning?

Having elicited the patient's perspective on her illness, we were much better able to understand the patient's complaints and to negotiate a plan of care which fit the different "clinical realities" of the patient and her physicians. The medical staff was primarily worried about hepatic function, but were puzzled by the fact that the patient focused almost entirely upon the pain in her legs. Our interviews to extract her explanatory model led to our understanding that, for the patient, pain in the legs was essentially unrelated to alcohol, despite numerous atttempts to "explain" to her otherwise. The patient saw her liver disease as a "punishment" by Indian gods for her violation of appropriate Indian behavior, and felt that the appropriate treatment was to return home for treatment by a medicine man (as she had done in the past, and which had resulted in periods of sobriety and "good health"). Thus, although the patient saw her liver disease as life-threatening, she focused on the pain in her legs because she felt that if the doctors in the hospital could presume to cure her serious liver disease, they should also be able to relieve her less serious pain. In fact, the patient felt that she was being purposely mistreated by the nurses who "laugh in the hall and talk about me but don't care about me when I cry."

The lack of shared understanding between patient and staff was revealed by the fact that the patient felt that she could not discuss her own attempts to treat her pain (Indian tea, sweating, eating dirt) with staff, despite the fact that such treatments "worked" for her. We were able to discuss these treatments with the staff, and encourage them to overtly include them in the treatment plan. This had the effect of heightening the staff's appreciation for the patient's desire to get well, as well as increasing rapport between the patient and the medical staff.

Finally, because of the strong traditional beliefs of the patient, which stressed the importance of spiritual healing for her problems, we orchestrated a case conference to discuss both hospitalization and long-term treatment planning. We invited a local Indian healer, an Indian alcohol counselor (who had prior knowledge of the patient), and an Indian psychiatrist. Not only did these professionals confirm our beliefs about appropriate approaches to the patient while in the hospital, but they also helped to arrange for treatment after discharge at an Indian alcohol rehabilitation facility in another state.

ANTHROPOLOGY AND CLINICAL INTERVENTION

In this specific case, some traditional anthropological knowledge was crucial, specifically, the fact that direct eye contact and a firm handshake are seen as aggressive acts by traditional native Americans. When the case was first presented to me, I was told that the patient had "psychomotor retardation" indicative of severe depression because she would not look up or shake hands. This information actually raised my "index of suspicion" that the patient was fairly traditional, and that her behavior could then be seen as normal, expected behavior. I knew, however, that the first task would be to determine how "behaviorally ethnic" (Harwood 1981) the patient was.

As I walked into the room, and observed the "prayer feather" by the bedside, I initiated the interview by "passing hands" in the traditional beliefs. The patient responded to my passing of hands by looking up quickly, and then looking back down, but began to answer all my questions in complete sentences, with only moderate speech latency. I questioned her about many things, but particularly asked questions which revealed that the patient often had returned to her tribal home some distance away for treatment in the traditional medicine of her tribe. In addition, the patient felt that she had not followed the "red way," and was being punished.

The psychiatrists on the team had been faced with a dilemma: feeling the patient to be severely depressed, they wanted to start her on large doses of antidepressant medications; this was potentially hazardous, however, because of the patient's impaired hepatic function. After discussing that a great deal of her "psychomotor retardation" might be culturally-based "normal" behavior, and after getting much better verbal responses in subsequent interviews, antidepressant medication was deferred until later in the hospitalization.

In the same interview, I asked questions to elicit the patient's explanatory model for symptoms. In so doing, I was able to better understand why she felt betrayed by the physicians, who were trying to convince her that her liver disease was quite severe and needed treatment, but who, from her perspective, should have been able to treat her "less severe" leg pains if they could presume to cure her serious liver disease. Of equal importance, we elicited the EMs of both the patient and her other physicians for the leg pains: the consultees saw the pain as a possibly irreversible neuropathy for which there was no specific treatment, save mild analgesics. In contrast, the patient saw her problem as vascular, and felt that it should be simple to treat by warming and massage "like she did for her feet as a child" when they were numb, tingling, and painful from being cold in the snow.

This explained the patient's practice of piling blankets on the bed at night (she told me it was to cause sweating) and covering her air conditioning vents with blankets, which had caused the nurses to think of her as "weird" and "confused." The patient was also keeping the drapes drawn tight on the windows, which further suggested depression to her physicians, and further disturbed the nurses. When the patient told me that the best treatment for her would be to do what she had done in the past — go home to the reservation and be shut alone into a hot teepee for three days — the rationale for her behavior became obvious. We were able to communicate this to the nurses who previously had seen the patient as "apathetic" and not willing to help herself, but now saw her as trying to help herself much more, which made her a more "desire-able" patient.

Finally, it is common knowledge in medical anthropology that behaviorally ethnic patients often use dual sources of treatment, both biomedical and traditional. During the interview, I simply asked her very nonjudgmentally about what other things or medicines she was using to help her — if she had any native American friends "who might be able to bring a traditional cure into the hospital for her." The patient readily admitted to drinking "Indian tea" and eating dirt, both brought to the hospital by friends, and willingly showed me the bottle in her bedside cabinet. I felt that this would further demonstrate to the nurses the patient's desire to "help herself," and received the patient's permission to show her nurses the tea. I also anticipated questions about its ingredients, and after being reassured by the patient that there was nothing toxic in the tea, and "that it is the only medicine that really works," communicated these details to both her physicians and nurses. They expressed surprise, but somewhat dubiously went along with my suggestion that *they* actually *encourage* her to use her medications along with theirs, in order to strengthen their therapeutic alliance with her.

I also gathered a great deal of life history data, some of it quite troubling, including the fact that two of her children had been killed by a schizophrenic ex-husband. Although currently provided emotional and social support from an Anglo boyfriend, the patient still felt that she needed to go back to her own people. These revelations further softened the nurses' attitude toward the patient.

Finally, because of the strong traditional beliefs of the patient, which stressed the importance of spiritual healing for her problems, I felt that specialized treatment needed to be arranged, and asked the patient if she knew any traditional healers in the area. After she told me about a "medicine man" she knew, who turned out to be both a native American and an alcohol counselor, we arranged for him to come to the medical school to consult on the case, invited a native American psychiatrist (albeit from another tribe) from the community to attend the case conference, and awanged a conference to discuss both hospitalization and long-term treatment planning. These consultants confirmed much of what we though about the patient and helped to arrange discharge to an alcohol rehabilitation facility in another state.

In addition to helping the patient in her hospitalization, the case presented an unparalleled opportunity to demonstrate a culturally sensitive approach to patient care to medical students, residents, and their attendings. It also was an opportunity to practice systemic consultation: the "patient" was actually the entire ward, and attention needed to be paid to staff and patient alike. Conflicts between the patient and staff, engendered by misunderstandings and biases stemming from both the patient's culture and the culture of biomedicine, needed to be brokered by an approach sensitive to each. The only negative aspect of the above case is that it may reinforce physician belief that the only time to "call the anthropologist" is when they have a patient with darker skin or who speaks with an accent, a stereotype that I always address directly when asked to see such a patient by emphatically stating that all patients have culturally derived health beliefs, and that most consultation requests result from system conflicts.

ANTHROPOLOGICAL LESSONS FOR PSYCHIATRIC CONSULTATION

The major point illustrated by this specific case, and which is essential to the practice of systemic consultation in the hospital, is that in order for psychiatrists to do consultation work oriented toward system conflicts as the ultimate cause of patient and staff problems, they must become clinical ethnographers. Although there are some psychiatrists who think even limited liaison work with other specialists is unrewarding, I would disagree. By engaging in participant-observation and consciously adopting an "inside-outsider" role (Agar 1980), it is possible to nonthreateningly penetrate the various "subcultures" of the hospital's subsystems and to understand their "daily round" (time demands and work schedules), patient care activities, social networks, sources of support and stress, sttitudes, values, and beliefs. Such a stranger role has long been recognized as extremely powerful (Simmel 1950), "inside" enough to encourage those in the setting to reveal their "secrets," but "outside" the system enough to be seen as neutral.

As a nonphysician anthropologist, it may be easier for me to achieve this desired ethnographic status of "marginal native" (Freilich 1970), because I truly am marginal and can more easily avoid being seen as an agent of vested, potentially competing, professional interests than can my psychiatry colleagues. But I would advocate that consultant psychiatrists consciously work to maintain, rather than reduce, status/role ambiguity. Good clinical ethnographers must constantly monitor the status and role perceptions of the "natives" (other professionals in the system), and not be seen as allied with one or another group. For example, by only relating to other physicians, psychiatrists run the risk of alienating nurses; by acting as unbridled "patient advocates" they may offend other physicians or nurses; by ignoring family members they may find their plans for the patient sabotaged.

Unfortunately, the inside-outsider role is difficult for some of my psychiatrist colleagues to adopt. Whereas anthropologists derive a positive professional self-image from, and are tolerant of status-role ambiguity, most physicians have strong needs to define roles and demonstrate competence. Such needs are particularly acute in psychiatry because this field is of relatively low status within the hierarchy of medical specialties. This leads some consultant psychiatrists (particularly residents who, as neophyte converts to the field, are its most zealous proponents) to define problems and offer professional opinions prematurely, forsaking data gathering in favor of "turf" negotiations, and being primarily oriented toward the patient rather than the ward social system.

Emphasis on the physician-patient dyad is, after all, the cornerstone of medical practice, and is "taught" as such in the process of professional socialization in medical school. A patient-centered approach may be reassuring, but may also establish a relationship between consultant and consultee which is as much a battle for professional status as it is for the patient's health, and which limits rather than expands areas of potential collaboration. The ethnographic approach would suggest that psychiatrists resist the knee-jerk reaction of "I am going to tell them what is going on with their patients" (thereby asserting professional competence and the importance of psychiatry) because such an approach, even if seemingly "asked for" by a consultation request, is often seen as judgmental and responded to defensively by other specialists. Instead of immediately telling consultees what is wrong, I would advocate further data gathering to elicit their perspectives, which are equally crucial to a systemic case formulation.

As in so many other consultations, the above case study illustrates how important it is to have access to all people in the system. Although the formal consultation request came from the patient's physicians, the nurses were also extremely upset by the patient's constant whimpering and crying. In situations like this, it is not unusual for the actual request for psychiatric consultation to originate with the nurses, and consultant psychiatrists who do not systematically gather data from them, as well as from the patient and the other physicians, will misunderstand the case. Similarly, it is common for consultation requests to be initiated by harried residents trying to get another clinical service to take over cases (called "turfing" the patient), or by physicians who are angry at patients or family members.

Good clinical ethnographers attempt to actively convey a general sense of "wanting to better understand the work that goes on here," as well as a sense of acceptance of "indigenous" cultural beliefs and practices. In this particular case, I actively solicited the nurses' EMs for the patient's problems. Some thought the patient was depressed, others thought she was lonely, and others said she was retarded. They all were frustrated by the patient, and were relieved to be able to "ventilate" to someone about their feelings. Such an open curiosity and nonjudgmentalism facilitates the flow of information from those in the system.

Naturally, the best rapport and information flow occurs on wards in which psychiatrists engage in liaison activities (such as joint research, teaching, case conferences, workshops, etc.). Once liaison efforts are conceived of as anthropological "fieldwork," several anthropological lessons apply in the hospital, as much as they do among the Nuer or the Yanomamo. First, good ethnographers pay particular attention to ritual events and try to participate in them, especially if the natives regard them as onerous (such as 7:00 a.m. bedside rounds, weekend and holiday rounds, or mortality conferences). My experience has been that staff on another clinical service view attendance at such events as signifying real commitment. My psychiatry colleagues have said to me, "Why should I get up to make rounds at 7:00 ... they're not necessary and I just stand around most of the time!", not realizing the symbolic significance of "sharing the burden" with staff. There is also tremendous potential value in "hanging around" because when crises occur the milieu is most fertile for change.

Second, as in any ethnographic endeavor, psychiatrists engaged in liason "fieldwork" must be alert for the "tests" which always occur. In traditional fieldwork, tests of the anthropologist's interest take the form of invitations to eat unusual food, to undergo tribal "initiation," or to make some other type of personal sacrifice. In the hospital, such tests may include being asked to interview an emotional patient with no advance warning, to help remove a drain from an abdominal incision, or to endure caustic remarks about psychiatry. "Natives" in both settings watch closely to see how the "ethnographer" responds: stoicism or willing participation is rewarded with respect; defensiveness or disdain will be seen as evidence of hostility and disinterest.

Third, since the goal of ethnography is an understanding of the culture, it is important to pay particular attention to language and meaning. It is particularly important to discern the "rules" of each hospital ward, including who is supposed to behave in what way in both intraprofessional and patient-practitioner interactions. In hospitals, many psychiatric consultation requests are the result of rules being broken (such as family members not observing visiting hours), setting off a chain reaction of discontent which is displaced onto the patient. For example, on the high-risk obstetrics team on which I worked, it is expected that the nurse specialist and the social worker participate actively in discussions during rounds and will take an active role in patient care, particularly in the areas of patient education and counseling. A psychiatrist or anthropologist in this setting must honor these rules and work *through* these team members in making diagnostic or therapeutic interventions.

Fourth, rules and regulations must also be evaluated as reflections of a higher-level ethos — systems of shared, implicit assumptions about what is "good" or "bad," "right" or "wrong." In the medical setting, such core values are frequently revealed through the telling of "war stories," almost mythical recountings of the most difficult situations which are handed down from generation to generation. Consultant psychiatrists and anthropologists alike should recognize that the content of such "myths" illustrate basic cultural "truths" and also that they betray areas of conflict which are threatening and otherwise repressed.

Fifth, certain ritual behaviors are also important in understanding the culture of a given hospital unit if the ethnographer gets beyond the manifest function of ritual activity and analyzes the latent, protective function of ritual. For example, some ritual practices (such as always taking vital signs at a particular time or always seeing patients in a particular order) serve to protect practitioners from the problem of becoming emotionally attached to specific patients. Even standard medical protocols have the latent function of reducing the ambiguity or uncertainty that attends the reality that patients are individuals and each may respond somewhat differently to the same treatment regimen.

In short, an understanding of language, rules, rituals, core values, and myths are techniques which any good ethnographer can use to better understand emic (insider) views of reality. It is only after such an understanding is achieved that an anthropologist or a consultant psychiatrist can implement programs of change which will not be antithetical to the "local culture," and thereby dismissed out of hand.

Ethnographers often analyze social systems from a structural-functional perspective. Understanding the structure and function of a hospital subsystem implies an understanding of role differentiation and specialization among staff, as well as the status hierarchy attendant to this structural and functional configuration. It is critical for consultant psychiatrists to have such an anthropological perspective, because in the hospital, structural and functional problem (such as disagreement about basic goals, role conflicts, procedural misunderstandings) are often seen as "personality problems," and frequently result in psychiatric consultation requests. "Symptoms" of such structural and functional problems include: patients who continue to do poorly but staff activities toward the patient do not change; inability to carry out expected roles; lack of coordination and leadership; overreliance on rules and regulations; nurse-M.D. role conflicts; ambiguity of roles, such as physicians or nurses also trying to be "friends" to patients; and rigidity and inflexibility of roles. Generally speaking, one of the earliest cues that there are problems in any complex social system will be complaints about "personality problems," a simultaneous overreliance on formal rules, and a lack of flexibility.

Another important aspect of ethnographic work is a commitment to inductive rather than deductive reasoning. Rather than asking *a priori* questions, collecting data to accept or reject predetermined hypotheses, and then analyzing data, the ethnographer engages in a constant dialectic of data collection and analysis which are done concurrently. This type of nonlinear thinking is not commonly taught in the "hard" science disciplines, but it is essential if one is to understand what the problems of a given setting are and to gradually make sense out of it through increasingly refined interpretations, without relying on preconceived ideas about the nature of problems and imposing those ideas on the setting. It may be reassuring for a psychiatrist to receive a consultation request and immediately formulate hypotheses about the nature of the problem (both because this is the way clinical reasoning is taught and because it provides a sense of confidence), but many psychiatrists and anthropologists have missed important data by premature hypothesis testing and have alienated "natives" by seeming imposition of problem-solving agendas from the "outside."

Finally, ethnographers and psychiatrists share a common practice — recognition of the importance of monitoring one's own personal reactions to the field situation as a source of data. Clearly, the ethnographic "myth" is that the anthropologist is a neutral observer who can move in among a group of strangers and understand their culture and its problems in a short period of time without affecting, or being affected by, that culture. Obviously, this is both arrogant and untrue. Members of a particular culture will give information to an anthropologist or to a consultant psychiatrist based in part upon on what they believe that the ethnographer wants to learn, and the ethnographer will inevitably react to group members affectively. Ethnographers and consultant psychiatrists alike must go into clinical situations with awareness of the biases they bring to it from their own "cultures" and personalities. Additionally, there is some sense that the less an ethnographer likes his or her own culture, the more favorably the alternatives may be viewed (Braroe and Hicks 1967); consultant psychiatrists must be aware of this phenomenon and monitor how ambivalence, hostility, or allegiance to the discipline of psychiatry may color their views of consultation work, other medical specialties, and consultees.

ANTHROPOLOGICAL LESSONS FOR ORGANIZATIONAL INTERVENTION

How can consultant psychiatrists bring about change at the level of social systems? Perhaps the most important step is the basic ethnographic understandings which result from "fieldwork" as just discussed (this ensures accurate "diagnosis" and "therapeutic alliance"). In fact, because there is some controversy within the discipline about the propriety of initiating programs of change within another culture, anthropology may not have as much to say about specific change techniques in the hospital. On the other hand, if one sees the goal of consultation at the level of social systems as an increase in understanding and flexibility of interaction between various subsystems in the hospital milieu, then the applied anthropological role of "culture broker" (Weidman 1982) may be eminently appropriate for a consulting psychiatrist. This position implies defining areas of misunderstanding and acting as a "translator" between various subsystems. In this way the culture broker can interpret for one group the meanings and understandings of another, and vice versa, while maintaining a relative neutrality. If a culture broker ha established credibility and trust through liason activities (fieldwork), recommendations are much more likely to be consistent with the needs of the groups and therefore accepted. Other strategies, such as the Explanatory Model (EM) paradigm (Kleinmen 1982), can be used with equal effectiveness with hospital staff as with patients, and it is a valuable tool in understanding and negotiating incongruities in perspectives which often lead to consultation requests.

CONCLUSIONS

Does anthropology have a contribution to make within psychiatry? Without question, there have been mutual interests in areas of transcultural and community psychiatry, but the value of my attempts to work in clinical psychiatry is still very much open to debate. In this overview and case study, I hope it is clear that my psychiatry colleagues and I share a commitment to the incorporation of psychosocial variables in the health care delivery equation and that we ought to share some basic clinical or "fieldwork" strategies. But it should also be clear that there are problems on a number of levels.

In some way, psychiatry must recognize the discrepancy between the reality of clinical medicine, which sees psychiatry as highly marginal, and the profession's fantasy of itself as central to modern medicine. Although consultation-liaison psychiatry is a potent opportunity to influence medicine, my work would suggest that psychiatry resist the dogmatic assertion of professional worth in such settings and adopt a more covert, anthropological approach to "fieldwork" with other clinical specialties. This demands that both psychiatrists and anthropologists embrace, rather than defend themselves against, the anxiety of status marginality.

Not every psychiatrist or anthropologist will be comfortable with this approach and will avoid consultation-liaison work. Some within consultation-liaison psychiatry will focus on individual patients, ignoring the potential for change at the level of medical systems and the potential for collaboration between anthropology and psychiatry that this approach implies. Anthropologists working in medicine must also resist bold assertions of competence and relevance in public forums such as this, because such messages may be more easily heard covertly in day-to-day clinical settings. Anthropological and psychiatric practice, particularly in the important area of systemic consultation in hospital settings, should be mutually supportive. Anthropologists working in clinical psychiatry and psychiatrists working with other clinical specialties are, after all, both "marginal natives."

ACKNOWLEDGMENTS

I would like to acknowledge the invaluable and continued support of two psychiatry colleagues, Dr. Pauline Powers and Dr. Barry Fenton. By incorporating me into their consultation-liaison teams and sharing their professional lives, they have provided me with unparalleled fieldwork opportunities in hospitals and taught me much about clinical medicine. I would also like to thank Ben Kracht, a graduate student in medical anthropology, for assistance in medical chart auditing for the case report presented.

Notes

1. This case occurred as part of normal work in consultation-liaison psychiatry. It is one of many which could be described.
2. I was first introduced to the concepts and encouraged to practice the techniques by Alice Murphree and Carol Taylor, two of my major professors at the University of Florida. Dr. Taylor has written a book about hospitals which should be required reading for anyone doing work in health care settings (Taylor 1969).
3. The bulk of early work was done by medical sociologists. Classic studies which should be consulted include Becker, et al. 1961; Fox's chapter in Merton, et al. 1957; Light 1980; and Coombs 1978.
4. I think it is important to be critical, but as anthropologists we must attempt to apply the same standards of analysis in our own culture as we do in others. Stein (1980) and McKinlay (1977) both discuss the common practice of "doctor bashing," a disciplinocentric and all-too-common practice in which social scientists fail to analyze physician behavior in the larger context. Physicians in our culture are extremely sensitive to the critiques of medical practice, some are actually advocates of a political-economic perspective, but most are understandably quick to personalize "criticism" from social scientists, particularly when working in the

clinical settings. I now defer any discussions of a theoretical nature about health economics and politics until I am with physician colleagues with whom I have a long working relationship (there is an old aphorism which states, "confrontation without a relationship is an attack.") and, unless they raise such issues in the context of seeing patients, until we are away from the clinical arena.

5. A more thorough discussion of the applied work I have done in the hospital is forthcoming in the second edition of *Applied Anthropology in America*, edited by Elizabeth Eddy and William Partridge, and published by Columbia University Press.

6. A more thorough and theoretical analysis of the field of consultation-liaison psychiatry can be found in an earlier work (Johnson 1985).

7. I have helped evaluate a grief counseling program for women who have stillbirths, a pain control technique for burn wound debridement, and have collected data for a study of psychiatric impairment in patients hospitalized on a high-risk obstetrics ward.

8. Of course, cultural relativism taken to the extreme may serve to legitimize some rather oppressive practices. For critiques of the concept of cultural relativism see Diamond (1974) and Hatch (1983). Nonetheless, I feel that my first responsibility in the clinical setting is to understand that setting, not to advocate for or against any of the constituents. To that end I have silently witnessed frank malpractice, as well as a host of other "objectionable" behaviors on the part of patients and practitioners alike, usually choosing not to act on my more activist impulses.

9. The question of whether anthropologists ought to actually practice in competition with psychiatrists or other practitioners is a complex one which involves issues such as training, credentialing, and marketing strategies to create a new niche in an already crowded health care arena. There is some precedent for, and there has been much discussion about such a "clinical anthropology" (Chrisman and Maretzki 1982; *M.A.N.* 1980; Shimkin and Golde 1983), but the growing political pressure to reduce medical spending makes me pessimistic about the potential for yet another medical "specialty" to compete successfully for positions in clinical settings. In addition to the "turf and territory" issues which would arise in jockeying for position with already established practitioners, such clinical medical anthropologists will have to convince hospital administrators and government regulators of the cost-effectiveness of their interventions. I think it could be done, and I have no doubts about the efficacy of the types of systemic interventions anthropologists can make in hospitals, but I am also afraid that the routinization of positions for hospital anthropologists and the maintenance of inside-outsider roles so critical for good ethnography are mutually incompatible.

REFERENCES

Agar, Michael H., 1980. *The Professional Stranger: An Informal Introduction to Ethnography*. New York: Academic Press.

Auerbach, O. B., 1975. Liaison Psychiatry and the Education of the Psychiatric Resident. In *Consultation Liaison Psychiatry*, ed. R. O. Pasnow, New York: Gruene and Stratton.

Becker, Howard S., *et al.*, 1961. *Boys in White: Student Culture in Medical School*. Chicago: The University of Chicago Press.

Braroe, N.W., and G.L. Hicks., 1967. Observations on the Mystique of Anthropology, *Sociological Quarterly* 8: 173–186.

Buckley, W., 1968. *Modern Systems Research for the Behavioral Scientist*. Chicgo: Aldine.

Chrisman, Noel J., and Thomas W. Maretzki, 1982. *Clinically Applied Anthropology*:

Anthropologists in Health Science Settings. Dordrecht, Holland: D. Reidel Company.

Coombs, R. H., 1978. *Mastering Medicine: Professional Socialization in Medical School*. New York: The Free Press.

Diamond, Stanley, 1974. *In Search of the Primitive: A Critique of Civilization*. New York: Transaction Books.

Engel, G. L., 1977. The Need for a New Medical Model: A Challenge for Biomedicine, *Science* 196: 129.

Engel, G. L., 1980. The Clinical Application of the Biopsychosocial Model, *American Journal of Psychiatry* 137: 535.

Favazza, A.R., and A.O. Faheem, 1982. *Themes in Cultural Psychiatry: An Annotated Bibliography*, 1975–1980. Columbia, MO: University of Missouri Press.

Favazza, A.R., and M. Oman, 1977. *Anthropological and Cross-Cultural Themes in Mental Health: An Annotated Bibliography*, 1925–1974. Columbia, MO: University of Missouri Press.

Freilich, M., 1970. *Marginal Natives: Anthropologists at Work*. New York: Harper and Row.

Greenbert, I., 1960. Approaches to Psychiatric Consultation in a Research Hospital Setting, *Archives of General Psychiatry* 3: 691–697.

Hackett, T. P., 1982. Consultation Psychiatry Held Valid, Liaison Held Invalid, *Clinical Psychiatric News* Jan. p. 36.

Harwood, Alan, 1981. *Ethnicity and Medical Care*. Cambridge, MA: Harvard University Press.

Hatch, Elvin, 1983. *Culture and Morality: The Relativity of Values in Anthropology*. New York: Columbia University Press.

Henry, G. W., 1929. Some Modern Aspects of Psychiatry in General Hospital Practice, *American Journal of Psychiatry* 86: 481–499.

Johnson, Thomas M., 1981. The Anthropologist as a Role Model for Medical Students, *Practicing Anthropology* 4: 8–10.

Johnson, Thomas M., 1985. Consultation-Liaison Psychiatry: Medicine as Patient, Marginality as Practice. In *Physicians of Western Medicine*, eds. R. A. Hahn and A. D. Gaines, 269–292. Dordrecht, Holland: D. Reidel.

Kennedy, Donald, 1979. Anthropologists in Medical Education, *Medical Anthropology* 3: 281–296.

Kleinman, Arthur, 1978. Culture, Illness, and Care: Clinical Lessons from Anthropologic and Cross-Cultural Research, *Annals of Internal Medicine* 88: 251–258.

Kleinman, Arthur, 1982. Teaching of Clinically Applied Anthropology on a Psychiatric Consultation-Liaison Service. In *Clinically Applied Anthropology*, eds. W. J. Chrisman and T. W. Maretzki 83–115. Boston: D. Reidel.

Light, Donald, 1980. *Becoming Psychiatrists: The Professional Transformation of Self*. New York: W. W. Norton and Co.

Lynaugh, Joan E. and Barbara Bates, 1979. The Two Languages of Nursing and Medicine. In *Culture, Curers, and Contagion*, ed. Norman Klein 129–137. Novato, CA: Chandler and Sharp Publishers, Inc.

M.A.N., 1980. Open Forum: Clinical Anthropology, *Medical Anthropology Newsletter* 12(1): 14–25.

McKinlay, John, 1977. The Business of Good Doctoring or Doctoring as Good Business, *International Journal of Health Services* 7(3): 459–486.

Merton, Robert K., George Reader, and Patricia L. Kendall, 1957. *The Student-Physician: Introductory Studies in the Sociology of Medical Education*. Cambridge, MA: Harvard University Press.

Meyer, E., and M. Mendelson, 1961. Psychiatric Consultations with Patients on Medical and Surgical Wards: Patterns and Processes, *Psychiatry* 24: 197–220.

Schiff, K.S., and M.L. Pilot, 1959. An Approach to Psychiatric Consultations in the General Hospital, *Archives of General Psychiatry* 1: 239.

Schwab, J.J., 1968 *Handbook of Psychiatric Consultation*. New York: Appleton-Century-Crofts.

Shimkin, Demitri and Peggy Golds, 1983. *Clinical Anthropology: A New Approach to America's Health Problems?* Lanham, MD: University Press of America.

Simmel, G., 1950. The Stranger. In *The Sociology of Georg Simmel*, ed. Kurt Wolg Glencoe, IL: The Free Press.

Stein, Howard F., 1980. Medical Anthropology and Western Medicine, *Journal of Psychological Anthropology* 3(2): 185–195.

Stein, Leonard, 1967. The Doctor-Nurse Game, *Archives of General Psychiatry* 16: 699–703.

Tarnow, J.D., and S.E. Gutstein, 1982. Systemic Consultation in a General Hospital, *International Journal of Psychiatry in Medicine* 12f: 161–185.

Taylor, Carol, 1969. *In Horizontal Orbit*. New York: Holt, Rinehart, and Winston.

Tilley, D., 1982. A Survey of Consultation-Liaison Psychiatry Program Characteristics and Functions, *General Hospital Psychiatry* 4: 265–270.

Weidman, Hazel, 1982. Research Strategies, Structural Alterations and Clinically Applied Anthropology. In *Clinically Applied Anthropology*, eds. N. J. Chrisman and T. W. Maretzki, 201–241. Boston: D. Reidel.

Fieldwork in a Clinical Setting: Negotiating Entree, the Investigator's Role and Problems of Data Collection

JOAN J. MATHEWS

Loyola University Medical Center

INTRODUCTION

Over the last decade anthropological interest in medical systems has broadened from an orientation of health related beliefs' and practices as part of a system of magical theories to studies of biomedical theory, practice and practitioners (Chrisman and Maretzki 1982; Hahn and Gaines 1985). There are many challenges, however, to conducting anthropological fieldwork in clinical settings. The most important challenge concerns the achievement of research credibility. This involves the establishment of scientific validity through the use of appropriate methodology and through the anthropologist's conduct as an investigator. Research credibility is important to achieve if the data are to be accepted by members of the health care community. This paper focuses on three vital issues which are faced by the anthropologist who conducts fieldwork in an in-patient clinical setting or hospital.

One issue concerns the gaining of entree into a clinical institution. This is a potential problem for two reasons. First, medical practitioners are reputed to resist analysis by outsiders. This resistance results partly because physicians historically have resisted any external review or regulation of their professional prerogatives (Freidson 1970) and also because social science analysts often have engaged in what McKinlay (1977: 459) calls "doctor-bashing," or deprecating physicians; at the same time these social science analysts purport to seek the perspectives and problems of clinicians, as well as of patients (see for example, Millman 1976; Danziger

1979). Second, the typical hospital is composed of several semi-autonomous administrative units that can control access to informants either formally as through a research review committee, or covertly through denial of access to particular areas, activities or potential informants. The anthropologist must determine how to secure administrative permission to enter the site and to gain the cooperation of many different individuals within the institution in order to observe clinical activities and to conduct interviews with informants. The second issue pertains to how to conduct oneself in a highly complex and rule-oriented environment. This aspect concerns the anthropologist's role and responsibility regarding the data he or she collects. The third issue examined in this paper concerns the impact of the anthropologist's presence on the clinical scene. In this regard, methods which minimize observer effect on data collection procedures are discussed.

Ward and Werner (1984:221) noted a lack of methodological rigor in anthropology in two areas: the paucity of methodological literature that focuses solely on ethnographic methods, and the sparseness of explanations of the methodology of fieldwork in ethnographic accounts. Anthropologists often enter fieldwork without having been formally taught how to systematically perform this task (Mead 1972:37; Agar 1980:2). The purposes of this paper are to describe some issues relevant to conducting fieldwork in the complex and sensitive environment of a medical facility and to consider some methodological problems associated with conducting fieldwork in such a setting.

FIELDWORK IN COMPLEX ORGANIZATIONS

Several methodological issues are involved in conducting ethnographic research in one's own culture. First, the research questions and plan must be formally structured. The anthropologist cannot go to the field with a roughly sketched notion of studying "the healing system" or "the doctor-patient relationship"; rather, he or she should formulate a systematic research plan which includes delineation of the hypotheses or research questions, study sample, data gathering, analysis techniques, and timetables. Explicit research questions and a plan are especially crucial in a medical setting because a research protocol must be approved by the Institutional Review Board for the Protection of Human Subjects (IRB). A formal plan is also necessary in order to establish research credibil-

ity in a medical setting which values formal methodology and repli-
cability. In clinical settings where physicians increasingly rely on
quantitative data to make clinical decisions, the anthropologist must
be prepared to explain the relevance of qualitative research with
respect to specific research questions and goals.

An initial methodological problem concerns the gaining of entree
into the culture to be studied and the establishment of trusting
relationships that allow the fieldworker to be included as a participant in actions and events. This is especially true when conducting
ethnographic research in one's own culture. Traditionally, anthropologists have entered the group informally by lurking at the edges of
cultural scenes and sometimes by making acquaintance with so-
called "marginal" members of the group, persons who view the
stranger as a potential ally in their conflicts with the main group. In
complex institutions, such side-entrance maneuvers may be damaging to the overall reseach effort because officials or powerful members of the group may halt the research. Anthropologists are often
naive about organizational power structures and hierarchies. The
anthropologist who plans to work in an institutional setting must
become knowledgeable about the organization's structure and
hierarchy in order to determine at which levels he or she should
enter, and how to negotiate his or her role within the group.

In a foreign culture, especially in small scale societies, the anthropologist usually tries to de-emphasize his or her role as a professional. This is achieved largely by living among one's informants and by
making even one's leisure time part of the fieldwork. In an organization in one's own culture, especially in an institution which is populated by professional persons, the ethnographer also must present
himself as a professional. Since he typically participates with the
organization only during working hours, the relationship with his
informants is to some extent a collegial one. Thus, the native
ethnographer must be sensitive to appropriate conduct since errors
in understanding the culture are usually not as well tolerated as they
may be in a foreign culture.

In summary, research in a complex organization demands of the
fieldworker a knowledge of formalized entree procedures, a willingness to establish research credibility, and the development of organ-
izationally and culturally appropriate behavior. The remainder of
this paper focuses on these issues. The processes of selecting and
gaining entrance to a site, obtaining IRB approval, and defining a
role and style of interaction with informants are described. Also
discussed are some critical issues such as overidentification, reci-

procity, observer effect on the environment, and the ethics of observation and handling of confidential information.

GAINING ENTREE TO THE SITE

This paper is based on a year's fieldwork experience in a university medical center, anonymously called University Hospital. It is located in a suburban area of a large Midwestern city where it serves not only as a general care hospital, but also as a regional center for trauma, burns and neonatal care. It also is a major facility for heart and kidney transplants, open heart surgery, and cancer treatment. The medical center provides training for residents and fellows in medical specialties, for doctoral students in the biological sciences, and for undergraduate and graduate nursing students. The goals of the study were to describe the processes of exchanges of clinically relevant information between physicians, patients and nurses, and to analyze the social factors which shape such transactions (see Mathews 1983).

The data from this study show that many patients view clinical information and patient participation in decision-making as a consumer's right. These patients tend to be younger (under 50 years), and many have heart disease. Patients who actively seek information believe the trajectory of their disease can be controlled with medical care and changes in their lifestyle. Older patients, and those with cancer, tend to want little or no clinically related information. Older patients tend to want passively to be cared for, while cancer patients tend to be fearful of information concerning their disease.

The physicians and nurses studied in this University hospital setting firmly believe the patient has a right to information, and most attempt to provide information in ways that are linguistically and conceptually appropriate to laypersons. This general philosophy and approach may be linked to the age of the staff who themselves are members of the consumer-oriented age. The median age of physicians at University Hospital is 40 years and of nurses is 28 years.

A university hospital was selected as the research site for several reasons. Although not well documented, common knowledge holds that physicians practicing at university centers are at the leading edge of clinical and technological practice. This suggests that these physicians also are responsive to societal forces such as consumer demands for clinical information and for participation in clinical decisions. In addition, several physicians in this study stated that physicians in private practice and at non-university hospitals tend to resist changes in clinical practice, including resistance to changes in the traditionally physician-dominated doctor-patient relationship, and also generally resist analysis by outsiders. This assessment is supported by a sociology graduate student who unsuccessfully attempted to gain access to seven community hospitals to do his research before obtaining permission to conduct his study at University Hospital.

The identification of formal procedures for entering a complex organization can be problematic on at least two fronts. First, there may be no formal protocol for the outsider to follow in obtaining permission to do research and establishing contact with key persons. For instance, individuals within University Hospital who wish to perform research are required to have their protocols signed by their department chairperson, and thus they have sponsorship within the institution. The outsider must find a sponsor in the institution. Often, this is achieved through referral by an acquaintance. I handled this requirement through a friend who was willing to sign as the sponsor of my study. Second, several structural units such as hospital administration, medical staff, nursing staff, academic units or a research committee, may control the researcher's access to the subjects of a study. It may not be at all clear which of these units gives formal approval for the conduct of a study by a person from outside the institution.

For my study, gaining entrance to University Hospital began at the top with the chief officer of the medical center, the provost. This was an arbitrary decision since the anthropologist may explore entering an institution at any of several hierarchical levels. The reason I chose this stratagem was that this request would fall outside the routine problems of a provost and therefore would likely not be ignored. The provost was sent my curriculum vita, an abstract of the proposed research and a letter requesting approval to conduct research. The provost responded that no formalized structure exists to grant research permission to an outsider. He recommended that a research protocol, prepared in accordance with IRB guidelines, be sent to that board, since in any case that committee must approve all research performed in a clinical area.

The formal charge of the IRB is to ensure that the benefits of proposed research outweigh any potential risks to the subjects involved in a study. This includes psychological, as well as medical risks to patients. The IRB also insures that the subjects are provided with an informed consent which is written in layperson's language.

The informed consent must describe the nature of the research, and must assure the patient of his right to refuse or withdraw participation. Informed consent must be obtained from both patients and staff volunteers. However, when experimental drugs or devices are not employed, professional staff may give their consent simply by agreeing to be observed, interviewed or accompanied in their daily work. The official IRB role does not, of course, prevent the committee from informally considering the merits of the problem, clarity of hypotheses or appropriateness of methodology. Some well-meaning nurse friends had warned that my research interest would pose a threat to physicians. I followed two strategies to lessen the chance of having the proposal rejected by influential physician members of the IRB.

First, the label for the research was carefully selected since terminology can make an important difference in how a project will be perceived by members of the organization. The title selected for this study was "The Informative Process in the Clinical Setting" (Mathews, 1985). Thus, while some writers, who view physicians as controlling information for their own ends, use the phrase "information control," I used the neutral terminology, "information process," to imply that both patients and clinicians can exercise control over the flow of information.

A second precaution taken to facilitate acceptance of the study was to contact two members of the IRB prior to the board's review of the proposal in order to informally discuss the intent and scope of problem to be investigated. One of these persons suggested modifications in the protocol that might pose less threat to physician members of the IRB. One suggestion was to modify a biased literature review to a very general overview of the major issues in doctor-patient communication. The second suggestion was to include a statement that the attending physician would be informed when his or her patient was selected for a formal interview. On the surface this suggestion appeared to be a matter of professional courtesy and not an issue of access control. At a deeper level, however, lies the physician's desire to maintain control over his patients. This is illustrated by the following case:

> A staff nurse who is engaged in research that involves interviewing patients is in trouble with the Institutional Review Board. The research protocol states that random sampling will be done by drawing bed numbers. The patient in a selected bed will be interviewed and the attending physician will *then* be informed that his patient has been enrolled in the study. An attending physician voiced his objection to one of his patient's participation. The nurse has been

informed that she is in violation of IRB rules because she must secure permission from the attending physician *prior* to interviewing the patient. Nurse members of the IRB objected to this interpretation of the approved protocol and the ensuing discussion centered on the "right of the physician to own the patient relationship."

Upon approval of the study by the IRB negotiations were started through other channels. First I met individually with the hospital administrator, chief of the medical staff and director of nursing service. The provost had forwarded my initial letter of request to each of these key persons. Prior to our appointment, each of these persons was mailed a copy of the full research proposal. Each believed that the research had potential for obtaining useful information which might be used for instructing health services personnel; each granted his support of the endeavor.

The chief of the medical staff and the director of nursing were queried as to the best way to secure cooperation through the ranks. The chief of staff facilitated introductions to the chairmen of the departments of medicine and surgery. These men in turn recruited an attending physician with whom I would start "on service" (i.e., accompany that physician on patient rounds).[1] I then introduced myself to the residents and medical students on the attending physician's service. After these initial introductions, I contacted other attending physicians to ask if time could be spent with them on their service.

Negotiations with the nurses entailed dealing with six organizational levels. The Director of Nursing instructed me to see the Associate Director who is responsible for special projects of any kind. She recommended that the Clinical Directors of Nursing, Nursing Supervisors, Head Nurses and staff nurses be contacted. Securing the cooperation of all these levels was essential in order to be accepted on the clinical units. The head nurses of the four units that were selected for intensive observation suggested that I meet with their staff to briefly explain the research prior to beginning study in these units. But this was not easily accomplished. In one instance the head nurse was off the day she had promised to introduce me to the staff; another head nurse simply told me to go to the clinical unit, gather the nurses together and give an explanation. In the ideal situation the head nurse facilitated me by inviting me to a staff meeting and allowing adequate time to explain the proposed study. She also suggested a mechanism for explaining my presence to staff who were off duty during the initial contact. This was to post a photograph of me on the wall of the nurses station along with a short explanation of the research. From this simple measure my presence was efficiently and effectively explained to nurses, resident house staff, unit secretaries, housekeeping staff and other curious personnel around the units.

A comment is in order concerning the wisdom of gaining the cooperation of all pertinent personnel in an organization. Some researchers mistakenly presume that negotiations with powerful persons will filter down through the ranks and be accepted by lower members of the staff hierarchy. This assumption often is incorrect because failure to secure the cooperation and good will of personnel at all levels may lead to suspicion, subterfuge or exploitation on their part. For example, the medical and nursing staff may be "too busy" to give interviews, "forget" to inform the researcher about an upcoming event, or neglect to relate some pertinent aspect that may be of interest. This situation may be true not only of the staff, but of patients as well. For instance, when I talked with the hospital administrator he warned that some patients might refuse to be interviewed "simply to exercise their consumer right to say 'no'."

Some social scientists who have studied patient care units have wrongly believed that they only needed to secure the approval of physicians and/or administrators. In so doing they ignored the group which protects and often serves as advocates for patients, i.e., the nurses (c.f., McIntosh, 1977). This error was witnessed at University Hospital. A fellow social science graduate student provoked the ire of nurses by showing up unannounced in patient rooms to conduct interviews. As far as the nurses were concerned, he was an unauthorized intruder and was called upon to explain his presence on many occasions. He complained to me of having difficulty in finding patients who could tolerate his lengthy interviews, a problem which he could have overcome had he secured the cooperation of the nurses in selecting suitable patients.

DEFINING THE ANTHROPOLOGIST'S ROLE

A native anthropologist studying some aspect of his or her own culture is faced with the problem of maintaining objectivity in spite of possessing intuitive understanding of values and meanings associated with the cultural unit under examination. In this study three concerns were identified regarding the anthropologist's role. These were (1) dealing with the hazards of being an "expert" observer, that is, having some knowledge of the clinical situation; (2) managing the balance between being an unbiased analyst and overidentifying with the subject and subjects of investigation; and (3) coping with ethical issues regarding observer bias and observer effect on the cultural scene. As experienced fieldworkers know, such issues are not resolved and then set aside, but are continually reassessed over the duration of fieldwork. Indeed, they may evolve during the course of different situations.

Expert Observation

As applied anthropologists have turned attention to studies of contemporary Western society, a literature has developed around the problem of maintaining analytic objectivity while at the same time making use of the knowledge and insights possessed by being a member of the culture. Neville (1978: 198–201) suggested that familiarity with one's own culture may create conflict between one's world view and that of members of the social institutions under investigation, thus enhancing analytic bias. She recommended that anthropologists studying their own cultural institutions should strive to maintain "cultural relativism," a posture that ideally prevents anthropologists from taking value-laden positions. My position, that anthropological studies should strive for research objectivity, echoes this view.

Medical anthropologists in particular must strive to overcome their possible biases toward medical practice and practitioners that may have been bred by the mystique of medicine in general, and specifically by the current well-publicized criticisms of medical costs, overuse of medical technology, allocations of health care resources, and medical professional dominance. Indeed, some writers have stated that knowledge of health care systems such as the organization of clinical practice and basic biomedical concepts and language is a pre-requisite for objectively studying clinical settings (Chrisman and Maretzki 1982: 22; Maretzki 1985: 29; Hufford 1985). My knowledge of health care systems stems from 20 years of experience in nursing education and administration. However, at the time of the study I had not been actively involved in a clinical setting for a number of years. Some issues related to my background are discussed in the last section of this paper.

There are both advantages and disadvantages of being an expert observer, that is, of possessing prior knowledge of medical science, language, actions, and values. An understanding of the actions and meanings of a clinical setting greatly reduces the time and cognitive effort necessary to adjust to an otherwise foreign culture and language. An understanding of medical language and practice also enhances the investigator's credibility as a serious observer of the clinical situation. It also may help dispel perceptions physicians and nurses may have about the anthropologist's intent to expose, criticize or disrupt the clinical system. However, one disadvantage of such foreknowledge is that it may reduce the objectivity of the anthropologist's observations. Thus, an objective investigator must constantly validate his or her understanding of clinical practice from the people who enact day-to-day clinical reality. This can be achieved by seeking explanations from individuals concerning the rationale for their actions even though the logic or motive may seem apparent by the action itself. Insight also can be obtained by asking two or more participants in an interaction to independently explain the meaning of the interaction.

Objectivity

The potential problem of overidentification with the topic and subjects of a clinical investigation may take two directions. One is the investigator's personal response to the intensely dramatic arena of the clinical setting. Ethnographers have reflected upon their feelings of inadequacy in the "really important" events of life and death which take place in the hospital environment (Sudnow 1967; McIntosh 1977). As an observer of the medical community, the investigator must acquire "affective neutrality" (Parsons 1951), and become accustomed to the reality of clinical problems. This requires depersonalization of patients' pain and suffering, and the development of an objective attitude regarding medical impossibility, privileged information, and even clinical error.

Second, as Bosk (1972: 203) noted, the fieldworker is poised between his debt to his discipline, and his personal obligations to his subjects. On one hand, he is bound to objectively report his findings, even if they reveal unflattering behavior. On the other, intense personal relationships may be generated between the fieldworker and his subjects. Moreover, the researcher must be alert to possible sources of observer bias such as subjective reactions to personalities, weighting the importance given to certain events, personal prejudices, and the vicissitudes of the researcher's own life. Ward and Werner (1984) referred to possible discrepancies and contradictions in data arising from such factors as "epistemological windows". These investigators recommended that such contradictory texts in the data base be analyzed for *how* and *why* they occur (Ward and Werner 1984: 102).

To some degree the structure of hospital life limits the opportunities that an investigator might have to develop overrapport and or to become overindebted to his subjects. Unlike the anthropologist in a small scale society who lives and works 24 hours a day with an unchanging population, the medical anthropologist in a contemporary hospital confines his relationships with his subjects to working hours. Moreover, at University Hospital the medical attending physicians are on clinical services for one month at time; they then rotate to other administrative and academic duties. The surgical attending physicians make sporadic visits to the patient care units. Resident house staff and medical students rotate through services every three months. The time spent with the nursing staff of a unit was also generally limited, the range being from one to four months. Patients in the sample selected usually were hospitalized for a few days to a few weeks.

The means by which I controlled overrapport, overindebtedness and other subjective biases was to have a clear definition of the role of the investigator in mind. Since I was not a hospital employee, I did not offer to be a helper or to run errands that would have ingratiated me to the staff. Similarly, patients sometimes asked for my opinion as to whether they were making correct medical decisions. Patients probably sought my advice because, in accordance with hospital rules, I wore a lab coat. This was handled by simply telling them that I was a social scientist and not in a position to make such judgments. In this way, it was possible to professionalize the research role to the greatest possible extent. This also was achieved by formalizing devices such as appointments for interviews, letters of appreciation for services rendered, and strict adherence to formal and informal institutional rules for the conduct of research.

Some researchers tell of concocting a "cover story" which is used to explain the observer's presence in the setting or to conceal the actual topic of interest (c.f., McIntosh 1977; Bosk 1979). This technique is usually defended as necessary to prevent subjects from altering their behavior with respect to the topic of study.[2] However, such camouflage presents an ethical dilemma in research with human subjects and is illegal according to federal guidelines on informed consent regarding research. In the present study a straightforward explanation was given of the purpose of the study. Furthermore, it was tacitly assumed in an environment which places prodigious demands on physicians' and nurses' time and energy, that these individuals simply would be motivated to conduct their work in a normal fashion rather than to alter their usual behavior in order to favorably impress an observer. But this may not have always been the case. A medical student admitted that several residents had been ordered by their attending physician to "clean up their language" when the investigator was present.

Patients also were given a straightforward explanation of the research goals and were assured of confidentiality. However, in some ways, my presence was helpful for patients for I was one of the few persons who had the interest and patience to listen to ailing and anxious patients for as long as they wanted to talk. These protracted discussions also provided data for they often reflected patient concerns that might not have been elicited by structured interviews.

In general, the doctors and nurses seemed pleased that *their* particular setting had been chosen for study, and they were eager to cooperate. This was partly because of carefully designed strategies for developing trust. During initial meetings, doctors, nurses and patients were assured that no information disclosed would be given to other physicians, nurses or patients. This decision was guided by the assumption that my presence constituted an artifact, and that such information normally would have to travel through usual channels. Another way that trust was established was by assuring informants that their behavior was not being judged, but rather was described objectively as usual clinical life. The staff cooperated during interviews and permitted close association with them when they interacted with patients, performed their work and chatted in their rest areas.

One issue faced by field researchers concerns the advisability of intervening in potentially harmful situations, and of revealing potentially damaging information. As stated above, in this study I remained entirely a neutral observer, for interventions disturb the very relationships which were under study. Nevertheless, on several occasions patients were interviewed following clinician-patient exchanges in order to assess their level of understanding and satisfaction with the information given. Sometimes the patient was confused and upset by apparently contradictory or incomprehensible information given to him. In these cases I repeated what the doctor or nurse had said, but did not recast the doctor's or nurse's comments in a form that would seem to make better sense.

On rare occasions I was a party to information that could have been used in a harmful way. Usually this concerned honest differences of professional opinion or alleged technical or judgment errors committed by physicians at other hospitals before the patients had been transferred to University Hospital. Since confidentiality had been promised to the informants in this study, this information was kept in trust. This was particularly appropriate since the physicians who discussed these cases stated that these were differences in professional opinion and that there was no specific evidence that these incidents involved medical negligence.

Observer Effect

The ethnographic methodological literature abounds with commentary concerning the impact of the anthropologist's presence in the research arena (Peterson 1978; Sayles 1978; Taylor 1978; Bosk 1979). Indeed, it has been suggested that the fieldworker's relationship with his subjects itself is a major methodological tool of ethnography (Bosk 1979: 202) and part of the cultural reality being studied (Cassell and Wax 1980: 261). Among the various roles that ethnographers have described for themselves are confidant, assistant, advocate for the underdog or exploited, and mediator between subgroups within a system. Some writers have claimed that such roles create solidarity with the group under study, and build trust which allows the investigator access to the inner throughts and workings of its members. Other writers have recognized that the assumption of such roles has lead to exploitation of the investigator by competing factions within the group, or to conflicts of interest which arise when attempting to satisfy the interests of two or more subgroups. Wax (1952) suggested that the anthropologist should be aware of what he or she may be providing informants, e.g., attention, relief of boredom, an audience for radical views. Such insight concerning reciprocity in field work relationships may assist the investigator in evaluating the veracity of data given by informants. As Mauss (1967) points out, the giver and recipient in an exchange are united in a sequence that involves reciprocal exchanges and creates mutual obligations among participants.

In this study I avoided creating non-investigator roles. This was achieved initially when I explained the study to patients, physicians and nurses. In addition to assuring these persons of confidentiality, as described above, I also stated that I would not engage as an intermediary between patients and clinicians or between staff and supervisory personnel. In addition, socializing with staff, that is, going to meals with them and attending staff parties, was kept to a minimum. On these rare occasions I maintained a neutral, observer profile. This establishment of mutual professional expectations be-

tween investigator and subjects probably excluded me from exposure to the "backstage reality" of social organization. For instance, I
seldom witnessed common gossip, backbiting, or the perjorative
slang which allegedly is common among house staff and nurses
(Shem 1978).

Backstage reality can provide the anthropologist with important
data about informal organizational culture. The relevance of such
data for the topic under study must be balanced against the potential risk of inappropriate involvement of the investigator in the
internal affairs of the staff. In this study, it was believed that
intimate knowledge of local gossip would not shed light on the
problems of the exchange of *clinically relevant* information between
clinicians or clinicians and patients.

COLLECTING DATA

One methodological problem is the handling of data collection as
unobtrusively as possible in the clinical arena. Three issues arose in
this study relative to this problem: (1) the recording of field notes, (2)
the use of tape recording, and (3) the effect of the observer's presence
on normal situations. In this study I spent six to ten hours each day in
the hospital. Observation was made of physicians' rounds, nurses'
report, nursing staff meetings, nursing patient care planning conferences, medical physicians' morning reports, surgeons' morbidity and
mortality conferences and other clinically related medical meetings. In
addition, time was spent conducting formal and informal interviews
with physicians, nurses and patients, as well as observing interactions
between these subjects. Although the day was divided into distinct
activities, it was difficult to remember all that goes on during these
meetings or during rounds in which physicians may talk with 15 or 20
patients over a two hour period.

Field notes were not written at the time of observations because I
wished to avoid distraction from the content, sequence and contextual fabric of the interactional process and to avoid arousing self-
conscious or atypical behavior on the part of the subjects. To keep
track of observations I used a pocket-size notebook in which to
record key words that were used to stimulate later recall of the
events observed. Some researchers leave the clinical area for
periods of time during the day in order to write journal entries. In
this study fieldnotes were not written while I was on the hospital
premises, but rather were entered directly into a personal computer.

Fieldnotes were content coded for later retrieval, using Software Publishing Corporation's PFS software program. Fieldnotes were entered as descriptively and as close to verbatim as possible. This procedure required an additional three to four hours of work each day.

Tape recording was used only for formal interviews with physicians and nurses. Some nurses initially resisted being tape recorded but permitted it when it was explained that I wished to concentrate on the interview without the distraction of notetaking. Formal interviews with patients were not tape recorded because an informal setting seemed to be less inhibiting to the patient. Moreover, the interviews usually were punctuated by interruptions and extraneous noises. It simply was easier to take shorthand notes as described above. All interviews were content coded and transcribed into the computer.

Last, I was concerned about minimizing observer effect on the natural course of events. In order to maintain as nearly normal an interactional environment as possible, I did not engage in conversation with physicians or nurses while they were interacting with each other or with patients. Instead, questions or comments were held until the interaction sequence appeared to be completed.

Observation of interactions between staff and physician-patient transactions presented no problems; during rounds I merely was one of several members of the group accompanying the attending physician. Observation of nurse-patient interactions was somewhat more difficult. First, nurses frequently enter and leave patients' rooms, and it is awkward to be continuously trailing them. It was felt to be ethically inapporopriate to lurk behind bed curtains while a nurse performed extended patient care, although often this is when most meaningful interactions may take place. Further, most nurses seemed intimidated by the observer's presence; if the observer simply lingered in a patient's room, the nurse usually went about her tasks without speaking to the patient at all. A method to overcome this problem was tested by means of a wireless microphone attached to a nurse which would transmit her conversations with patients over distance. The nurse-patient transactions would be monitored by the investigator located in the corridor. This change in methodology required submission of a protocol revision to the IRB and a new informed consent which advised the patient that his conversation would be overheard whenever the nurse was in the room. This system, however, requires an open channel on an FM radio band for receiving the signal and does not work in a large metropolitan area where the entire radio band is occupied by commercial broadcasting stations. In the end, nurse-patient interactions were best observed when the investigator accompanied nurses on planned nurse-patient encounters. These included patient admission assessments, discharge planning and patient teaching sessions.

THE PERSONAL EQUATION

This paper has emphasized the goal of an objective and professional research role. This posture is vital to achieve scientific validity and research credibility of anthropologic studies. In spite of this goal, complete objectivity and observer neutrality may never be fully obtained in social science research. This occurs partly because research is never value-free and also because the researcher's observations are inevitably colored by his or her own background and perspectives. Anthropological research is particularly subject to personal influences because of the tradition of intense participation by the anthropologist in the lives of the group under study (c.f. Hymes 1972). In this section I will discuss some personal variables and how I handled these over the course of study.

On a personal level I faced two critical issues relative to conducting research in a clinical setting. One problem required confrontation before entering the field. This was my negative bias toward physicians. The second involved the resolution of role conflict between my two identities as a nurse and as an anthropologist. My personal view of physicians arose from my background as a nurse and was enhanced by the critical nature of social science literature on the medical profession and on doctor-patient relationships. Doctor-nurse relationships are often characterized by tension, due, in part, to asymmetrical statuses, sexual politics, and a general lack of understanding of each other's methods, logic and priorities (Mathews 1985). It is inevitable that unresolved personal conflicts taken into the field often result in a lack of observer objectivity.

Resolution of my bias was handled pragmatically and cognitively. From a practical viewpoint I anticipated that a negative attitude would prevent my gaining access to, or cooperation from, physicians. In addition, a major justification for the study was to describe how recent societal changes (e.g., consumerism, litigation, greater public education) have influenced professional ideologies and the interactional processes. It is meaningless to propose to study the processes and outcomes of change while adhering to old prejudices. Thus, I determined to lay my bias aside and to objectively observe clinical reality as it is enacted. As a result of this neutral posture, I gained an appreciation of the problems, logic and methods of physicians that I had not previously experienced. In addition, I was never denied access to any physician or to any medical activity that I wished to attend.

For several reasons, I did not want people to know of my clinical background. First, I wanted members of the group to view me as non-partisan. I did not want physicians' or nurses' attitudes toward my clinical identity to limit their willingness to speak freely about physician-nurse relationships. Second, I did not want patients to cast me in the role of someone from whom they could request services because this would place me in the position of having to deny their requests or of improperly practicing nursing. Last, I wanted freedom to ask physicians and nurses questions about their work world. The answers to many of these questions might be expected to be common knowledge to a clinician who understands many premises and procedures of the clinical culture. These questions were important because I wanted to elicit the perspectives of the informants rather than to impose upon the analysis my sense of how things are. Thus I elected to conceal my background as a nurse.

A few doctors and nurses guessed that I was a nurse. When they were asked why they assumed this, each one stated that it was because I was a woman in the health care environment. Each was asked not to reveal my clinical background to others, and to my knowledge they complied with this request. The detail with which most of the attending physicians, house staff and medical students explained to me pathology, the use of various pieces of apparatus, and patient cases indicated they did not recognized me as a member of the medical culture and instead were providing knowledge that would enhance the meaning of my experience.

Patients were not aware of my clinical status. When I made physicians' rounds patients may have assumed that I was a doctor. This is partly because, in accordance with institutional policy, I wore a white labcoat, as do physicians. One attending physician routinely introduced me as "doctor", as he did all of the house staff and medical students on his service. Another attending physician introduced me by name and added, "She's working with us." Usually, however, I was part of the nonintroduced entourage. Whenever I saw a patient alone or in the company of only one physician or nurse, I introduced myself as a social scientist or anthropologist.

CONCLUSIONS

This chapter has had two major goals: first, to describe procedures for gaining entree and negotiating a role in a highly complex and sensitive clinical organization, and second, to discuss some fundamental methodological and ethical issues faced by a fieldworker in such an organization.

Qualitative description can yield results that are phenomenologically rich, and may provide theoretical insights as well as suggest better physician-nurse-patient interaction. At the same time, this method provides no formal procedures to control validity and reliability. The merits and deficits of a qualitative approach in the clinical setting may work for or against the anthropologist depending on his or her ability to sustain effective fieldwork among a group of professional persons. This places upon the anthropologist the responsibility to work within the formal research framework of the institution as well as the informal rules of conduct that will generate cooperation from members of the organization.

One of the most difficult analytic tasks faced by the anthropologist is to elucidate the common themes in the infinite ways by which individuals express their values and logic. The seriousness of this task is matched only by the importance of letting the data tell the story rather than being influenced by one's preconceived notions generated from the literature, past experience or folk beliefs. For these reasons the anthropologist should be aware of the potential for biases, overgeneralizations and overindebtedness, and he or she should plan strategies for dealing with these issues before entering the field. The ethnographic record should include a description of how the fieldworker avoided succumbing to these potential problems. A clear account of the writer's insights and strategies will permit the reader to judge objectivity and validity for himself and, at the same time, can help other fieldworkers plan to deal with these issues.

ACKNOWLEDGEMENTS

The research upon which this article is based was supported by a fellowship from the National Institutes of Mental Health (National Research Service Award Institutional Training Grant T32 MH 16136) and a fellowship from the National Institutes of Health (National Research Service Award NU 05629–02).

NOTES

1. An attending physician is one who has faculty rank in one of the Departments of the University's School of Medicine, and has a private practice with admitting privileges to University Hospital. A resident is a graduate physician who is training in an area of clinical specialization such as internal medicine or surgery.
2. McIntosh's study was conducted in Scotland; Bosk's study did not deal explicitly with patients. These factors may explain why they were able to use a cover story.

REFERENCES

Agar, Michael H., 1980. *The Professional Stranger: An Informal Introduction to Ethnography*. New York: Academic Press.

Bosk, Charles L., 1979. *Forgive and Remember: Managing Medical Failure*. Chicago: University of Chicago Press.

Cassell, Joan and Murray L. Wax, 1980. Editorial Introduction: Toward A Moral Science of Human Beings, *Social Problems* 27: 259–264.

Chrisman, Noel J., and Thomas W. Maretzki, 1982a. Anthropology in Health Science Settings. In *Clinically Applied Anthropology*, eds. Noel J. Chrisman and Thomas W. Maretzki, 1–31. Boston: D. Riedel.

Chrisman, Noel J., and Thomas W. Maretzki, 1982b. *Clinically Applied Anthropology*. Boston: D. Reidel.

Danziger, Sandra K., 1979. On Doctor-Watching: Fieldwork in Medical Settings, *Urban Life* 7: 513–531.

Freidson, Eliot, 1970. *Professional Dominance*. Chicago: Aldine.

Gaines, Atwood D., and Robert A. Hahn, 1985. Among the Physicians. In *Physicians of Western Medicine*, eds. Robert A. Hahn and Atwood D. Gaines, 3–22. Boston: D. Reidel.

Hahn, Robert A. and Atwood D. Gaines, 1985. *Physicians of Western Medicine*. Boston: D. Reidel.

Hymes, Dell, 1972. *Reinventing Anthropology*. New York: Pantheon.

Hufford, David J., 1985. Folk Studies and Health, *Practicing Anthropology* March: 23–24.

Maretzki, Thomas W., 1985. Including the Physician in Healer-Centered Research: Retrospect and Prospect. In *Physicians of Western Medicine*, eds. Robert A. Hahn and Atwood D. Gaines, 23–50. Boston: D. Reidel.

Mathews, Joan J., 1983. The Communication Process in Clinical Settings, *Social Science and Medicine* 19: 1371–1378.

Mathews, Joan J., 1985. The Informative Process in the Clinical Setting, Doctoral Dissertation, Ann Arbor, Michigan: University Microfilms.

Mauss, Marcel, 1967. *The Gift*, New York: W. W. Norton.

McIntosh, John, 1977. *Communication and Awareness in a Cancer Ward*. New York: Prodist.

McKinlay, John B., 1977. The Business of Good Doctoring or Doctoring as Good Business: Reflections on Freidson's View of the Medical Game, *International Journal of Health Services* 7: 459–483.

Mead, Margaret, 1972. *Blackberry Winter: My Earlier Years*. New York: Morrow.

Millman, Marsha, 1976. *The Unkindest Cut: Life in the Backrooms of Medicine*. New York: Morrow.

Neville, Gwen K., 1978. Marginal Communicant: The Anthropologist in Religious Groups and Agencies. In *Applied Anthropology in America*, eds. Elizabeth M. Eddy and William L. Partridge, 197–209.

Parsons, Talcott, 1951. *The Social System*, Glencoe, Illinois: Free Press.
Peterson, John H., 1978. The Changing Role of an Applied Anthropologist. In *Applied Anthropology in America*, eds. Elizabeth M. Eddy and William L. Partridge, 165–181., New York: Columbia University Press.
Sayles, Myrna, 1978. Behind Locked Doors. In *Applied Anthropology in America*, eds. Elizabeth M. Eddy and William L. Partridge, 210–228.
Shem, Samuel, 1978. *House of God*. New York: Dell.
Sudnow, David, 1967. *Passing On*. Englewood Cliffs, NJ: Prentice-Hall.
Taylor, Carol, 1978. Anthropologist-in-Residence. In *Applied Anthropology in America*, eds. Elizabeth J. Eddy and William L. Partridge, 229–244., New York: Columbia University Press.
Ward, John and Oswald Werner, 1984. Difference and Dissonance in Ethnographic Data, *Communication and Cognition* 17: 219–243.
Wax, Rosalie, 1952. Reciprocity as a Field Technique, *Human Organization* 11: 34–37.

Biomedicine as a Cultural System: An Anthropologist in the Kingdom of the Sick

SUSAN M. DiGIACOMO

Cornell University

Illness is the night-side of life, a more onerous citizenship. Everyone who is born holds dual citizenship, in the kingdom of the well and in the kingdom of the sick.

Susan Sontag, *Illness as Metaphor* (1978:3)

INTRODUCTION

It is no mere literary turn of phrase to say that the seriously ill take up residence in another country for the duration. When emigration also means prolonged or periodic exile in the hospital, the sense of being a stranger in a strange land is further heightened. Distinctive forms of language, institutional organization, authority structures, and shared beliefs make such places as foreign as any unknown culture. This essay chronicles the adventures of an anthropologist in the kingdom of the sick, and suggests some ways in which the experience of that illness may be turned to anthropological account.

In late June 1980, a few weeks before the completion of my dissertation research in Barcelona, Spain, my doctor discovered a swollen node in my neck. A biopsy confirmed his suspicions: it was Hodgkin's disease, a cancer of the lymphatic system. Ten days later, I flew home, and on July 5 was admitted to a major research hospital for tests and surgery to determine the extent of my disease. Following my release, I returned daily to the hospital for six weeks of radiation treatments, was allowed to rest for six weeks, then

315

resumed daily radiation treatments for another six weeks. Radiotherapy ended three days before Christmas. A remission of nearly four years followed, ending in late May 1984 with chest surgery to remove a tumor attached to my heart. At the end of June, the surgical wound sufficiently healed; I embarked on a program of aggressive chemotherapy scheduled over a period of 12 months. On April, 1, 1985, my chemotherapist and I made a joint decision to end this regimen several treatments short of the total prescribed course of therapy because of my unusual (and dangerous) physiological response to the drugs. The prognosis is uncertain. Further treatment in the event of a second recurrence remains a possibility, at least in my doctor's mind.

I decided before being hospitalized in 1980 that my best chance of staying sane lay in using my skills as a researcher and ethnographer to demystify my disease and its treatment, and thereby to restore some sense of control. Treatments of indefinite length and uncertain outcome invariably inspire fear and rage, and rob the cancer patient of much of his personal autonomy. In such circumstances knowledge is the only kind of power available. It imposed order, pattern and meaning on a life that had suddenly taken on a frighteningly random character, and so made it possible to manage the fear. Hospital staff and professionals soon made it clear that they found my curiosity inappropriate, and their disapproval led me to formulate other kinds of questions. What began as a method of coping with an otherwise intolerable situation developed into an interest in the hospital as an institution possessed of an organizational culture that defines categories of persons — doctors and patients — and shapes their relationship to each other.

Few social scientists have written sociologically or anthropologically about their illnesses.[1] Only three examples have come to hand. Julius Roth's book *Timetables* (1963), a study of the structuring of the passage of time in hospital treatment, was the outcome of a siege of tuberculosis that began just after he had completed his Ph.D. Lewis Killian's successful career in sociology was interrupted at its mid-point by a stay in a mental hospital. What he observed and participated in there touched his intellect as well as his emotions, and his 1975 article entitled "Rebirth in a Therapeutic Community" reexamines the nature of the total institution. Roth's dominant area of interest in graduate school had been the sociology and social psychology of institutions and occupations, so he was able to see his hospitalization as a research opportunity instead of a major interruption of his life. Killian's professional interests also included social psychology, though not specifically the sociology of mental health. Irving Kenneth Zola suffered two major traumas in late adolescence — first polio, then a car crash that shattered his femur and his fragile sense of wholeness. Many years later, during a sabbatical year as consultant-in-residence to the Netherlands Institute of Preventive Medicine, he was offered an opportunity to visit Het Dorp, a community conceived and constructed to promote the dignity and independence of its 400 severely disabled adult residents. As a resident visitor in Het Dorp, Zola began to reexamine his own life as well as observing the lives of the permanent residents, and eventually produced a "socio-autobiography," *Missing Pieces* (1982).

Like Roth, Killian and Zola, I had the rare opportunity to be both a complete participant and an observer. And, as they began to think sociologically about their experiences along already established lines of interest, so did I. Doing fieldwork in a factory had given me an interest in the structure of organizations and the ways in which they process people, and I had only recently been engaged in untangling the web of nationalist politics in Catalonia. When I was able to stand a little away from my own experience and talk about it objectively, it was in these terms that I spoke.

The theoretical lens through which I view the world is that of symbolic/interpretive anthropology in the Geertzian sense: cultural systems as ways of constructing reality, and social action as a way of commenting upon that reality. I believe biomedicine can profitably be treated as such a system, and that this system is reproduced (and sometimes, as in my case, renegotiated) in interaction between doctors and patients. I want to shed some light on what this process means to those involved in it.

It is the office of the ethnographer to "rescue the 'said' of social discourse from its perishing occasions and fix it in perusable terms" (Geertz 1973: 20) by means of "thick description," a sort of cultural *explication de texte* in which texture and context are as vital to understanding as the text itself. Geertz (1973: 10) likens the ethnographic enterprise to "trying to read (in the sense of 'construct a reading of') a manuscript — foreign, faded, full of ellipses, incoherencies, suspicious emendations, and tendentious commentaries, but written not in conventionalized graphs of sound but in transient examples of shaped behavior." As "shaped behavior," social action is itself a reading, a first-order interpretation, of the "ordered clusters of significant symbols" that "individuals and groups of individuals employ to orient themselves in a world

otherwise opaque" (Geertz 1973:363). The cultural anthropologist
reads these structures of meaning out of the social text — a second-
order interpretation — and recasts them in terms of the anthropological universe of discourse: a third-order interpretation.
The result of this exercise is not Meaning — a "General Theory
of Cultural Interpretation" (Geertz 1973:26) — but meaning,
explanatory rather than predictive, permitting generalization
within a case rather than across cases.

Appropriately enough for my purposes here, I am applying to the
practice of medicine as a cultural system the same mode of analysis
that the clinician applies to a set of disease symptoms. The
uninitiated may object that medicine is a "hard" science, its practice
based on such objective indicators as hematology laboratories and
sophisticated radiological and surgical techniques can provide, while
cultural analysis is "soft," subjective, and not susceptible of
verification. However, the etiology of most cancers is as little
understood as the genesis of any given culture.[2] Because the
mechanism whereby normal cells become cancerous remains
unknown, cancer treatment remains as brutally primitive as any
inflicted by the leeches and barber-surgeons of old. And, as often as
not, no clear and obvious course of action emerges from the
application of even the most advanced diagnostic tools. The
treatment of cancer is at least as much an interpretive art as a hard
science, and possibly more so. Generalizing across cases is nearly
impossible for the clinical oncologist, and even generalizing within a
single case can be extraordinarily difficult.

Which brings me to the next thing that is *not* being said. Although
cultural systems find expression in social action, there is no easy
one-to-one correspondence between them. If the social "text" is full
of indeterminacies, ambiguities and even contradictions, it is
because both the cultural order and the social order are likewise
pervaded by indeterminacy, and the relation between the two is
necessarily imprecise and non-congruent. Individuals make selective
use of this ambiguity to suit their own immediate purposes — either
to fix social reality, or to change it to their advantage (Moore 1975).
Social discourse in clinical settings is no exception.

A final disclaimer. The semiotic approach to culture is often
attacked on the grounds that it may all too easily "lose touch with
the hard surfaces of life" (Geertz 1973:30) in the pursuit of
meaning. Its detractors describe it as an attempt to "get inside the
natives' heads" in order to "see things from the natives' point of

view" — a dubious undertaking at best, and a misapprehension of the nature of anthropological knowledge. Cultural analysis is not a variety of mental telepathy. The interpretations it generates are, though "essentially contestable" (Geertz 1973: 29), based on a view of the cultural construction of reality as a shared public enterprise whose "natural habitat is the house yard, the marketplace, and the town square" (Geertz 1973: 45) — and, I would add, the hospital.

FIELDWORK AS PERSONAL GROWTH

When my doctor presented me with his diagnosis, my first reaction was a combination of fear and outrage at having my work and my life interrupted. In the hospital, my identity was assailed. It is difficult to be anything but what a total institution makes of you, and it is doubly difficult when the heavy symbolic charge of cancer is added to institutional requirements. A friend of mine, also an anthropologist, remarked to me that having cancer is like being black: you are totally defined by a single characteristic. It is a stigma, an attribute that reduces the afflicted person "in our minds from a whole and usual person to a tainted, discounted one" (Goffman 1963: 3). Goffman's analysis, however, requires "a language of relationships, not attributes," since "an attribute that stigmatizes one type of possessor can confirm the usualness of another, and therefore is neither creditable nor discreditable as a thing in itself" (1963: 3). Goffman's interest is in the social organization of identity; the symbolic content of that identity is of secondary importance. It is my position that the symbolic freight that cancer bears has much to do with the way social relationships between cancer patients and others — specifically, their doctors — are structured. Cancer is a root metaphor, a symbol which provides "an almost endless set of categories for conceptualizing and responding to the subtleties of experience" (Ortner 1973: 1340). As Susan Sontag (1978) has eloquently pointed out, the dominant idiom in which cancer and its treatment are described is military. At the same time, the metaphorical extensions of cancer include the whole range of social deviance, social injustice, and political corruption. The accumulated layers of meaning then redound upon the individual sufferer, with all their intimations of fatality, of catastrophe, of evil.

Identity, however, seemed to be the one area in which I could retain some control. I certainly could not control my body; that was

now in the hands of my doctors. Nor would I be able to control the
progress of my work for some time. I was already too sick to begin
writing my dissertation, and treatment would, I knew, only make
me sicker. Even my place of residence would be determined by the
location of treatment facilities for the duration. But I still had my
anthropologist's perspective on the world, and so I entered the
hospital feeling more conscious of my professional identity than I
had ever felt. I did not wear it lightly; I clung to it as to a life
preserver.

Before I left Barcelona, I determined that I would not be an
ignorant patient, waiting passively for things to happen to me. I
spent an evening with a medical sociologist friend, pulling out all his
sources on cancer and looking up Hodgkin's disease. By the end of
the evening, we had pieced together basic definitions, distributions
by age, sex and geography, disease characteristics from cell types
to symptoms, stages of progression, and strategies of treatment.
On my return home, before going into the hospital, I read a few
recent articles in the *New England Journal of Medicine* provided by
a pathologist friend on trends in the staging and treatment of Hodgkin's disease. The knowledge was sobering, but would, I felt, reduce
the surprise factor and make me less a victim.

I took a notebook with me to the hospital with the intention of
keeping a journal. I wanted to record in ethnographic detail as
much as possible — what people did and said, and to whom; what
happened to me; and what I thought and felt about it. I had no
particular use in mind for this journal, but I knew that at some point
I would want to remember. And the discipine of keeping a journal
would structure my days and provide some continuity between my
life as a field anthropologist, which I had been until only a week
before I was admitted, and my new life as a cancer patient.

In the hospital, and later as an outpatient, I asked questions. I
used the vocabulary of medicine to the extent that I knew it, and
approached doctors as colleagues rather than as superiors.
Generally, their first reaction was surprise at my failure to defer to
them, then disapproval. Occasionally, when I persisted, conflict
resulted. These disagreements first prompted me to think of my
relationships with my doctors in anthropological terms.

PERSONAL GROWTH AS FIELDWORK

I had progressed from ignorance to a degree of knowledge about my
own condition that took at least some of the uncertainty out of my

life. I took my first step toward a critical understanding of medical culture when one of my doctors came to visit me a few days after I had been admitted. He was the hospital's most illustrious in-house Hodgkin's disease expert, and a member of that small select group of doctors who are clinical investigators, engaged in both research and treatment (Lax 1984: 116). His research, going back 20 years, had helped to make possible the new treatments that had transformed Hodgkin's disease from a death sentence to one of the more tractable cancers, and one of the *New England Journal* articles I had read was his. He had only come to reassure me that I had a "good disease" (one with a high rate of long-duration remissions), but I detained him for at least 20 minutes, peppering him with questions about differential survival rates obtained through the use of different treatment strategies. My aggressive questioning made him more and more ill at ease, and finally he interrupted me.

"Look," he said, "I don't like telling you these things, because you won't understand them properly. This is *statistical* information, and you must not think it applies to you as an individual."

"Of course not," I answered. "I know that. I'm a scientist too, not the same kind as you, but I understand the difference between a statistical statement and a statement about an individual."

He continued, as though I had not spoken, "I don't think it's wise for you to try to become an expert on your own disease. It could be very damaging psychologically."

I was surprised into silence, and he stood up and left. My questions had been intelligent and informed, but his response was to assume, in spite of that, that not only did I really *not* want to hear the answers, but that hearing them might make me come unhinged. On another day, again after a fairly lengthy question-and-answer session, the same doctor called me an "intelligent, difficult patient," his word order suggesting that the latter was a direct consequence of the former. His smile took the edge off the implied criticism, but it was there nonetheless.

There were to be several more tests of will and challenges to medical authority, and all of them reinforced the conclusions I drew from that first interview. The day before surgery to biopsy my liver and remove my spleen and several lymph nodes, I met the anaesthesiologist. Unsmiling and unwilling to provide much specific information, he told me very briefly what his function would be during the operation. My main concern at that point, however, was where I would wake up. I did not want to be alone. I wanted to know where the recovery room was so that my husband could be there when I came to.

"That's impossible," he said flatly. When I asked him to explain why, he trotted out a series of hackneyed excuses I could almost have predicted: the recovery room was too crowded, people unaccustomed to the sights there were likely to faint, etc., ending with, "It's not our policy to allow relatives into the recovery room." The surgeon, when approached with the same request, reacted in the same way. Frustrated at being denied what I saw as a basic human kindness (and with the memory of very different treatment in a Catalan hospital still fresh in my mind) because of the sheer arbitrariness of rules, I told the anaesthesiologist what I thought of his policy: it was nothing but custom, clothed in all sorts of pseudo-hygienic and pseudo-practical nonsense, and there is nothing absolute about custom; it varies from place to place. It was apparent in his manner and tone of voice that he regarded his authrity as absolute (my life would, after all, be quite literally in his hands for a few hours) and my behavior as an inexcusable challenge to it. He was so angry that he very nearly refused to tell me where my family could speak to the surgeon after the operation.

Doctors (and nurses as well) expect to do their work according to established hospital routine. The resulting standardization and depersonalization of patient care is rationalized as necessary for the "efficient" functioning of the hospital and the benefit of the patient (Freidson 1970; 1967). Patients are expected to accept routines, even those they dislike or do not understand, for these two reasons. Patients who take issue with hospital rules incur the wrath of hospital staff, and in consequence are labeled "bad" patients (Lorber 1975). I have no doubt that I was so labeled after this encounter.

I was never told that after surgery I would be a walking hardware store of stainless steel clips, left to mark excised lymph nodes and the place where my spleen had been. I found this out by overhearing a casual remark by a technician who was taking an abdominal X-ray. Later, I confronted my surgeon with this piece of information and demanded to know what the clips were for, how many, how big, and what possible side effects they might produce. He was surprised and a little offended by my aggressive inquisitiveness. He told me that clips were small, the size of half a fingernail paring, and that there were no side effects. And, he added, one simply cannot explain to a patient every cut and stitch; the procedures are entirely routine, and there is no need for patients to know, or time to explain.

The most serious confrontations were about my treatment. Two weeks after my release from the hospital, I returned for a treatment simulation. This had been represented to me by a nurse as a sort of dress rehearsal, its purpose being to take some of the strangeness and fear out of the massive technology (a linear accelerator) used in radiotherapy. I realized quickly enough, however, that this is incidental to the real purpose of the simulation: mapping out those areas of the body to be treated, and determining appropriate dosages with the assistance of a nuclear physicist. At the end of the simulation, I was told peremptorily to appear the next day for my first treatment. I got angry. I lived more than two hours' drive from the hospital and needed advance notice in order to organize my new commuter life. I refused to come in until the following Monday, and the reaction was one of surprise and indignation. It did not matter that no time frame had been specified; I should simply do what I was told without argument, regardless of the dislocation and inconvenience it caused me.

There were side effects from the treatment, among them the loss of all the hair on the back of my head and burning, blistering skin. I knew this was a mild version of the radiation burns suffered by atomic bomb victims. My radiologist corrected my choice of words. "You're having a radiation *reaction*." I retorted that it was quite obviously a burn, and she answered, "We don't call it that."

I had been told to expect to lose some hair, but only an inch and a half from the back of my neck. When I lost a full five inches, I called my radiologist's attention to the discrepancy between what she had told me and what actually happened. Her answer was that my waist-length hair, heavier than short hair, had caused more "traction" and hence more loss. I was aghast at the falsehood. Anyone who looked at the back of my head could clearly see the line that was the top of the radiation field. She added, "You are losing your *tumors*, too. You should be glad." Her reaction to my observations on the changes in my body again reinforced my impression that doctors believe patients are unable to handle the truth, and must be sheltered from it.

I had to fight for every piece of information I got, even though, by their own lights, my doctors believed they were being extraordinarily open and frank with me. I prepared for my weekly visits with my radiologist as I would prepare for any interview I would do as a field anthropologist. I thought out my questions beforehand, and conducted the interview from notes. I had to talk fast, because after the first five or ten minutes, my doctor began edging toward the examining room door, an indication that she felt she had spent enough time answering my questions and had other important things to do. These visits were clearly for her benefit, so she could gauge my progress, not for mine.

I persisted with my questions, and got a fair amount of information. But, as it turned out, not enough. I never knew, until the day I returned to the hospital for a check-up six weeks after what I believed was the end of treatment, that I was scheduled for six more weeks of radiotherapy as soon as my body had recovered sufficiently from the trauma of the first six. Everyone else knew, including the X-ray technicians, who greeted me with, "Oh, I see you're back for the rest of your treatments!"

My oncologist astonished me by casually mentioning continuing radiotherapy, as if it were a foregone conclusion, during my office appointment. It surprised *him* that my radiologist hadn't prepared me for this, but he suggested to me that perhaps I had failed to understand her "stilted English way of saying things." In retrospect, I saw that this remark might be construed generously as an attempt to offer me a graceful exit from a situation in which I ran a risk of looking foolish. In the heat of the moment, however, I was in no mood to be patronized. I insisted on seeing my radiologist at once, and he telephoned ahead to Radiation Medicine to warn her of my approach. His interpretation of their conversation was that they were (and always had been) in agreement about the need to continue radiotherapy, and somehow I had misjudged the situation. As I was leaving his office, my oncologist reminded me that it was important for me to understand that no one had ever foreclosed the possibility of further treatment. I was only too aware of the need to allow treatment decisions to be dictated by changes in the patient's condition; but there is a difference, I pointed out, between that and failing to inform the patient about part of the programmed treatment sequence. My oncologist shook his head. I was drawing too fine a distinction, he said, "being legalistic."

I was furious. I felt cheated, and demanded an explanation from my radiologist. Besides the prospect of physical misery over a much longer time than I had been led to expect, I would have to face more practical problems of transportation, lodging and money to pay for bus trips and subway and taxi fares. Had I been working, there would have been serious difficulties in arranging to be absent for another six-week stretch on a moment's notice. I explained all this to my radiologist.

She replied, unruffled, "The question of further treatment was always left indefinite." (In fact, I had been told that further treatment would depend on the reappearance of active disease.) "Besides," she continued, "we simply cannot explain everything to patients. We've found that they just can't absorb much information at any given time. And anyway, this isn't a post-graduate course in radiology."

I slammed my fist on the examining table. "Well, I have a post-graduate mind. Now tell me!"

She did, but with the air of someone responding politely to an outrageous and bad-tempered demand. There were three treatment options at that point:

(1) Use chemotherapy, and "clean the patient out." This is the most drastic, and the least recommended course of action. It is hardest on the patient, and the possible complications of combined-modality treatment are very dangerous: leukemia; secondary, non-Hodgkin's lymphoma; and long-term immune suppression (Desforges et al. 1979: 1218–1219).

(2) Do nothing, and wait. As a radiologist who prefers to treat conservatively, she had some sympathy with this point of view, but in cases like mine, she explained, 15 to 20 percent of patients develop recurrent disease in areas contiguous to the mantle (upper body) treatment field within a few years.

(3) To prevent this, there is a third option: an additional five or six weeks of radiotherapy directed at abdominal and pelvic lymph nodes. This, she said, reduces the risk of a relapse to two or three percent.

Objectively considering the matter, I had to concede that the rational course of action was to sacrifice six more weeks and agree to more radiotherapy. But, whatever the reality of the situation, by this point I felt I was being bullied into accepting more treatment with the most effective of threats, that I had been made to submit, to comply, through the strategic manipulation of information.

To be fair, at least part of this was the result of what I came to understand is an extremely loose institutional structure, a reality considerably at odds with the image that hospital personnel prefer to project to the public. Communication between departments, even ones as closely linked as Radiation Medicine and Medical Oncology, is fragmentary at best. During the second week of my hospitalization, my oncologist went on holiday. Any message he left for my radiologist reached her late, and only in part. I saw her almost by chance, just before I was discharged. No doubt a similar failure in communication between my two doctors played a part in my having been kept out of the picture until the last moment. This is still enough reason to be angry, but my doctors did not think so.

There were several other instances of this kind of slippage. When it came time for me to be discharged, no one seemed to know the proper procedure, or to want to take responsibility for getting me out. Each doctor I spoke to suggested that I speak to another. The day of my operation, no one was able to tell me whether I would be taken to a surgical floor or returned to the medical oncology floor afterwards. Blood samples and X-rays got lost in transit and had to be repeated. After seven days on IV, my doctors allowed me to eat. A breakfast replete with acid and grease, in the form of orange juice and fried eggs, appeared, and the results were predictable: I vomited all day and all night, not an easy thing after abdominal surgery. Someone had simply forgotten to tell the kitchen that I should be on a bland, semi-liquid diet. But to get angry, to assert oneself in the only way possible, by refusing to surrender one's arm for a replacement blood sample, was to step out of one's assigned role, and thus to threaten the entire institution. Of all the transgressions a patient may commit, non-compliance is the worst (Zola 1980: 241).

TOWARD A NEGOTIATION MODEL OF CLINICAL PRACTICE

On August 15, 1983, I returned to the hospital for a routine semi-annual check-up, which included a routine chest X-ray. As usual when nothing is amiss, I heard nothing afterwards from my doctors, and quickly became immersed in my dissertation, scheduled for completion the following May. Apart from ongoing digestive problems as a consequence of abdominal surgery and radiotherapy, I felt reasonably well and my return visit to the hospital had occasioned only the normal level of tension and anxiety that accompanies such a visit.

In late September, my doctor at home, a family practitioner at the University Health Services, telephoned me. He had called my oncologist to try to get a sense of how usual my digestive problems were in people who had had abdominal radiotherapy, but he never got a chance to ask his question. As soon as he identified himself, my oncologist launched into a ten-minute explanation of why my suspicious X-ray film had lain on his desk for a month, unattended to. Clearly on the defensive, he assumed my doctor had somehow found out about the X-ray and was calling to press him for a decision about further testing. There was a shadow at the apex of my heart. My radiologist had expressed some concern about it, but my oncologist disagreed with her reading of the film. Shortly thereafter, my radiologist went on holiday, leaving the problematic X-ray in my oncologist's care. With a sense of *déjà vu* I recalled my first, near-fortuitous meeting with my radiologist after my oncologist had left to take *his* vacation.

The X-ray was repeated immediately, overpenetrated for better contrast, and read both at the University Health Services and at the hospital. Both readings were, I was told, unequivocally negative; nothing to worry about. Nothing further was said about the matter until I returned to the hospital six months later for another routine check-up. I took my oncologist to task for hiding from me any doubts or concerns, no matter how small. He commented only that the X-ray "didn't seem all that bad" in his judgment, a rather defensive response that suggested to me that he himself was not entirely comfortable with the way he had handled the situation. To be on the safe side, he suggested that we repeat the X-ray that day.

I scarcely had any time to wonder whether my angry reaction would have any effect. A letter dated twelve days after my hospital visit informed me that the shadow at the apex of my heart was still there, and the radiologist who had interpreted the film recommended a CAT scan as soon as possible. Later, when I thanked my oncologist for letting me know with such dispatch that something was wrong, he replied wryly that he wouldn't dream of doing otherwise, after our last conversation on the subject.

I was encouraged, but not convinced, that this one event signaled a major shift in my oncologist's willingness to communicate with me. I had always found him harder to talk to than my radiologist. He impressed me as more hurried and distracted by other obligations, less sensitive to individual character and psychology, and generally less talkative. It occurred to me that doctors and academicians talk in fundamentally different ways. Where a professor will discourse at length on all the implications of a student's question, the doctor's tendency is to give the shortest, simplest possible answer to a patient's question — in fact, to oversimplify in the interest of brevity. This would have to change if I were to survive a year of chemotherapy coinciding with my first, full-time teaching position. I had the professor-student relation explicitly in mind as the model on which I wanted to restructure our relationship.

Zola (1980) has analyzed the structural difficulties in the doctor-patient relationship that make learning impossible for the patient and create an adversary relationship around the issue of compliance rather than a "therapeutic alliance." At an early stage in the proceedings I managed, with help from my doctor at the University Health Services, to dispose of two of these: the problem of territory and social support, and the overloading of the clinical encounter. Zola argues that facing a doctor alone in unfamiliar and generally inhospitable surroundings is disorienting and intimidating, and suggests the presence of a family member or friend as "advocate" to defuse the situation. Some separation in time between the examination and the presentation of a diagnosis, prognosis, and treatment regimen would give the patient time to assimilate new information and formulate appropriate questions.

Although I had never felt intimidated, and had long since ceased to feel disoriented in the hospital, I did feel the need of an ally of sorts. My doctor at the University Health Services was uniquely well situated to be such an ally. Trained in family medicine and an individual of exceptional sensitivity, he fully understood and supported my need to comprehend my disease and its treatment to the fullest possible extent — particularly in view of my responsibility fully to inform my new department chairman of my state of health. Had I known him four years earlier, I might have had less difficulty getting information. A physician rather than a non-medically-trained friend, he shared large areas of medical knowledge and basic premises with my chemotherapist, so that his views and opinions had to be taken seriously. While he made it clear that he and the University Health Services staff would cooperate fully with the recommendations of my oncologist through the course of my treatment, it was also clear that he saw himself in the role of interpreter and advocate on my behalf. His letter to my oncologist reads in part:

> "As one would expect, the current events have triggered for Susan a lot of unpleasant memories around her initial treatment. What she appears to remember with the most distaste is the feeling of being out of control and not in a position to make an informed decision. I think she fears this almost more than the pathology itself. She feels the chance to sit and talk with you before final decisions are made would be helpful in attacking this fear."

The response reads in part:

> "Thank you for your sensitive letter regarding Susan DiGiacomo's anxieties and concerns. I certainly will try to sit down with Susan and go over all the information and bring [her radiologist] into the equation ..."

The result, in fact, was an hour-long "summit conference" with both my oncologist and my radiologist present — an unprecedented willingness on their part to invest large amounts of their time in my peace of mind. In preparation for this conference, I typed out my questions and discussed them in advance with my UHS doctor. At his suggestion I sent them to my oncologist before our meeting. When I arrived he had read the letter, and as we spoke, he tape-recorded his answers and later sent me a transcript so that I would not have to rely on memory or notes taken in a moment of emotion. The letter ends, "We both understand your effort to assume control of your destiny" — the first time I had known him to voice such a sentiment.

The forms of chemotherapy developed in the 1950s and current into the 1970s relied on the use of one, or at most two drugs. The most recent thinking in cancer treatment is that combinations of drugs, as many as eight, are more effective, provided (1) each drug has a different toxic effect on normal cells; and (2) the drugs are non-cross-resistant; that is, different enough in chemical composition so that a tumor that has become resistant to one drug will not automatically become resistant to them all. In theory, the tendency is toward shorter, more intensive periods of treatment, and the result, for the patient, is a wider range of toxic side effects of diminished severity compared to fewer, but more dangerous sequelae of treatment with one or two drugs.

At the writing of Henry Kaplan's classic treatise *Hodgkin's Disease* (1972), the four-drug combination MOPP (nitrogen mustard, vincristine [oncovin], procarbazine and prednisone) had not yet become standard, but its high remission induction rate seemed to hold out promise, despite the severe and varied complications it produced (Kaplan 1972: 359). Its curative potential was firmly established by the publication of the second edition (Kaplan 1980: 454–458).

Two years later, a group of researchers at Italy's National Cancer Institute in Milan published the results of their experiments with an eight-drug protocol administered in alternating groups of four — MOPP alternating with ABVD (adriamycin, bleomycin, vinblastine and dacarbazine). A comparison (Santoro et al. 1982) of 12 monthly cycles of MOPP to 12 monthly cycles of MOPP alternating with ABVD yielded a 20 percent rise in complete remission induction for the latter — a result so dramatic that my oncologist had instituted a clinical trial comparing MOPP alone vs. ABVD alone vs. MOPP alternating with ABVD in the hope of replicating the Milan group's

results. It was his personal conviction (and the recommendation of
the hospital's Joint Radiation Medicine/Medical Oncology Conference) that the MOPP/ABVD combination was the likeliest to
achieve a lasting remission in my case. The choice of participation in
the study, however, remained mine (I declined it). Then he did
something extraordinary: he handed me photocopies not only of the
consent form for experimental subjects, which described the side
effects of all the drugs in general (sometimes vague) layman's terms,
but also of the entire experimental protocol, normally intended only
for the consumption of other doctors.[3]

Thus far, a much more auspicious start than I had experienced
four years earlier. But there remained a question (which, as treatment progressed, ramified into a series of related questions) for
which I was not able to elicit an answer that satisfied me. The
surgeon who opened my chest had discovered only one tumor, with
no spread beyond that site, and he was able to remove it entirely.
Further, the locus of the tumor had been outside the treatment field
when I received radiotherapy, deliberately shielded to prevent
severe heart damage. In retrospect, it seemed possible that microscopic disease had been present but undetected, and therefore un-
treated, though this is an unusual sort of recurrence. If this were in
fact the case (although there was no way of knowing for certain), it
was also possible that there were other extensions of microscopic
disease lurking elsewhere; and equally possible that there were
none. The limitations of the available diagnostic techniques were
painfully obvious. When I began chemotherapy, there would be no
measurable cancer in my body; yet I would be given the same
treatment as people with end-stage, metastasized disease receive.
To me, this seemed like overkill, and I wondered aloud whether less
— perhaps six months rather than twelve — might be enough, particularly in light of the fact that the standard "salvage" chemotherapy for
people who have "failed" radiotherapy is six cycles of MOPP.

The response seemed calculated to cut off that line of inquiry and
reminded me of my radiologist's presentation of the case for six
more weeks of radiotherapy: "This is what will give you the best
chance to live." I tried again, but my oncologist would say only that
there was no statistical basis for knowing whether less would be
sufficient in cases like mine. He did not have to remind me that we
could not afford to make a mistake this time. Still, it seemed to me
that overestimating the required dosages might be as serious as
underestimating them, given what I knew about the toxic properties

of the drugs in question. I could not get him to comment on this.

It was not long before this very question became a constant preoccupation for both of us. The first injection of nitrogen mustard and vincristine (prednisone and procarbazine are taken by mouth in pill form) produced agonizing pain in my face, ears, and throat, and a sensation of crushing pressure around my chest. Vincristine is specifically toxic to nerves, and often produces some degree of peripheral neuropathy, usually numbness or tingling in the fingers and toes. Rarely does it produce the kind of incapacitating facial pain that I experienced. When I returned to the hospital a week later for the second injection of the cycle, my oncologist (who had heard about the pain not only from me, but from my UHS doctor as well) halved the dosage of vincristine. "Her face fell off last week," he joked to the technician as she prepared the drugs, making sure at the same time that I knew he had got the message. The second injection produced less facial pain, but precipitated a major gastrointestinal crisis. Already a spare 95 pounds at the start of treatment, I lost five pounds the first week because eating caused more pain than I could bear, and five more the second week because I could digest nothing but clear soups.

The first cycle of ABVD was no more auspicious. After the first of the two injections my white blood cell counts, which had proved more resistant than expected to nitrogen mustard, dropped precipitously and my fever soared to 102°. I spent five days in a local hospital in isolation — without immune defenses I might have died of any infection — receiving intravenous antibiotics on a preemptive basis, for no bacterial infection could be detected. This crisis set the pattern for the others that followed. As the treatment progressed, the fevers increased in both severity and duration.

Bleomycin is known to produce fever, but only during the 24 to 48 hours immediately following an injection; my fevers lasted from three to six *weeks*. In the course of one such fever crisis, my blood was cultured at the University Health Services in an attempt to locate an infection. The culture grew staph, and I was rushed to the hospital emergency room for fear that bacteria had lodged in a faulty valve in my heart. This turned out to be a false alarm. My blood was cultured repeatedly over two days, and no staph grew, leading the heart and infectious disease specialists to the conclusion that the UHS blood culture had become contaminated. I met with my oncologist to discuss this sequence of events and what effect it might have on the course of my treatment.

"What do *you* think happened to me?" I asked. He shrugged. "Some infection," he said vaguely. "But there *was* no infection."

"Then perhaps the fever was a disease symptom." Rising and falling fevers in ten-day cycles, called the Pel-Epstein fever, are a characteristic symptom of Hodgkin's disease, and one that I had experienced in 1980. Two thoughts crowded into my mind at once. The pattern was wrong for a Pel-Epstein fever; both the fever-free intervals and the periods of fever were too long. Or perhaps I had microscopic disease, undetectable in X-rays and CAT scans, that was resistant to chemotherapy.

I pointed out the problem of pattern, then took a deep breath and asked, "What happens to people for whom chemotherapy doesn't work? Are there any therapeutic alternatives?"

He answered evenly, "They live for a few months, sometimes a few years. Do you mean holistic medicine?" There was a touch of contempt in his voice.

He should know better, I thought, than to suggest that. "No, I mean *real* medicine. Experimental immunotherapy, that sort of thing." The chance to snap at him restored some of my composure. Discussing the possibility of one's own imminent death is a deeply unsettling experience. Later, I realized that the fact that we had had such a conversation signified a further development in our changing relationship. Most doctors shrink from the subject of death, in part because of their own complicated emotions (Artiss and Levine 1973) and in part because they do not wish to deny their patients hope (cf. Novack et al. 1979). Earlier, my oncologist had been resolutely upbeat, confining his misgivings to the notes he made for his own file and cheerfully denying that I was experiencing anything unusual, even on the day that I appeared for a treatment weighing a skeletal 86 pounds and announcing in a hoarse whisper that I thought I was dying of chemotherapy. He called me a "tough kid," a gruffly affectionate epithet I had heard him apply to some of his other patients. Not everyone could live up to it, though; one of his patients died the same night I was admitted to the hospital through the emergency room, and three days later I could still see the effect of the loss in his face. Each of us had begun to see the other in three dimensions instead of two.

At the second ABVD treatment the following week, the dosages of adriamycin and vinblastine were cut back in view of the leukopenia induced by the previous injection. Dosages of chemotherapeutic drugs arc not the same for everyone as, for example, a course of penicillin would be. Because of their extreme toxicity to normal tissues an attempt is made to minimize the damage by calculating an optimum dosage for each individual according to height and weight (body mass). Thus, the dosage varies not only from patient to patient, but for the same patient from treatment to treatment according to gain and loss of weight and the degree of bone marrow suppression as reflected in white blood cell counts. The dosage I was given at my first treatment was already at the low end of the range for adults; this was revised downward for the second injection because of my weight loss. Similarly, I began the second cycle with the optimum dosages, only to have them decreased at the second treatment because of the severe hematologic toxicity. Throughout the nine months of treatment, the dosages were pushed up and down in an effort to find the balance that would kill the disease without killing the patient. Baldly put, this is the core of the chemotherapeutic enterprise. In my case, the point of equilibrium was never located.

In the course of searching for it, my relationship with my oncologist continued to change, involving more and more negotiation and compromise on the dosages I received as my understanding of the treatment process expanded and my physical condition deteriorated. I brought all my capacities for identifying and analyzing pattern to bear on my body's increasingly violent response to chemotherapy, using every treatment as an opportunity to try out my theories on my oncologist. He came to respect my ability to observe and report sensitively and accurately and even, I think, to enjoy the intellectual fencing as I began to negotiate more aggressively (and more successfully) for lower doses. This was no fiction of participation; it was based on a mutual understanding of chemotherapy as a necessarily and inherently indeterminate process. I knew, and my oncologist knew that I knew, that each one of my treatments was an experiment.

By helping me to become a collaborator in rather than an object of treatment, he made it at once easier and harder for me to go on with it — easier because the sense of empowerment was an antidote to depression and fear; harder because I had to participate as well in my oncologist's worries. In my case, there was no direct measure of progress. The absence of macroscopic disease at the start of treatment meant that we could not judge the correctness of treatment decisions by the shrinking of a tumor. There was only a negative measure: no measurable evidence that the treatment was *not* working. Even this, however, was ambiguous; a non-specific blood assay called a LASA, thought to be correlated with active Hodgkin's disease, turned out positive. Partly on the basis of this result, my oncologist leaned in the direction of interpreting my persistent fevers and night sweats as disease symptoms. I persisted in seeing them instead as symptoms of gross damage at the cellular level as a result of chemotherapy. The implications of both theories were alarming. Either way, the armamentarium of biomedicine was exhausted.

After six months of chemotherapy, my blood counts (white blood cell, platelet and hematocrit counts are the ones chemotherapists pay closest attention to) began to rise and fall dramatically and inexplicably. Treatments had to be postponed one, two, and even three weeks to allow the blood counts to reach minimally acceptable levels, thus lengthening the total period of chemotherapy, for missed treatments had to be made up. This suggested severe bone marrow depression, a bad sign and at least potentially grounds for curtailing the treatments. Longer intervals between treatments also diminish the effectiveness of the drugs; more or less continuous bombardment keeps the cancer cells retreating. I could already see the treatments extending indefinitely beyond the originally planned twelve months, and the purpose of going on with them was becoming less and less clear. Again I raised the question of how much chemotherapy it was necessary (or even possible) for me to have. My oncologist thought six cycles insufficient; he could live with nine, but would push for all twelve if he thought my bone marrow could tolerate that much. In any case, he said, when I had completed nine cycles we could do more X-rays and blood work, reassess the matter, and decide then whether to stop there or go on. I had already learned that decisions in chemotherapy can never be made in the abstract or in advance of the moment in which they must be taken, with all the data in.

On February 22, 1985, I had the first injection of my eighth cycle of chemotherapy (ABVD). I had been running a low-to-middle-grade fever for two weeks; that afternoon it reached 100.7°. The treatment had been postponed for a week because of it. It seemed to me (and I said so to my oncologist) that, given my appalling history of bad reactions, treatment could only go forward if nothing else were wrong with me at the time it was administered: no viruses, no low-grade fevers, no marginal blood counts. Proceeding on this basis, however, raised serious questions about the value of proceeding at all. My oncologist, clearly at a loss to interpret my symptoms, made a further concession: we would not go on with the treatments past twelve months, no matter how many of the twelve treatment cycles I had completed by then.

As if to prove me right, my body reacted swiftly and violently to the drugs I received that day. I vomited afterwards as usual, but then lost consciousness for three or four hours, and on waking, found it very difficult to speak. Within 48 hours I was overcome by weakness, and my fever shot up to 102°, then to 103°, and remained at these levels for nearly a month. I took Tylenol constantly, then a stronger anti-inflammatory drug, Indocin, to keep the fever low enough so that I could continue teaching. I continued to experience drenching sweats at night, and my white blood cell count fell sharply. The day before the next scheduled treatment I spoke to my oncologist by telephone. It was my intention to insist on a cease-fire of at least a week; he surprised me by giving me four. "Send me weekly records of your temperature," he said, "and come back in a month; then we'll talk." I had won this round, but not in the way I wanted to; he seemed convinced that my symptoms were manifestations of active disease.

I was desperately ill; yet there was nothing apparently wrong with me. My oncologist's alternative explanation for my fever — an infection — was intellectually unsatisfying. In the absence of any shred of evidence, it was like asking me to believe that it was being caused by demons. There seemed to be more and better evidence for my theory than for his. Not only the fever, night sweats, erratic blood counts and weakness, but also the violent cough, the nerve damage, the constant mouth sores, the classic symptoms of menopause, and the unmanageable digestive problems suggested to me that the destructive power of the drugs, acting each time on an increasingly damaged body, had finally outstripped the body's ability to heal sufficiently after each assault — that I was, in fact, being poisoned to death. With every record of fever I sent a letter to my oncologist describing and analyzing my condition. The last letter deliberately subverts the military metaphors that provide so much of the imagery for cancer treatment:

> I think of my body as a city in a war zone — Beirut, if you like. It is impossible to rebuild while the bombs are still falling. After months of continuous bombardment, more and more buildings are reduced to rubble, and there is not enough of a foundation left on which to set even one stone. Another image of war comes chillingly to mind. I hope I am not like the village in Vietnam that had to be destroyed in order to be "saved".

I had no idea of the accuracy of my aim until I met my oncologist in the hospital a week later. It seemed to me that continuing the treatments would be at least as dangerous as stopping, and perhaps even more dangerous. The pattern of my response had, after nine months, been established, as well as a trend of more violent and longer-lasting toxic reactions. Simply put, things would only get worse. My University Health Services doctor and I had spent a long time agonizing over the question of going on or stopping, and he advised me to go on if my oncologist could see any advantage in doing so, even if only for another cycle or two. I wanted liberation, and was prepared to argue my way out of my oncologist's office if necessary.

I did not have to. He opened with, "The quality of your life has been pretty miserable for a long time. I think we've gotten as much chemotherapy into you as will do any good. How's your temperature?"

I could hardly believe what I had heard, and responded only to the question. "Almost normal. What do you think caused it?"

"Maybe a kidney infection that resolved itself spontaneously. There were a few white blood cells in your urine specimen."

"But the culture itself was negative. And there was no pain, no symptoms. Do those infections usually go away spontaneously?"

"No," he conceded lamely. He had no explanation. I knew he had no explanation, and he knew I knew he had no explanation.

I found myself forced back upon the very imprecise notion of "constitution" in order to explain my body's apparent inability to tolerate chemotherapy. "I know you think I'm a survivor, a "tough kid," just like _____ , who made it through all twelve cycles, but the reality of it is that, even if I was strong when I started, I'm frail now, and I'm afraid I wouldn't survive any more chemotherapy." Before I began my course of treatment, my oncologist had, on his own initiative, put me in touch with another Hodgkin's disease patient of his, a woman my age who was finishing the identical protocol I was about to start, and had got through it all in relatively good physical and psychological shape. He had wanted me to see that it was possible.

Now he had to admit that perhaps it was not. "She dropped dead," he responded without preamble. At her last check-up, he had formed the impression that she was in "great" shape. But some weeks later, she developed a cough, which she "neglected" for about a month. Then her trachea became infected; then she was admitted to the hospital; then she died.

In 1985 in the United States people do not die of sore throats unless their immune system has been hopelessly compromised. The obvious question hung in the air between us, and as soon as I could control my voice I asked it, as gently as I could. "How much did the chemotherapy have to do with it?"

He was evasive, stressing that the immediate cause of death was sepsis, adding, though, that her treatment probably had something to do with the fact that she became ill in that particualr fashion. Then he let it drop. I could see the pain and the guilt, and pursued the matter no farther. I had been vindicated in the worst possible way.

CONCLUSIONS

The above narrative enhances our understanding of the relationship between doctors and patients in the hospital setting, and suggests some implications for fieldwork and future research in that setting. I base my analysis on my own personal trajectory because it is both representative and singular. At the outset I had no reason to believe that my treatment was being managed any differently from that of anyone else going through the same course of radiotherapy; I now have many excellent reasons to believe that I am treated very differently from most other patients, and may even be unique. My intrusion into medical settings as both patient and anthropologist, my refusal to participate in the system of roles as these are usually constructed and played out, and the eventual redefinition of my relationship with my oncologist, caused the meanings that both reflect and inform this system to stand out in sharp relief.

Hospital patients commonly complain that they "become their disease," and it is instructive to examine exactly how this transformation takes place in the case of cancer patients, where the process is particularly clearly defined. Depersonalization is often ascribed to the presence of high technology, but this is only a part of the picture.

Interactions with the patient are highly routinized; on the other hand, treatment of the patient's disease is highly individualized. The transformation of a person into a case of stage II-B Hodgkin's disease begins with a belief shared by her doctors that the very knowledge of having cancer renders the patient so emotionally unstable that she is unable to confront and live with any reminders of the severity of her condition. The patient is also assumed to be too ignorant to understand any explanation a doctor could offer (Ley and Spelman 1967; McKinlay 1975; Bloom 1981). Together, these beliefs form the justification for withholding information from the patient. At the same time, the use of high technology makes possible the detailed and accurate staging and treatment of the patient's disease, resulting in improved chances of achieving a remission. Meaningful contact with the patient is sacrificed to the need to arrest her cancer.

The patient's role is defined for him through interactions with doctors and other staff[4] in the hospital. In many cases, fear of death and the desire to be rid of the disease spreading unseen through their bodies are sufficient to make patients submissive and unargumentative in the presence of their doctors. Confronted by an angry patient, a doctor characterizes him as "hostile" and "resentful," rather than as a person who may have a legitimate grievance about the manner in which his treatment is being managed. The responsibility for conflict is always placed on the patient. The doctor absolves himself from responsibility by invoking the patient's ignorance: "You failed to understand what I meant."

An example from my own experience illustrates the power of the doctor to make a patient accept this characterization of himself. Another Hodgkin's disease patient, a woman about my age, who at first agreed with me that neither of us had been adequately prepared by our doctors for the side effects of radiotherapy, suddenly switched sides when her radiologist appeared in the waiting room and entered the conversation. With her doctor, she insisted that I had misunderstood what I had been told and unfairly blamed my doctor. It was my responsibility to approach her and resolve the misunderstanding. The radiologist warned me (and his patient echoed him) that I might jeopardize the success of my treatment if I persisted in my "resentment" towards my doctor. I interpreted this remark as an oblique reference to the theory that resentment is an emotional state that "feeds" cancers and, if not addressed and resolved, can undermine the best of medical treatment (Simonton, Matthews-Simonton and Creighton 1978).

The structure of time and work in the hospital contributes to the routinization of contact with the patient. No time is built into consultations and check-ups for the patient to ask questions. Appointments are only 15 minutes long, and by the time the physical examination has been completed, there is very little time left for discussion of aspects of either disease or treatment that the patient finds particularly troubling or incomprehensible. When they feel the interview has gone on long enough, doctors begin to shuffle papers, move towards the door, open it, and stand in the hallway, forcing the patient to continue the discussion in a public place, which, of course, silences him.

The "'said' of social discourse" (Geertz 1973:20) in doctor-patient encounters in general and in the treatment of cancer in particular has primarily to do with relative positions of power. The doctor has a vested interest in preserving the ignorance of his patient, for it preserves and enhances his own power (Waitzkin and Stoeckle 1972:187). And power is particularly important in securing cooperation with forms of treatment — chemotherapy — that are arduous, extremely unpleasant, and dangerous, possibly even lethal. The doctor emerges as omniscient and omnipotent, and the ambiguity inherent in the relationship between treatment and prognosis is, if not eliminated, substantially reduced.

Cancer, it will be recalled, is an exceedingly potent metaphor, and metaphors "reverberate through patterns of thought, experience, and action" (Childress 1982:7). In a society that has declared a "war on cancer" (in much the same way that an earlier "war on poverty" — a social cancer — was declared), the cancer patient is a victim, held hostage by a disease that has invaded his body, which becomes the battlefield on which the war is fought. The dissimilar meanings of corruption and battle combine to promote medical paternalism and even authoritarianism. No effort is spared to defeat so evil an enemy, and no general needs to explain his orders.

Medical tradition supports this model of the doctor-patient relation. Medical authoritarianism can be traced all the way back to Hippocrates, who believed that the patient's state of ill health, his ignorance of its causes, and his emotional involvement with it all rendered him unsound of judgment (Hippocrates, cited in Freidson 1961:184). Hence the interpretation of the Hippocratic injunction *primum non nocere* (first of all, to do no harm) to mean, in practice, engaging in paternalistic, benevolent deception: withholding information if there is reason to suppose that disclosing it would impair the patient's emotional or physical well-being by depriving him of the hope of recovery and consequently of the "will to live," causing him to refuse treatment, etc.

Although there has been a marked increase over the past 25 years in physicians' expressed willingness to inform their patients of a diagnosis of cancer (Oken 1961; Novack et al. 1979), there is still a great deal of reluctance to provide information *beyond* the diagnosis. This position has been aided and abetted by a large body of sociological literature on the subject of doctor-patient relationships in which breakdowns in communication between patients and practitioners are ascribed to patients' failings: psychological unpreparedness to receive bad news, ignorance of medical terminology, inhibitions arising from low socioeconomic status and/or ethnic group membership, etc. (McKinlay 1975). Even the doctor-patient negotiation strategy proposed by Katon and Kleinman (1980) is substantially based on the patient's relative ignorance.

It is abundantly clear that treatment strategies that rely on the physician's control of information in order to force compliance from patients have misfired. Beneath the public image of technological (and therefore efficacious) biomedicine lies a different reality, one fraught with uncertainty, ambiguity, and contradiction. Patients who have never been allowed to see biomedicine's clay feet feel defrauded if treatment fails to achieve the desired result. They know only *that* something has gone wrong, not *why*, and make their physicians accountable by suing them for malpractice. The American Medical Association has only just begun to understand the nature of the problem, but the proposed solution — seminars, leaflets and speeches aimed at doctors, urging them to lower patients' expectations by projecting a less confident image ("Physicians Have an Image Problem — It's Too Good," *New York Times*, February 10, 1985) — is only an attempted short cut to lower malpractice insurance rates. Until doctors become teachers as well as healers, and make their patients genuinely informed partners in an uncertain enterprise, the practice of medicine will continue to take place in an atmosphere of mutual distrust and fear, with litigation as the outcome.

The challenge for anthropologists — particularly applied anthropologists working in clinical settings — is to find ways of studying an institution as important and powerful as biomedicine without validating and perpetuating existing forms. As Laura Nader (1974: 284) pointed out in her essay on the importance of "studying up" in American society, indignation is a legitimate motive for anthropological investigation. But it must not become an exposé; it must lead somewhere. And it must be framed in the anthropological universe of discourse, not in the conceptual framework of the institution itself. Judging by the lead article in the February 1985 issue of *Medical Anthropology Quarterly*, this issue seems to be at the heart of current concerns in the subdiscipline. Anthropologists fear that clinicians will not take them seriously unless they accept "biomedical disease concepts as the gold standard" (Philips 1985: 33); on the other hand, they worry that such acceptance reduces them to social engineers, adjusting patients to the prevailing clinical model instead of helping to transform it into something more humane. It is possible, as Victor Turner did in *The Forest of Symbols* (1967), to examine affliction without making the analysis of it dependent on the concepts and beliefs that guide the practitioner. This is precisely what a focus on the symbolic structures, events, processes, and relationships involved in biomedicine can do for us. The goal here is not medical anthropology, but an anthropology of medicine.[5]

Laura Nader (1974: 307–308) has suggested that, given the problems of entry and access involved in "studying up," anthropology may have to reassess the value placed on participant-observation, and focus instead on "using our knowledge of others as a mirror for ourselves and allowing questions to lead us to methodology (rather than vice versa)" (1974: 308). I am not promoting cancer as a tool of research, but I think my experience and the uses to which I have put it suggest some ways in which maximum advantage can be made of otherwise calamitous events.

Treatment for cancer, whether by surgery, radiotherapy, or chemotherapy, is isolating.[6] Cancer patients have minimal opportunity for contact with their fellow sufferers, meeting them only briefly in waiting rooms or in the corridors of cancer wards. Often, all they know about their disease comes from their own experience. The implication here for fieldwork is that the anthropologist's experience of the self can provide vitally important clues where experience is highly individualized. In most kinds of anthropological writing, the ethnographer carefully erases all traces of the self in order to provide an insider's eye view. But when the observer is also perforce a participant, and experience takes place mainly at the individual level, the ethnographer becomes an informant as well.

In this regard, emotions are important tools of research, especially strong emotions like anger, as Jean Briggs discovered and recounted in *Never in Anger* (1970). Disputes of any kind, like rituals, distill the essence from aspects of culture and social organization that remain relatively obscure in more mundane forms of interaction. For most of five years, I have been an angry patient, and it was that anger that opened the way to an anthropological understanding of my experience. Jules Henry (1963: 146) put the matter this way:

> To think deeply in our culture is to grow angry and to anger others; and if you cannot tolerate this anger, you are wasting the time you spend thinking deeply. One of the rewards of deep thought is the hot glow of anger at discovering a wrong, but if anger is taboo, thought will starve to death.

As Susan Sontag (1978) and others have pointed out, cancer stigmatizes its victims. It is a synonym for humiliation, degeneration and corruption, and those afflicted with it often refuse to discuss it, as if it were a shameful secret. In my contacts with other cancer patients, I have found that being one of their number gives me a kind of instant rapport that an outsider, no matter how sympathetic, probably could never achieve. There is no need to perform the usual wary dance of two strangers deciding how much of themselves to reveal; we go straight to intimacy.

Precisely because of the symbolic load the disease carries, it is important to an understanding of biomedicine to study *cancer* patients and their doctors. An anthropology of biomedicine should be an anthropology of biomedical specialties. Whatever the problem, doctors tend generally toward authoritarianism and patients to submission (Hilfiker 1985), but these behaviors reach extremes when the problem is cancer. It is worth noting here that the 1966 Freedom of Information Act specifically exempts doctors from the responsibility fully to inform their cancer patients (and this is the only disease mentioned) where, in the physician's judgment, disclosing information would be "an unwarranted invasion of personal privacy." Cancer has the power to magnify and clarify the dimensions of power and authority in doctor-patient interaction.

It may also be that the doctor-patient relationship in cancer treatment is the most amenable to change precisely because right answers are so elusive in this domain of clinical practice. My own case history is proof that it is possible to rewrite this social text. The revised version is an essay on shared control and responsibility, more suited to a society that professes democratic values than the first draft, which was a tract on power and manipulation.

ACKNOWLEDGEMENTS

I am grateful to the following people for various forms of assistance in the writing of this chapter: Hans Baer, Robert Carey, Paul Donato, Davydd Greenwood, Rita Linggood, Ross Midler, Oriol Pi-Sunyer, Jennifer Robertson, and Jonas Rosenthal.

NOTES

1. There is a "survival literature" by victims of cancer and other potentially fatal diseases, but much of it is introspective, consisting of personal narratives which treat the experience of illness as a journey into the self and do not attempt to generalize. An exception to this is Rose Kushner's 1975 book *Breast Cancer: A Personal History and an Investigative Report.* Susan Sontag's *Illness as Metaphor* (1978) and Norman Cousins' *Anatomy of an Illness as Perceived by the Patient* (1981) are probably the two best-known efforts to intellectualize an encounter

with mortality. Readers familiar with the Cousins book may be tempted to read into this essay his conclusions — that the "will to live," of which creativity is one aspect, is "not a theoretical abstraction, but a physiologic reality with therapeutic characteristics" that a doctor may engage and sustain by treating his patient as a "respected partner in the total undertaking" (Cousins 1981: 44–48). Such conclusions are neither explicit nor implicit in what I have written here. Having cancer is a domain of experience that has remained too long in the dark, and has thereby become mystified. The work of interpretation is demystification. This too is a form of healing, though not of the sort Cousins envisages.

2. Specifically, the etiology of Hodgkin's disease remains a mystery. This was one of the first things I asked my doctors about, but beyond telling me that Hodgkin's disease co-occurs with diminished immune competence (though a causal relationship in either direction has yet to be established), they were not interested in discussing past and present theories of its origin. What I know of these is the result of my own research.

In the late nineteenth and early twentieth centuries, the frequency of the association between Hodgkin's disease and tuberculosis suggested to some researchers that Hodgkin's disease was inflammatory rather than neoplastic in nature. Bacteria and viruses were investigated as possible etiologic agents (for a fuller discussion of these theories, see Kaplan 1972). The discovery of the HTLV (human T-cell leukemia/lymphoma virus) in 1980 stimulated further research into the relationship between viruses and human cancers (such a link had already been established for some nonhuman species). A study published in 1981 by epidemiologists at the Harvard University School of Public Health suggested that, like poliomyelitis before the vaccine, Hodgkin's disease is a consequence of an age-related response to a common virus. Increased risk was associated with higher socioeconomic status. Children of small, higher-income, often Jewish families living in single-family suburban dwellings, overprotected by their anxious parents and having fewer neighborhood playmates, were less likely to acquire immunity to the virus in childhood than were children of larger, lower-income, often Catholic families living in more densely populated urban environments (cited in the *New York Times*, January 18, 1981).

This stereotype-based and guilt-inducing theory forms part of a tradition of placing blame largely on the victim's shoulders. In 1957 Lawrence LeShan published "A Psychosomatic Hypothesis Concerning the Etiology of Hodgkins' [sic] Disease", asserting that the life histories and personality characteristics of Hodgkin's disease patients predispose them to their affliction. Old resentments, unmet emotional needs, and unresolved conflicts are said to block the effective functioning of the immune system, opening the way to cancer. LeShan later generalized his theory to include all cancer sufferers (LeShan 1977), and his work forms one of the principal theoretical supports for the popular book *Getting Well Again* (Simonton, Matthews-Simonton and Creighton 1978). If the mind can make the body ill, the authors reason, then the process can also be made to work in the other direction: right thinking can help the physician restore health (they are careful to avoid promising miracles). But the patient must acknowledge his "participation" in the emotional states that led to his illness, and make a conscious and conscientious effort to overcome them.

A detailed examination of the flaws in this line of reasoning is outside the scope of this paper. It is sufficient to point out here that it offers the cancer patient a ready answer to the inevitable question "Why *me*?", and it offers the physician a ready escape hatch should treatment prove ineffective. It can also be pressed into service to bring a "bad" patient under control, as in the example from my own experience offered above. I note with relief that the highly respected *New England Journal of Medicine* has recently (June 13, 1985) published an article condemning the belief in disease as a direct outcome of mental states as "largely folklore," and the "corollary view of sickness and death as a personal failure" as a "particularly unfortunate form of blaming the victim" (Angell 1985: 1572).

3. The extent to which biomedical knowledge is regarded as the private property of the medical profession is illustrated by the experience of a friend, a fellow academic. The recurrence of his renal cell carcinoma after 21 years was a highly unusual circumstance, and represented almost certain death even after the surgical removal of the tumor, for the standard forms of follow-up therapy were useless against his cancer. His surgeon, recognizing his intelligence and need to understand as much as possible about his illness, offered him two recently published articles on an experimental immune therapy, leaving to his patient the decision of whether to become an experimental subject.

A few months later, in the same spirit of collegiality that had characterized his relationship with his surgeon, my friend wrote an article detailing the intellectual process whereby he had decided in favor of the experimental therapy. The paper is nothing if not a confirmation of the accuracy of his doctor's judgment in encouraging his active participation in the treatment process. He intended the piece for publication in the same journal that had published the two articles his surgeon had given him. Before submitting it, he sent a copy to his surgeon and asked him to check the technical parts for accuracy. To his confusion and distress, the surgeon recommended that he not submit the article because it would expose him (the surgeon) to the censure of his colleagues for imprudently providing his patient with access to professional literature. Sadly — and, I believe, to the detriment of clinical practice — my friend withheld his article, unwilling to reward his doctor's openmindedness with apparent ingratitude and disregard for his professional standing.

4. Absent from this account are the people who actually administer the treatment — the X-ray and chemotherapy technicians — partly because of space limitations and partly because only my doctors could address the questions I was raising. However, it is worth digressing briefly on the nature of the technicians' participation in the treatment process, because it affects the patient's experience of treatment. Radiotherapy technicians press buttons from behind three feet of lead and concrete, and the entire treatment lasts a minute and a half. A few more minutes just prior to treatment suffice to position the patient on the treatment couch. Chemotherapy technicians, on the other hand, must touch their patients in order to administer treatment. They remain in the treatment room with the patient for most of the 20 to 60 minutes that chemotherapy requires, and are aware that, despite their very considerable skill in inserting IV needles and minimizing the corrosive effect of the drugs on the veins, the treatment is sometimes unavoidably painful. In contrast to the X-ray technicians, they are neither physically nor emotionally remote. Their formal training also appears to be more extensive, including graduate degrees, and, unlike X-ray technicians, they respond knowledgeably to questions about the substances they administer.

5. For this formulation I am indebted to Paul Donato (personal communication).

6. Support groups have grown up around the victims of certain cancers, primarily breast cancer and ostomy patients. However, sufferers of less common cancers often find themselves alone, or obliged to seek out cancer support groups on their own. In the hospital where I was treated, the social services staff organized support groups and orientation sessions for chemotherapy and radiotherapy patients from time to time, but these were never in operation during either of my courses of treatment. What Zola (1980: 250) calls the "overprivatization of the medical interview" usually prevents doctors from arranging for their patients to meet. My oncologist's offer of the name, address and telephone number of a patient he hoped could help me (with her consent, of course) is probably highly unusual. Having done this, however, did not prevent him from looking uneasy when I told him later that I had met another of his patients quite by chance. His reaction suggested to me that doctors may not like the idea of their patients comparing notes about them.

REFERENCES

Angell, Marcia, M.D., 1985. Disease as a Reflection of the Psyche, *The New England Journal of Medicine* 312(24): 1570–1572.

Artiss, K.L., and A.S. Levine, 1973. Doctor-Patient Relation in Severe Illness, *The New England Journal of Medicine* 288: 1210–1214.

Bloom, Joan R., 1981. Cancer Care Providers and the Medical Care System: Facilitators or Inhibitors of Patient Coping Responses? In *Living and Dying With Cancer*, ed. Paul Ahmed, 253–272., New York: Elsevier North Holland.

Briggs, Jean, 1970. *Never in Anger: Portrait of an Eskimo Family*. Cambridge, Mass.: Harvard University Press.

Brinkley, Joel, 1985. Physicians Have an Image Problem: It's Too Good, *New York Times*, February 10.

Childress, James F., 1982. *Who Should Decide? Paternalism in Health Care*. New York: Oxford University Press.

Cousins, Norman, 1981. Anatomy of an Illness as Perceived by the Patient. New York: Bantam Books.

Desforges, Jane F., *et al.*, 1979. Hodgkin's Disease, *The New England Journal of Medicine*, November 29: 1212–1221.

Freidson, Eliot, 1961. *Patients' View of Medical Practice*. New York: Russell Sage Foundation.

Freidson, Eliot, 1967. Review Essay: Health Factories, the New Industrial Sociology, *Social Problems* 14 (Spring): 493–500.

Freidson, Eliot, 1970. *Profession of Medicine*. New York: Dodd, Mead.

Geertz, Clifford, 1973. *The Interpretation of Cultures*. New York: Basic Books.

Goffman, Erving, 1963. *Stigma: Notes on the Management of Spoiled Identity*. Englewood Cliffs, NJ: Prentice-Hall.

Henry, Jules, 1963. *Culture Against Man*. New York: Random House.

Hilfiker, David, M.D., 1985. *Healing the Wounds: A Physician Looks at His Work*. New York: Pantheon Books.

Kaplan, Henry S., 1972 and 1980. *Hodgkin's Disease*. Cambridge, MA: Harvard University Press.

Katon, Wayne and Arthur Kleinman, 1981. Doctor-Patient Negotiation and Other Social Science Strategies in Patient Care. In *The Relevance of Social Science for Medicine*, eds. Leon Eisenberg and Arthur Kleinman, 253–279. Dordrecht, Holland: D. Reidel.

Killian, Lewis and Sanford Bloomberg, 1975. Rebirth in a Therapeutic Community: A Case Study, *Psychiatry* 38(1): 39–54.

Kushner, Rose, 1975. *Breast Cancer: A Personal History and an Investigative Report*. New York: Harcourt Brace Jovanovich.

Lax, Eric, 1985. *Life and Death on 10 West*. New York: Dell/Laurel.

LeShan, Lawrence L., 1957. A Psychosomatic Hypothesis Concerning the Etiology of Hodgkins' Disease, *Psychological Reports* 3: 565–575.

LeShan, Lawrence L., 1977. *You Can Fight For Your Life*. New York: M. Evans & Company.

Ley, P., and M.S. Spelman, 1967. *Communicating With the Patient*. St. Louis, Missouri: Warren H. Green, Inc.

Lorber, Judith, 1975. Good Patients and Problem Patients: Conformity and Deviance in a General Hospital, *Journal of Health and Social Behavior* 16: 213–225.

McKinlay, John B., 1975. Who Is Really Ignorant — Physician or Patient?, *Journal of Health and Social Behavior* 16(1): 3–11.

Moore, Sally Falk, 1975. Epilogue: Uncertainties in Situations, Indeterminacies in Culture. In *Symbol and Politics in Communal Ideology: Cases and Questions*, eds. Sally Falk Moore and Barbara G. Myerhoff, Ithaca, N.Y.: Cornell University Press.

Nader, Laura, 1974. Up the Anthropologist — Perspectives Gained from Studying

Up. In *Reinventing Anthropology*, ed. Dell Hymes, 284–311. New York: Vintage Books.

New York Times, 1981. Childhood Clues to an Adult Disease, January 18.

Novack, Dennis H., *et al.*, 1979. Changes in Physicians' Attitudes toward Telling the Cancer Patient, *Journal of the American Medical Association* 241 (March 2): 897–900.

Oken, Donald, 1961. What to Tell Cancer Patients: A Study of Medical Attitudes, *Journal of the American Medical Association* 175: 1120–1128.

Ortner, Sherry B., 1973. On Key Symbols, *American Anthropologist* 75(5): 1338–1346.

Philips, Michael R., 1985. Can "Clinically Applied Anthropology" Survive in Medical Care Settings?, *Medical Anthropology Quarterly* 16(2): 31–36.

Roth, Julius A., 1963. *Timetables: Structuring the Passage of Time in Hospital Treatment and Other Careers*. New York: Bobbs-Merrill.

Santoro, A., G. Bonadonna, V. Bonfante, and P. Valagussa, 1982. Alternating Drug Combinations in the Treatment of Hodgkin's Disease, *The New England Journal of Medicine* 306: 770–774.

Simonton, O. Carl, Stephanie Matthews-Simonton, and James Creighton, 1978. *Getting Well Again*. Los Angeles: J.P. Tarcher, Inc.

Sontag, Susan, 1978. *Illness as Metaphor*. New York: Farrar, Straus and Giroux.

Turner, Victor, 1967. *The Forest of Symbols: Aspects of Ndembu Ritual*. Ithaca, N.Y.: Cornell University Press.

Waitzkin, Howard, and John D. Stoeckle, 1972. The Communication of Information about Illness, *Advances in Psychosomatic Medicine* 8: 185–189.

Zola, Irving Kenneth, 1980. Structural Constraints in the Doctor-Patient Relationship: The Case of Non-Compliance. In *The Relevance of Social Science for Medicine*, eds. Leon Eisenberg and Arthur Kleinman, 241–252. Dordrecht, Holland: D. Reidel.

Zola, Irving Kenneth, 1982. *Missing Pieces: A Chronicle of Living With a Disability*. Philadelphia, PA: Temple University Press.

Index

Adiposity 49, 59–62
Administrative structures 87–88, 95
Adoption 136–137
Affective neutrality 304
Aggressiveness 129
Alcoholism 277–279
American Cancer Society 201, 210–211, 223–225
American Medical Association 340
Appalachia 37, 50
Asthma 232

"Bag ladies" 77
Baker Act 78–79, 89–95
Birth as a medical event 193, 197
Birth control 136
Blood glucose level 42, 46, 58, 61, 65
"Boat people" 147
Body image 61–62
Boston Women's Health Book Collective 253
Bureaucracy 23, 79, 87, 260
Buddhism 154, 175

Cancer 201–225, 315–343
Cancer, etiology of 207, 318
Cancer, Japanese conception of 202
Capitalist class 18–23
Cesarean section 185–198
Cherokee Indians 43–66
Chinantec Indians 13–14, 21
Chest physiotherapy (CPT) 233–245
Client advocates 90
Clinic,
    campus 102
    cystic fibrosis 238

rural health 6–7
Community Mental Health Centers 75, 83–84
Compliance 229–246, 250
Consultation psychiatry 269–290
Coping strategies 120, 202–204, 212
COPLAMAR 5–25
Crosscultural obstertrics 185
Cultural theme 61–62
Culture brokers 131, 277, 289
Culture shock 148
Curandero 9
Curative medicine 20
Cystic fibrosis 229–246

Deinstutionalization 76,. 86–87, 90
Delayed diabetogenic effect 59
Diabetes,
    type II 43–66
    type I 44
Diseases of poverty 11, 16
"Doctor-bashing" 295
Doctor-nurse relationship 310–311
Doctor-patient relationship 251, 296
Drinking 119, 129–130, 133
Dual system of authority 35–36

Eclecticism 11
Ecotopic pregnancy 249–263
Educational Commission for Foreign Medical Graduates 148
Epidemic 43
Emic view 287
Explanatory model (EM) 198, 276, 278, 281, 285, 289

Family medicine ward   171–174
Fetal monitor   188
Fecundity   63
Fertility   63
Fiduciary relationship   195
Florida Mental Health Act   73–95
Foreign medical graduates
   (FMG)   147–179
"Foreign student syndrome"   103, 106
Freedom of Information Act   342
Functional health   245

General practitioners   37
Genotype, type II diabetic   63
"Gentiles"   32
Geertz, Clifford   213, 317–319, 339
Ghosts   125
Goffman, Irving   212

Health maintanence organization
   (HMO)   253, 256, 261–263
Hegemony   260–262
Hill-Burton Act   30
Hodgkin's disease   209, 224, 315, 320–
   343
Holistic approach   245
Hospital,
   Indian   45–47
   referral   12
   rural   7, 30
   state mental   76, 80
   university   102, 298–312
Hunters and gatherers   62–63, 66
Hypoxia   233

Illich, Ivan   29, 250, 259
Indian Territory   51–53
Industrial economy   62
Institutional, definition of   30
Institutional Review Board for the
   Protection of Human Subjects   296
Intermediate nursing facility   32
International Classification of Mental
   Disorders   104
International students   101–117
Internship   150, 157–179

Joint Commission of Mental Illness and
   Health   75, 96

Long-term care facility   30
Low-technology health care delivery   17

Macro-level   21, 108, 274
Mean parity   64
Medex   33
Medical Ethics Case Conference   185
Medical establishment   29
Medical militarization   201–225
Medical profession,   149, 303
Medicalization   121, 252, 259
Medicineman, Navajo   32, 280, 283
Mental Health Associations,
   Florida   83, 91
Methodology 41, 49–50, 202–204, 245,
   270, 295–312
Metropolis   17
Mexican Revolution   4
Micro-level   108
Midwifery   138
Monochronism   112–113
Mormons   31–32, 36–37
Multiparity   63–66

National Cancer Act   202
National Institute of Mental Health   75
National Residency Matching
   Program   156
Native American   277–280
Navarro, Vicente   18, 260–261
Navajo   31, 38, 40
Neonatal intersive care unit
   (NICU)   160–171
Noncompliance   229–246
"Nostaglic-depressive" reaction   103,
   115
Nurses   38, 126, 301
Nurse practitioner   254–256
Nurse-intern relationship   104
Nursing home   33

Obesity   48, 58–61, 66
Objectivity   304–307
Obstetrics   249–263
Obstetrics/gyncecology department
   252–257

Parsons, Talcott   120, 205
Pasante   9

Patient Management Conference   172
Patient self-determination   195
Pharmauceutical companies   2
Phenotype   62
Physician/officer   219
Policy cycle   81–86
Policy science   73
Political economic perspective   4, 23,
   260
Poverty   55, 66
Prediabetic   65
Pregnancy   119–143, 249–263 (See
   ecotopic)
Preventive health   40, 116
"Problem" (or "bad") patient   250, 322
Psychiatry, clinical   272
Psychotropic medication   80
Public health departments   37–38
Public health district   38, 40

Quasi-doctor   114

Reification of illness   202
Reinstitutionalization   77
Residency   150, 154–157
Revitalization movement   88
Ruling class   18, 20, 22, 24

Satellite   17

Scientific medicine   20, 29
Self-treatment (and self-diagnosis)   104,
   108, 114, 244
Sick role   120, 140, 205
Skilled nursing facility   30, 34
"Snake pit"   81–82
Social support network   255
Sontag, Susan   201, 225, 315, 319, 341
Sorcery   125
Spanish-Americans   32
Stigma of labelling   212
Students,
   African   106–109
   international   101–117
   Latin American   109–115
   Micronesian   129–143
Symbolic anthropology   317

Therapists, respiratory   234
Therapeutic alliance   231
Thrifty gene   62–63, 66
Transcultural psychiatry   269

Underdevelopment of health   18
"Uprooting disorder"   103–104, 110,
   115
Utah Cost Improvement Program
   30–41
Utah State Division of Health   34
Utes   40